T0284932

THE

HOLOCAUST

THE

HOLOCAUST

HISTORY AND MEMORY
NEW EDITION

JEREMY BLACK

INDIANA UNIVERSITY PRESS

This book is a publication of

INDIANA UNIVERSITY PRESS
Office of Scholarly Publishing
Herman B Wells Library 350
1320 East 10th Street
Bloomington, Indiana 47405 USA

iupress.org

Manufactured in the
United States of America

First Printing 2024

Cataloging information is available
from the Library of Congress:
978-0-253-06990-0 (hardback)
978-0-253-06989-4 (paperback)
978-0-253-06991-7 (e-book)

For a Branch of My Family I Never Met

Contents

Preface

THE HISTORY OF THE HOLOCAUST, OR SHOAH, CONSTANTLY
needs revisiting and emphasizing in the face of continuing attempts to
deny its veracity or scope. The arrest of David Irving in Austria in 2005
on the charge of Holocaust denial served as a pointed reminder of its
contentious character, and that year, Mahmoud Ahmadinejad, the new
president of Iran, publicly joined the sordid ranks of the deniers. In fact,
Adolf Hitler's determination to rid Europe of Jews and what he saw as
Jewish culture in all its manifestations was central to his ultimate goal of
establishing a thousand-year Reich (German empire). The opportunity
was provided by the extensive German conquests in the early stages of
World War II (1939–45), and the history of the Holocaust in part properly
belongs to that of the war. Although this might seem an obvious point, it
is challenged by the range of work on aspects of the war that underplays
or ignores the Holocaust and other Jewish themes.[1] Indeed, I deliberately
included a volume on the Holocaust in the seven-volume collection of
articles and essays on the war by various scholars that I edited in 2007.
The present book, which builds on an earlier book published in 2008 and
on an earlier edition of this book published in 2016, was written in part
in response to the continuation of Holocaust denial and also because of
the need for a short introductory study.

The spate of Holocaust denial during the 1990s and the 2000s was
the clarion call for the writing and publication of my 2008 book. The context for it was the mounting evasiveness, downplaying, and even denial of
the Holocaust across the world; the challenges these vexatious developments posed to human civilization; and apprehension over what these

foibles could portend for civil society. It is alarming that in the years following 2008, the implications of these developments have become even more palpable. Antisemitism is increasingly visible in certain European states—for example, Hungary. There are also efforts to decontextualize the Holocaust that are part of attempts to erase and deny Jews and Judaism. The diminishment of the Holocaust draws on antisemitism. This book seeks to bring to readers' attention—through direct, detailed, and thematically oriented prose—the backdrop, the events, and the history of memories and perspectives of the Holocaust, so as to educate readers and would-be skeptics of one of the most defining events of World War II and the modern era and to warn them of the costs of ignoring it. This study clearly demonstrates the perils that flow from embracing historical fallacies and inattentiveness and the horrendous civilizational costs that result from such acceptances.

The complex roots of the slaughter are discussed in the first two chapters. The German extermination policies that led to the Holocaust that consumed much of European Jewry were the culmination of powerful currents in nineteenth-century thought, as refracted through the prism of Nazi ideology and Hitler's messianic fantasies. There is an emphasis in the book on the extent to which Hitler's military strategy and the one-sided genocidal war against Jews cannot be detached from each other. Indeed, the slaughter of Jews should be part of the analysis of the German conduct of the war. This study underlines the importance of the killings by *Einsatzgruppen* (mobile killing squads), especially mass shootings, and, to a different extent, by the *Wehrmacht*, alongside the more usual emphasis on slaughter in the extermination camps.

This genocide reflected the extent to which the war was a brutal struggle between different visions and practices of modernism and modernization: Nazi ideology, therefore, was antimodernist in that it sought to destroy other visions and practices but also had modernist visions and practices in its own way. In Nazi minds, Jews represented and personified at once an anachronistic past, in their traditional customs and separateness from the modern unitary nation, and, far more dangerously, a different and threatening modernism—or rather modernisms, for Jews were seen by the Nazis as highly prominent in and shaping, if not directing, capitalism, Communism, cosmopolitanism, liberalism, socialism, and much of modern culture and thought. This Nazi paranoia captured the extent to which Jews were spread across much of the world and, particularly, allegedly prominent in its most dominant economy and most active culture, the United States. Moreover, although many Jews were not part of modernization, a large number, especially among those who assimilated, were influential precisely because they were involved in modern and liberal projects. The role of Jews in both physics and Hollywood was indicative of the wider situation. The Holocaust is of separate significance not only as the most brutal episode of antisemitism and a warning of where that most stupid of attitudes can lead but also as one formative background to the creation and ethos of the state of Israel.

The treatment of the Holocaust in these pages requires explanation because so much space is devoted to postwar discussion and memorialization (a lengthy chap. 5) and to consideration of the Holocaust today (chap. 6). This emphasis is not in pursuit of some absurd postmodern relativism but, rather, because the subject of the Holocaust is at once the brutal mass slaughter of the Jews perpetrated by the Germans and their allies and also the postwar consideration of this slaughter.

Discussion of the consideration does not in any way lessen the slaughter but simply notes that, as personal recollection fades with the passing generations, it is through this consideration that the Holocaust is grasped. It is, for example, through postwar publications, such as Anne Frank's *The Diary of a Young Girl* (1947; English edition 1952), that the Holocaust has been understood by many. It is through postwar films such as *Schindler's List* (1993) as much as, if not far more than, through wartime photography that the Holocaust is understood visually, and that process is increasingly important—both for a society for which the visual is supplanting the literary as means and medium of thought and in order to confront the widespread loss of shock. Given the dominance of German documentation in the surviving written official sources on the Holocaust, the subsequent publication of memoirs and the visual account were and are of even greater consequence. Free showings for schools of *Schindler's List* in the United States helped make it an apparently canonical "text" on the Holocaust.

Moreover, memorialization of the Holocaust throws light on postwar societies, on the contentious nature of World War II, and on the widespread persistence of antisemitism. Most obviously, in postwar Germany and among its wartime allies, recognition of the Holocaust was often suppressed or downplayed in an attempt to minimize the consequences of collaboration, notably connivance in or acceptance of the murderous treatment of Jews. As such, however ahistorically, this response also offers gleams of understanding about the policies and attitudes that made the Holocaust not only a possibility but also a terrible reality. Thus, the Holocaust was not just an event that reflected short-term elements and a multiplicity of factors that ranged more widely in time, but also a process with short-term and long-term implications. How this situation and process was then treated by subsequent generations is of major significance.

Since writing my earlier study in 2007, I have had the opportunity for additional work, not least as a result of visits to Bulgaria, Estonia, France, Germany, Greece, Hungary, Latvia, Lithuania, Poland, Romania, Russia, Serbia, Slovakia, Slovenia, and Ukraine. Europe is covered with Holocaust sites and, increasingly, memorials and museums. Each is different—Salonika (Thessaloniki) is not Paris—reflecting not only the contrasting experiences of the local Jews but also styles and contexts of memorialization. The common theme is loss: the loss of individual life, the loss of Jewish communities, and the loss for Europe.

It is appropriate to be emotive when writing about the Holocaust—how else to treat genocide, an abstraction that means smashing living babies' skulls against walls—and yet, that emotional response also is both less and more than the story.

Compared to the horror of the subject, the problems posed by toponyms (place names) are of lesser consequence and certainly were not responsible for the persistent painful headache I had while researching and writing this book. Nevertheless, given that some readers seem to find the spelling of place names a more serious topic, it is important to note that these are arbitrary realities imbued with implicit national or ethnic narratives often divergent from, if not in outright opposition to, other narratives. The spelling of Eastern European toponyms can automatically be taken as a diminution, neglect, or even denigration of a people's identity, history, and even calamity. Indeed, the conundrum of Eastern

European history is seen with the issue of how to express sensitively multiple narratives of suffering and memory without short-changing engraved, collective historical memories and causing offense through what will always be an arbitrary choice for toponymic selection. There is no easy resolution since, typically, everything has a name, names do mean a lot, and one must choose a name. The magnitude of Eastern European suffering can overwhelm even the most conscientious lexicographical and syntactical formulations of historians.

Take Kaunas (Yiddish: Kovne; Polish: Kowno; Russian: Kovno), currently the second-largest city in Lithuania after Vilnius (Yiddish: Vilne; Polish: Wilno; Russian: Vil'na). Kaunas was the Lithuanian capital during the interwar period. Disconcertingly pleasant when I visited, Kovno, like Vilnius, was a major Holocaust execution site and is thus inscribed in Jewish memory. However, historians generally adopt as place names the political-administrative formulations currently found on up-to-date maps and employed by whatever states govern particular places. As Kaunas was named and has continued to be named Kaunas since the creation of a Lithuanian state in 1918 and during the existence of the Lithuanian Soviet Socialist Republic, Kaunas, not Kovno, should be used. Moreover, Kaunas is the older name, since it dates at least to the thirteenth century. At the same time, the 1941 *Kovno massacres* is a term that is employed to describe the slaughter of Jews in Kaunas.

In light of the likely readership of this book, note references are restricted to English-language literature. There is also extensive and important scholarship in German, as well as other languages, and the quality of much of this literature in recent years is among the few heartening signs to emerge from this mentally difficult subject. Readers who wish to pursue this literature can consult the notes and bibliographies of the English-language literature.

For this edition, I would like to thank Pete Brown, Guy Chet, Bill Gibson, Peter Hoffenberg, and Jeremy Noakes for their most valuable comments. I greatly appreciate the major commitment and the large amount of time this effort involves. I would like to thank Mike Mosbacher for giving me permission to use material from my 2008 work for the Social Affairs Unit on the Holocaust. I am grateful for the opportunity to speak on the subject at a number of places, including the University of Hawaii, Oundle School, Radley College, and the Foreign Policy Research Institute in Philadelphia.

This book is dedicated to a branch of my family I only knew through flickering memories and fading photographs in my grandmother's flat. She was a lovely woman and a very kind grandmother and great-grandmother.

THE

HOLOCAUST

ONE

Until Barbarossa

ANTISEMITIC BACKGROUND

In a horrific form, the Holocaust, particularly the mass executions and extermination and concentration camps, testified to a persistent and widespread use of concepts of race in order to rank peoples and develop and express national cohesion. This approach was more common in the political thought and practice of the twentieth century than is generally appreciated and was particularly important in state-building and also in the creation of new political allegiances.

In Europe, toward the close of the nineteenth century, the proponents of increasingly insistent organic notions of nation became readier to draw on, if not to create, an often-mystical sense of identity between people and place or, as it more generally was expressed, between race and country. Organic notions of nation drew on and sustained a range of potent political and cultural notions and ideas, including Romanticism and social Darwinism, which, in turn, fed into early fascism. The corresponding claim that peoples' thoughts and actions do not follow universal and timeless patterns but, instead, are shaped by time and place lent itself to the idea of distinctive cultures. This stress on distinctive cultures could be part of an antihumanistic ideology, although the latter could vary. There is the claim that racial characteristics are timeless or potentially timeless, the latter a view about potential that could lead to the idea that these characteristics are subject to change and that might most obviously threaten the emphasis on "purity of blood." This concern became an obsessive theme masking a questionable reality.

The stress on distinctive cultures potentially but not inevitably or always undermined universalism and, thus, the idea of tolerance and rights for others; this undermining was certainly apparent in the Nazi case. Indeed, the Nazis had little interest in the theme of the protection of minorities that was important to the post–World War II peace settlement, unless it involved Germans. Instead, of universal themes such as class or religion, the organizing narrative became the nation. Although in particular cultures, that approach could encompass a strong commitment to tolerance, the function of history as a process and subject often became that of providing the vision of a single people with a national destiny, a destiny that linked past, present, and future and demanded sacrifices. The emphasis on nation was linked to belief in the nation, the latter being frequently though not always presented as necessarily different from, and superior to, other nations. This emphasis affected attitudes toward those who could be seen and defined as weakening the nation and its supposed purity: the "enemy within" made it harder to deal with the rival abroad, and Jews were frequently and wrongly typecast in this form. International rivalry encouraged this analysis.

Concern about the enemy within was linked to a politics of paranoia. The conspiracy theories that had been pushed to the fore in Europe at the time of the French Revolutionary Wars in the 1790s, a period in which there was a widespread belief in secret societies, some allegedly long lasting, influenced the subsequent account of both present politics and the recent past. Earlier concerns about secret movements, notably the Freemasons and the Illuminati—both, in the eyes of some counterrevolutionaries, supposedly responsible for the French Revolution—were played through a new context from the 1790s, and these concerns were made more open and "democratic," in large part through the culture of print and rising literacy.[1]

These beliefs proved the easiest way to address anxieties stemming from the unexpected extent and unwelcome character of political, economic, social, and cultural change, change that was readily apparent from the late nineteenth century.[2] A sense of racial tension became more pronounced. In part, this tension reflected the increased rate of migration and the ideas of inherent racial competition. As well as concern about immigration into states, there was the issue of migration within them. The volatility of societies contributed greatly to racism. Large-scale urbanization was accompanied by the breakdown of previous patterns of social linkage and by the disruptive impact of economic cycles. On the one hand, in response, there was a wish to understand and fix social patterns, and on the other, racism served to express, focus, and formulate society's fears, anxieties, hatreds, and fantasies.

The role of conspiracy was a consequence of a sense of flux and ideological polarization and, in turn, contributed to this polarization. For example, in France, Théodore Garnier, a priest, founded the *Union Nationale* in 1892. This populist corporatist party (falsely) claimed that Jews, Freemasons, and Protestants were running the French Third Republic (1870–1940) and needed to be overthrown. Moreover, Garnier frequently referred to a (nonexistent) secret plot devised in 1846 by Henry, 3rd Viscount Palmerston, the British foreign secretary and, according to Garnier, a Jew (he was not)—a plot supposedly seeking to use Jews and Freemasons to destroy France and Catholicism. Garnier also spread the inaccurate idea, advanced in France in 1881 in the Catholic journal *Le Contemporain*, that a Jewish conclave the previous year had decided to take vengeance for Jews' historic oppression. The emancipation of France's Jews by the revolutionaries in 1791 was presented by Garnier as a deliberately anti-Catholic step he and others used to condemn both Jews and revolutionaries.[3] Other prominent social Catholics, such as the Abbé Léon Dehon, were also strident antisemites. This Catholic assault on the Third Republic and Jews looked directly forward to Vichy cooperation with Nazi Germany during World War II and was a potent instance of the manner in which widespread and virulent Catholic antisemitism prepared the context for abetting genocide.

Those who could be excluded from the national narrative sometimes faced persecution, if not violence, in the nineteenth century. Irrespective of legal emancipation, which occurred in Germany in 1871, and the opportunities it brought, Jews, who were frequently presented as different, were a major category for exclusion; this was the case both for secular Jews and for religious ones. In the late nineteenth century, some nationalist bodies, such as the Union of the Russian People, provided the context for pogroms, large-scale antisemitic violence that notably occurred in 1881–84 and 1903–6. The context for the Union of the Russian People and the pogroms included the ethnic policies of Czar Alexander III (r. 1881–94) directed against non-Russians, policies continued by his anti-semitic son, Czar Nicholas II (r. 1894–1917), as an aspect of consolidating the state around a Russian nationalism. Indeed, Russian developments demonstrate the linkage between political policy and violent social con-sequences. In Germany, where Jews were comparatively well integrated, there could be antisemitic riots, but there were no pogroms on a Russian scale in the late nineteenth century or the first decade of the twentieth century. This contrast provides a qualification to the process of a simple reading from the past onto the 1940s.

Racism drew on essentialist notions of identity. As an aspect of a widespread struggle over its character and presentation, nationalism frequently changed in the second half of the nineteenth century from being regarded as progressive and liberal to being presented as having a "blood and soil" character, and increasingly so in the last decades of the century. Other states and nations were the prime targets of nationalism, but there was also a process of discrimination against groups that might offer contrasting values, as well as against citizens who could be presented as different. Thus, there was opposition to international movements with national and local representation, such as trade unions and the Catholic Church, an opposition that looked toward later hostility to communism.

The increase of antisemitism in the late nineteenth and early twenti-eth centuries was partly the result of conditions specific to that time. In this age of nationalism, there was the rise of an antisemitism that, along-side traditional religious and ethnic themes, presented Jews as a foreign people and was concerned about Jewish immigration as well as Jewish cultural movements. In itself, the concept of community is inclusive and a possible agent for progress, not the inherently racial or racist idea that was to be conceptualized by the Nazis as a basis for their implementation of the idea as the rationale for removing outsiders. Nevertheless, the con-cept, which was strong throughout Germany, was frequently employed to suggest an inherent value for a coherence that verged on homogeneity and, accordingly, a critique of a modern life that supposedly led, at the service of a worthless cosmopolitanism, to an atomizing divisiveness of individual communities and, indeed, individuals. Antisemitism was more potent across Europe from the 1880s, as it became central to a language of social commentary and criticism that was an increasingly automatic reflex for many of those unhappy with social, economic, and cultural change.[4] Jews were decried as cosmopolitan and plutocratic. This was a critique very different from that of Jews as backward traditionalists, but antisemitism, which was directed against both secular and religious Jews, and thus against Jews as a race, readily proved able to encompass and exacerbate very different and frequently contradictory attitudes and tendencies, which widened its constituency. This situation abetted the Holocaust, affected subsequent attitudes to it, and continues to do so. Racism also seemed to be endorsed by science, including the concept of natural selection and the development of ethnography, and thus appeared to be progressive while appealing to the antiscientific antimodernism that was a powerful feature of the period.

Racism, moreover, with its stress on immutable characteristics, offered a vehicle for older identities and prejudices, not least a religious aversion on the part of many Christians that was important to long-standing antisemitism.[5] Ridiculous accounts of supposed Eucharistic host desecration and ritual murders by Jews had led to show trials and slaughter and were incorporated into public myths centuries later.[6] Thus, in central Brussels, the Shrine of the Sacrament of the Holy Miracle in the Church of St. Michael and St. Gudula (now Brussels Cathedral) commemorated the Eucharistic hosts allegedly desecrated by Jews in 1370, hosts that supposedly had bled miraculously when stabbed.

In 1871, the charge of ritual murder was revived by August Rohling, a professor of Catholic theology at the German University of Prague, with the publication of his *Der Talmudjude* (*The Jew According to the Talmud*). In such literature, fiction published in the guise of historical fact overlapped with crude sensationalism, as in *The Protocols of the Elders of Zion*, an untrue, incendiary 1902–3 work of Russian propaganda that reported Jewish plans for world domination and that Nicholas II read to his family. Scare literature served to affirm identity through strife. This element contributed, for example, to the frequency of pogroms in Russia during Easter week.

Throughout the nineteenth and into the twentieth century, the hierarchy of the Catholic Church was divided over attitudes toward Jews. Philosemitism was often a fig leaf for promoting the return of Jews to

Palestine as a means to fulfill an Old Testament prophecy and therefore advance the end of the world. In 1926, a clerical association, Friends of Israel, was founded to forward the conversion of Jews by taking anti-semitism out of the Church. However, in 1928, the year in which the association petitioned Pope Pius XI to drop the prayer for "the perfidious Jews" from the Good Friday liturgy, it was dissolved as a result of pressure from the Vatican's Congregation of the Holy Office. The head of the latter emphasized the "facts" of Jewish history, including collective guilt for the murder of Christ as well as for alleged commercial exploitation of Christians in the present.[7]

During the interwar years (1918–39), many Catholics blamed Jews for the harsh treatment of the Church in Russia, Spain, and elsewhere, an analysis that brought together traditional antisemitism with a very frequent, indeed insistent, presentation of communism as dominated by Jews. Such attitudes help to explain why it was possible for so many first to accept existential and violent antisemitic rhetoric and then to turn with such violence against Jews. The concept of national community and culture as Christian served to exclude Jews and drew on a long anti- or nonsemitic practice. This concept took different forms across Europe and led to a Christian nationalism in, for example, Hungary, Portugal, and Spain. In the case of converts to Christianity, there was a clash with those who put the emphasis on racial criteria as the reason for, and form of, antisemitism. In effect, however, the emphasis on converts excluded most Jews from Church concern.

In scholarship on the Holocaust, the major emphasis is on racism, which is correct as far as the Nazis were concerned, as the harsh fate of Jewish converts to Christianity indicates. However, a strand of Christian antisemitism was also important to the Holocaust. This not only helps explain the background of the Holocaust, both in terms of the isolation of Jews and the antipathy of some elements in Germany and Austria, not least the emphasis on Jewish deicide of Christ and on Jews as thereby cut off from divine grace.[8] Christian antisemitism was also important in terms of the response to the Holocaust within occupied and pro-Axis Europe. Thus, in 1941, in the face of the vicious Ustasha terror by the Croatian fascist movement, Jews in Croatia who converted to Catholicism were not killed, which was not an option offered to Jews by the Germans. Drawing attention to Croatia underlines the attempt in this book to weld together exterminations by the Germans and those by certain of their allies, thus presenting a panscopic view of the events feeding into the Holocaust and the interconnectivities of collaborationist and occupational regimes from France to the Eastern Baltic and the Balkans. For example, in June 1941, Romania, a country noted for decades for its antisemitism, joined the attack on the Soviet Union, declaring a holy war to free Bessarabia, which the Soviet Union had annexed the previous year. In this war, Jews were brutalized by the Romanians, and large numbers died.

Christian antisemitism was downplayed after World War II due to the focus on Nazi perpetrators rather than Germans and allies as a whole. In part, this downplaying was an aspect of the postwar attempt to "normalize" Western Europe by developing the political parties of Christian Democracy, and thus creating a new historical narrative to match the new plan for a new Western Europe. It seemed more necessary, and proved easier, to concentrate on the Nazi origins and direction of the slaughter.

If the focus is, however, on "bystanders"—those whose acceptance/compliance/consent helped make the Holocaust possible—and also on the killing by Germany's allies, then the situation appears different. Although a range of factors, including expediency, played a role in individual responses, religious antisemitism was, for many, very important in creating a sense of Jews as different, alien, and threatening.

Alongside the powerful religious theme were other strands of antisemitism. These included both hostility to Jewish efforts to assimilate and the biological-racist competitiveness associated with social Darwinism. Based in large part on a revival of antisemitism that was founded on biological-racial views, the rise of antisemitism in the later nineteenth and early twentieth centuries was readily apparent. Nationalist hostility to the cosmopolitan—and, thus, alien—influences that critics associated with Judaism was important, as was a sense that Jews were central to an unwelcome, indeed threatening, modernism.[9] Thus, the Holocaust has been seen as part of Hitler's revolt against the modern world, although in both rhetoric and practice, he was only in revolt against certain aspects of the modern world and, indeed, provided a prospectus for a Germanic future.

Ironically, there was also a long-standing habit of viewing Jews as opposed to progress. This notion did not begin in the nineteenth century. Emperor Joseph II, ruler in the 1780s of the Habsburg lands (including what became Austria, Hungary, the Czech Republic and Slovakia, northwestern Romania, southern Poland, and part of northern Italy) and a model of "enlightened despotism" who saw himself as a supporter of religious toleration, left little scope for those Jews whose wish to maintain a separate identity led them to seek more than freedom to worship. Jewish emancipation was believed to entail not only the cessation of legal restrictions on Jews on the part of government but also the end of Jewish customary practices, such as the wearing of traditional clothes, as well as the end of autonomous Jewish institutions, which were seen as barriers to integration. Indeed, liberal German commentators were affected by a sense that Jews were opposed to their concept of progress, especially from the 1870s—particularly when they looked at Jewish communities in Eastern Europe, which, indeed, tended to be more conservative and less assimilated than Jews in Germany and Austria. In this perspective, Eastern European Jews were seen as an obstacle to development and assimilation through cooperation in progress, and their communities as proof that the cooperation and progress were not occurring. This was an acute instance of a more general prejudice, notably in Protestant Anglo-German views, against Eastern and southern Europeans, a prejudice that was in part adopted in these areas but used against particular groups there, notably Jews.

German nationalism led in the nineteenth century to a powerful state, the German Empire, proclaimed in 1871 on the back of the defeat of France. Germany controlled the strongest economy in continental Europe. However, the idea that this state should be based on the supposed community of *Das deutsche Volk* (the German people) was abhorrent to Otto von Bismarck, who played a key role in the creation of the empire and effectively ran it for twenty years, resigning the chancellorship in 1890. Instead, this kind of ethnic nationalism was advanced by the Pan-German League (Alldeutscher Verband), which emerged in the 1890s and drew on bold assertions of a racial nationalism that were to be seen in schoolbooks and maps.[10] Such views were increasingly influential among the educated middle class, and by 1914, they were becoming more important among conservatives. Moreover, there was an increasing

"Christian-centric sense of German nationhood," one that excluded Jewish citizens.[11] Antisemitism was also widespread and popular in Austria, notably in Vienna, where it was used by the Christian Social Party to build support. In practice, a large number of German and Austrian reserve officers were Jews, and, despite being inaccurately criticized as shirkers, Jews served faithfully in the war.

The German Empire, or Second Reich (the first was the medieval Holy Roman Empire that ended in 1806 at the hands of Napoleon, fueling German nationalism), collapsed, however, as a result of its defeat in World War I (1914–18). This collapse was accompanied by the fall of ruling families, such as the Wittelsbachs of Bavaria, and ensured that loyalty and identity shifted from the dynasties, particularly the Hohenzollerns of Prussia, that had ruled the empire. Germany's major ally, Austria, was also defeated, and the Habsburg Empire collapsed as a result.

WORLD WAR I AND THE EMERGENCE OF HITLER

German defeat led to a largely grim emphasis on the history of the *Volk* (people) and the hardship and dispossession they suffered as a consequence of this defeat. For many, nationalism became a key way to understand and confront that history. Whereas failure at the hands of Napoleon in 1805–7 had been followed in 1813 by what was presented as a "German War of Liberation," a conflict linked to nationalist rhetoric that brought rapid success to Prussia and Austria, the situation was very different in 1918. Defeat then was presented by right-wing populists as undeserved and as a consequence of betrayal from within, particularly by Jews and communists. This account distracted attention from the extent to which Germany's defeat was the result of being totally outfought on the Western Front by British, French, and US forces. In the spring and early summer of 1918, with Russia defeated and the Germans launching attacks on the Western Front, victory had appeared within Germany's grasp, but the situation had rapidly changed. This sudden shift encouraged the belief that the army, in practice defeated, had, instead, been stabbed in the back by traitors at home.

In this account, Jews and communists were repeatedly linked by critics such as Alfred Rosenberg, since several prominent communists, including Marx and Trotsky, were indeed Jews, although Marx converted to Protestantism and most Jews were not communists and most communists not Jews. Moreover, Jews had responded to the national cause. More than 100,000 German Jewish and 320,000 Austro-Hungarian Jewish soldiers served during the war, and one in eight died. Most Jews were not pacifists, and the calls of nationalism, duty, and honor had encouraged military service. However, by 1916, antisemitism had increased on the home front with inaccurate claims that Jewish service and sacrifice were not comparable. There was also antisemitism in the military.[12]

The war, indeed, proved a key experience in the development of antisemitism. It was only in 1919 that Adolf Hitler (1889–1945), an Austrian-born veteran of the German army in the trenches, defined his virulent antisemitic views. Many officers of the SS (*Schutzstaffel*, protective force) who were to play a key role in the Nazi regime were linked by experiences of war and defeat, which ensured a bitter generational cohort.[13]

So also was the case with fascism and antisemitism elsewhere in that year. Defeat led to a marked exacerbation of the challenge from communism, both from the Soviet Union and independently. In 1919, the short-lived communist takeovers of Hungary and Bavaria, with Jewish leaders prominent in both (for example, Eugen Leviné and Ernst Toller in Munich), encouraged the misleading identification of communism with Jews. The radical and yet capitalist and cosmopolitan character of Budapest, where many of Hungary's Jews lived, helped ensure that the agrarian populists who opposed the communist regime were hostile to the city.

The Austrian background to Hitler's ideas is important. In part, he drew on Austrian antisemitism that had become much stronger in the two decades preceding World War I, notably in response to the social and economic fluidity of a rapidly changing empire. Hostility to Jews was important in itself, as well as being a way to express potent concerns about the roles and demands of Slavs within the Habsburg Empire, roles and demands that appeared to threaten it with dissolution. Indeed, Hitler's assumptions represented the refraction of pre-1914 right-wing nationalist and racist views through the prism of Austrian and German defeat and disintegration of Habsburg (Austrian) hegemony over part of Slavic Europe. Slavs were widely blamed for this disintegration. The year 1918 not only saw the collapse of the defeated Habsburg Empire but also the creation of new states in Eastern Europe—Yugoslavia, Czechoslovakia, and Poland—although only around one-third of the newly created Polish state came from the Habsburg Empire. The other parts came from the Russian and German empires. More generally, the borders of Eastern Europe were in flux, with an accompanying challenge to senses of identity and hierarchy and with the use of national self-determination as a key rhetoric and means, a use that looked toward a new emphasis on Germanness in an aggressive *völkisch* rhetoric.[14]

In turn, the collapse of Imperial Russia in 1917 and the failure of the Bolsheviks (the victorious communist faction), once successful in Russia, to recreate the entire former empire ensured that Finland, Estonia, Latvia, and Lithuania became independent states, although Ukraine was conquered by the communists. The Russian Civil War there proved particularly deadly for Jews, over 100,000 of whom died as a consequence of over 1,000 pogroms between 1918 and 1921, in large part due to violence by Polish, Russian, and Ukrainian forces who saw Jews as supporters of communism but whose actions also brought to the fore their violent antisemitism.

Germany's defeat and loss in World War I inspired, energized, and focused Hitler's antisemitism. Accordingly, he aspired to reverse Germany's defeat, both morally and territorially, and to recreate an acceptable (i.e., German-dominated) Europe, specifically by controlling Eastern Europe, where *Lebensraum* (living space) was to be pursued for Germans. Although there was tension between Nazi views and conservative geopolitics, Hitler's arguments drew on a long-standing nationalist belief that Germany's destiny included domination of Eastern Europe. This belief, in part, drew on Prussian attitudes, notably toward Poland, but also entailed a transference of Austrian assumptions. The racial inflections of these beliefs focused on a supposed struggle between Germans, defined as Aryans, and non-Germans, a struggle in which there was no uncertainty where virtue, progress, and destiny lay. Nor, to Hitler, was there any doubt about who the villains were. He saw Jews as the active force behind opposition to Germany, whereas other peoples, such as Slavs and Roma (Gypsies), were, in his eyes, far more passive insofar as they were not stirred up by Jews.

The belief in German destiny and redemption had a mythic as well as ideological dimension and dynamic that helped mold more particular and pragmatic nationalist expressions of German interest. The mythic component appealed to Nazi destiny makers. Thus, Eastern Europe offered the prospect for a conflation of nationalism and racist imperialism, and German conquest of the region was to make the prospect operative. The quest for an Aryan geography had some surprising aspects. In *Die Entdeckung des Paradieses* (The discovery of paradise, 1924), Franz von Wendrin argued that the Garden of Eden had been in Germany but that Jews had falsely claimed that it was in Asia. His cartographic claims were accompanied by statements on the need to liberate Germany from the inferior races. Atlases presented Germany as under threat from Jews and communists. For example, the opening page of maps in the 1931 edition of *F. W. Putzgers Historischer SchulAtlas*, the standard German school atlas, included a map of Germany as the bulwark of European culture against the Asiatic hordes, the latter depicted in terms of Huns, Avars, Arabs, Magyars, Turks, Mongols, Jews, Czarist Russians, and communists. Thus, with a crusading mentality, the past was recruited to the service of the present, with racial groups and ideologies melded together. Archaeologists were among those also expected to demonstrate Aryan cultural and economic superiority over others, and Heinrich Himmler was to take a strong interest in archaeology.

These themes were powerfully present in the 1920s as an aspect of a determination to overturn the Versailles peace settlement that had followed World War I and, instead, to ensure German domination of east-central Europe and, thus, Eastern Europe as a whole. Hitler did not invent the racial prospectus of reordering the East, a prospectus that included expelling the allegedly undesirable from Germany, but he benefited from the extent to which the idea was already widely in circulation. This was to make the implementation of his aspirations far easier, not least by discouraging opposition to them.

Germany provided a vehicle for the central European nationalism that Hitler expressed and, in many respects, encapsulated because his was a German nationalism of a particular type. This type was a consequence of the advent of Western European–style nation-states in multiethnic Eastern Europe, a process in which Jews were to be the prime victims but not the only ones. Despite discrimination, Jews had earlier benefited considerably from the opportunities provided by the multi-ethnic Habsburg Empire, also the Ottoman (Turkish) Empire in the Balkans. The central European aspect of Hitler's nationalism linked antisemitic German policy in World War II with that of allies such as Slovakia and Croatia, which became independent (as German client states) in 1939 and 1941, respectively, as a result of Hitler's destruction of Czechoslovakia and Yugoslavia. These and other German allies, such as Hungary and Romania, also benefited from Hitler's support not only in the creation of what appeared as ethnically coherent territories but also in gains by them at the expense of other peoples. Austria provided a crucial link because it helped bring a central European nationalism to Germany, as well as providing key personnel for the pursuance of the Holocaust. A very different but still instructive contribution to the Holocaust came from antisemitic racists in the former Austrian and German empires who found the political changes from 1938 an opportunity to maneuver to their benefit and to push forward ideas. Alongside well-known instances of antisemitic racism from within the former Austrian empire, as in Slovakia, came the less well-known contribution of Czech antisemites to the course of the Holocaust in Bohemia and Moravia.[15]

Racism and the Holocaust were a central drive for Nazi Germany, one that sat alongside other elements that have attracted attention, such as theories of fascist politics or analyses of the Nazi state as a political system. The aggressive racial nationalism at issue was also actively anti-liberal, not least because it opposed the liberal protection for freedoms and liberal toleration that, in guaranteeing rights for all, gave space to individualism and minorities. As a result, the fate of Jews was an aspect of the crisis of European liberalism and, more particularly, the weakness of German liberalism from 1848. Hitler presented liberalism as the cause and product of weakness, both immediate and longer term, in Germany and also more generally. His redemption of Germany entailed a belief in the refashioning of a stronger people and state.

Although Hitler himself made several statements explicitly rejecting the personality cult, he made many more accepting and promoting the cult of himself. National Socialism, in practice, rested on such a cult, not to say political religion, based on the pivotal figure of the *Führer* (leader), as well as on a confused, indeed incoherent, mixture of racialism, nationalism, and belief in modernization through force. Force certainly characterized Hitler's regime with, from the outset, a brutal attitude toward those judged unacceptable—an attitude that culminated in a genocidal attack on Jews. His was a vicious antisemitism that would not be satisfied with discrimination. For Hitler, there had to be persecution, and it had to be not an ongoing aspect of Nazi rule but a decisive and total step that would end what he saw as the Jewish challenge. To Hitler, this was a metahistorical issue, not an add-on designed to fulfill other policies, such as the redistribution of territory, raising of funds, or rallying of popular support. Jew hatred became crucial to Hitler's psychology and rulership, the basis of his decision making; it gave energy to his rhetoric and purpose to his foreign policy and, indeed, his territorial expansionism. In a classic instance of German Romanticism, the pronounced cult of personality was linked to a sense of historical mission. History, to Hitler, was a lived process that he embodied, so that his personal drama became an aspect of the historic—and, thus, at once historical and timeless—mission of the German people. Racial purity was a key aspect of this mission, at once means and goal.

Hitler was not interested in the light that scientific advances threw, and subsequently were to throw, on the complexities of racial identity: namely, that no race possesses a discrete package of characteristics; that there are more genetic variations within than between races; and that the genes responsible for morphological features, such as skin color, are atypical. Races, indeed, are constructed as much as described, and this was the case with the Nazi construction of both Aryans and Jews. However, the Nazis were convinced of the elemental characteristics of race and overlooked the extent to which their definitions were the result of construction. With his organic concept of the German people, Hitler was strongly opposed to biracial marriages and unions, which help to underline the very fluidity of ethnic identity and challenge classification in terms of race.

Jew hatred was integral, indeed necessary, to Hitler's thought. Prior to his gaining power on January 30, 1933, Hitler's policies were not clearly worked out, but he certainly wanted the Jews to emigrate from Germany. Their challenge, in his eyes, underpinned communism, which he saw as a cover for Jewish goals and the prime opposition to Germany in Europe. In his book *Mein Kampf* (*My Struggle*), which Hitler dictated in 1924 while imprisoned after the total failure of his 1923 attempt to overthrow the Bavarian government, the dual nature of the struggle is clearly outlined. Hitler blamed Jews for the German defeat in 1918 and for the problems that emerged thereafter. Under the Nazi regime, Germans were expected to read this book. Jews were seen by Hitler as universally malign and responsible for radical, political, economic, financial, and cultural threats to Germany, European culture, and humanity.

Indeed, to Hitler, who had read *The Protocols of the Elders of Zion*, the ubiquity of Jews was readily apparent because they were depicted as responsible both for trade union activism and for plutocratic oppression. If the Jews were allegedly powerful in the Soviet Union, indeed central to communism and thus to what he presented as a Judeo-Bolshevist conspiracy,[16] Hitler also claimed they were so elsewhere—for example, in France, where there was, in his eyes, both communist Judaism and plutocratic counterpart. Thus, the widespread nature of Jews and the degree of assimilation they showed were, to Hitler, aspects of their threat; Jews could be held responsible for whatever international forces he saw as a challenge and, ultimately, for all of them. Moreover, in training the German people for an external enemy, an enemy within was a useful prelude.

This adaptability was to be useful when Hitler came to explain the problems eventually posed in World War II by conflict with what was a very dissimilar coalition. Jewry to him provided the link that bound together Britain, the Soviet Union, and the United States in enmity to Germany. Churchill, Roosevelt, and Stalin were presented as manipulated, if not controlled, by Jews, which would have come as a surprise to all three of them.

Although Hitler's ideology and vocabulary were often vague, he did not display vagueness in the case of Jews and argued that there was no room for ambiguity or equivocation in German thought and society. To him, both were obfuscations of the existential nature of the struggle between the national mission and its opponents. They were also aspects of the individualism he deplored as a threat to what he presented as a necessary conformism. It was scarcely surprising that irony was as unwelcome to him as ambiguity.

On October 24, 1933, Hitler received General Wilhelm von Dommes, a representative of the Hohenzollern (Prussian imperial) dynasty, who pressed for its restoration. Hitler replied by emphasizing the need to save Germany from Bolshevism and from Jewish domination and by doubting that the monarchy could be tough enough to take on the bloody conflicts such a program would entail. Hitler added that Jews were responsible for Bolshevism and would have to be eliminated.[17] The exiled Wilhelm II was also antisemitic, but Hitler kept him at arm's length.

Hitler's long-term views about the fate of Jews interacted with short-term opportunities, problems, and anxieties presented by developments. Thus, prior to the outbreak of World War II with the German invasion of Poland on September 1, 1939, international relations were a key issue, particularly for Hitler. In seeking to further his goals, Hitler sought to minimize international hostility and, thus, downplayed aspects of antisemitism as put forward by radical Nazis. In 1936, for example, during the Berlin Olympics, there was an attempt to avoid giving cause for international criticism, underlining an awareness that in many other countries, antisemitism of this type was not acceptable. This degree of covering up might imply a consciousness of guilt and wrongdoing, but there is scant sign of it. As another instance of the role of opportunities and problems, events—specifically the number of Jews brought under German control by successive advances in 1939–41—were to be important to the chronology and contours of the Holocaust.

Opportunities, problems, and anxieties, however, do not exist in the abstract but are sensed and created, and Hitler's views largely conditioned the process. Although it is difficult to establish a consistently coherent account of Hitler's views, he came, as a long-term goal, to believe it his mission to extirpate what he (inaccurately) regarded as the Jewish-dominated Communist Soviet Union, which he felt would secure his notions of racial superiority and living space. This was to be accompanied by the removal of Jews, the two acts creating a Europe that would be dominated by Germans. They were to be a master race over the Slavs and others and thus able to act as a world power capable of standing against other world powers. The resources of the East were to be seized in a radical-utopian vision different in character from that of the communists, one inherently involving mass slaughter. To the Nazis and, indeed, to many Germans, the Slavs were identified as an inferior, if not subhuman, race, but the Jews were apparently more threatening. German dominance in Eastern Europe was thus to have a linked political and racial complexion, an outlook that brought Nazi views together with preexisting German ideas on Eastern Europe from a variety of perspectives.

SUPPORTING IDEAS

Hitler alone was not the issue. There was also support for the extermination of all Jews, support which interacted with and paralleled that of many enthusiastic circles for the Nazi regime, not least because it provided the Nazis with the opportunity to fulfill their aspirations. Alongside Hitler's frequent interventions, there was a large cohort of enthusiastic followers, many of whom were willing to be very active and push the bounds of the possible. This helped to ensure that an ideological imperative was transformed into an operational system. To the Nazis, Jews were different but not separate, and this situation had to be ended.

The basis of support for genocidal policies was varied, as was, indeed, the genesis of those policies. Adolf Eichmann, a key figure in the Holocaust, in the 1950s described himself in the third person: "This cautious bureaucrat was joined by the fanatical warrior for the freedom of the blood from which I descend."[18] There were antimodernist aspects of Nazi ideology, not least the mystical focus on symbol and ritual and strong aspirations to being, and controlling, the future. Aspects of self-consciously modernizing beliefs, such as demographics and eugenics, led, or were used, to these ends. For example, ideas about how best to deal with epidemics and to destroy parasites, which played a role in medical thinking, were focused on Jews. Echoes of these views continued to resonate after World War II. Wilhelm Schier's *Atlas zur Allgemeinen und Osterreichischen Geschichte* (1982) used the same map to show the movement of Jews in the Middle Ages and the spread of plague—the black death. There was, in fact, no connection between the two, but a link between Jews and disease was central to Nazi ideas and focused their pronounced notions of racial purification.

These notions drew on widely diffused antisemitic images seen frequently in 1920s publications and even more so from 1933. Jews were depicted as ugly, subhuman, malevolent, and threatening.[19] As such, they apparently needed stopping, and this allegedly could only be achieved by crushing and extirpating the force they represented. The Nazis saw this as their destiny. The attempt by Himmler—the head of the SS (*Schutzstaffel*, protective force), which he turned into the key Nazi coercive force—to make the SS an ethnically pure corps of Aryans rested on ideas of Aryan triumphalism. These involved much pseudoscience, as well as a quest to discover the roots of Aryanism in the mountains of central Asia, particularly the Pamirs and Tibet (a quest of which I noted some legacies when visiting Afghanistan in 1976).

Many of the features seen with Nazi attitudes were also apparent in other countries, not least in the commitment to an aggressive stance on territorial destiny, the concern with a racist attitude to nationhood, and a potent hostility to Jews, who were presented as alien, threatening, and overly powerful. The ethnic cleansing seen at the end of World War I, as states were redefined and borders contested, served as an example for fresh drives and ideas for racial homogeneity, notably in Romania.[20]

NAZI ANTISEMITISM, 1933–39

Prior to gaining control in Germany (1933) and Austria (1938), Nazi thugs engaged in a high level of intimidation and violence directed in particular against Jews. Attacks were frequent on Jewish targets, or what were held to be Jewish targets. Thus, in 1932, alongside attacks in Germany, members of the Austrian SS violently sought to stop the playing of tango and swing music in dance halls, presenting the music as Jewish and un-German. In 1933, there were numerous attacks in Austria on synagogues and Jewish-owned shops and cinemas. The Nazis presented German nationalism very much in terms of the *Volk* (people) and concentrated on ethnic rivalry with non-Aryans, especially Jews and the idea of racial destiny. Jews were treated as a threat to the organic, ethnic concept of *Germanness* and as automatically antithetical to the *Volksgemeinschaft* (people's, or national, community) that was the Nazi goal.

These were the themes of works produced in Germany. The *Atlas zur Deutschen Geschichte der Jahre 1914 bis 1933* (1934), by Konrad Frenzel and the virulently antisemitic Nazi "intellectual" Johann von Leers, opened with a passage from *Mein Kampf* and included pages headed *Versklavung* (The enslaving of Germans as a result of the postwar peace conferences), *Die Ausbreitung der Juden* (The spread of the Jews) and *Chaos*, the last dealing with reparations and inflation. Leers fled to Egypt after the war and under the name Omar Amin became the political adviser of the Information Department under Gamal Abdel Nasser, president from 1954 to 1970. Leers was one of many links between the Nazis and Arab nationalists that were particularly strong in Egypt. In the *Neuer deutscher Geschichts-und Kulturatlas* (New German history and cultural atlas, 1937), edited by Fritz Eberhardt, conflict between "Indogermanic" peoples and Semites in the ancient world was stressed, while the Jews, described as an excrescence, were presented as a threat to modern Germany. The spread of the Jews was also presented as a challenge in Bernhard Kumsteller's *Werden und Wachsen: Ein Geschichtsatlas auf volkischer Grundlage* (1938), a work that saw the Germans as upholders of civilization.

The cosmopolitanism of the Jews was presented as an antithesis to nationalism and, thus, as making necessary the assault on their prominent cultural role in German values—or, indeed, on any role or employment. Doing so allegedly served to protect the "pure" values of German art, music, and so forth. Culture was appropriated and classified from the Nazi perspective. "Degenerate" art and music were castigated, not least for Jewishness, with prominent critical exhibitions in 1937 and 1938, respectively. Both science and the arts were purged of obvious Jewish influences, with 4,000 paintings and drawings burned in Berlin in 1939, and the Western tradition was presented as inherently and necessarily antisemitic.[21] Emigration led to an enormous loss of cultural energy and diversity and scientific originality, one that was of particular benefit to Britain and the United States.

An emphasis on race led to the criticism, indeed dehumanization, of the racial outsider, with Aryans and non-Aryans ("the blood enemy") treated as clear-cut and antagonistic categories, superhumans and subhumans. The association of the Jews with modernity as well was treated as a challenge although, conversely, some Nazis regarded them as a primitive constraint on Nazi modernity. The two approaches combined in the idea that Jews were preventing Germans from achieving their innate potential and fulfilling their necessary destiny and mission, and doing so deliberately.

In focusing on an Aryan *Volk*, the Nazis downplayed the earlier tradition of studying classical (i.e., non-German) influences in German history. Moreover, a stress on the *Volk* challenged individualism and notions of progress and liberty in terms of the celebration and protection of the self, which were associated with a now-damned liberalism and individualism. The focus on Aryans ensured that serious regional, political, religious, social, and economic differences and divisions within Germany were deliberately downplayed. This was an extreme accentuation of the process by which in 1871 the German state created the Second Reich, overlaid with earlier identities and loyalties. The Nazi agendas of national strength and racial consciousness answered the same historical consciousness and set of references. A focus on apparent external threats was linked to the goal of a necessary depoliticization within a newly united and assertive Germany, a depoliticization that, in practice, was a product of a totalitarian drive. The Nazis drew on but redirected Bismarck's *Kulturkampf*, the anti-Catholic policy followed from 1871 to 1887.

Yet, under the Nazis, past themes of national history were also linked to a very different determination to prove Aryan superiority and, at the same time, to take it as a given. As with Nazi geopolitics, there was a meshing of national and racial themes. In a process that was already established, history served to give force to long-term myths about Germany's role and destiny in Eastern Europe.[22] For the Nazis, the present was positioned to take forward a vision of the past that was at once national and racial. They were not unique in this belief, but there was a strong millenarian flavor to their project as well as an extremism in implementation. Excising Judaism, a central element in Nazi policy, was not only about controlling the present and future but also about building a racial civilization by extinguishing the symbolic authority over the past embedded in Judaism and the Bible. Jews were presented as rival and dangerous drivers of world history.[23]

In the short term, prior to the outbreak of World War II in Europe in 1939, propaganda, legislation, and action against the more than half a million German Jews (about 0.75 percent of the German population) provided opportunities to radicalize German society toward Nazi goals, as well as to divert attention from the serious economics strains created by the ambitious rearmament launched by Hitler. His linkage of Jews with communism drew on, and stimulated, a widespread tendency to link the two and to see each as a greater threat as a result. In his novel *Mr Norris Changes Trains* (1935), Christopher Isherwood, who had been there, described from the viewpoint of Berlin those who were pleased with the Nazi takeover: "They smiled approvingly at these youngsters in their big wagering boots who were going to upset the Treaty of Versailles . . . they thrilled with a furtive, sensual pleasure, like schoolboys, because the Jews, their business rivals, and the Marxists, a vaguely defined minority of people who didn't concern them, had been satisfactorily found guilty of the defeat and the inflation, and were going to catch it." There were always large numbers of Germans, notably in Berlin, who rejected Nazi thought and policy. In particular, there was opposition on political grounds to the Nazis and to compliance with them, while many Christians did not share in the compliance of others.

Most German Jews were not communists. They were politically liberal, on the Left, and saw themselves as patriots and as assimilated into German society. As in Austria and Hungary, many were veterans of World War I. Jewish organizations emphasized this patriotism when seeking to persuade the Nazi regime of their good intentions. Zionism (interest in Israel and support for the idea of it as a Jewish homeland and state) was very weak among German Jews, and intermarriage was high: about one-quarter of Jewish men and one-sixth of Jewish women, with higher percentages in certain cities, notably Hamburg.

Nazi legislation and the practice of power, however, turned German Jews into persecuted people and outsiders, and far more rapidly than Jewish leaders had anticipated. Many had assumed that the Nazi government would not last long, which was certainly the pattern of the governments under the previous Weimar Republic. The extent and objectives of Nazi antisemitism were not initially widely understood, and the compliance and indifference of most of the Christian population was not anticipated.

As a result of this compliance and indifference, and of the accompanying ostracism and segregation of Jews, civic culture collapsed because it had very few defenders. Continuing from appalling violence by Nazi thugs under the Weimar Republic, there were acts of violence—indeed numerous violent physical attacks on individual Jews—from the outset of Hitler's rule. These were an aspect of the very violent nature of Nazi government even in the years of peace. Attempts to use the legal system to punish such acts failed.

The process of discrimination and exclusion as the national community was created essentially rested on legislation and administrative acts, for example, the 1933 Law for the Restoration of the Professional Civil Service, and on institutional and popular acceptance, if not enthusiasm. In 1933, Jews were removed from much of professional life, the number of Jewish pupils in schools and universities was limited, and Jews were banned from owning land or being journalists. Such practices were also seen elsewhere. In Romania, there was similar legislation in 1938, with Jews deprived of basic civil rights and banished from the public sector, in an attempt to use legislation to push a Romanization that excluded Jewish Romanians. That year, Jews were excluded from certain professions in Hungary and Italy.

The pace of legislative action varied in Germany, with little new legislative discrimination occurring in 1934 or during the run-up to the 1936 Berlin Olympics, a period of particular concern among the Nazis about their international reputation. Indeed, the slowed pace encouraged discontented radical Nazis to press for more antisemitic measures. There were also marked variations in the rate of incarceration in concentration camps, not that this related principally to Jews at this juncture. Nevertheless, the hostile thrust of policy in order to ensure a national purification, a key theme of Himmler's, was clear, as was the application to Jews. Among the legislation, the Nuremberg Laws of September 15, 1935, were particularly important. Drawing to a limited extent on US state laws about mixed marriages and sexual relations between whites and nonwhites,[24] the Nuremberg Laws defined a Jew as anyone with at least three Jewish grandparents, or anyone with two Jewish grandparents who was also a member of the Jewish faith. The Nuremberg Law for the Protection of German Blood and Honor banned marriage between Jews and non-Jews (as they were in Italy in 1938). The ban on sexual relations was very important for couples who wanted to sustain a relationship despite not being able to get married. There were numerous cases of denunciation to the Gestapo.

Full citizenship was restricted to Jews, which was seen as a clear signal to Jews to emigrate. In 1935, Jews were banned from military service. The process of legal discrimination continued, with a mass of antisemitic legislation during 1938–39, including the decree of December 1938 forcing Jews to live in specially designated Jewish houses and another in May 1939 permitting the abrogation of leases with Jews. This inequality before the law was a crucial feature of the treatment of Jews. Depriving Jews of pension benefits also encouraged emigration. Philanthropy was redefined with Jewish philanthropic foundations (many of which in practice catered also to Christians) brought under Aryan control, while Jews were excluded from receiving support. This was a key erosion of the public sphere, and an institutionalization of a new discrimination that marked Jews apart. It was particularly significant in cities, where the network of philanthropy had helped underpin and express the civic culture.

Furthermore, alongside brutal thuggery, the potential of a police state was increasingly focused on Germany's Jews. Political police systems and practices had developed in Europe from the late nineteenth century in response to concern about political instability and social volatility. The tendency to control public opinion, and thus information, was present in the twentieth century, most prominently with totalitarian regimes, notably those, such as Nazi Germany, that focused on pushing through change rather than simply maintaining authoritarian control. The Nazi regime pursued its purposes through focusing populist support and energy by means of a demonology fueled by hostile information and a millenarianism that rested on a process of ruthless selection.[25] This approach required the classification of individuals and the identification of intended victims. Indeed, Nazi racial policy was implemented in part through modernity in the shape of the machine technologies for classification, registration, ordering, filtering, and retrieving developed by IBM.[26] In 1939, the census definition of Jewishness was transferred from religious to racial criteria. The latter reflected the "biological" aspect of Nazism and of Hitler's thinking in particular. There were ideas of purging the national body, ideas that drew together pseudoscience with quasi-religious notions of redemption.

Initially, in response to the so-called Jewish question, there was pressure to make much of Germany "Jew-free." This entailed driving Jews out from much of Germany, particularly rural small-town Germany, which tended to be the part of Germany most sympathetic to the Nazis.[27] The Jews moved to larger towns, where sympathy for the Nazis was less pronounced or at least less consistent, or emigrated. The latter was permitted by the government until October 1941, although not for men of military age after the outbreak of World War II in 1939. Emigration was, indeed, encouraged as a means to achieve racial purity and create opportunities for non-Jewish Germans. It was one of the "solutions" en route to what became the "Final Solution." Prewar discrimination against, and brutality toward, German Jews had led some to commit suicide and many to flee, giving effect to the policy of expulsion, with the SD (Sicherheitsdienst, the security service of the SS) developing the concept of forced emigration as, by 1938, the solution to what was termed the "Jewish question."[28] This solution was restricted by the many obstacles placed in the path of those seeking to leave, not least by bureaucrats.

By 1938, nevertheless, more than half of the Jewish population of Germany had emigrated; in the end, about 60 percent did. Many fortunately reached the New World, including 102,200 to the United States and 63,500 to Argentina, or destinations that, despite Nazi plans, were not to be overrun by the Germans during World War II: 52,000 to Britain and 33,400 to Palestine, then a British-ruled territory. In addition, 26,000 German Jews went to South Africa and 8,600 to Australia, lessening the extent to which Jews lived in Europe. Unfortunately, others had to take refuge in lands that were to be overrun by the Germans, particularly 30,000 (including Anne Frank) in the Netherlands, 30,000 in France, and 25,000 in Poland. This scarcely fulfilled Hitler's hope that all Jews would leave Europe. That many Jews sought to avoid persecution by fleeing when they could was a key instance of the extent to which there was no simple, passive response to persecution and the threat of more.

Instead, refugees fled from Germany and the newly expanded Germany. Although many hoped to make their way to Palestine or the United States, they, on the pattern of flight from earlier persecutions, took shelter where they could. About half of those who fled to Belgium, the Netherlands, and France, and most of those who fled to Poland, were to be murdered during the Holocaust. These countries were variously seen as refuges, expedients, and transit places, but the refugees generally lacked the opportunity and means to further their hopes.

Opportunities for emigration were limited: the cost and the possibilities of finding employment and shelter (which arose, in part, from existing contacts, especially family links) were important in determining the rate and destinations of emigration. In many states, there were restrictions on immigration—restrictions that reflected the seriousness of the world depression and the resulting high levels of unemployment. Immigration at a time of worldwide economic depression was very difficult. Antisemitism as a generally pronounced and frequently virulent aspect of broader xenophobia in potential host countries also played a role in limiting emigration from Germany.

Concerns over refugee numbers led to the enforcement of restrictions on immigration in some countries, for example, in Britain and the United States, a point that was subsequently minimized in postwar discussion in both countries. Jewish refugees faced difficult conditions in countries to which they could flee, for example, in France and Poland. In France, in 1933 and 1938, there were major drives against immigration. In 1938, Poland refused entry to Jews expelled from Germany who had not been born in Poland.

American antisemitism, which was widespread, was echoed in the State Department, while, from 1930, there was a standing instruction to US consuls not to issue visas to those "likely to become a public charge," that is, to require financial support, a category the size of which was expanded by German policies of expropriation directed at Jews. The US State Department pressed its consuls to be cautious in granting visas, and those who ignored this pressure suffered in terms of their careers.[29] Prominent antisemites included Joseph Kennedy, ambassador to Britain in 1938–40 and a politician with ambitions to be the Democratic Party presidential candidate in 1940. At the same time, all would-be emigrants, regardless of religion, found great difficulty immigrating to the United States, Canada, and other countries during the Great Depression of the 1930s; these attitudes and policies were given a new edge in wartime.

Partly as a result of restrictions overseas, there were worries among German Jews about the possibility of a successful new start elsewhere, and these anxieties exacerbated an unwillingness to abandon assets that were owned in Germany. The German government did not allow Jews to take their monetary and other possessions with them. More generally, the rate of emigration was higher among younger Jews and, conversely, lower among older Jews, particularly those who hoped to see out the crisis, believing that the Nazis would change policy or be replaced—or who had less confidence in a new start abroad. Indeed, in the early years of the Nazi regime, in response to the apparent balance of problems, there was some Jewish emigration back to Germany. Many Jews, notably veterans, also retained a German patriotism, which often was strong. The higher rate of emigration among younger Jews affected the percentage slaughtered on arrival at death camps as opposed to those worked to death.

Jewish emigration provided the German government and German civilians with opportunities to seize assets or acquire them at greatly reduced prices. At a larger scale, what the regime termed its "Aryaniza-tion and de-Jewification" policy drove out Jewish businessmen through discrimination (in taxation and much else) and expulsion. There was an attempt to transform the marketplace. This policy provided many opportunities for greed and envy and, more specifically, for banks and for industrialists such as Friedrich Flick. The policy also offered much to ordinary small-scale businessmen who acquired vacant Jewish real estate throughout the country. Some were opportunists, others antisem-ites, many both.[30] This was a combination also seen in informing on Jews to the authorities in order to gain the benefit of being allocated houses owned or occupied by Jews.[31] As an aspect of Aryanization, new eco-nomic and financial activities were profitably established: for example, the brokering of takeovers by banks[32] and their role in managing Jewish bank accounts. These accounts were blocked on the orders of the govern-ment, and high fees were charged by the banks for access to the accounts for approved purposes such as emigration. Far from policy emerging simply from government, many businessmen were frustrated by the slow pace of the dispossession of Jews. Similar processes were to be seen in Germany's allies. Thus, in Romania, the National Bank, which managed the economic side of expropriation, was a key element in the traditional economic and financial structure.

Antisemitic legislation and Jewish emigration also greatly widened the pool of those who benefited from discrimination against Jews by opening up jobs. For example, as a testimony to their concern about the Jews as the enemy within, an enemy of great potency, the Nazis were obsessed with the idea that education provided Jews with an opportunity to pollute the young with liberal ideas. Jews were, therefore, purged from higher educational institutions that, in turn, provided opportunities for many of the second-rate "intellectuals" who congregated around Nazism and further encouraged them to publish their views and to present them as normative. Similarly, in 1938, Jews were banned from teaching in Italy.

At this stage, mass murder was not a policy aimed at German Jews, but the callousness, not to say brutality, of the government and its supporters was already apparent. Violence was also directed against individual Jews, with the *Anschluss*, the takeover of Austria on March 12, 1938, involving much violence against Jews and their property in Vienna and encouraging more action in Germany, notably Goebbels's drive against the remaining Jews in Berlin, which contained Germany's largest Jewish community. Thuggery became normative and increasingly organized, most prominently in the vandalism in June linked to the decree obliging Jews to register their wealth and, even more, in the *Kristallnacht*— Night of the Broken Glass—pogroms in Germany on November 9–10, 1938. Ordered by Hitler, this violence, which had drawn in part on the antisemitic persecution in Austria after the *Anschluss*, served, in turn, to lower barriers against fresh violence as well as to draw participants and bystanders into a web of complicity, a process seen, for example, in Berlin. On the *Kristallnacht*, synagogues and Jewish businesses and homes across Germany were attacked, destroyed, and damaged without the police intervening. This was a deliberate attempt not only to intimidate Jews, so as to speed up their emigration, but also to destroy their presence in society and thus to annihilate their identity in Germany. About 1,000 synagogues were destroyed, and as many as 7,500 businesses attacked. The figures for destruction and casualties are all uncertain. There was considerable looting, as well as much deliberate destruction of property. The looting was a matter of the seizure of goods as well as the extortion of money. In addition, Germany's Jews were "fined" one billion *Reichsmarks*.[33] Individual violence, theft, and corruption combined with that of the state. Insurance companies sought to lessen their liability for the damage.

Attacking Jewish communities by destroying their synagogues was a crucial precursor to the Holocaust, as it was an open attempt to wreck Jewish cohesion and invite the non-Jewish population to antisemitic violence as much as to destroy a presence that was different and yet also integrated physically into the center of German society. This violence had already been seen in June 1938 when the Nazi leader in Upper Bavaria, Adolf Wagner, ordered the destruction of the main synagogue in Munich. Located on Herzog-Max-Strasse, close to the Marienplatz, the main square in the old town, this was a major building (to Hitler an "eyesore") that Wagner wanted totally destroyed and replaced by a parking lot. Other centers of German Jewish culture and activity were also destroyed—for example, the main synagogue in Dresden. This was an organized process. The destruction of synagogues was accompanied by that of the sacred scrolls of the Torah, as well as of other objects, including prayer shawls. The violence was at once brutal and symbolic, humiliating and complete.[34]

After the *Kristallnacht*, in which possibly several hundred Jews were killed, the number of Jews held in concentration camps sharply increased by about 30,000—so also did the killing of Jews in the camps. Whereas fewer than one hundred had been murdered there prior to the *Kristallnacht*, possibly one thousand were killed in the next six months. Furthermore, after the *Kristallnacht*, economic measures against Jews were stepped up, not least with the expropriation of businesses in December 1938. The number of Jewish-owned businesses fell rapidly. Measures to encourage emigration were also pushed forward, but Hitler, at this stage, turned down Reinhard Heydrich's idea for Jews to be made to wear an identifying badge, as well as Goebbels's suggestion for the establishment of ghettos. It was not until September 1, 1941, that a decree was issued requiring German Jews to wear a yellow star.

Concentration camps serve as central sites for discussion of the Holocaust, but when they were established after Hitler gained power in January 1933, they were primarily intended as detention centers for those the Nazis wished to incarcerate rather than as central places for a war against Jewry, let alone for genocide. The focus for those in "protective custody," which meant detention without trial, was initially on political opponents of the Nazis; by the summer of 1935, there were about 3,500 prisoners, with Dachau, opened near Munich in March 1933, as the most prominent camp. It swiftly witnessed the introduction of an arbitrary policing designed to sow terror and fulfill fantasies of brutality that sought to destroy the threat allegedly posed by those the Nazis disliked. Theodor Eicke, the second commandant in 1933–34, propagated this Dachau spirit, which he disseminated on becoming chief of the Inspectorate of Concentration Camps from 1934 to 1939, then becoming a commander of a division of SS troops before being shot down and killed in 1943.[35] However, the system expanded from 1935, not least in order to use the forced labor of the larger numbers of the regime's real or apparent opponents who were detained. Major camps included Sachsenhausen, opened in 1936, Buchenwald in 1937, and Mauthausen in Austria (established after the *Anschluss*) in 1938. The development of the camps was to provide an important element in the institutional genesis of the Final Solution.[36]

The policy of forced emigration had been followed when Austria was occupied in March 1938, after which, with the two states united, German antisemitic legislation was applied, with considerable success, in a society that, anyway, was strongly antisemitic. Under the ruthless pressure of Adolf Eichmann, the SD official responsible, more than 100,000 of the 160,000 Austrian Jews emigrated in 1938–39; in turn, this served as a model for policy within Germany. Austria's Jews mostly emigrated to Britain, the United States, and Palestine. In December 1938, Hermann Göring, the second most powerful figure in the Reich, announced that Hitler had decided that forced emigration was to be pressed forward rapidly.

Arab pressure in Palestine, not least violent opposition to British policies and control, both in the Western Wall riots of 1929 and, more seriously, in the Arab Rising of 1936–39, however, helped limit emigration to Palestine, which after World War I was a League of Nations mandate administered by Britain. This emigration was actively sponsored by Jewish agencies and, indeed, approved by Nazis, who wanted Jews to leave Europe. The British were concerned about Arab views elsewhere in the Middle East, not least because their position in both Egypt and Iraq was fragile, and Whitehall was also concerned over Arab discontent in Saudi Arabia and Transjordan. Moreover, the heavy commitment of troops in Palestine to contain and eventually overcome the Arab Rising was disproportionate to Britain's general military requirements. The White Paper of May 1939 about the future of Palestine reflected British concerns about Arab views on and in Palestine. As a result, the idea of a Jewish state in Palestine was put aside while Jewish immigration was limited. Nevertheless, the Arab Rising helped lead many Arab leaders to support German policies.[37]

Forced emigration remained the policy pushed by the Germans. The deportation of Jews from occupied areas was the policy envisaged for Bohemia and Moravia (the modern Czech Republic), which were seized by the Germans on March 15, 1939. Eichmann was sent to Prague in July to encourage emigration through the Central Office for Jewish Emigration, as he had done in Vienna in 1938. "Encourage" is a misnomer for the harassment involved in what was often really forced migration and expropriation.

POLAND INVADED

Hitler was keen on conflict and determined not to be denied, as he had been with the Munich Agreement of September 29, 1938, about the fate of Czechoslovakia. In turn, the Poles were determined not to respond to German pressure by making concessions. The German attack on Poland on September 1, 1939, led Britain and France to declare war two days later. Poland had a population of about 3.3 million Jews, a larger percentage of the population than their German counterparts had been. As with Germany, Austria, Bohemia, and Moravia, the German conquerors wanted Jewish emigration from Poland. That policy, however, proved unrealistic there and also for the vast majority of Jews in areas that the Germans conquered from 1939.

The murderous but not yet clearly genocidal intent of German policy became readily apparent that year. Having rapidly overrun Poland in September, the Germans and the Soviets, who cooperated in the conquest (Soviet forces overran eastern Poland from September 17), at once began to kill Poland's leaders and intelligentsia in order to further their ends of creating a docile slave population. In addition, several thousand Jews were killed by the Germans during or soon after the conquest, some of them burned alive in synagogues.

This killing proved a key episode in eroding inhibitions and encouraging slaughter as a means of policy and, therefore, as a wider option. Indeed, on September 8, Heydrich, an SS *Gruppenführer* who was head of the Security Police and SD and who now also became head of the Reich Security Main Office established that month, noted of Poland: "We want to leave the little people alone. The nobility, the priests and the Jews have to be done away with." The killings in Poland show that genocidal intentions and actions were apparent as part of military operations from the start of World War II and from the beginning of German occupation policies. Many army officers proved willing or eager to support the slaughter of Jews.[38] Although Jews were not the sole target, Operation Tannenberg, the mass shooting of Poles on proscription lists and others (including hospital patients) by special task units supported by Germans living in Poland and by the German army, was in part an experiment to determine if genocide was feasible in terms of manpower, resources, and the time required to carry it out. The geographic parameters of Tannenberg were clearly defined for a specific purpose but had a wider applicability. Tannenberg was purposefully named as vengeance for the Polish defeat of the Teutonic Knights in 1410 and a reference to a major victory over the Russians in 1914. The naming of Operation Barbarossa, the 1941 invasion of the Soviet Union, after a valiant medieval German emperor was also significant.

Alongside an initial mixture of fear, fatalism, simple survival, and resignation based on the experience of German rule in 1915–18, killings in Poland continued after the conquest. Indeed, on November 11, 1939, Jews were killed in Ostrów Mazowiecka, the first total destruction and slaughter of a Jewish community during the war. This was a conspicuous instance of a wider pattern of killing.[39]

For brutality, there was also the example of the Soviet Union. Thousands of Jews were killed there, although the killing was not directed specifically against Jews. Following the earlier mistreatment and slaughter of those judged opponents of communism, notably in Ukraine in the early 1930s, in 1939–40, 1.17 million people were deported from Soviet-occupied eastern Poland to Soviet labor camps, and in 1940, about 127,000 more were deported from the Baltic states—Estonia, Latvia, and Lithuania—which were occupied by Soviet forces that year. Many who were not deported were slaughtered.

The Nazis had been happy to see Polish Jews flee into exile as they overran the country, but once Poland was conquered, Nazi policy, from September 1939, called for a comprehensive transfer of Poland's Jews in what was one of the biggest moves of civilians hitherto in Europe. Jews were to be removed from the areas annexed to Germany in 1938–39— Austria, Czechoslovakia, and western Poland—and sent to the General Government, the part of Poland (central Poland) that was occupied by the Germans but not annexed, and to a Jewish reservation in Poland's eastern borderlands.

In the General Government, Jews were to be controlled and exploited by being made to live in urban ghettos, a medieval practice of formal discrimination and exclusion that had come to an end in the nineteenth century: the Prague ghetto was ended in 1852 and that in Rome in 1870. The first new ghetto was established in Piotrków in October 1939. Among other cities, Łódź followed in April 1940 and Warsaw that November: it contained a third of the city's people, 380,000, in slightly more than 2 percent of the area. Deportation to these small, crowded ghettos also entailed the movement of large numbers of Jews (including those who had converted to Christianity) from other parts of the same cities. It was a serious undertaking for the German administration, although one lessened by the use of Jewish elders' councils for the internal control of the ghettos and as their intermediaries with the German authorities. From December 1, 1939, Polish Jews were to be distinguished by wearing armbands with the Star of David.

The ghetto inhabitants were subject to harsh conditions, especially limited food, poor sanitation, and forced labor in cruel conditions, and these circumstances became increasingly bad. They were accompanied by vicious, random violence.[40] All Jewish men between twelve and sixty were now under an obligation for forced labor, and forced-labor camps were established from October 1939. Those who were caught trying to leave the 300 ghettos or 437 labor camps or to cross into Soviet-occupied Poland were killed, and others were tortured. In addition, some German Jews were deported to Polish ghettos. These ghettos and labor camps, like the later concentration camps, proved to be incubators of high levels of death through epidemics, particularly typhus, as the inhabitants were exposed to serious levels of malnutrition, overcrowding, totally inadequate heating, major problems with water supplies and sanitation, and a shortage of medical supplies.

These living conditions confirmed the antisemitic prejudices of German leaders. The German doctors supposedly responsible for overseeing public health in occupied areas saw Jews as natural carriers of disease, and their attitudes and actions reflected the extent to which the profession was open to Nazi penetration, in large part enthusiastically so. The destitution of the harshly treated Jews was then used to justify mistreatment.

In some respects, this was a halfway stage to the more deliberate slaughter of the Final Solution. Starvation certainly was accomplishing this end, although, at the level of ghetto managers, many of the responsible Germans sought to provide Jews with minimal food, primarily in order to ensure that the ghetto population could work,[41] a procedure also seen in concentration camps. This was an important and instructive instance of the often sharply contradictory crosscurrents in German policy. By June 1941, 2,000 Jews were dying monthly from starvation in the Warsaw ghetto (and 800 in Lódź), and by August, the monthly death rate in Warsaw was 5,500. Indeed, over the period of the Holocaust as a whole, a large number of Jews starved to death or died of diseases that could easily have been prevented or for which they could readily have been treated. Ghetto life was a slow death that, in the meantime, left a large supply of forced labor, the latter a key and developing element of the German war economy. Thus, the Lódź ghetto specialized in uniforms for the German army (in June 1941, Himmler visited the plant of a uniform manufacturer there) as well as other military supplies.[42] In the labor camps, large numbers died. Himmler was not only head of the SS but also, from October 1939, Reich Commissioner for the Consolidation of German Nationality. The latter entailed the repatriation of ethnic Germans living abroad and their settlement in areas such as the *Reichsgau Wartheland*, as well as the prevention of any harmful influence from other nationalities.

The ghettos were initially intended as a stage in the path to the expulsion of Jews, in effect, a storage stage. Indeed, in September 1939, the Germans expelled thousands of Jews from their part of Poland to the Soviet occupation zone. Himmler was opposed, at this stage, to the large-scale slaughter of Jews. Instead, the emphasis was on the creation of a Jewish reservation in Poland's eastern borderlands, a policy Hitler advocated from late September. The new German-Soviet border in Poland was revised accordingly on September 28, 1939. On October 6, Hitler told the *Reichstag* that the new racial order in Europe would include the resettlement of peoples and the regulation of the Jewish problem. This declaration provided the opportunity for Eichmann, still the SS officer in charge of the Central Office for Jewish Emigration, to implement his plans to deport Jews to Poland's eastern borderlands. The attainment of *Lebensraum* appeared imminent.

Nisko, a town on the River San in what is now southeast Poland, and the surrounding area was the first designated destination. It was seen by the Germans as a Jewish reservation, where Jews could be deported prior to further movement to the east, but the plan failed, in part due to competing pressures on land (for settlement) and rail transport and in part because of opposition by Hans Frank, the newly appointed governor of the General Government, who wished to control developments.[43] Moreover, Jews, many from Vienna, dispatched to this infertile area were maltreated and lacked the necessary farming tools, let alone experience. Some were shot or sent into Soviet territory. The Nisko experiment was followed, in 1940, by the Lublin Plan. The Jews sent to Lublin were housed in camps and used as slave labor, a policy instituted by Odilo Globocnik, an SS protégé of Himmler who was later prominent as a brutal organizer of mass slaughter.

As an aspect of Hitler's chaotic bureaucratic Darwinism—namely, giving far-reaching and clashing powers to rival satraps—the poorly organized and brutally administered deportation plans fell afoul of

competing schemes to populate occupied territories with German settlers. These settlers were to be drawn from German refugees from Soviet
rule and those whose repatriation from Soviet territories was arranged
by the German government in cooperation with the Soviet Union. These
schemes drew on a long-standing agrarian Romanticism that had been
directed by right-wingers and then the Nazis to focus on strengthening Germany's borders and what was presented as the German race.
Farming was seen as a healthier way to build up the German master
race. Himmler, who, as Reich Commissioner for the Consolidation of
German Nationality, was also in charge of German settlement outside
Germany, sought an SS-based population of farmers and warriors as
a way to incorporate the new territories, as well as to develop his own
power, the last a key theme. In practice, few Germans wished to settle
in Poland, but Himmler repeatedly saw it as an opportunity to provide
land for those of German descent who were to be repatriated, sometimes
unwillingly, from communities further east. This repatriation was to ensure that they were not under the control of the Soviet Union. Jews were
not welcome in this prospectus, and this greatly limited the options for
them, as many were moved from areas designated for German settlers,
especially in the Warthegau, which had been part of Poland but was now
annexed to Germany.

The option of expelling Europe's Jews to the French colony of Madagascar in the Indian Ocean was discussed in 1940 and approved by Hitler
in June, the month in which France surrendered to the successful German invaders. A pro-German government based in Vichy took over the
part of France not occupied by the Germans and initially controlled
most of the French colonies, including Madagascar, until it was captured
from Vichy forces by the British in 1942. The option of expelling the Jews
to Madagascar drew on a long-standing idea that European colonial expansion should provide the solution to the question of a separate Jewish
homeland, possibly Uganda, within the British Empire. With Hitler, the
emphasis was antisemitic and designed to facilitate the movement of
Jews from Europe and, indeed, had been employed in that sense by Hitler
in a conversation with Göring in November 1938 and with Polish foreign
minister Joséf Beck in January 1939. Heydrich wrote to Foreign Minister
Joachim von Ribbentrop about the idea in June 1940. It was hoped that

Vichy could be persuaded to cede Madagascar to Germany, which could then use it to deport Jews. Such deportation was not intended to provide a pleasant exile, not least because Madagascar was noted as an unhealthy environment, with yellow fever being particularly deadly there, as it had been for the French when they conquered the island in the mid-1890s. Furthermore, the infrastructure and economy would not be able to support the millions of Jews who were to be sent there. Similarly, later plans to complete an invasion of the Soviet Union by marching Jews to Siberia, an area not envisaged for German settlement, were intended to lead to their death.

The Madagascar option, however, was rendered impossible in the short term by British naval power, which was also to be the basis for the British conquest of the island from Vichy forces in May–November 1942. As a result, in part possibly as a cover-up for genocide, the Germans, instead, came to think of Madagascar as an eventual postwar destination for Jews. It was mentioned under this head, alongside Siberia, by Hitler when he met Marshal Slavko Kvaternik of Croatia on July 21, 1941. Other parts of Africa were sometimes considered, Hitler telling Goebbels on May 29, 1942, that central Africa would be a sensible destination, not least as the climate would weaken Jews.

However, the deportation of Jews from the Axis sphere, the policy apparently sought by Hitler in February 1941,[44] was not feasible. Meanwhile, the conquest, from April 9, 1940, of Denmark (1940), Norway (1940), Luxembourg (1940), the Netherlands (1940), Belgium (1940), France (1940), Yugoslavia (1941), and Greece (1941) had brought, by May 1941, large numbers of Jews under German control—or, at least, direction, via allies and client states. The largest Jewish populations were in France, with 283,000, and the Netherlands, with 126,000.

Aside from the Jews born or brought up in these countries, many Jews who had already fled Germany, Austria, and other areas now also came under German control. At the same time, refugee movements continued within German-dominated Europe, as Jews left areas where their fate seemed particularly bleak, notably Germany and Austria, and headed to others, especially France and the Benelux countries, from where they hoped to move to countries outside the German-dominated region. Some managed to reach neutral states, notably Portugal, Spain,

Switzerland, and Turkey, or to emigrate outside Europe, especially if married to citizens of neutral countries, which then included the United States. Desperate expedients were often necessary in order to leave German-controlled regions.

In Germany, the popularity of the Nazi regime, already high as a consequence of overcoming the Versailles terms and ending unemployment, was greatly enhanced by the defeat of France, a success conspicuously lacking during World War I but not in 1870–71. At the same time, preparations escalated for the attack on the Soviet Union by Germany and its allies, to be launched in June 1941. The military's schemes and contingency plans for a war designed to keep the Soviet Union in its place were co-opted by Hitler into a broader war designed to fulfill his hopes for the destruction of Jewish Bolshevism and to create a new German territorial system able to ensure a "new order" that was to fulfill the goals of Germany's destiny to lead Europe and rescue culture.[45]

While this was being prepared, all arrangements for Jews seemed transitional, as this attack would alter the international situation, as well as provide more land that could be seen as a solution for the Jewish question, if land was indeed to offer a solution. In the event, alongside the mass slaughter of Jews in Soviet territory as the Germans advanced in 1941, the failures or problems of deportation hopes and plans, combined with the fact that the attack on the Soviet Union led to control over many Jews and was not to provide the Germans with a solution for the Jews elsewhere in Europe, encouraged a stress on schemes for immediate mass murder in order to produce a solution. So also did the extent to which conquest brought greater power and centrality to the SS, and with far fewer institutional and practical restraints than in Germany. Conquest also brought forward the possibility for utopian Nazi thoughts and plans, while enhancing their violence through the practicalities and ideology of repression. In this conflation, military operations and occupation policy were to be linked.

CONCLUSIONS

The plans already mentioned reflect the extent to which there was no clear-cut path toward genocide. Instead, the treatment of Jews was an aspect of a wider characteristic of German policy. It was, at once, confused, divided, haphazard, and brutal, a mismatch between broad antisemitic aspirations that lacked clear formulation and, indeed, coherence and, on the other hand, an absence of clarity over prioritization and execution. At the same time, changes within the German state, society, and culture, notably the isolation and exclusion of the Jews, had removed the barriers—first, to active and violent discrimination against fellow Germans and other Jews and, finally, to their mass murder. Thus, the judiciary and press had been brought under Nazi control, while the police had been militarized, and legal restraints on killing had been removed. In early 1941, Operation T4 doctors were dispatched into the concentration camps. Those prisoners selected from the camps were then sent to T4 asylums to be gassed.

Moreover, these changes interacted with ideological pressures and international developments that made the Holocaust seem not only possible and acceptable but also necessary—indeed, essential. Hitler told the *Reichstag* on January 30, 1939: "If the international Jewish money power in Europe and beyond again succeeds in enmeshing the peoples in a world war, the result will not be the Bolshevization of the world and a victory for Jewry, but the annihilation of the Jewish race in Europe." This was at once a (totally misleading) account of the outcome of World War I and a prospectus for a second world war. Hitler was to refer to this speech in 1941, and Goebbels recorded in his diary in March 1942 that the prospectus was beginning to come true.

This annihilation was clearly a prospect in 1939 in anticipation of the first step in the attainment of *Lebensraum*, which was sought in part in Poland but more particularly in Ukraine and Crimea. The ideal of settlement in the East went back into the nineteenth century. Hugely important in shaping Nazi ideas was the Oberost Empire created by the German high command in the Baltic states, Belarus, and Ukraine in 1918 after the Peace of Brest-Litovsk—so also with the Free Corps actions in the Baltic states during 1919 against the communists. These brutal actions were very important in creating a climate that produced the paramilitary movements of the post-1918 period and their culture of violence. Many of these Free Corps members and Baltic Germans, for example Rosenberg and Scheubner-Richter, ended up in Bavaria. This movement was more important than imperialism in Africa in shaping subsequent German actions.

However, the method and the time to the completion of *Lebensraum* remained under debate, with several means under consideration, notably forms of exile and of comprehensive slaughter. Madagascan and Siberian relocation plans were understood as placing Jews in a region with harsh climates and disease that would do the killing. The killing of Jews in Poland in 1939 and the T4 euthanasia program in 1939–40 for the slaughter of psychiatric patients were such that the notion of mass murder was not a difficult chasm to cross in policy and action. Thus, what became the Final Solution was not so much a question of annihilating the Jews in Europe but determining how to kill them more effectively.

Global war brought under Hitler's control areas where most of Europe's Jews had settled, brought forward the millenarian strain in Nazism, and encouraged Hitler to give deadly effect to his aspirations and fears with an urgency that reflected his sense of challenge for Germany and his forebodings of an early death. The slaughter of Jews became a major war aim in a war that was seen and presented by Hitler as an existential struggle for racial and cultural identity as well as superiority. Indeed, this identity was presented as a guarantee of superiority, one that could only be achieved by the prompt, total, and irrevocable removal of Jews from a German-dominated Europe.

TWO

Toward Genocide

ARMY GROUP CENTER ACHIEVED RAPID SUCCESS WHEN GERMAN armored forces outmaneuvered the Soviet West Front (army group) near the city of Białystok, which, until September 1939, had been in eastern Poland before becoming part of the Soviet Union. Once Białystok was occupied, on June 27, the Germans attacked the city's Jews. German police battalions slaughtered the patients in the Jewish hospital and filled the main synagogue with Jews, set it on fire, and shot dead those who attempted to jump out.

The German invasion of the Soviet Union in 1941—Operation Barbarossa, launched on June 22—brought far more people judged unsuitable by Hitler, both Jews and Slavs, under his control. This provided opportunities for the implementation of Nazi plans, which entailed not only fulfilling Nazi views of Germany's destiny but also overcoming problems as they arose that apparently challenged these plans and this destiny. The war against the Soviet Union was conceived from the outset as a genocidal war, and the *Wehrmacht* (German armed forces), in conjunction with German civilian authorities such as the Ministries of the Eastern Territories and Agriculture, planned for thirty million Soviet deaths. In part, this death rate estimation was intended in order to pursue plans for a complete ethnic and geopolitical recasting of the Soviet Union and, in part for more immediate reasons, in order to ensure food for the invading army. The focus was on killing Jews. As they did not intend to occupy distant Siberia, which they regarded as being in faraway Asia, the Germans planned to detain and deport Jews there. At the same time, SS task forces (*Einsatzgruppen*) advancing close behind the troops from the opening day of the invasion killed Jews, political commissars, and others deemed undesirable.[1] Other SS units also played a major role, particularly the *Kommandostab* brigades. German special police battalions, moreover, took a prominent part in the killing, as they also did with mass shootings in Polish Galicia, for example, in the city of Kolomea, where the police shot around 15,000 Jews. Both the SS and the police received special antisemitic indoctrination to this murderous end.

THE GERMAN ARMY

In general, in contrast to postwar propaganda that suggested that it did not participate, the German army cooperated in the killing, whereas in Ukraine, the army was willing to complain about the brutal treatment of non-Jewish Ukrainians. Indeed, the German army supported the slaughter of Jews and saw them as the key source of resistance, which they certainly were not. The harsh content and tone of orders for the day by many army commanders to their units did not encourage reasonable treatment of Jews, communists, and prisoners. Indeed, many called on their troops to annihilate Hitler's targets. SS task forces were particularly murderous, but the army also killed many Jews. This was particularly the case in Serbia, where Jews were killed in mass shootings in late 1941 and early 1942. They were the prime group shot in response to Serbian partisan activity, with army officers accepting the Nazi identification of communists and Jews and willingly having the latter shot because they could not catch the former or other partisans.

In the Soviet Union, as the Germans advanced, frontline troops frequently killed Jews. This was done notably, but not only, in response to difficulties in the campaign that led to the killing of Jews as a way to strike at concerns about partisans and communists. Attributing opposition to Jewish Bolshevism encouraged a brutal response, which was particularly marked among young soldiers. One German soldier subsequently recalled his colleagues in the infantry regiment seizing twenty Jewish men in the city of Lida, part of Poland occupied by the Soviet Union in 1939: "They were beaten with rifle butts and tortured with bayonets; blood was flowing from both nose and mouth. Then they had to, under further mistreatment, dig a pit. When it was finished they had to stand one after the other before the pit and were executed in the presence of all. There was no reason for this killing."[2]

Moreover, in Greece and France, the army played a role in the deportation and murder of Jews. Field Marshal Wilhelm List, the commander of German forces in the Balkans in 1941 (and of Army Group A on the Eastern Front in 1942), was sentenced in 1948 to life imprisonment by a US military tribunal for war crimes in the Balkans, notably his instructions for murderous antipartisan warfare including the reprisal killings of hostages. However, he was released in 1952 on the grounds of ill health, a typical outcome, and lived until 1971.

Violence by the German military against civilians harked back to a recent tradition of such actions by German forces in Europe and overseas. Crucially, the Franco-Prussian War (1870–71) had not proved the swift and cheap victory the Germans had anticipated, unlike their victory at the expense of Austria in 1866. Problems in 1870–71 included supply difficulties, continuing French resistance, and opposition from a hostile population. The Germans responded harshly to the *francs-tireurs* (free shooters), deserters, or civilians who fought back and whom the Germans treated as criminals, not soldiers. Summary executions helped dampen opposition in this war but were also part of a pattern of German brutality, which included the taking of hostages, the shooting of suspects (as well as of those actually in arms when captured), the mutilation of prisoners, and the destruction of towns and villages, such as the town of Chateaudun. In part, this practice reflected the problems posed for the Germans by hostile French citizen volunteers who did not wear uniforms and were impossible to identify once they had discarded their rifles. In response, the Germans adopted a social typology that prefigured those of the following century, treating every "blue smock," the customary clothes of the French worker, as a potential guerrilla.[3]

In turn, murderous German atrocities in Belgium and France in 1914, during the opening campaign of World War I, in part appear to have reflected fury that Belgium had unexpectedly resisted German attack and, therefore, affected the ease and pace of the German advance. German losses at the hands of Belgian regular units led to reprisals against civilians as well as to the killing of military prisoners, while a high degree of drunkenness, confusion, and friendly fire among German units contributed directly to their belief that they were under civilian attack, which reinforced their attitude that it was acceptable and, indeed, sensible to inflict reprisals on the innocent. This killing was then defended by strategies of deception and propaganda that were organized by the German army and government in 1914.[4] In the case of the Austrian army, and on the pattern of brutality in occupying Bosnia in 1878, the invasion of Serbia in 1914 and its occupation in 1915 were followed by guerrilla opposition that led the army to kill many civilians.

While indicative, these instances were very different from the overlap between operational and genocidal warfare seen in World War II. Earlier, violence against civilians was not the German goal but, rather, a response to an uncertainty and fear that German soldiers could not accept psychologically. The use by regulars of violence against civilians suspected of opposition was deadly when it was seen as necessary and became an automatic response, but prior to 1941, this was generally a secondary aspect of German military conduct in Europe.

A different background was that of German campaigning in Africa, particularly in the 1900s, when practices with genocidal consequences— such as driving people into a waterless desert in German South West Africa—were followed. In responding to the Herero rebellion in German South West Africa (now Namibia) in 1904–5, the Nama rebellions there in 1890 and 1905–9, and the Maji Maji Rebellion in German East Africa (now Tanzania) in 1905, the German army had become used to seeing entire ethnic groups as race enemies and had developed the practice of racial conflict. The Herero prisoners sent to prison and labor camps were treated with great cruelty, such that large numbers died: indeed, about 45 percent of those in military custody by 1908. About 250,000 people died in the suppression of the Maji Maji Rebellion.

In part, these assumptions and practices were transferred to Europe in the twentieth century, first with the massacres in Belgium during World War I and, far more clearly, consistently, violently, and on a larger scale, in Eastern Europe during World War II, but the genesis of the latter was more clearly European circumstances. A key prelude to German policy in Eastern Europe during World War II was possibly set by the extensive German campaigning on the Eastern Front in World War I. A disparaging sense of the people overrun, not least seeing them as weak, dirty, and diseased, became commonplace. This attitude was in response not only to those who were conquered, a response that was racist as well as cultural, but also to the vast areas that now had to be psychologically understood and overcome. Jews were numerically prominent in the Russian borderlands that were overrun, and their fate was an aspect of the extent to which the war made violence an experience of Eastern Europe's Jews. The Russian Empire had then included central and eastern Poland, Lithuania, and Ukraine, all of which were overrun by the Germans in 1915–18.

This episode has been seen as important to the development of a hostile and violent response to conquered peoples as a central aspect of German war policies. However, it is possible that, in part, this approach represents a retrospective perspective, owing something to knowledge of what was to happen in World War II. Indeed, a less critical view of the German army in World War I has been advanced,[5] and although there was often harsh treatment of civilians, the Nazi dimension was, of course, absent then.

Furthermore, rather than emphasizing racism, Isabel Hull has argued that genocide against the Herero developed out of standard German military practices and assumptions, so that genocide in South West Africa was in any event not the product of ideology but of institutional action. This is a conclusion that casts an instructive light on the German army's quest for a crushing victory in a battle of annihilation, a form of total war. Civilians were dispensable in this view, while there was also an emphasis on the punitive treatment of Germany's enemies, treatment that was unconstrained by international law. Defeat in World War I enhanced the brutality of the German army, including its Austrian units.[6]

In World War II, racial violence was displayed by the Germans from the outset, in Poland in 1939. The army executed about 16,000 Poles as well as cooperating closely with the SS in murderous operations to enforce control. Moreover, the massacres of about 3,000 French African soldiers by both the regular army and the SS in France in 1940 showed that the German military was also willing in Western Europe to embrace the Nazi notion of racialized warfare and its murderous applications. These massacres were not a response to official policy but, instead, were a sporadic product of racial violence from below, albeit a violence that reflected Nazi ideology and also propaganda from 1914 onward against the French use of African soldiers.

On the Eastern Front from 1941, building on the examples of conquering and ruling Poland—the first Eastern Front of World War II—the institutionalized ruthlessness of the German army was accentuated by Nazi ideology. As a result, there was a far greater willingness to ignore, indeed mock, international laws and to respond almost instinctively in a brutal fashion that reflected a belief that the population was subhuman and that, therefore, German violence was appropriate, indeed necessary. Many members of the army appear to have accepted the identification and conflation of Jews with communism. This was a conflation stemming readily from the antisemitism that was central to Nazi ideology, a conflation relevant to the Nazi prospectus for Germany but apparently also relevant for conquered and occupied areas. The conflation was interpreted to mean that the slaughter of the Jews would ensure the weakening of communism and, thus, stabilize German conquest and ensure an easy occupation.

German generals also personally benefited greatly, as Hitler felt it necessary to bribe them, notably with the property of German Jews and of Poles. This was an aspect of the close relationship between Hitler and the military elite and one the latter played down after the war, as did many historians. The navy also provided eager support for the regime, while the major role of the SS in creating military units—the Waffen-SS—indicated the eventually close relationship between ideology and the German war effort. Over 800,000 men served in the Waffen-SS, and it became an important part of Germany's fighting forces, serving under the operational command of the army, although it was a separate structure.

THE *EINSATZGRUPPEN*

Close to one million Jews were killed within six months of the start of Operation Barbarossa in the territories conquered by the Germans—in other words, before the January 20, 1942, Wannsee conference that receives so much attention. This was also the period of most killing of Jews in the occupied Soviet Union during the war. The majority were killed by Germans, although Romanians did their malign part in the area they overran, slaughtering thousands in Odessa. This was one of the cosmopolitan cities the Germans found so abhorrent because it encapsulated the cosmopolitanism they deplored. Vienna, Salonika (Thessaloniki), and Riga were other examples, and Alexandria would have been one had it been captured in 1942 by German forces advancing from Libya. Jewish cosmopolitanism in major cities was long-standing. In 1772, Dean Mahomet, an Indian in the service of an officer of the Bengal army, wrote of Calcutta, the port the British made the capital of Bengal: "The greatest concourse of English, French, Dutch, Armenians, Abyssinians [Ethiopians], and Jews, assemble here; besides merchants, manufacturers, and tradesmen, from the most remote parts of India."[7] This was not an acceptable outcome for German imperialism.

In Lithuania, Belarus, Ukraine, and Latvia, the Germans had much local support. While most antisemitic violence in these areas took place under German supervision or with the active encouragement or toleration of Germans, they did not always need to intervene. The Germans were able to draw on widespread antisemitism, as in the city of Lwów, where Ukrainians did much of the killing. A German eyewitness in Złoczów, in the Tarnopol province of southeast Poland, reported on July 3, 1941: "I saw that in the ditches, about 5 meters deep and 20 meters wide, stood and lay about 60–80 men, women, and children, predominantly Jewish. I heard the wailing and screaming of the children and women, hand grenades bursting in their midst. Beyond the ditches waited many hundreds of people for execution. In front of the ditches stood 10–20 men in civilian clothes [right-wing Ukrainian nationalists] who were throwing grenades into the ditch."[8] The Waffen-SS were also active in this particular massacre.

The large-scale slaughter developed as the Germans advanced, particularly from July 1, 1941, when Heydrich, having visited Grodno, pressed for more activity, and again from mid-August. Aside from instructions, the particular decisions of commanders, both as how best to implement orders and concerning initiatives of their own, were important. The mass slaughter was not a product of the slowing down, still less failure, of Barbarossa in November–December 1941 later in the year (which left the Germans with an apparently intractable struggle with the

Soviet Union), as is sometimes suggested. Instead, the mass slaughter began in the heady and optimistic days (for some Germans, euphoric days) of advancing panzers (armored vehicles, especially tanks) and apparently imminent victory. Written instructions came from Heydrich, backed by Himmler, that local pogroms were to be encouraged. Hitler certainly sought and received the *Einsatzgruppen* reports. From August, the killing, which initially focused on male Jews, escalated to include large numbers of women and children, again in response to instructions from Himmler and Heydrich, which were conveyed with the assurance that they had Hitler's support. The process began from the end of July with *Einsatzkommando* 9 under SS *Obersturmbannführer* Alfred Filbert, who operated in Lithuania and Belarus. At the start of August, Himmler ordered the killing of all Jews in the town of Pinsk. Mass slaughter now appeared a realistic option to those who wanted it.[9] Unlike in Poland in 1939, this was genocide.

Similarly, although there was, at this stage, little real partisan threat, the Germans used indiscriminate brutality against those whom they alleged to be partisans or their supporters. Jews who were very clearly not partisans were routinely slaughtered in what were presented as antipartisan operations. This was an important aspect of the antisemitic convictions and assumptions that were widespread among ordinary Germans.

At the same time, from the outset, Barbarossa proved more difficult, and German casualties higher, than had been anticipated. Motivated by ideological and ethnic contempt, seriously overconfident after earlier successes (particularly against France), and certain that their armed forces were better in every respect, the Germans gravely underestimated Soviet capability, effectiveness, determination, and resilience. The poor Soviet performance in the early stages of the Winter War with Finland in 1939–40 appeared to confirm views that the Soviet military had been greatly weakened by the brutal and wide-ranging purges of the services that began in 1937. The overconfident Germans devoted insufficient attention to the eventual Soviet success over Finland and to the Soviet defeat of Japan in border fighting in 1939. To the surprise of Hitler and many of his generals, some Soviet forces fought well and effectively from the outset in 1941, resistance did not break down, and the Germans had higher casualties than expected.[10]

Stalin had a nervous collapse of will after the Germans attacked, notably, for three days from June 28 when the advancing Germans reached Minsk. There was possibly consideration on his part of a settlement with Germany similar to the Treaty of Brest-Litovsk accepted by Lenin in 1918. However, he fought on. There was also a panic in Moscow in mid-October, but Stalin decided not to flee, and the ruthless NKVD secret police was successfully used to restore order.

Soviet resistance accentuated the consequences of a prior German failure to settle strategic choices. Furthermore, as Filippo Anfuso, head of staff of the Italian Foreign Ministry, noted when on August 25, 1941, he accompanied Mussolini to Hitler's headquarters—the Wolf's Lair in East Prussia—the space of the Soviet Union had not been conceptually overcome.[11] Hitler told Mussolini then that Franklin Delano Roosevelt, the US president, was controlled by a Jewish cabal—a belief that contributed to Hitler's sense that, even before the Japanese attack on Pearl Harbor, he was in effect already at war with the United States. By late August, German logistics, as well as the crucial armored divisions, were experiencing rapidly mounting problems. In addition, the Germans suffered from a lack of strategic and operational consistency, with goals shifting over the emphases between seizing territory or defeating Soviet forces and also over the question of which axes of advance to concentrate on. This lack of consistency in German policy led to a delay in the central thrust on Moscow in September 1941, an advance already meeting serious difficulties, while forces, instead, were sent south to overrun Ukraine and destroy the Soviet forces there. Both these goals were accomplished, but the delay in the advance on Moscow hindered the Germans when they resumed the movement. Moreover, Hitler did not offer the Soviet Union terms likely to open the way to a peace.

In Lithuania, mass killings of all Jews by the Germans, as opposed to simply of adult males, began in August 1941. Food and security issues interacted with racist assumptions about the desirability of such a slaughter, but the latter were foremost. The killings there were in open country, not in extermination camps, and Lithuanians played a major role in them. On December 1, 1941, Karl Jäger, commander of the 150 men in *Einsatzkommando* 3 of *Einsatzgruppe* A, produced a list of Jews killed daily from July 2 to the end of November. The total came to

133,346, including from the middle of August large numbers of children. He claimed to have "solved the Jewish problem in Lithuania. In Lithuania there are no more Jews except for work-Jews."[12] Many of the Jews of the city of Vilnius, the largest city in Lithuania and a major center of Jewish life known as the "Jerusalem of the North," were taken the six miles to Ponary, a former holiday resort, where they were shot by both Germans and Lithuanians at the edge of deep fuel pits already dug by the Soviet forces in nearby woods. Some were stabbed or bludgeoned. Infants were frequently flung into the pits. Between 50,000 and 60,000 Jews were killed there. Also in Lithuania, 10,000 Jews from the city of Kaunas (Kovno) were marched to nearby Forts VII and IX, where they were shot at the edge of pits. Whereas there were approximately 240,000 Jews in Lithuania in early June 1941, only 20,000 remained in 1945. The largest group was slaughtered in 1941.[13]

Similarly, at the ravine of Babi Yar, outside Kiev, the major city of Ukraine, the Germans—*Einsatzkommandos* helped by the army and by some Ukrainians—recorded slaughtering 33,771 Jews in three days at the close of September: they were machine-gunned. A standard German technique as they advanced was to make the victims dig a ditch or pit; shoot them, individually or in groups, on the edge of it, so that they fell in; and then shoot other victims so that they fell in on top, suffocating any survivors. Thus, for example, about 18,000 Jews were shot at the edge of a ditch at Berdichev on September 15–16. The use of ravines, as when 1,500 Jews were killed near the town of Taganrog in Ukraine on October 27, speeded up the process by ensuring that there were no ditches to be dug.

Such killings were designed to ensure that the outcome in the former Soviet Union would not be a large number of ghettos, as in Poland. However, some ghettos were created as Jews were confined, notably in Lwów and Vilnius. The determination to kill extended to the murder of the ill and the old in their beds. As the Germans moved further east, there were additional mass murders, notably after the capture of Kharkov, the fifth-largest Soviet city and the major administrative center in eastern Ukraine, on October 24, 1941.

Those who carried out killings were sufficiently without shame, indeed were proud, to take photographs of their murders, often posing with the corpses. Such photographs were part of a wider recording of mistreatment. In this posing, soldiers frequently counterpointed their power and the humiliation of their victims. The photographs of killings were displayed in barracks, and copies could be ordered. Soldiers not directly involved were often aware of what was going on, not least because the killings were public. Many Germans captured by the Allies during the war made reference to mass executions. This was the case not only with prisoners who had served in the army but also with captured members of the Luftwaffe (air force). News of Babi Yar, for example, spread rapidly, including to German officers stationed in France. Some wives and lovers accompanied the police battalions and watched murders, including from deck chairs.

The mass shootings led to the destruction of many existing ghettos. Thus, in Belarus, 7,000 Jews were slaughtered on October 20, 1941, as the Borisov ghetto was destroyed with the active complicity of Belarus auxiliary police. On November 15, many members of the Minsk ghetto were slaughtered with the active participation of Lithuanian militia. The Ratomskaya ravine was the site of most killing there. On November 30 and December 7–8, all but 2,500 of the 30,000 Jews from the ghetto in the Latvian capital, Riga, were killed: with 1,035 Jews from Berlin, who arrived by train on November 30, they were marched to the Rumbuli woods, made to undress, and forced into pits, where they had to lie down on top of the dead, to be shot in the back of the head. Latvian collaborators assisted the Germans in this operation. Latvians also helped in the shooting of about 3,000 Jews from Daugavpils (Dvinsk) on November 7–9, the little children held up by their hair, shot, and then thrown into the mass grave.[14] Moving on from Ukraine, *Einsatzgruppe* D slaughtered the Crimean Jews while General Erich von Manstein's Eleventh Army cleared Crimea, except for Sevastopol, between September 26 and November 16; there were large-scale massacres at Bakhchiserai and Simferopol.

After Babi Yar, Field Marshal Walter von Reichenau, on October 10, issued an order urging soldiers to support the systematic killing of Jews as "a hard but just punishment for the Jewish subhumans," an instruction at total variance with international law. He presented it as a way to preempt resistance in the rear of the German advance, although there was no significant resistance at this stage. Reichenau's instruction was praised by Hitler. As an instance of the increasingly complicit nature of the army command, Reichenau's superior officer, Field Marshal Gerd von Rundstedt, the commander of Army Group South, signed a directive to his other subordinate commanders suggesting they issue comparable instructions, although he favored leaving the killing to the *Einsatzgruppen*. At the Nuremberg trial, where he was a witness, Rundstedt explicitly denied any knowledge of the episode.

It is typical of conventional military history that his role is not mentioned in standard guides. For example, the entry in Trevor Dupuy's *Encyclopedia of Military Biography* (1992) refers to Rundstedt as "an example of the best of the old Prussian officer corps."[15] Similarly, in his biography of Josef "Sepp" Dietrich, one-time commander of Hitler's bodyguard—who commanded an SS division on the Eastern Front in 1941–43 and then an SS corps and who was later twice imprisoned for war crimes—Charles Messenger displays what can be considered as a worrying failure of critical judgment seen in too much work on the Waffen-SS. From this author's personal experience in work on compendia like that of Dupuy, publishers do not like reference to the serious complicity of many *Wehrmacht* commanders in atrocities.

In 1941, this complicity was true both of Nazi sympathizers, such as Reichenau, who ordered the killing of Jewish children under five when a staff officer tried to postpone it, and of others who were not sympathizers. The latter included Field Marshal Wilhelm von Leeb, the commander of Army Group North until January 1942, who knew about the massacres outside Kaunas. He was later sentenced by the Allies to three years imprisonment in the High Command Trial at Nuremberg for transmitting the Barbarossa Decree authorizing the murderous treatment of civilians. General Erich Hoepner, the commander of Fourth Panzer Group, referred, in May 1941, to the forthcoming war as the "warding off of Jewish Bolshevism." The order he issued to his units emphasized the need for the "total annihilation of the enemy" and the supporters of the "Russo-Bolshevik system."[16] Hoepner, who had been given the task of disarming the SS in the abortive military plot to overthrow Hitler in 1938, was to be tortured and hanged for his role in the July bomb plot of 1944 against Hitler.

More commonly on the part of the generals, although there was a degree of variety in individual response,[17] there was frequently not only a lack of interest in the fate of civilians and prisoners of war, as with Leeb, but also a wish to see them removed so as to make military operations easier. The military high command in Berlin was aware of the killings, not least because Lieutenant-General Rudolf Schniewindt had forwarded a report from an army major who had observed the killing of about 2,000 Jews near Zhitomir by a *Einsatzkommando*. However, antisemitism was important in the thought of the German military leadership, not least because of a belief that a Jewish Bolshevik conspiracy had undermined Germany in 1918 and threatened it thereafter. As a result of this challenge from the Soviet Union, established social prejudices in military circles against Jews had been given a clear political and ideological direction, and antisemitic ideas circulated already prior to the war. In Barbarossa, this direction was to be accompanied by the shaming or disciplining of some soldiers who sought to take no part in violence against Jews.[18]

In some circumstances, German generals were willing to defy orders, which shows that they were not automata and that the postwar defense of "only following orders" was invalid. When, in December 1941, Hitler ordered Rundstedt, at the furthest point of his advance, to stand fast at the city of Rostov rather than to retreat to a better defensive position further west so as to avoid being cut off by counterattacking Soviet forces, he refused and was dismissed, to be reappointed in 1944. Reichenau succeeded Rundstedt but died of a heart attack in January 1942. More generally, in the face of the Soviet winter counteroffensive that began on December 5–6, 1941, commanders who responded to Hitler's "no retreat" order by advocating withdrawal were ignored, even dismissed. In total, thirty-five generals were removed, including Heinz Guderian, Hoepner, and Leeb. However, Hitler did not face comparable opposition over his treatment of the Jews.

This, indeed, casts a light on the postwar justification of German generals, such as support in Britain for Manstein when tried by the British occupation authorities and convicted of war crimes. In the event, he was sentenced to eighteen years' imprisonment, of which he served four. Manstein served as a key general on the Eastern Front from 1941 to 1944. As commander of the Eleventh Army in the Crimea in 1941–42, he had known about the slaughter of local Jews, and he provided support for the *Einsatzgruppen*, including supplies. His army order of November 20, 1941, declared: "The Jewish Bolshevist system must now once and forever be exterminated. Never again must it be allowed to interfere in our European *Lebensraum*." Guderian, who like Manstein, was given bribes by Hitler, added that Jewry was the progenitor of Bolshevik terror.

Basil Liddell Hart, an influential British ex-military supporter of German generals, such as Rundstedt (who was not tried), who wrote a foreword to the 1952 translation of Guderian's memoirs, stressing the need to obey orders as an aspect of "the essential requirements of military discipline" in response to a complaint by Sir James Butler, the editor of the British official history of the war, who had written "it doesn't seem to me that there is any comparison, for instance, between reprehensible acts which British and American commanders may have been instructed to carry out in the nineteenth century and the sort of things which Guderian and his fellows put up with on the part of the Nazi government without protest or without effective protest."[19]

As far as the bulk of the German military was concerned, it was not until 1943 that it was felt necessary to introduce the National Socialist leadership officers, who were designed to act like Nazi commissars. In 1941, servicemen's letters suggest that antisemitic propaganda had been widely internalized and become a dominant consensus. This is an instructive aspect of the engagement of the German population as a whole. As conscripts, soldiers in the army were very much an aspect of this society. Moreover, that society had already witnessed violent assaults on Jews in Germany, with very few, if any, seeking to intervene.[20]

The support of many soldiers for antisemitic action, by themselves or by others, was far from universal in the *Wehrmacht*, but it was frequent and a key element of a more general arrogance and contempt for other nations, notably when conquered. Indeed, the conquests of 1939–42 fueled the racial arrogance and sense of entitlement to rule and direct that Nazi ideology encouraged. It is instructive that German prisoners of war mostly knew about the Holocaust. The killing of Jews became a common feature of operations against partisans irrespective of the lack of any link between the Jews in question and partisans, or indeed of partisan activity at all. Army units operating on their own began killing Jews in the Soviet Union in the autumn of 1941, and this conduct soon became more frequent, indeed routine. Aside from the role of officers, soldiers increasingly proved willing to slaughter civilians, in part due to group dynamics but also because many believed in the cause.[21]

The conversations of German prisoners bugged and recorded by the British after their capture, especially at Trent Park, revealed a widespread lack of any remorse or sense of responsibility. Instead, there was a feeling that, if mistaken, the killings were only so for being committed publicly or before final victory was obtained. Moreover, on the part of many who were bugged, there was a view that the shooters had shown a commendable determination and, in some cases, laughter as mass executions were described. Some *Wehrmacht* veterans recalled different attitudes, but the awareness of killing encompassed many forms of savagery. Walter Sanders, a communications officer on the Eastern Front, noted SS men throwing live Jews down a mine shaft and beating to death and shooting Jews unable to keep up when being marched to a camp.[22]

On September 1, 1941, Ulas Samchuk, the leader of the Ukrainian movement OUN (Organization of Ukrainian Nationals), which sought an independent Ukraine, declared in the newspaper *Volyn*: "The Jewish problem is already in the process of being solved." The slaying by the *Einsatzgruppen* and other killers is of great significance not only for the numbers killed but also for the general understanding of the Holocaust. It is all too easy to treat the killing of Jews in the field as a prequel to the Final Solution of the extermination camps, and then to focus on the latter. Indeed, that is the general tendency of public attention and of memorialization—understandably so, in part because the sources for the camps, however limited, are better than for the killings in the field, particularly insofar as Auschwitz remains as a central site to mark all the extermination camps and is readily visited.

Other source factors are also pertinent. The testimony of survivors is particularly crucial. By the nature of things, the extermination camps left very few indeed, but, in the public mind, there was an elision between them and the concentration camps. Very brutal as the latter were, and particularly prone as the Germans were to killing Jews, there were survivors from the concentration camps, and their testimony misleadingly served for all Jews sent to the camps. Moreover, several of the concentration camps were liberated by US or British forces, whereas none of the extermination camps were. In contrast, there were very few survivors of the massacres by the *Einsatzgruppen* and allied killers. This was because of the care the killers took to ensure that none should survive. In addition, Jews who managed to flee the killings in the Soviet Union in 1941, for example, those from eastern Belarus, faced several years of murderous circumstances, not least genocidal German antipartisan sweeps.

In terms of finality, the slaughters in late 1941 were a form of the Final Solution for large numbers of Jews and for many important Jewish communities, not least that of Kiev and many of the communities in Belarus and the Baltic states, both large and small. The relationship between this slaughter, the Final Solution, and the general perception of the Holocaust is, therefore, significant. The extent to which the slaughter of the second half of 1941 should be disentangled from the industrialized killing that followed can be questioned, not least because this slaughter encouraged bringing ideas for the industrialized killing to fruition. It was integral to the Holocaust.

Although there was no difference in goal, the slaughter by the *Einsatzgruppen* in late 1941 did not, however, provide a model for the destruction of the Jews across much of Europe. However docile, collaborationist, and/or antisemitic many of the Dutch or French may have been, it is difficult to imagine all of their authorities cooperating in marching the Jews of Amsterdam and Paris into the surrounding countryside and slaughtering them there. Nor would such a process have matched German assumptions about Western Europe. Furthermore, in organizational terms, there was a contrast between killing Jews close to where they lived in newly conquered lands with the cooperation of part of the local population, as happened in the Soviet Union in late 1941, and, on the other hand, moving them across much of Europe in order to be slaughtered in specially created killing facilities.

The emphasis on the later events is not simply one on the centrality of the extermination camps but also on the fact that these camps were designed to ensure the slaughter of all of Europe's Jews, who were to be brought to the sites, whereas the killings in the field in late 1941 were an attempt to kill all of the victims concerned but with most of these being from the locality. The killing of Jews in the field was far more "total" than the comparable slaughter of peoples in Eastern Europe (e.g., Serbs by Croats or Poles by Ukrainians) because, although their treatment was murderous and brutal, a smaller percentage of the latter was killed in this manner. This point is also valid for the Nazi killing of non-Jewish Germans.

A difference in the manner of killing, however, was more the case with the extermination camps: the overwhelming percentage of those killed in Auschwitz and the other camps, and notably by deliberate slaughter, were Jews. As a result, these camps represent the uniqueness of the Holocaust as a genocide to a degree that the killings in the field cannot. Nevertheless, this is misleading, because, as already indicated, for Jewish communities involved in the latter, the experience of violence and destruction was comparable. Indeed, there is a need to devote more attention to these killings in the field than they generally receive in public reference to the Holocaust. Moreover, these killings did not stop when the extermination camps were established but remained important, especially in 1942, when very large numbers were killed in this fashion, and in the death marches in 1945.

The killings in the field indicate that the model of industrialized killing seen in the extermination camps was not applicable to all of the slaughter. Taking this point further, alongside the murderous use of gas, there were large-scale shootings at Auschwitz. A focus on the killing fields and the other sites of killings in the field therefore qualifies the notion that the Holocaust was in some respects an aspect of modernity, more specifically of new technology and processes—railways, gas, applied knowledge—as seen in the planning of camps, the killing there, and the attempt to ensure an efficient administration.

Aside from the deeply troubling moral dimensions of this issue, not least as modernity is usually seen as, in some way, positive and progressive, there are also fundamental empirical qualifications to this thesis. For example, far from being modern, the coerced labor of severely malnourished and appallingly maltreated Jews in the concentration camps was far less efficient than the labor employed in the essentially free-market United States and Britain, or even the far harsher example of the Soviet Union, where controlled and coercive labor systems were dominant.

Subsequent events have also indicated that controlled labor forces are less effective than free-labor markets. Furthermore, the slaughter by the Germans of so many intelligent and productive people scarcely suggests a search for efficiency; although, as a key purpose of this labor was to kill the workers, a different, warped type of effectiveness was at issue. Indeed, murderous antisemitism was the determinant drive. Separately, it is not clear how the insistent brutality of the treatment of the victims prior to slaughter is supposed to relate to modernity.

The activities of the *Einsatzgruppen* lowered restraints on mass killing of Jews elsewhere. These activities, and the approach to killing, at once casual and systematic, reflected the degree to which restraints on slaughter had already collapsed in key sectors of the regime, with, in addition, important complicity by others, particularly the army. Soldiers were acclimatized to killing Jews or to cooperating in their slaughter. The chaos of the campaign and the euphoria of a triumphant advance provided an opportunity for what was clearly killing that, in goal and intention, was pursued in a fashion that was methodical and far from chaotic. This ethos of killing could then be generalized. In practice, as far as the *Einsatzgruppen* were concerned, there was a fair amount of inconsistency and chaos in the detention and slaughter of Jews alongside, of course, the fundamental chaos represented by the very process and goal.

"EUTHANASIA" AND GAS

In addition to the earlier killing of Jews in Poland and during Operation Barbarossa, an important background to the new form of slaughter was provided by the "euthanasia" program for the slaughter of mentally ill and disabled Germans unable to work. Authorized verbally by Hitler in July 1939 and later that year by private written authorization, and reflecting his long-standing support for euthanasia, this program indicated that mass murderers could be readily found.

Much of the practice of the Holocaust, such as its secrecy, can be seen in these killings. The euthanasia program also provided experience in such killing in specially designated mental hospitals such as Hadamar in Hesse, Germany, with its gas chamber and crematorium, in which over 10,000 people were slaughtered in 1941 (and about 15,000 overall), as well as in Eastern Europe through shooting or by gassing in gas vans. The gas used was carbon monoxide. Initially, lethal injection was employed, but, from January 1940, gas was used as it was better suited to slaughtering large numbers. Aside from gas vans, converted shower rooms were also employed. The centrally directed killing of the mentally ill and handicapped was officially halted on August 24, 1941, possibly as a result of growing popular concern as news of the killings leaked and in response to critical sermons by Clemens von Galen, the Catholic bishop of Münster. However, the murder of the mentally handicapped and ill continued, particularly from the summer of 1942, although by injection and starvation (notably a nonfat diet), not by gas.

As with the slaughter of Jews, there was, alongside an apparent desire for disguise that possibly implied some sense of the wrongness of what was being done, no shortage of willing killers, while a perverted view of progress through racial purification led to enthusiastic support for the policy rather than any sense of dull acceptance of some sort of necessity contributing to it. As a parallel to the different means of slaughtering Jews, there was, in 1939–40—alongside the structure for killing the physically and mentally ill that turned to the use of gas—the so-called T-4 Program, a large-scale killing by the SS of considerable numbers of psychiatric patients in Poland and northeast Germany. In total, about 212,000 Germans were killed in the euthanasia program, as well as at least 80,000 from psychiatric institutions in German-occupied areas.

The development of German policy toward Jews also led to experiments in how best to kill people. The Germans sought to find a means of gassing that would give Jews little warning of their fate so that they had no opportunity to resist. The Germans were confident that they could overcome any resistance but did not wish to see disruption to the planned processes of predictable slaughter. The Germans also wanted a method that required relatively few operatives or killers. Furthermore, mass killings in the field were considered to be too public as well as overly traumatic for some of the personnel involved, and indeed expensive, for example, in the use of ammunition. This was cost-benefit analysis steeped in blood. Gas was a cheap means. The difference was that to achieve the result, the victims had to be concentrated rather than spread out over a front or in cities and towns. Diffusion on the battlefield was not terribly effective; the use of gas in a confined space was.

At the Polish camp based on a converted barracks at Auschwitz (Oświęcim), west of Cracow, on September 5, 1941, Zyklon-B (prussic acid) poison-gas crystals were used as a test on 600 Soviet prisoners, instead of on the lice for which these crystals were intended in the fumigation of clothes and housing. From September 1941, the Germans also had a gas van that was more deadly than their earlier model, which had used carbon monoxide from bottles. The gas used in the sealed rear compartments of the vans was exhaust fumes (not Zyklon-B), and the victims suffocated to death. Having been tested on Soviet prisoners of war, these vans were employed at Poltava in Ukraine in November as part of the *Einsatzgruppen* killings. Other gas vans were then used in Belarus, the Baltic republics, and Serbia.

From December 7, 1941, Jews were killed in gas vans en route between the newly opened extermination camp at Chełmno and nearby woods, where the corpses were buried. Gas vans were a method already employed earlier that year by the Soviet NKVD when killing political prisoners but not on the scale that was to be employed at Chełmno and elsewhere. In turn, gas chambers were to be even more effective in killing large numbers than in the camp at Chełmno, which was the prototype for the subsequent extermination camps. At Chełmno, most of the Jews transferred from the Łódź ghetto were gassed as soon as they arrived. About 1,000 people could be killed there daily. Aside from the gas, there was much sadistic violence from the SS guards at Chełmno. Eventually, about 152,000 people, the vast majority Jews but including several thousand Gypsies (Roma) and a few hundred others, were killed at Chełmno. Only six people survived the camp.[23] The establishment of other camps swiftly followed.

A NEW GEOGRAPHY

The killing of those deemed unwanted was central to German plans for the future of Europe. The Nazi leadership planned a "new order," with Germany central to a European system and the Germans at the top of a racial hierarchy. The economy of Europe was to be made subservient to

German interests, with the rest of Europe providing Germany with labor, raw materials, and food, on German terms, and also taking German
industrial products, both processes contributing to German prosperity.
Moreover, Jewish assets were to be seized. Indeed, the despoliation of
Jews, first in Germany and then throughout Europe, was a vital component of the Nazi war economy and its finances. This was the case in both
the narrow but crucial sense of funding the production of armaments as
well as providing forced labor and in the wider sense of injecting cash
or goods into the economies of Germany and allied and occupied countries in order to stave off the worst effects of shortages and to cement the
Axis system. Hitler's vision of the future for the German-led European
sphere assumed an inherently competitive world economic system with
the United States as the major rival for control in, and of, this system.

The despoliation was not simply a matter of state action. Members of
the regime and military commanders also participated actively, seizing
property and other assets, including estates, jewelry, and paintings. The
last proved of totemic interest to prominent Nazis such as Göring. Furthermore, many ordinary Germans sought to benefit from the property
and other assets owned by Jews and also from opportunities for promo-
tion or employment created by their removal. This was an important
aspect of the extent to which participation in the Holocaust was far more
extensive than the actual deportation and killing. Moreover, the rationale advanced for deporting and killing Jews testified to the strength of
antisemitism. This was true of the presentation of Jews as communists,
partisans, consumers of food, spreaders of disease, or encouragers of
Allied bombing.

Hitler was increasingly committed to a demographic revolution of
slaughter and widespread resettlement, a revolution accompanied by
the economy of plunder that was to lubricate Germany's war effort. His
remarks about Jews became more frequent and more vicious, and, in
order to demonstrate to himself and others his own sense of purpose, he
returned to his prediction in January 1939 that another world war would
lead to the destruction of European Jews. There was not only in his own
mind a consistency of attitude and single-mindedness of purpose but
also a policy that was brought to the fore by circumstances including
the expansion of the war.

The development and implementation of policy led to a geography of killing in pursuit of what was presented as spatial purification. This was a key aspect of Nazi population policy, although the idea was on record already in the 1920s. Much of the former Soviet Union was designated by the Nazis for occupation and its population classified for Germanization, extermination, or, if not appropriate for either, forcible transfer to Siberia, which was not intended for occupation. Under the *Ost* (General Plan, East), German settlers from the *Herrenvolk* (master race) were to replace Slavs and Jews across Eastern Europe. Crimea was referred to by the Nazis as a German Gibraltar, a German Riviera, or, for Hitler, with his interest in a supposed racial provenance, a Gotengau, the land of the ancient Goths. In Crimea, German South Tyroleans, displaced to satisfy Hitler's Italian ally, Mussolini, were to replace the native population. Ukraine was to be devoted to SS *latifundia* (estates) supported by subjugated peasants. A settler colony of ethnic Germans in Ukraine was planned by Himmler under the name of Hegewald.

Like the Madagascar option, however, the possibility of transfer to Siberia, also seen as deadly and as a means both intended and functioning to ensure a Jew-free Europe, was thwarted by Allied resilience. Thus, this idea was not to be the direction of the war on Jews. The slaughter of Jews was apparently the means available to give immediate effect to German plans. Moreover, whatever the long-term possibilities for German policy, a sense of racial geography as already and increasingly under pressure was suggested by the deportation of Western European Jews to already-crowded Polish ghettos.

Such deportation also reflected suggestions from officials seeking either to address issues of antisemitic policy, such as sustaining the rate of rounding up French Jews, or to handle other problems, for example, the availability of housing, at the expense of Jews. The question of housing became urgent because of Germans being displaced by Allied bombing. This bombing became more of an issue from 1941 and more effective from 1942. Officials addressed issues and advanced expedients within the context of an increasingly brutal antisemitic ideology, encouraged and legitimated by Hitler's rhetoric and instructions. The deportation of Jews could, thus, be seen as the solution to more problems, both immediate and long term, than that which was fundamental for Hitler—namely, their very existence.

AN IMPORTANT TURNING POINT

Terrible as the killings in the field were, a still more comprehensive and drastic (in scale) Final Solution was being planned from late 1941. Initially, Poland was seen as a destination, indeed a dumping ground, for Jews from elsewhere in Europe, one where they could be treated harshly and made to work, but it soon became the setting for total slaughter. The Germans did not have to rely on the cooperation of a national government in conquered Poland and were able to operate as they chose in that brutally treated country, one in which there was also a large-scale slaughter of non-Jewish Poles as part of the program of German murders that was broadly based within their occupation system.[24] There was scant interest in finding Polish collaborators and no Polish quisling-type government to provide room for confusion or differences over the implementation of policy. Instead, seen as inferior, the non-Jewish Poles were part of the German target for racial violence.

Moreover, Poland's location and rail links were convenient for the deportation of Jews from all over Europe and notably from Western and central Europe, as well as for Poland's Jews.[25] The location of concentration camps in Poland was known by non-Nazis, being depicted in *Oświęcim Camp of Death* (New York, 1944), a translation of a Polish underground pamphlet published in 1942. Oświęcim is the Polish for Auschwitz.

Mid-September 1941 proved a key moment, as these issues were referred to Hitler. In an important turning point, he determined to deport Jews to Poland on September 17, deciding to deport the German, Austrian, and Czech Jews at once to Łódź. This was seen as likely to lead to the death of many of them that winter. Indeed, the idea of deportation was both a means to an end and a deception about what was intended, which was a characteristic fusion in Nazi policy and execution. This decision—to implement the long-held plans for a new racial order—was taken in the midst of optimism, and among some, euphoria, about the progress of the war. Indeed, on September 16, the Germans completed their encirclement of the Soviet Southwest Front forces near Kiev, an encirclement that was to yield 665,000 prisoners, the largest number in any encirclement that year. In accordance with Hitler's decision, mass deportations from outside what had been Poland were to begin, even though the war was not yet over. Both Łódź and Chełmno were part of the expanded German territory, while German (and Austrian) Jews transported there were technically still subjects of the Reich, but such points were of no importance in the face of the murderous intent of Hitler's policy.

The decision in mid-September 1941 was crucial, not least because it established the policy of moving Jews rapidly from throughout German-controlled Europe, thereby putting more Jews into position for mass slaughter. Eichmann, who was in charge of the Race and Resettlement Office of the Reich Security Main Office's Amt IV, was ordered to prepare the details for the new policy. In October, he used the term *Final Solution* to refer to the Jewish problem, and it appeared thereafter in many documents. The first deportations from Hamburg's large Jewish community, the second largest in Germany after Berlin, occurred in October. In December, Hanover's Jews, another large community, were deported by train to Riga.

The contrast between the official stopping of the euthanasia murders on August 24, 1941, and the decision to encourage the willing murderers on the Eastern Front and in the occupied East to step up their slaughter is instructive. The first reflected a concern about German public opinion and the second a response to it. It was apparent, from the Eastern Front and Germany, that the treatment of Jews would arouse scant opposition. Indeed, this situation suggested that the slaughter might serve to further affirm public support for the regime as well as maintain its sense of dynamic. The exclusion of Jews from society helped clear the way to embarking on the Final Solution. This exclusion and the acceptance of mass murder drew on the widespread beliefs that Jews were different and evil and on the sense of empowerment many Germans derived by behaving cruelly toward them.

THE INTERNATIONAL CONTEXT

Although both Hitler and Stalin were very aware that they were engaged in a struggle between Nazism and communism, they recognized that both ideologies were diametrically opposed to the liberal values of Britain and the United States. In each case, Hitler and Stalin were not only hostile to Britain's political position but also rejected its liberalism and the global economic and financial order it coordinated, not least its cosmopolitan character. This rejection was a product of a total opposition to liberal capitalism, which antisemites associated with Jews and decried as plutocracy, and hostility to Britain for its encouragement of an international agenda focused on resistance to dictatorial expansionism. Hitler's cooperation with the Soviet Union from the Molotov-Ribbentrop Pact in August 1939 until the launching of Operation Barbarossa in June 1941 can be linked to an anti-Western turn in Nazi antisemitism in 1938–41, such that "the war in the West against Churchill and Roosevelt was no less an ideological war than the war for *Lebensraum* in the East."[26] So also for Germany's opponents—indeed, on September 3, 1939, as the British declaration of war was briefly debated in the House of Commons, Churchill said, "This is not a question of fighting for Danzig [Gdansk] or fighting for Poland. We are fighting to save the whole world from the pestilence of Nazi tyranny and in defence of all that is most sacred to man. This is no war for domination or imperial aggrandizement or material gain, no war to shut any country out of its sunlight and means of progress. It is a war, viewed in its inherent quality, to establish on impregnable rocks, the rights of the individual, and it is a war to establish and revive the stature of man."[27]

While Germany's allies and enemies changed, the alleged threat from Jews remained a constant in Hitler's view and rhetoric. In his broadcast to the German people on June 22, 1941, to mark the launching of Operation Barbarossa, Hitler managed, in his characteristic fashion, to blame Jews for both British and Soviet policy. This approach influenced some of his closest supporters, such as Robert Ley, a wounded veteran of World War I and virulent antisemite who, from 1933, was head of the German Labor Front. Before Ley committed suicide in 1945, he wrote of the Allies as being tools of the Jews and of the war as being a conflict with the latter. Publications and the media spread this theme, and many Germans were influenced by it, believing in this "Jewish control," a long-standing component of antisemitism, and the alleged need to overthrow it.

The extension of the war in December 1941 to include the United States may have further energized Hitler's attitudes to Jews, encouraging him to push forward European mass murder; it has been suggested that the announcement on August 14, 1941, of the Atlantic Charter agreed on by Churchill and Roosevelt had already contributed to the same end. Hitler claimed that US policy was dictated by Jewish financial interests, an inaccurate argument he also used about Britain. The passage through Congress in March 1941 of the Lend-Lease Act had earlier led Hitler to the same conclusion.

Japanese forces attacked Pearl Harbor on December 7; the United States declared war on Japan on December 8, and Germany and Italy declared war on the United States on December 11, Hitler taking the view that Germany and the United States were already in effect at war in the western Atlantic, where US warships escorted convoys to Britain and were becoming targets of German submarine attacks. To Hitler, the subsequent American focus on war with Germany rather than Japan—Roosevelt's "Germany First" policy confirmed by the Washington Conference that began on December 22, 1941—demonstrated the role of Jewish interests in US policy and more generally, and thus justified and made necessary his escalation of his war with Jewry. This war was not separate from military and international policies for Hitler but central to both. His speeches and meetings, and references by other Nazi leaders, all from mid-December 1941, make this apparent and suggest that Hitler had decided to instigate genocide.

Indeed, Hitler's speech of December 12 to the *Gauleiters* and *Reichsleiters* has been seen as crucial for the Wannsee conference. He was happy to anticipate the end of Jewry when giving radio addresses in January, February, and November 1942.

One extreme and convicted commentator, the antisemitic David Irving, who was imprisoned in Austria in 2005 under the law prohibiting Nazi activities, argued that Hitler did not order the Holocaust and, instead, put forward the proposition that it was a product of a momentum or dynamic latent within Nazism and its antisemitism. The reality is that Hitler was central to the Third Reich, and no major initiative would have been possible without his direct support, while many actions were taken in a context in which his approval was explicit or implicit. The idea of "working toward the *Führer*" helped provide a dynamic in which, in order to justify their position and fulfill their potential as Germans, large numbers sought not only to carry out what they knew to be Hitler's will but even went further to anticipate his objectives, both declared and believed.[28] This helped produce an integration of the society with the state, an integration for which Hitler's influence in both was crucial. The process was directly relevant to the treatment of Jews. For example, the *Gauleiters* competed to be first to tell Hitler that their *gau* (region of government) had no Jews. Individual *Gauleiters* pushed through deportations. Thus, in the autumn of 1940, Josef Bürckel was a keen supporter of the *Aktion Bürckel*, the deportation of Jews from the Saarland and Palatinate.

There is no sign of Hitler having issued any written order for the Holocaust, but Göring and Heydrich cited him as their authority for mass murder. The early autumn of 1941 was the key period. Aside from authorizing the deportations, Hitler allowed the SS to gain the control in Poland that made the organization of genocide there possible. He was also kept informed of the mass slaughter and "made *ad hoc* interventions in it."[29] On December 18, 1941, Hitler told Himmler that Jews were to be killed "like partisans"—in German terms, at once and without any legal process or restraint.

Hitler himself never witnessed any of the killings. In contrast, in August 1941, Himmler saw a mass shooting in Minsk and decided on that visit to increase the personnel available for slaughtering Jews. During his inspection of Auschwitz in July 1942, he saw a gassing. In 1943, Himmler had quarters prepared for himself in the house of the Waffen-SS at Auschwitz, but he never occupied them, although he visited the extermination camp at Sobibor in July 1943. In 1946, Joachim von Ribbentrop, German foreign minister under Hitler (and a decorated veteran of World War I), told Leon Goldensohn, a US army psychiatrist responsible for monitoring those charged at Nuremberg, that

> Hitler was off balance in regard to the Jewish question. He [Ribbentrop] told me often that the Jews caused the war, and that there was a complicity between Jewish capitalism and Jewish Bolshevism. I know for a fact that this idea of the Jews causing the war and the Jews being so all important is nonsense. But that was Hitler's idea, and as time went on he became more

and more obsessed with this idea. He [Ribbentrop] also said that in the long view, historically, the Jews' extermination would always be a blot on German history, but that it was in a way attributable to the fact that Hitler had lost his sense of proportion and, because he was losing the war, went "wild" on the subject of the Jews.[30]

Ribbentrop was being self-serving: all senior German officials were well aware of Hitler's genocidal policy. Ribbentrop felt it unnecessary to tell Goldensohn that in April 1943, he had informed the Hungarian regent, Admiral Miklós Horthy, that Jews should either be slaughtered or put into concentration camps—that is, before Hitler pressed on to say that Jews faced the choice of work and death and then compared them to tuberculosis bacilli, which left no doubt of the context and nature of the choice.[31] Made an honorary SS-*Gruppenführer* (major general) in 1936, Ribbentrop was sentenced to death at Nuremberg for the Foreign Office's role in the Final Solution. At Nuremberg, Hans Frank, who was in charge of the General Government of Poland, sought to avoid punishment by denying knowledge of the extermination camps. He, too, was convicted and hanged.

The nature of German policy formation, with partially autonomous bodies implementing Nazi beliefs and responding to problems and their perception of problems, ensured that there was no one moment when the Holocaust of all European Jewry was settled, although Hitler appears to have given a verbal order in 1941. Hitler initially planned to use the Jews as hostages in an attempt to keep America out of the war. However, the growing cooperation of Britain and America, for example with the signing of the Atlantic Charter, issued on August 14, 1941, a total rejection of German assumptions and policy, alongside other developments, such as the Soviet deportation of the Volga Germans, prompted Hitler to agree to the deportation of the German Jews. Although the decisions reached in mid-September were clearly very important, there was no single moment when the mass killing of men, women, and children in the field in the German-occupied Soviet Union was determined to be a stage in the comprehensive and industrialized slaughter of all of Europe's Jews, which, in turn, was to be a prospectus for the fate of all Jews in the world.

Instead, policymaking was more ad hoc, and killing was incremental and cumulative. Given that background, the shift occurred in late 1941, as ideology, opportunity, and need were brought together, with Himmler and Heydrich as the key implementers of Hitler's will and coordinators of the results. They were instrumental in introducing a new policy, as well as in generalizing regional policies of murder and turning them into a strategy, but this process was dependent on Hitler's approval.[32] Heydrich's plan, worked out in response to Göring's request, was one for deportation to the Soviet Union, but the failure to end the war with the Soviet Union produced the chaos in Poland that prompted Himmler to go along with local German initiatives in carrying on extermination in Poland.

INITIATIVES TOWARD SLAUGHTER

Ian Kershaw indicates, with his study of the Warthegau (Wartheland), that there was also a complex relationship between central direction and local initiatives, with the latter reflecting a range of factors. The Warthegau was the part of Poland annexed by Germany as part of the Greater German Reich in 1939 and thus intended for Germanization. The Warthegau included the Łódź ghetto. Arthur Greiser, the *Gauleiter* of the Warthegau (who was to be convicted of genocide and hanged in Poznán in 1946), agreed to take the large numbers of deportees who were to follow Hitler's decision on September 17 but, in return, received approval for the establishment of the killing facilities at Chełmno. They were to be administered by the *Gauleiter*, who was to be answerable to Himmler. Similarly, in the region of the German-created General Government of Poland (which covered much of Poland, including the major cities of Cracow, Lublin, and Warsaw), the demographic situation changed. This was not, initially, a result of deportation thither from elsewhere in Europe, which took a while to become large scale, but rather because of the end of the certainty of moving Jews from there into what had been part of the Soviet Union.

This shift helped lead to an accentuation of the already homicidally harsh treatment of Jews in the General Government, as well as particular violent initiatives. The beginning of the construction of an extermination camp at Belzec in November 1941 was a consequence. This camp was the result of an initiative by SS Brigadier Odilo Globocnik, the head of the SS and police in Lublin district; he had presumably been authorized to take that initiative when he met Himmler on October 13. Knowledge of such policies, and support for them, helped ensure that when those at the center spoke of deportation to the East, they meant slaughter and not, as earlier, a territorial, albeit harsh, solution to the Jewish issue. Deportation was eliding into destruction, and "allowing to die" into killing, and killing very large numbers.

Kershaw argues that Hitler was content to permit others to turn the ideological imperatives he expressed into practical policy objectives and, in doing so, to please him.[33] Officials rationalized their policies by claiming that Jews posed a threat, whether as partisans, black marketeers, or spreaders of infection, or that they posed a problem as consumers of food and housing and as inefficient workers. These claims were preposterous, and that of Jews as consumers of food was a stark contrast to the reality of their subminimal rations. These rationalizations reflected the concerns of officials, but such concerns and their contexts were not simply bureaucratic. Instead, ideological imperatives ensured that issues and problems were interpreted in a violently antisemitic fashion. German policy made Jews a problem and then used mass murder to solve the alleged problem, to address the uncertainties of war and the need for a new order, to satisfy a quest for violent solutions and solutions through violence, and to further aspirational hopes and plans for a particular future.

Nazi propaganda, determined at the most senior level, emphasized that Jewry was to be destroyed. A press briefing by Alfred Rosenberg—the highly antisemitic minister of the Eastern Occupied Territories (convicted and executed at Nuremberg in 1946)—on November 18, made after he had seen Himmler, referred to the "biological eradication of the entire Jewry of Europe," while Goebbels, in the newspaper *Das Reich* on November 16, wrote of the annihilation of world Jewry. This article, entitled "The Jews Are to Blame," (frequently translated as "The Jews Are Guilty") was reprinted elsewhere in the German press.

This reprinting is instructive with reference to the question of German popular knowledge of the Holocaust. There should have been little doubt about the intention of government policy. No qualification, on grounds of occupation, geography, religion, or any other criterion, was offered. The Jews were to be destroyed as a race, and without exception. This was

a goal different from that of the murderous treatment of political categories deemed to be opponents, although that treatment also involved
appalling cruelty and misery.

Fourteen senior state, party, and SS officials from relevant agencies met
on January 20, 1942, in a suburban villa at Wannsee on the outskirts of
Berlin, a guest house of the Security Police and a building preserved
today as a museum with instructive displays about the meeting and the
Holocaust. The meeting helped coordinate the organization of what was
intended as a Final Solution. In this, all European Jews, including those
not hitherto under German control, were to be deported to death camps
and slaughtered. Such an interministerial gathering of specialists was
important because Hitler did not use cabinet government. This meeting has been seen as definitive in policymaking by some scholars but as
more transitional by others. It has been argued that the first invitation
to Wannsee was to discuss only deportations to the East, forced labor,
and selective mass murder. The eventual Wannsee protocol (minutes),
however, indicate agreement on genocide, although the decision was
not taken there.

At the Wannsee meeting, Heydrich announced that Jews were to be
deported to the East and worked to death, with those who survived to be
dealt with. Survivors were seen as a threat because they were presented
as likely to be stronger than those worked to death. Thus, the slaughter of the survivors was regarded as particularly necessary in Nazi race
warfare. The fate of those unable to work was left unstated. Heydrich
was still hoping that his plan for deadly deportation to the Soviet Union
could be carried out and described the genocidal measures in Poland as
"Ausweichmöglichkeiten," or "stopgap measures."[34] The minutes suggest
that much of the proceedings, which may have lasted between an hour
and ninety minutes, was taken up by a lecture by Heydrich in which he
pressed for the coordination of an effective response to the task of the
Final Solution, a task to which, he pointed out, he had been entrusted by
Göring, the minister nominally responsible for policy toward the Jews.
Heydrich sought to reassert his plan against the focus on Poland.

Heydrich underlined the central role of the SS and of himself personally by pointing out his instructions; the conference thus established that Himmler, the head of the SS and police, and Heydrich, as his representative, were in charge. This was a prime example of the institutional and personal empire building so important in Nazi governance and so weakening to it. However, the role of the SS also put pressure on other branches of government to cooperate, and that was important in a governmental system in which, due to endemic competition, cooperation was limited. The calling of the conference reflected the contrast between the situation in the occupied Soviet Union, where the *Einsatzgruppen* could operate readily, and that elsewhere in Europe, where it was necessary for the SS to take greater account of a range of other branches of government. Indeed, the SS resolution to control the situation and the determination to make others complicit in the genocide were probably the key purposes of the Wannsee meeting. It served to make clear the subordination of the fussy Frank and of Rosenberg, the minister for the Eastern Occupied Territories.

In his speech at Wannsee, Heydrich reviewed earlier policy, specifically the use of emigration to clear Germany of Jews, but noted that this policy had been stopped by Himmler in October 1941 because it posed problems and also due to new possibilities. Instead, Jews were to be deported to Eastern Europe to prepare for the Final Solution. It was estimated that over eleven million Jews were to be involved, including 330,000 in Britain and eight million in the Soviet Union (including Ukraine). Josef Bühler, the representative from the General Government of Poland, asked for the solution to be rapid and claimed that there was no real need for additional manpower there. Characteristic of German interest in classification was the fact that the questions of mixed marriages and their progeny took up nearly a third of the Wannsee minutes. The SS wanted to send the progeny (i.e., children) to the East with the other Jews. This was a radical solution, and one at variance with the policies of the Ministry of the Interior, which wanted to protect them. In the event, concerned about the possible implications for public opinion, Hitler decided it was not worth deporting those in and from mixed marriages, especially those with Aryan relations.[35] Plans to dissolve forcibly all mixed marriages were not pursued. Many of the German Jews who survived the war in Germany did so because they were in mixed marriages. In Hamburg, 5,880 Jews were deported, the overwhelming majority to their slaughter; of the 674 Jews remaining in the city at the end of the war, 631 were in mixed marriages.[36] At the same time, this was to be a category that ceased to grow. In Hungary, marriage between Christians and Jews had been prohibited in 1941. Considered a source of racial and social infection, Jewish blood and characteristics were not to be permitted to spread.

GENOCIDE AND THE WAR

Deciding on genocide, on the key issue that all must die, still, however, left the question of implementation. Should the key be forced labor to the death, either in road building, such as the projected highway across Ukraine, or in work camps, not least with the possibility of taking over some of the Stalinist sites of forced labor in the Soviet Union? Or should gassing be the main method of operation? In the event, gassing became the preferred method of implementation.

By the Wannsee meeting on January 20, 1942, the flow of the war was increasingly complex, and the news far less welcome to the Germans than at any stage hitherto. Japan, Germany's new and far more active ally, was doing very well, capturing Manila in the Philippines on January 2, 1942, and Kuala Lumpur in Malaya on January 11. The German attacks on Moscow and Leningrad, however, had stalled by early December 1941, and, on December 5–6, the Soviets launched a major counteroffensive. This initially highly successful counterattack revealed the extent to which the Germans, aside from suffering from an inadequate logistical support system, were not prepared for defense and found it difficult to fight well in that role. Moreover, the counterattack encouraged partisan action in the German rear because it made it clear that German success was uncertain. In turn, this partisan action spurred German troops to ever-more violent action, not least as this action reduced the extent of cooperation with the conquerors, a cooperation the Germans despised.

Nevertheless, the impact of the Soviet attacks that winter was lessened because, instead of focusing on sections of the front where his forces enjoyed a clear advantage, Stalin mistakenly sought to attack along the entire front. In this context, and with Soviet forces less well prepared than they were to be a year later, Hitler's December 21, 1941 "no retreat" order to his forward forces helped stabilize the front, albeit at a heavy cost in German manpower, which left many divisions short of troops.

Furthermore, Hitler planned a fresh offensive for the summer of 1942, one designed to destroy Soviet forces west of the Don, to seize the oilfields in the Caucasus, and to capture Stalingrad on the River Volga. These gains, it was suggested, could be exploited by crossing the Volga and advancing to the northeast to outflank Moscow from the east and, despite logistical problems, by advancing from the Caucasus into Syria and Iran to put pressure on Allied interests in the Near and Middle East. The latter advance would be supported by the invasion of Egypt by German and Italian forces from Libya. Thus, the auspices could be seen as favorable for the Axis. As yet, Britain and the United States did not appear in a position to challenge the German occupation of Western Europe.

OPERATION REINHARD

The Wannsee meeting helped indicate to a range of officials that genocide was now policy and that the SS leadership was committed to it. It was followed by the escalation of the practice of mass murder by gassing, already seen at Chełmno as those brought from the Łódź ghetto and nearby towns were murdered. Jews throughout Europe, wherever they lived, were to be detained, held in local holding camps, and then moved by train to camps far from where they lived, where they would be killed by gassing. The SS scheme to exterminate the Polish Jews and also Jews deported there was codenamed Operation Reinhard.

Secrecy was to play a key role in order to minimize possible Jewish resistance or critical public reaction. In place of deportation, there was to be "resettlement," effected by "special resettlement trains," en route to secret camps. As far as the killing was concerned, gas vans were presented as if transporting Jews to labor duty, while the gas chambers were made to look like shower rooms and thus to appear as the entry, after the serious disruption, total misery, and utter squalor of the rail journeys, to a more predictable and safer environment, albeit an arduous one.

Three more extermination camps (not that this term was employed at the time), Belzec, Sobibor, and Treblinka, were established to give effect to Operation Reinhard. At Belzec, the construction of which had begun on November 1, 1941, the Germans began gassing Jews on March 17, 1942, and could kill 1,500 people daily. Jews from Lublin were followed by those from Lwów and then Cracow. In the event, over 600,000 Jews were slaughtered there. More generally, in the eleven months from the beginning of the killing at Belzec in mid-March 1942, over half the Jews who would be slaughtered by the Germans were killed. In March, construction began at Sobibor, and, in May 1942, the month in which a major Soviet offensive near Kharkov was crushed with very heavy Soviet casualties, the new camp opened. About 300,000 Jews, mostly from central Poland but also from Austria, Bohemia, and Germany, were killed in Sobibor. In July 1942, the month in which German successes in the Don campaign led Hitler to declare "The Russian is finished," Treblinka was opened. It was to be the camp in which the second-largest number of Jews was killed—over 900,000—mainly from the nearby Warsaw ghetto. Pressure for the food from conquered territories encouraged the drive to kill Jews, but it was not the cause.

The naming of Operation Reinhard is attributed to honoring Reinhard Heydrich, Himmler's deputy, who had been fatally wounded by the Czech resistance on May 27, 1942 (he died a week later). This assassination led to the slaughter of many Czechs, both those already held in prison and the population of the village of Lidice, which was destroyed on Hitler's orders as a reprisal intended to deter resistance: the men and dogs were shot, the women sent to concentration camps, the children selected for gassing or Germanization, and the village destroyed. This serves to underline the extent to which many non-Jews were killed by the Germans. The naming of the operation has also been attributed to Fritz Reinhardt, a long-standing Nazi who was state secretary, a key functionary, in the Ministry of Finance, which was one of the bodies involved in the system. An early Nazi, former leader of the training school for party speakers and SA-*Obergruppenführer*, Reinhardt's roles included seizing gold from Jews. He was imprisoned from 1945 to 1950.

The operation was commanded by SS Brigadier Odilo Globocnik, who was answerable to Himmler. Like a disproportionately large number of those involved in the Holocaust, Globocnik was Austrian. These camps concentrated on killing Jews on their arrival, as soon as they had undressed. The camps did not focus on forced labor. The exhaust fumes used for the killing, a slow way to die, were generated by large tank diesel engines.[37] There were also some mass executions as part of Operation Reinhard, which presumably reflected not only the zeal for killing but also the extent to which it was impossible for the gassing to keep up with the demand. Moreover, the killers may have been less committed to relying simply on gassing than popular understanding of the Holocaust suggests.

THE EXTERMINATION CAMPS

Other extermination camps were not part of Operation Reinhard. Aside from Chełmno, another at Majdanek, near Lublin, had been constructed as a prisoner-of-war camp but in August 1942 was equipped with gas chambers and became both a concentration and extermination camp. Large numbers of Jews were killed there, notably 40,000 in just two days in Operation Harvest Festival in November 1943. Majdanek was also the center of *Ostindustrie*, a major project in the SS economic plans, as well as being the central store for the belongings of those slaughtered in the Reinhard camps.

Also combining the two roles of concentration and extermination camp, Auschwitz was where the largest number of Jews was killed. Due to lacunae in the evidence arising from the German failure to keep accurate numbers of those killed there, the total number is controversial, but it was about 1.5 million. In 1942–43, a train carrying Jews arrived at Auschwitz about every hour.[38] The variety of the operations at Auschwitz reflected the different levels of German oppression. There were three camps: Auschwitz I, opened in June 1940, initially as an internment center for Polish political prisoners, rather like Dachau and Buchenwald; Auschwitz II, or Birkenau (built over land that had been that village), on which work began in October 1941 (although not at that stage as an extermination camp), in order to raise the overall number of inmates to 100,000; and Auschwitz III, opened in October 1942, at first to supply forced labor for nearby industrial facilities run by the company

I. G. Farben, which also owned the largest stake in Degesch, the maker of the Zyklon-B gas used in the extermination camps, 23.8 tons of which went to Auschwitz. The initial gassings, first of Soviet prisoners and ill Poles from September 3–5, 1941, and then, on February 15, 1942, of elderly Silesian Jews, took place in Auschwitz I. Then, facilities for killing large numbers—gas chambers, using Zyklon-B gas—and, eventually, crematoria were constructed at Birkenau. Birkenau was designed for killing far more than the very large number that was actually slaughtered there. The first gassing there, again of elderly Silesian Jews, occurred on March 20, 1942.[39]

This was the industrialized mass murder seen only in German antisemitism. Zyklon-B, a hydrogen-cyanide compound, was at least quicker than exhaust fumes, although it still took several minutes to kill. The bodies taken from the chambers, the sounds heard from them, and the scratches on walls and ceilings left no doubt of the great pain and terrible anguish suffered by the dying. Aside from the contortions of the corpses, the bodily fluids on the corpses were also indicative.

In contrast, other than by the Japanese in China, gas was not used in conflict in World War II. This was different from the situation in World War I. Then, gas was extensively employed in conflict from 1915, with chlorine gas, and, from 1917, mustard gas, first used by the Germans. During the interwar years, a major reliance on gas had been envisaged in the event of a future great-power war. Furthermore, gas was employed as a weapon in the interwar period, notably by the Spaniards in Morocco and the Italians in Libya and Abyssinia (Ethiopia). Although gas was used as part of military operations, there were civilian casualties, particularly because mustard-gas bombs could not be aimed accurately, and also because much of the opposition was by irregulars who could not be readily distinguished from civilians, while there was scant interest in making that distinction.

However, the gas masks distributed to British civilians at the outbreak of World War II were not made necessary by German bombing with gas, as had been feared. American tests on the effectiveness of phosgene, hydrogen cyanide, cyanogens, chloride, and mustard gas were similarly not taken forward. The British also tested gas bombs as well as anthrax and briefly considered using them in 1944 in reprisal for the German use of V-rocketry against Britain (the first V-rocket was launched against London on June 13) but did not do so. Thus, in Europe, the Germans were unique in employing gas.

The use of gas was seen as a necessary way to kill the large numbers assigned to slaughter in order to ensure the Final Solution. Gas served other purposes as well. In their mass shootings, some members of the *Einsatzgruppen* had made clear their preference for a less obvious and direct way (to them, not to the victims) to murder women and children; the use of gas vans and then gas chambers appeared to provide this. German depersonalization of extermination—depersonalization of both victims and murderers, or at least depersonalization very much in their eyes and on their terms—was taken further in the camps when Jewish inmates, rather than Germans, were made to move the corpses from the gas chambers to the crematoria. In the brutal pathology of killing, gas seemed a modern and effective way to kill, yet another aspect of the Nazi identification with modernity, and it linked with the reiterated Nazi assumption that the Jews were a form of vermin, for Zyklon-B was also used for fumigation.

Not all Jews were killed at once in the extermination camps, and there were important variations in individual circumstances. Nevertheless, slaughter was the objective, and callousness, brutality, sadism, and depravity characterized the treatment of the victims, from their deportation to their slaughter. There were many beatings as the Jews were crammed into extremely crowded cattle cars. In the rail journeys, which were lengthy, Jews were denied food, water, light, warmth, sanitation, space, and bedding. Those who died on the journey were left in the shut cattle cars. The use of cattle cars was emblematic, as the camps were abattoirs for those judged nonhuman, albeit not for meat production. Both on the journeys and on arrival at the camps, Jews were exposed to acute levels of pain, fear, and disorientation. Moreover, those manning the camps were often extremely violent thugs, and there were no restraints on their cruelty and arbitrariness. Violence and cruelty built up group identity and dynamics among the guards and thus helped encourage their brutal treatment of the victims.

The degradation and humiliation already commonplace in the deportations were carried forward into an attempted depersonalization and dehumanizing of the victims. This was a matter not only of the living—and acutely so, both in the camps and during the killing—but also of the dead. Their bodies were treated as raw materials or rubbish, with hair, for example, shaved off to be used in textile production in Germany. Gold dental fillings were torn out with hooks. The mutilated bodies were burned and the ashes turned into bags of fertilizer. Spectacles, shoes, watches, wedding rings, and false limbs were among the items systematically collected. Moreover, the smell from the crematoria lay over the camps. Rudolf Höss, the Auschwitz camp commandant, referred later to the "ghastly stench."[40]

This sadism and degradation followed from that of the killings in the field. There, it became the practice to make the victims take their clothes off. In part, this was in order to derive use from their belongings, use without any restraint for privacy or other reasons, but there was also a strong wish to demonstrate the weakness of the victims and to humiliate them totally. This was clearly very important to the killers and an element recorded in their photographs. Other forms of humiliation included cutting off beards, which were often a sign of Orthodox belief, forcing Orthodox Jews to dance, and urinating on captives. Women were made to clean lavatories with their blouses. Particular pleasure seems to have been taken in humiliating the Orthodox and those who, in German eyes, were most clearly Jewish. Conversely, German witnesses sometimes expressed surprise that all Jewish victims, in their eyes, did not look Jewish, and notably so of attractive women.

If not killed on arrival at the camps, as many were, women were stripped and shaved, and some were sexually abused and raped despite the racial strictures of the Nazi ideology against sex with Jews. The crowded barracks of the women in the camps were particularly neglected. Women also had to face the loss of children and husbands, of being parted from them and of the likelihood of their death. Any babies they gave birth to were killed at once, commonly drowned in a bucket. Such killing was also common with babies born to non-Jewish female forced laborers, but the latter was less consistent, and many of those babies were seized for adoption as German children. Sexual abuse was a frequent characteristic of German wartime conduct. It was seen in the interrogation of women by German security services, in frequent rape by German units in the field, and in the brutal use of women for prostitution. Casualty rates among women in German army brothels were high: many died or were infected with venereal disease.

There is an emphasis in the literature on the disorganized and frequently incoherent nature of Nazi administration and policymakers. Variation, even contradictions, in the treatment of Jews, for example between the goals of slaughter and labor, provide an instance. Nevertheless, the establishment of the camps and the related logistical, technical, and procedural steps indicate the high degree of central coordination involved in the launching of the Holocaust and the extent to which it was not simply initially dependent on local initiatives by middle-rank officials, although such officials were not without considerable significance.

Aside from Jews, large numbers of Gypsies (Roma) were killed in the extermination camps in what was also genocide. Homosexuals, in contrast, were not targeted for mass destruction or killed in extermination camps. However, they were sent to concentration camps, where they suffered particularly brutal treatment from which many died. The same was true of Jehovah's Witnesses, who were actively persecuted because of their opposition to military service and to the Nazi system. Their murderous persecution and that of political prisoners underline the extent to which German killing was not only directed at Jews.

Moreover, about 3.3 million Soviet prisoners of war died in German captivity, likewise dehumanized, deprived of their dignity, and subjected to brutality and degradation, largely from starvation and the resulting exposure to disease—in total defiance of international conventions on the treatment of prisoners of war. These prisoners were in the custody of the *Wehrmacht*, which completely failed to show any care for them. They were left without cover, with their greatcoats and hats taken, and were exposed to the cold of a particularly harsh winter. In contrast, for example, out of the over half a million Japanese troops and civilians captured by the Soviets in 1945 who were sent to camps in Eastern Siberia, more than 60,000 died: the ratio would have been worse for those captured by the Axis.

Also, specific German orders in the Russian campaign displayed great fierceness. Thus, Georg von Küchler was ordered to wipe Leningrad off the face of the earth by bombing and artillery fire and to reject any surrender terms that might be offered. As commander of the Eighteenth Army, Küchler in 1940 had ordered support for the measures taken for the "final ethnic solution" in Poland. In January 1942, he succeeded Field Marshal Leeb as commander of Army Group North. In 1948, in the High Command Trial, Küchler was sentenced to twenty years imprisonment for war crimes and crimes against humanity, but he was released in 1953.

In 1942, the cruel treatment of Jews was increasingly focused not on their killing in the field (although that continued to be very important) but on their deportation from the ghettos that had been created by the Germans, as well as from conquered Western Europe, to camps run by the SS, which helped to increase the centrality of the SS in the Nazi regime. As the regime became a killing machine, so it needed killers who could be trusted not to ask questions. The SS was certainly unwilling to accept bureaucratic restraints and constraints, for example over the status of mixed marriages and the role of other agencies. On January 29, 1942, Himmler wrote: "All measures with respect to the Jewish question in the eastern territories are to be carried out with a view to a general solution of the Jewish question in Europe. In consequence, in the eastern territories such measures which lead to the final solution of the Jewish question and thus the extermination of Jewry are in no way to be obstructed."

He followed up on July 28: "I urgently request that no ordinance be issued about the concept of the Jew with all these foolish definitions. We are only tying our hands. The occupied eastern territories will be cleared of Jews. The implementation of this very hard order has been placed on my shoulders by the Fuhrer. No one can release me from this responsibility in any case, so I forbid interference."[41]

In September 1942, the newly appointed German minister of justice, Otto Thierack, a keen Nazi, handed over his remaining responsibility for Germany's Jews to the SS, deliberately doing so in order that they could be exterminated. He was to commit suicide in 1946.

The large number of camps established by the Germans included not only the extermination camps where gas was used but also slave-labor camps—in the case of Jews, *Judenlager*. These camps were important to the Nazi economy, specifically to the key need to supply the military, and in the spring of 1942, the organization of the camps was changed in order to reflect the emphasis on economic needs and labor. These needs became far more apparent and urgent as the war continued.

Jews, however, were treated more viciously than the other forced labor on which Germany so heavily depended. Most of the harshly treated Jews in these labor camps died as a result of serious malnutrition, physical violence, and disease, or were killed. Aside from the harsh working conditions, the lack of sufficient food, clothing, bedding, and shoes, and the frequent epidemics, there were brutal punishments, including public floggings and hangings, for minor infractions of arbitrary rules. Roll calls were murderous affairs, and brutal and theatrical executions were part of the litany of terror. The SS, which was particularly responsible for the extermination and concentration camps, assumed that most prisoners would die anyway in these conditions in under three months, and they were frequently correct. As a result, it may be more helpful to term them *death labor camps* or *extermination labor camps*.

The distinction between those judged able to work, in other words, to be worked to death, and those chosen for immediate killing, many of whom, of course, were able to work, was an aspect of the degree to which what were seen by the Germans as rational considerations, especially attitudes toward age and gender,[42] played a role in the slaughter. Jews were allocated to one or the other category. The differentiation was carried out in a number of locations, including the ghettos, where it proved the basis of deportation to the camps. Trains carrying deportees from Germany and Slovakia were stopped at Lublin in 1942 and able-bodied Jews removed for work. At Auschwitz, doctors inspected the deportees, driven by whip-carrying guards from the rail transports, as they were lined up for entry. Those chosen for immediate slaughter included pregnant women, young children, and "the unfit." As a result, some children arriving at the camps tried to appear as tall as possible, and there was lying about age.

The killing of children and pregnant women was not simply an issue of usefulness but also underlined the genocidal character of the slaughter, which contrasted with that of non-Jewish Polish and Russian victims as well as with non-Jewish German victims of the Third Reich. More generally, Jewish children were a prime target for murder throughout the Holocaust, one that underlines its shocking character. The destruction of any future for Jews focused on the slaughter of children (including babies), the killing of pregnant women, and the sterilization of men and women. In Pinsk, in October 1942, Adam Grolsch, a radio operator in the *Wehrmacht*, saw the shooting of 25,000 Jews in two days: "I saw how they had to undress in front of the tank traps how this man took a screaming baby and beat it headfirst against a wall until it was dead. Mothers were still carrying their children they shot them."[43]

Children were more vulnerable to privation and disease than were fit adults, and deliberate German purposes ensured that the survival rate of Jewish children from the war was lower than that for adults, with the exception of those concealed through adoption by Christians and in Christian orphanages. An aspect of supposedly rational German criteria, and, in practice, planned viciousness, was seen with the calculation of food availability. This aspect led to a conviction that killing Jews, as well as other Soviet civilians and, indeed, prisoners, would free foodstuffs for the German army and later settlers—an issue, already present in 1941, that became more acute in 1942. These and other ideas, however, were subordinated to the logic of antisemitic murder.[44] This war against Jews took precedence over utilitarian considerations, such as the provision of effective labor for the German war economy or the use of rail (or in the Aegean, maritime) transport for military ends rather than transporting Jews to the camps. Indeed, the SS found it difficult to integrate its functions of genocidal slaughter and raising economic benefit from Jewish slave labor. If an emphasis was often on the latter, the murderous treatment of this labor did not contribute to its effectiveness. Moreover, the course of World War II helped further radicalize Hitler's already rabid antisemitism.

The year 1942 saw renewed German advances, largely as part of Operation *Blau* (Blue) launched on June 28. German forces captured besieged Sevastopol in the Crimea on July 4, rapidly overran eastern Ukraine, and advanced into the Kuban and the northern Caucasus, capturing Stavropol on August 5 and Maikop four days later. On August 23, German tanks reached the River Volga north of Stalingrad. As far as Hitler was concerned, his forces were fighting Jewry, because communism was one of its products. On April 26, in his speech to the *Reichstag* on what was to be its last meeting, Hitler presented the war as a struggle with Jews, who, describing them as parasites, he blamed for German defeat in 1918 for being "the carriers of that Bolshevist infection" and for directing British and US policy.

German advances in 1942 brought a large number of Jews under German control, although far fewer than in 1939, 1940, or 1941. Distant extermination camps were not readily accessible from eastern Ukraine and beyond. Instead, many Jews were killed there. This killing in the field in 1942 tends to be underrated in the literature on the Holocaust. In the northern Caucasus, for example, there were killings of over 1,000 Jews at Essentuki, Kislovodsk, and Piatigorsk each. They were killed rather than being used for slave labor, their killing in part excused by the German identification of Jews with "bandits" (i.e., partisans) opposing their activities, an identification that, despite the presence of Jewish partisans, was mostly inaccurate. The German army played a major role in these killings,[45] and a 1995–99 traveling exhibition of photographs of *Wehrmacht* soldiers involved in atrocities included photographs of troops from the Sixth Army in their 1942 offensive. The advance into the Caucasus was intended to provide the opportunity for killing even more Jews, although the "Mountain Jews," whom Himmler's "scholars" had been trying to classify, posed a problem, as they were not seen as racial Jews. In the event, the Islamic influences they showed led to a relatively favorable response on the part of the German army, although over 1,000 were still murdered. There was no comparable slaughter in the field when German troops occupied the Vichy zone of France from November 11, 1942. Instead, the Germans relied on the already established system of deporting Jews from France to the extermination camps.[46]

In the Soviet Union and Eastern Europe, in contrast, at the same time in 1942 as advancing German forces slaughtered Jews in the field without sending them to extermination camps, the same process was seen in areas already under control. In part, this killing reflected the extent to which, although very murderous, the *Einsatzgruppen* in 1941 had not been sufficiently numerous to kill all Jews, while "work Jews" had not been killed, and, in addition, Jews lived across a broad area. This was the case in particular in Belarus and eastern Poland, which lacked the system of concentration and extermination camps seen further west.

As a result, large-scale slaughter continued in 1942. For example, at Tuczyn in eastern Poland, where Jews had been confined to a ghetto in the summer of 1942, a local resident described their slaughter that autumn:

> For the span of a few days I observed the massive influx of Ukrainian militiamen and German gendarmes, not SS but the regulars with those brown collars, who cordoned off the ghetto. The militiamen led the Jews out in large groups to the village of Rzeczyca. There they were told to dig ditches, to get undressed, and as they were kneeling along these ditches, they were shot in the back of the head.
>
> The ditches, filled to the brim with bodies, were then covered with lime and a thin layer of earth. The stench from the decaying cadavers which pervaded the entire area was simply indescribable. No one knows from where came the myriad of hungry dogs that circled these massive graves and fed on the human flesh.[47]

This was a dystopian reality as horrific as the extermination camps.

In Belarus, the ghettos destroyed included Baranowicze on March 5, 1942, and Lachwa on September 3, the latter after resistance: 3,300 and 1,000 Jews, respectively, were killed. Close to 2,000 Jews were killed in July 1942 when the Smolensk ghetto was destroyed. In eastern Poland, there were major massacres at the city of Brest-Litovsk in October and at Białystok in November. At Brest-Litovsk, during the ghetto "clearance" on October 15–16, 16,000–20,000 Jews (German estimates varied) were shot. In Lithuania, where large-scale killings continued at Ponary,[48] the large Vilnius ghetto was destroyed on August 16–22, 1943: the women, children, and old men were murdered, and the younger men taken for slave labor. When I visited in the mid-1990s, the rebuilt site of the ghetto gave very few indications of its earlier identity.

Jews were also frequently killed in antipartisan sweeps, which became increasingly important and large-scale for the German army in early 1942, with some sweeps involving several divisions. These sweeps brought the German army into areas it hitherto had only passed through perfunctorily, if at all, and also led to the slaughter of large numbers of civilians who had fled to the forests and marshes that covered large areas. Thus, over 8,000 Jews were killed in Operation Swamp Fever in the Pripet Marshes in August–September 1942. This killing of Jews in antipartisan operations continued during the war, as these operations served as an opportunity for the slaughter of all judged unacceptable, and within a context in which brutality and indiscriminate violence were at the fore. There was scant restraint on the part of the army. The 1995–99 exhibition of photographs of *Wehrmacht* soldiers involved in atrocities included photographs from these operations in Belarus, and they showed the SS and the *Wehrmacht* as virtually one and the same, although that was not the case with the camps.

The slaughter of Jews also played a role in strategic and operational planning by the military. Thus, had the *Afrika Korps* under Erwin Rommel driven the British from Egypt, as they unsuccessfully attempted to do in July and, again, September 1942, it was intended that it should advance across the Suez Canal into Palestine, in part in order to destroy the Jewish settlements there before the area was handed over to Italy: there were about 470,000 Jews in Palestine. Before that, the Germans, had they successfully overrun all of Egypt, would have slaughtered the Jews of another cosmopolitan city, Alexandria. Rommel's entourage included an SS colonel who was responsible for compiling lists of Jews in Alexandria and Cairo. Later, when German forces occupied Tunis, the SS rounded up Jews.

In the event, there was no German capture of Alexandria and no invasion of Palestine, while Jewish soldiers, earlier, played a role in strengthening the British position in the Near East, including in the hard-fought conquest of Vichy-run Syria and Lebanon in 1941. Had the *Afrika Korps* advanced, it would have found itself in conflict with the *Haganah*, the Jewish defense organization in Palestine. The plans to slaughter the Jews in Palestine, where there were not the alleged pressures of food and deportations encountered in Poland, underlined the truly genocidal character of German policy.

This genocidal character was clearly on display in Europe. Paul Roser, a French prisoner of war held in a disciplinary camp at Rawa-Ruska in Poland as a punishment for escape attempts, told the Nuremberg tribunal:

> The Germans had transformed the area of Lvov-Rawa-Ruska into a kind of immense ghetto. Into that area, where the Jews were already quite numerous, had been brought the Jews from all the countries of Europe.

One night in July 1942 we heard shots of submachine guns throughout
the entire night and the moans of women and children. The following
morning, bands of German soldiers were going through the fields of rye
on the very edge of our camp, their bayonets pointed downward, seeking
people hiding in the fields. Those of our comrades who went out that day
to go to their work told us that they saw corpses everywhere in the town, in
the gutters, in the barns, in the houses. Later some of our guards, who had
participated in this operation, quite good-humoredly explained to us that
2,000 Jews had been killed that night under the pretext that two SS men
had been murdered in the region.[49]

THREE

Genocide

He had come from Auschwitz, where his job had been to separate new arrivals into the ones that were to be worked to death and the ones that went straight to the gas chambers. I asked him if he would do it again, and to my astonishment he said yes.

Captain Eric Brown recalling his 1945 interrogation of the commandant of the concentration camp at Bergen-Belsen, SS *Hauptsturmführer* Josef Kramer, later hanged for war crimes.[1]

HITLER TRIED HARD TO GIVE FORCE TO HIS PREDICTION IN A speech on February 24, 1943, stating, "It is not the Aryan race that will be destroyed in this war, but rather it is the Jew who will be exterminated." This prediction was not new, but now German policy was clearly designed to give it immediate effect. Indeed, alongside the slaughter of Jews from elsewhere in Europe, a major effort had been made in 1942 to wipe out Polish Jewry, the largest population under German control, one far larger than the Jewish population in Germany. That year, about 1.7 million Jews were killed at the camps at Bełzec, Sobibor, and Treblinka alone as part of *Aktion Reinhardt* (Operation Reinhardt), the attempt to clear the General Government area of Jews judged unfit for labor.

WARSAW

The pace of slaughter was pushed forward from July 16, 1942, after a meeting between Himmler and Hitler. All Jews in the General Government were to be killed by the end of 1942. In July–September 1942, 300,000

Jews were deported from Warsaw alone, mostly to the death camp at Treblinka, about sixty-five miles away. The process by which Jews were removed from Warsaw indicated their limited options in the face of SS power. On July 22–30, 1942, the Jewish ghetto authorities played a significant role in persuading and forcing Jews to go to the Umschlagplatz for "resettlement." In an extraordinarily difficult position, one that drew on vain hopes for rationality on the part of the Germans as well as a tradition of trying to cope with antisemitism and its violence by lessening the blows, a tradition that also led to the petitioning of German authorities and their allies, the Jewish Council (*Judenrat*) and the ghetto police (*Ordnungsdienst*) cooperated. They hoped that the Germans were only after the "surplus," or unemployed and indigent, Jews, although on July 23, Adam Czerniakow, the head of the Jewish Council, concerned by his failure to save the orphans, committed suicide.[2]

During the first half of August 1942, information and rumors began to trickle into the Warsaw ghetto. There was great confusion about the meaning of the deportations, although there were many stories of the worst happening, and it was no longer credible to believe that somehow normal life would resume at the end of the German occupation. The ghetto police were now working with the SS and their auxiliaries. From mid-August, apprehension hardened as the truth about Treblinka became known to Warsaw's Jews; it, therefore, became more difficult to round up Jews for removal.

The Nazi commanders, in turn, relied more on SS units and sheer terror. The Germans used sanctions against the ghetto police so that the role they played was not at all voluntary. If they failed to deliver a certain quota, they and their families were sent to Treblinka. In the last phase of the deportations, from early September 1942, the ghetto police played a minor part. Indeed, by the last days of the action, the 2,000 *Ordnungsdienst* had been reduced to about 400.

RESISTANCE

By the first half of August 1942, the newly formed Jewish underground had declared war on the ghetto police in Warsaw, and on August 21, leaflets were distributed against them on the grounds that they had aided the mass execution of Jews. The attempt of Jewish authorities to use their position in order to benefit the Jewish community was to fail completely in light of their weakness and of the direction of German policy, which left no room for moderation or compromise. There is the question of whether any other conduct would have altered the murderous outcome, but the action of the police was shameful.[3] Similarly, in Kaunas, the ghetto police faced the pressures of German demands, ghetto anger and fear, and their own fear. The ghetto police were responsible for providing workers for the local airfield as well as for helping the SS deport Jews to the Riga ghetto in 1942.[4]

Underlining the variety of Jewish responses to German persecution, the Jewish Fighting Organization in Warsaw resolved to resist and, accordingly, stockpiled weapons. Created on July 28, 1942, this organization was seriously disrupted by German action that August and September. Nevertheless, after armed resistance to forcible removal by Warsaw Jews in January 1943—an attack on German escorts—the Germans initially withdrew. This was a period when the Germans needed all available troops to shore up their collapsing Eastern Front. On February 2, the last German troops besieged in Stalingrad surrendered; on January 13, the Soviets had launched a new offensive, seeking both to advance on Kharkov, moving into Ukraine, and against Rostov, cutting off the German retreat from the Caucasus. The Soviets were swiftly successful, capturing the cities of Voronezh (January 26), Kursk (February 8), and Kharkov (February 16).

Benefiting from Soviet exhaustion, however, Field Marshal Erich von Manstein, with great skill, stabilized the front and counterattacked from February 20, 1943, recapturing Kharkov on March 15 and Belgorod on March 18. On April 19, the Germans also launched a campaign to destroy the Warsaw ghetto. Despite being in a hopeless situation, outnumbered, and with few arms, the 1,000 members of the Jewish Fighting Organization and the Jewish Military Union, fighting from bunkers and underground positions, resisted until May 16, killing about 400 Germans. Although, in the face of grave danger due to deadly German reprisals, many individual Poles provided assistance to Polish Jews during the Holocaust, the situation was less happy for the Warsaw Ghetto Rising. It received scant support from the Polish Resistance, either directly or

in terms of diversionary attacks on the Germans. The Polish Resistance
could have done much more. The following year, the Warsaw Rising was
to indicate its strength but also its vulnerability to German counterattack. In May 1943, after the Jewish resistance was suppressed by the
Germans, with many Jews burned to death in their hideouts, the surviving Jews of Warsaw were sent to their deaths in Treblinka and Majdanek, and the synagogues were demolished. This was followed by the
flattening of the ghetto.[5] The suppression of the rising indicated that a
lack of troops was not the rationale for extraordinary violence as, in this
case, German brutality was well in evidence when they had a very clear
military advantage.

Jews also employed armed resistance in the Białystok and Minsk
ghettos, as well as in at least eighteen other ghettos, including Cracow,
Lublin, Lwów, Lutsk, and Vilnius. It was at the last that the United Partisans Organization was formed in January 1942 in response to a manifesto
by the poet Abba Kovner, which declared that the Germans were aiming
to kill all Europe's Jews and called for armed resistance. This was a rejection of the misleading claim that the massacres of Jews were a retaliation
for alleged Jewish support for the Soviet Union.

In the face of German power, most resistance was unsuccessful, but
some Jews were able to escape and join partisan groups in the countryside. As a result of German attacks, and of the brutality of German
antiguerrilla warfare, survival rates there were not high, but they were
higher than in the ghettos. In August 1942, for example, many Jews were
able to flee into the partisan-dominated countryside after a partisan
brigade defeated the Germans in and near Kosow (Ukrainian Kosiv,
Yiddish Tcosov), in eastern Poland: the brigade included a Jewish unit
formed that summer.

Circumstances within the ghettos varied greatly. Whereas in many
ghettos, the emphasis was on resistance within the ghetto, in some there
were possibilities for escaping from the ghetto in order to link up with
partisans. This was particularly the case with Minsk, the major city in
Belarus, where the ghetto was segregated by a barbed-wire fence rather
than a brick wall and where dense forests dominated by partisans were
close. Moreover, the communist-led resistance movement near Minsk
proved relatively supportive to recruiting and sheltering Jews. Up to

10,000 Jews out of a ghetto population of 100,000 in Minsk survived the war as a result.[6] In France, Jews took a significant role in the Resistance.

On a smaller scale, Jews also resisted elsewhere, including in the extermination camps at Auschwitz, Sobibor, and Treblinka. Given the disparity of forces present, it is not surprising, however, that the resistance was suppressed. At Treblinka on August 2, 1943, fifteen guards were killed in a major revolt, and about 400 Jewish prisoners fled, although most were captured and killed. At Sobibor, on October 14, 1943, a revolt led to the killing of a few guards and the escape of about 600 prisoners, but most were swiftly captured and killed, in part through the assistance of antisemitic Polish villagers. In 1943, the Warsaw, Treblinka, and Sobibor risings led Himmler to press for the killing of Jewish workers, including 18,400 held in Majdanek who were slaughtered on November 3. A large-scale revolt at Auschwitz II on October 7, 1944, by the *Sonderkommandos*, Jews forced to work in disposing of the bodies (who, in turn, were killed), led to the blowing up of a crematorium and escape of about 250 inmates, but they were all killed. There were also revolts in the camps at Chełmno and Ponary.

Options only improved as the Nazi regime collapsed, and in Buchenwald the inmates successfully revolted on April 11, 1945, just before US troops arrived.[7] This independent activity continued as the regime collapsed, not least with guards killed in some camps (e.g., Bergen-Belsen). This was resistance eliding into retributive justice. In addition, appalled by what they saw, Allied troops killed some of the guards.

In the majority of cases, however, the swiftness and completeness of German dominance ensured that there was no possibility of armed Jewish resistance, which helps answer the question of why there was not more resistance. The German practice of brutal reprisals, particularly mass shootings, may also have acted as a restraint. There was, however, not only no proportionality at all between resistance and retaliation but also no suggestion that retaliations ordered from the top of the German regime were intended to be seen by Jews as a cause for compliance. Instead, the drive was to kill Jews, all Jews. German attacks were not to prove a new bout of pogroms, one that left Jewish communities battered but not destroyed. Indeed, the contrast between the Holocaust and the pogroms of the late nineteenth and early twentieth centuries underline the distinctive character of German wartime policy and practice. The contrast with the First World War is also readily apparent.

The explosion of a small incendiary device in the Lustgarten in the city center of Berlin on May 18, 1942, the work of the procommunist Herbert Baum group, which had Jewish members, led to the execution of the group and the shooting, as a reprisal, of 250 Jewish men held at the concentration camp at Sachsenhausen. This explosion also led Hitler to heed Goebbels's advice that the Jews be deported from Berlin, including those involved in munitions production, whose retention had been pressed.

Instead of resisting, most Jews both outside the camps and also within them, including those forced to dispose of the bodies, adjusted to suffering in a harsh and destructive environment in which their fearful options were pitifully few: "The misleading assumption is that people had the power to choose whether or not to be robbed of their dignity in the first place."[8] German deception also played a role. The Jews being transported to extermination camps or marched out of towns in order to be shot were not told that they were going to be killed. Instead, they were informed that they were being moved to work. Similarly, the shower chambers at the extermination camps were presented as a disinfection stage for Jews prior to their allocation to labor tasks; before the "disinfection," clothes and shoes were hung on numbered hooks, implying that they would be retrieved. The degree to which those about to be murdered were taken in is contested.

Alongside the ending for most of any options for life, there were also, for a comparative few, possibilities for survival, although the opportunities to postpone, evade, or escape were all restricted. Chance played a key role: some potential victims were able to hide or flee, but these options were very limited, and each option was made risky by murderous German action. Suicide, which was frequent, was another avenue used by Jews to reject the German attempt to control them and, thus, an act of resistance as well as of despair and fear—so also were attempts to pass on news of the killing to the outside world and, moreover, to record what was happening. Indeed, keeping diaries was seen as a means to testify against, and thus reject, German control, as well as to preserve tradition.

Vandalism and sabotage in industrial works were also important and affected the efficiency of the German war economy. This element appears to have become more important as the war continued. Resistance of some type was more frequent than is often appreciated. It occurred more easily in the ghettos than in the camps, as German control in the ghettos, though pernicious, was indirect, and it was possible to maintain central aspects of Jewish culture, especially education and religious observance.[9] The latter was a way to testify belief, the former to ensure continuity, and each affirmed Jewish identity and the very timelessness that contested Hitler's view of history.

The absence of large-scale Jewish resistance troubled later commentators, many of whom were confused by the apparent fatalism of the victims. This fatalism could be linked to strong religious belief, to a failure to understand what was going on, or to a sense of inevitability and despair. Witnesses of mass shootings sometimes commented on the last factor. As a result, the resistance that is known is celebrated. Martin Gilbert, in his *Atlas of Jewish History* (1969), produced a map of Jewish partisans and resistance fighters, followed by another on Jewish revolts, which he described as "among the most noble and courageous episodes not only of Jewish, but of world history." He followed with an *Atlas of the Holocaust* (1988).

The scale and brutality of German oppression was a key factor in limiting resistance. The Holocaust is not the sole instance for which it is pertinent to consider this factor when assessing the extent of Jewish resistance to threats to their communities. For example, pogroms in Russia in the early twentieth century, such as the brutal one at Kishinev in 1903, led to the organization and arming of Jewish self-defense units. However, in 1919–21, when the Russian Civil War resulted in a fresh bout of deadly pogroms, with at least 50,000 Jews killed, the White armies that helped carry them out, especially in Ukraine, were strong enough that self-defense against them was not an effective option.[10] Jewish military experience, moreover, was essentially within the context of national armies.[11]

There was also very little effort by non-Jews forcibly to disrupt the deportation and killings, although across Europe, a large number of individuals were responsible for helping Jews to avoid capture by giving them shelter and food and contributing to their disguise or escape. This help was provided at great personal risk and in the face of surveillance and of the risk of betrayal and of murderous German reprisals. On April 19, 1943, unusually, a train carrying deportees en route for Auschwitz was attacked near Boortmeerbeek, between Mechelen and Leuven in Belgium. Three young men used a hurricane lamp covered with red paper to bring the train to a standstill before employing wire cutters to open one of the goods wagons, releasing seventeen prisoners. Such brave and impressive action was exceptional, although many people across Europe helped Jews threatened with deportation, notably Jewish children. Many were placed in adoption as Christians, both in orphanages and with individuals, in order to provide shelter.

It is important to note the horrible reprisals that were visited on Christians in response to any assistance they provided to Jews—in Poland, for example, but not only there. Prejudices aside, fear of certain death should one help fellow human beings is a major obstacle to helping them, especially if combined with certain death for others, notably family members. The testimony of those who helped hide Jews recorded their terror, an indicator of the total inversion of value represented by the nature of German rule.

THE PACE OF SLAUGHTER

At the same time, the Germans were driven on not only by their vicious ideology but also by a sense of the challenge posed by the large populations and extensive areas they now controlled. Thus, paradoxically, the weakness of the German authorities played a major role in the Holocaust and led to a use of the ethos and practice of work, system, and routine to confront the murderous task they had set themselves. Similarly, both at the level of the Holocaust as a whole and at that of individual perpetrators, the cruelty and sadism often displayed provided pleasure and a sense of power against a troubling presence as the new reality the Germans were seeking to implement was pursued. Slaughter was intended both to effectuate and to overcome a racist paranoia, a paranoia that ensured that the Germans lacked the willingness and ability to elicit consent from other than the few groups in occupied Eastern Europe designated for collaboration, a situation already seen with the army in Serbia in 1941. Photographs from the massacres of civilians were displayed in the major 1995–99 exhibition on *Wehrmacht* atrocities.[12] The standard rate was a hundred civilians from other countries slaughtered for every German soldier killed.

The sense of challenge reflected a belief in the potential strength of Judaism, as in October 1940, when the Reich Security Main Office issued a decree banning the emigration of Jews from Poland on the grounds that doing so threatened to allow a "lasting spiritual regeneration of world Jewry" by enabling Jewish religious leaders to reach the United States.[13] This decree was instructive in seeing the United States as the key safeguard for Jewry and also because the religious dimension was presented as crucial to Jewish viability.

Hitler's linkage of Jewry and communism reflected his fears about both and gave a particular character to these fears. He was especially anxious that a Jewish-led and inspired communism might result in a repetition of the challenge posed by the communist risings in Europe in the late 1910s. Agitation then in Germany provided a warning, in Hitler's eyes, as it had led, he believed, to defeat in World War I and showed that Germans could be infected by communism, a threat that Hitler argued required Jewish intermediary action. Fear about the internal threat allegedly posed by Jews was a response to any sign of opposition with which Jews could be linked—for example, the explosion in the Lustgarten in Berlin on May 18, 1942, carried out by the Herbert Baum group. Indeed, this attempt and the assassination of Heydrich in Prague (which was not carried out by Jews) appear to have encouraged Hitler and Himmler to press on to complete the Final Solution.[14] In a major speech given at the Berlin Sportpalast on February 18, 1943, and carried across Germany by radio, Goebbels strongly pressed the case for "total war" and attacked the Jews for guiding Germany's enemies.

It was not only Polish Jews who were to be slaughtered, with the ghettos in Cracow and Lwów destroyed in March and June 1943, respectively. The extermination camps in Poland were also used for Jews deported from elsewhere in Europe, with "evacuation to the East" employed by the Germans as a euphemism for slaughter. In June 1943, Himmler ordered the destruction of the remaining ghettos in Belarus

and the Baltic republics, with the deportation of Jews to the extermination camps. The Jews of Belgium, France, and the Netherlands, already
rounded up and held in camps (Malines/Mechelen, Drancy, and Westerbork, respectively), were deported to be killed in the extermination
camps in Poland, as well as in Kaunas and Riga. Deportations from
Western Europe had become more important in 1942, with French Jews
deported to Auschwitz from March, Dutch from July 14, Belgian from
August 4, and Norwegian from October, the last also using the local
police. Deportation from Greece followed in March 1943 and from Italy
that October. Most of the French and Dutch Jews killed in the war were
slaughtered that year.

In most cases, gas chambers were used in killing the Jews, but at
Chełmno, Riga, Zemun (near Belgrade), and Maly Trostenets, an extermination camp near Minsk, gas vans were used. At Bełzec, Maly Trostenets, Sobibor, and Treblinka, the vast majority of Jews were killed as
soon as they arrived, even if they were able to work. Only a small number
of very fit Jews were kept, under heavy guard in special detachments, in
order to help sort the effects of the slaughtered or to move their bodies
for cremation. In turn, they were killed. There were also important execution sites where shooting, not gas, was used, for example, Bronnaya
Góra, where most of the Jews from nearby Brest-Litovsk were killed from
October 1942. Brought by rail, they were forced to run down corridors
of death defined by barbed wire fences, and from these inclined ramps
into pits where they were machine gunned.[15]

SLAVE LABOR

When Auschwitz II (or Birkenau) and Majdanek were established in
1942, there was a different priority: each was both a concentration and
extermination camp. By then, it was clear that the war would not be
rapidly settled with a German victory, as had seemed possible, and
even likely, in the autumn of 1941. Instead, Germany was now at war
with a Soviet Union that had been capable of mounting a major winter counteroffensive in 1941–42, as well as facing the unprecedented
industrial might of the United States and a resilient Britain while having to assist Italy. This situation suggested that the conflict would be

attritional, which put a key focus on industrial production and, thus, on labor.

Auschwitz had a place in this new military and geopolitical prospectus because, unlike the other extermination camps, it was located in a key economic region, that of coal-rich Upper Silesia, control over which had been highly contentious at the end of World War I as the Polish-German frontier was settled. Aside from the coal mines, this was a major and well-connected industrial area that required a large slave-labor force, not least because the Germans were increasingly conscripting their own men for the army and, notably, after heavy losses in 1941 and 1942. Auschwitz thus acted as a nexus of the cooperation between Himmler and Albert Speer, minister for armaments and munitions from February 1942—cooperation that was to be important to the German ability to sustain the conflict in the face of US and Soviet power.

The I. G. Farben plant constructed near Auschwitz for the manufacture of synthetic rubber and oil was one of the largest German industrial projects and the largest for these products. Synthetic rubber and oil were crucial to the German war economy, the latter especially so after Operation Barbarossa brought about the end of the delivery of Soviet oil that had been so significant in 1939–41. This plant deliberately drew on local slave labor, the promise of which Himmler originally had used to persuade the company to locate there, as well as the availability of local coal.[16] Moreover, the exhausted nature of the I. G. Farben workers, and specifically the impact of the daily march to the plants, led the managers in late 1942 to have a camp constructed nearby at Monowitz (which became Auschwitz III). The SS had not been keen on this additional facility, but they accepted the outcome, guarding what, in effect, was a private concentration camp. The arduous and cruel nature of work and life in these camps was such that many prisoners fell sick, and those who did not recover speedily were sent to the gas chambers at Auschwitz II.

If Auschwitz represented the culmination of German extermination policies, it is also pertinent to note that the use of slave labor there was the end result in another narrative of the brutal treatment of Jews. Forced labor had become an important theme from 1938, not least because in Germany, German persecution, in seizing Jewish businesses and closing down Jewish employment opportunities, made it possible to direct Jewish labor. Having been made unemployed, Jews were given state welfare only on condition that they accept employment in difficult and demeaning conditions that were designed to remove them from fellow Germans. Thus, Jews were made to work on processing rubbish or in projects in which they were segregated in camps.

From 1939, this program was expanded in response to the rising need for non-Jewish German manpower for the army. Non-Jewish women were encouraged to remain at home and both have and bring up children, which were presented as ways to strengthen German society on a pattern also seen elsewhere, as in Italy. The Reich Labor Office recruited Jews for skilled work, a process that continued to be important and not under SS control, until large-scale deportations from Germany occurred in 1941. Even after that, some Jewish workers were retained in Germany by influential employers, for example, the armaments division of the German army, until they were finally all seized for deportation in February 1943. That June, Germany was declared *judenfrei*.

In practice, possibly 10,000–12,000 German Jews had gone into hiding, of whom 3,000–5,000 survived the war. Known as "U-boats" (a reference to German submarines), they faced hazardous conditions. While some Germans provided shelter, in many cases knowing that those they sheltered were Jews, which was a very risky practice, others denounced hidden Jews, for whom the Gestapo searched with great vigor. Hiding in dangerous circumstances, short of food, and without medical attention, other Jews died. Some were killed by Allied bombing, while for yet others, bombing provided an excellent opportunity to explain loss of papers otherwise identifying them as Jews.

The use of Jewish labor was a more important issue for Germany as it became clear that the war would be a lengthy, arduous, and total one. Jewish labor was particularly significant in both the Warthegau part of Poland, which was annexed to Germany, and the General Government of Poland. Large numbers of Jews were used for forced labor in Poland and at the disposal of other labor agencies that were not under SS control; although in Upper Silesia, the eventual site of Auschwitz, the SS controlled and profited from Jewish forced labor from the outset. SS control of Jewish labor elsewhere became dominant, as the Jewish question moved toward the Final Solution, with the allocation of Jews for slaughter or work a central means and display of SS power. This allocation was increasingly insistent and immediate for the Jews in Poland, as well as for those deported there.[17]

In some respects, as with the slaughter, forced labor was a continuum that did not only include Jews. Millions of foreign workers, especially Soviet, Polish, and French, were brought to Germany, while elsewhere in occupied Europe, civilians were forced to work in their home countries in often brutal conditions in order to produce resources for Germany. Aside from prisoners of war, 5.7 million foreign workers were registered in the Greater German Reich in August 1944; combined with the prisoners of war, 7.1 million men and women provided 24 percent of the workforce.[18] Moreover, German prisoners categorized as asocial or social misfits were allocated to the SS from 1942 and deliberately worked to death. Many were petty thieves, work shy, tramps, alcoholics, or, rather, those categorized as such, and thus reflected Himmler's drive to "purify" German society.

This perspective might seem to diminish the specific issue of Jewish suffering. Such an argument can particularly be made if the focus is on 1940 or early 1941, not least because it was not clear at that stage that this forced labor would not be the final solution for Jews, at least until forced emigration could be resumed at the close of the war. However, in the case of Jews, although SS attitudes with regard to the choice between murder and slave work moved back and forth from 1941, there was to be a major shift in 1941–42 toward killing some at once and working the remainder to death. The latter outcome, moreover, was presented as an explicit goal, not as a by-product of exploitation. There was to be murder, either quickly or slowly, but murder nonetheless. The concern was replacing dead workers with new ones whose work worthiness was also to be expended as soon as possible: replacement costs were less of a factor than production and genocide.

In contrast, the need for the labor of prisoners led the Germans to cease being so murderous to Soviet prisoners of war in October 1941; although their working conditions, which, from 1944, included fewer than 1,000 calories of food daily (in comparison to the official German civilian ration of 2,100 calories), were such as to lead to high death rates, and knowingly so. This "silent killing" was deliberate and intentional.

The calculation of rations reflected the cost assessments involved in the management and subdivision of labor in the camps.

However, Soviet prisoners of war who were Jewish were automatically slaughtered. Such comparisons ensure that any emphasis, as is frequently made in Eastern Europe in particular, on the large number of non-Jews slaughtered by the Germans (and, to a lesser extent, their allies), or indeed on other Germans killed by the Nazis, has to be matched by a focus on the distinctive fate allocated Jews and Roma (Gypsies)— and notably the Jews, as they were seen in the world of Nazi paranoia as far more threatening than the Roma.

An exception was made for the Jewish soldiers in the British and US forces, including the Palestine Brigade. They were treated like other British and American prisoners, including after the SS took over the prisoner-of-war camps in late 1944. This contrast reflected the German willingness to conform to the Geneva Convention's stipulations about prisoners, a willingness not extended to Polish and Soviet prisoners. Linked to this contrast, the Germans were interested in exchanges of prisoners with the British and Americans, exchanges dependent on observing the convention.[19]

The labor force at Auschwitz was not solely Jewish, but Jews were very important in it. As a result, although those deemed unable to work hard were gassed on arrival, fit men and women were selected for labor. With a serial number tattooed on their forearm, subsequently a readily understood and emblematic feature of the suffering, they were sent to crowded barracks to live while they worked. Most were subsequently killed, gassed when ill, or worked to death. The treatment of Jews, both by SS guards and by non-Jewish prisoner-overseers, most of whom were convicts, was generally worse, indeed far worse, than that of other prisoners.[20] The far-harsher treatment of Jews was seen across the entire system of Nazi brutality and incarceration, not simply in issues of life and death but also in the very few chances of relief, for example, in the very limited opportunities for music making in the concentration camps.[21]

The deliberate and deadly neglect of Jewish workers is a major reason why the term *slave labor* is problematic, not least because it can be made to imply a comparison with other systems of slavery, such as those of African slaves in the European, Islamic, and, indeed, African worlds.

Such a comparison is inappropriate, as these slaves had a clear financial value, expressed in sale and purchase, and for that reason, as well as to fulfill productive tasks, it was useful to keep them alive. Indeed, there was added value from slaves having children, and castration of slaves was only normal in the Islamic world. Some racists, such as the Nazi Manfred Sell, in his *Die schwarze Volkerwanderung* (The black migration, 1940), opposed the slave trade because of the possibilities it offered for intermarriage and deracination.

Nor is the comparison with governmental slave systems, such as that of communist North Korea, pertinent. Such comparisons may be relevant up to a point in the case of much of the forced labor deployed by the Germans and may also capture the emphasis on productivism not capitalism, goods not profit, but in the case of Jews, there was a distinct genocidal intent. The term *slave labor* thus describes the very one-sided nature of control experienced by Jews but does not suggest any equivalence with other slave systems. For some German authorities, Jews, indeed, had considerable economic value, as when these agencies protested against the killing of skilled workers. The conflicts between German authorities over this issue highlighted the fact that, for some of the fervent believers, the rejection of economic (as well as traditional military strategic) thinking was part of the point: pursuing racial goals was higher than pursuing traditionally conceived pragmatic purposes.

Profit from Jews was not simply sought in the form of slave labor, a profit seen in the large number of satellite camps attached to industrial sites. Many German companies also profited from the construction, maintenance, and supply of the camps. Some, such as Topf and Sons, crematorium specialists of Erfurt, had a readily apparent role, but in fact hundreds of companies were involved, as were their bankers, suppliers, and insurers. The German railways charged the SS for the transportation of Jews, although they offered credit and discounts due to the scale of the operation. The profit seeking was fully compliant with the SS, understood what was involved, and was bureaucratically sophisticated.[22] This underlines the extent, indeed the major extent, of German knowledge of and profit in the Holocaust. Profit and knowledge were frequently linked. Auschwitz was also a major transport center and, like Chełmno, the first of the extermination camps, was in an annexed part of Germany, not a site in the supposedly obscure "East."

Transport and slave labor were not only brought together in the carrying of Jews to concentration and extermination camps. In addition, the "new order" sought by the Nazis required new transport links, notably to move raw materials and food to Germany. The unusually harsh winter of 1941–42 revealed the serious inadequacies of the road system in the western Soviet Union. These inadequacies encouraged the Germans in the spring of 1942 to begin to build a series of strategic roads to supply their forces and link their territories. As part of an ambitious network, a highway termed DG IV and designed to link Lwów and Stalino with a spur crossing the Crimea and the Straits of Kerch into the Caucasus was the most important, and Himmler's personal involvement led to the road being called the "Highway of the SS." Such roads were also seen as a way to kill Jews through very cruel forced labor, and mass graves marked the route. As an instance of the role of modernization, the road was seen as a setting for new model towns.[23] Comparably cruel forced labor was also seen in communist states, notably with canal construction, including in the Soviet Union in the 1930s and Romania in the 1950s. In each case, tens of thousands died.

German propaganda, for example the popular film *Ohm Kruger* (1941), referred to the British establishment of concentration camps during the Second Anglo-Boer War of 1899–1902, between the British and the Boers of Transvaal and Orange Free State, republics that would become part of the Union of South Africa. This was a totally misleading comparison, as the intention of the camps was very different. To deprive the Boer guerrillas of civilian support, the British army moved their families into detention camps. A total of 27,927 Boer civilians died there from disease, but there was no active mistreatment of the civilians, the British forces themselves suffered heavily from disease, and the camps were criticized in Britain, not least because of the deaths, with a freedom to speak out that scarcely bears comparison with Nazi Germany—nor, indeed, did the public opposition to the Boer War in Britain and the government's willingness to face a general election in 1900. The German film presented it as unacceptable to put Boers in the camps; the camps themselves were not the object of criticism. The reality of the large number of Boer deaths caught the attention of Nazi officials, not the intentions of the British government, which were quite different from those of the Germans and from the devious obfuscating arguments that the Nazi regime used for deflection purposes. In practice, German policy and public attitudes were in stark contrast to those of the British in the Boer War. Like the Spanish "concentration camps" in Cuba prior to the Spanish-American War of 1898, this distinction serves as a dramatic illustration of the point about the misuse of comparisons, notably between British imperialism and the Holocaust, discussed in chapter 6.

THE KILLING CONTINUES

Knowledge of the slaughter could scarcely have been limited.[24] The bodies of the murdered at Auschwitz were burned in the open air until the crematoria came into service in 1943. Burned flesh has a distinctive smell. Indeed, Rudolf Höss, the camp commandant at Auschwitz, referred to the "ghastly stench," an all-too-typical instance of blaming victims for one's own crimes. Families visited or lived with SS guards and presumably observed and understood at least part of what was going on, as had also happened with the killings by the *Einsatzgruppen*. Rumors of mass slaughter were widespread in Germany.

Aside from providing labor, the processing system at Auschwitz was also designed to ensure that there were no Jewish children: nearly 1.5 million Jews under fourteen were killed in the Holocaust. It is the accounts of the slaughter of children that are most affecting. Conversely, non-Jewish German women were encouraged to have babies. This concept was linked to domestic policies, with a healthier race understood in explicitly racial terms. From 1939, women received the Honor Cross of the German Mother for having numerous children.[25] Thus, the Holocaust and the German Home Front were both in the front line of race war.

In order to ensure that there were no Jewish children, Himmler pressed doctors to develop an easy method of sterilization. This was a brutal example of the conflation between Nazism and medical murder, one that was widespread. Medical experiments, such as Josef Mengele's at Auschwitz, Kurt Heissemeyer's injection of Jewish children (aged five to twelve) to further his work on tuberculosis, and many others, were cruel and murderous.

These experiments were not the only aspect of a more general perversion of reason. Other sciences were also used to forward Nazi themes. For example, the anthropologist Bruno Beger was sent to Auschwitz in 1943 to undertake research on Jewish skulls—for the advance of which eighty-six Jews were killed. The role of "experts" on race policy in German planning and administration was another aspect of the extent to which an allegedly rational and modern dimension characterized German policy toward Jews. In practice, this was the very opposite of the case, and both ends and means were murderous in intent and barbaric in character, however rational their apparent language.

Auschwitz II was solely for Jews and Roma, an aspect of the way in which they were treated more harshly than other victims of the Germans. Alongside the huts and barracks, Auschwitz II contained gas chambers and linked crematoria. It was expanded rapidly after Himmler inspected the camp on July 17–18, 1942. This camp was fed by train with Jews from throughout occupied Europe, the first from Slovakia arriving on March 26, 1942. Prominent groups killed there included, after a long train journey, the community of over 40,000 from Salonika (Thessaloniki), a key step in German antisemitic violence in Greece.[26] Italian diplomatic representations on behalf of some of the Salonika Jews were rejected. The killing was also a fundamental blow in the decline of Salonika as a multiethnic community, a character that had helped give it a particular vibrancy and cultural importance. The former Jewish quarter there remains somewhat spectral, and the heat of the day does not stir the quiet. The university was built on a Jewish cemetery. The 1,800 Jews from Corfu made up another Greek community slaughtered in Auschwitz.

Aside from the specific viciousness of German intentions, the position of Jews, segregated by the Germans in ghettos, made them far more vulnerable to attack, deportation, and murder than the non-Jewish population, particularly if the latter were dispersed across the countryside. This helps explain the contrast in levels of resistance, but, however much levels of race violence were different, a common feature was the total failure of the Germans to negotiate any outcome or seek any meaningful compromise with those they despised.

This situation also helped ensure the more general failure of the German war effort. Particularly from 1942, the German inability to deal with practical difficulties stemming from insufficient resources, overextended front lines, and the strength of their opponents' war making and fighting quality owed much to the extent to which the inherently irrational, as well as vicious, Nazi regime had an essentially flawed decision making further warped by ideological megalomania and strategic wishful thinking.[27] The Germans were not alone in failing to consider adequately the nature of the likely response to their policy and in not matching operational planning to feasible strategic goals. However, their war making proved particularly flawed under both categories. The harsh treatment of the conquered, not least but not only the slaughter of Jews, was a central aspect of this megalomania and wishful thinking, as it presupposed that cooperation was unnecessary and that a new order did not need to be grounded in acceptance, however coerced.

Yet this critical point is unhelpful in this context because it presupposes for Nazi Germany a functional end and analysis for what was in fact ideological—and with this ideological dimension far from being an optional add-on. I pointed out to a German Waffen-SS veteran, when listening in Afghanistan in 1976 to his remarks, that Germany might have done better had it not turned on Jews; doing so served my purpose of riling him but was also knowingly foolish as that attack was a central aspect of German policy. Indeed, it took precedence over the tensions and rivalries between German agencies because they cooperated in the slaughter, even though that made it more difficult to fund the slave labor to pursue the goal of constructing a new Europe.[28] To Hitler, war with Jews was destiny, an existential and metahistorical struggle, one in which the Germans would clearly earn their right to survive and triumph. Moreover, considering a Germany that did not pursue genocide entails a politicized presentism, as that approach focuses, at least implicitly, on the idea of an acceptable Germany resisting the Soviet Union, which was not a possibility while Germany was a Nazi state. Hitler's racial paranoia and prospectus gave German policy in World War II a distinctive character and helped ensure that in 1944 Germany did not negotiate an end to the war, as it had done during and after defeat in 1918.

The killing went on to the close of the war—notably so in Hungary, a German ally that joined in the war with the Soviet Union in June 1941. In August 1941, refugee Polish Jews were detained by the Hungarian police and handed over to the SS for slaughter. However, the lack of opportunity provided by the attitude of the Hungarian government ensured that there was no comprehensive slaughter of Hungarian Jews until 1944, although large numbers of Jews were sent as forced laborers with the Hungarian troops that took part in the invasion of the Soviet Union, and many were killed in the Soviet counteroffensive in winter 1942–43. The deportations of Jews from Hungary to extermination camps largely occurred after Germany occupied the country on March 19, 1944. This was in order both to prevent its defection to the Allies (a potential defection that reflected the collapsing position of the Germans on the Eastern Front and threatened to take it further) and also so that the Germans could make more effective use of the Hungarian economy.[29]

From May 15, 437,000 Hungarian Jews were deported by the Germans to Auschwitz. Some were used for labor there, but about three-quarters were killed at once as the result of a very high rate of deportation and slaughter that summer: an average of over 8,000 killed daily. Indeed, a rail spur was constructed so that the trains could go directly to Auschwitz II. This rail spur helped reflect and ensure the preponderant role of this camp in the killing. Already from the spring of 1943, when large new crematoria there came into operation, the mass factory-style killing at Auschwitz II was at an unprecedented rate. Partly as a result, while other extermination camps were closed down, facilities at Auschwitz II were maintained.

The flow of the conflict was moving strongly against the Germans by the time the Hungarian Jews were deported. In the right-bank Dnieper/ Ukraine campaign, launched on December 24, 1943, the Soviets proved very successful. Subsequently, breakthrough attacks in Ukraine in March 1944 forced the Germans back, and in April–May, Crimea was reconquered by Soviet forces. From June 1944, there was to be much more success in maintaining the pace of advance, in large part because, with increased operational effectiveness, Soviet forces had acquired the means (including US-supplied trucks) and developed the doctrine to fulfill these goals. This was not simply a Soviet advance on one axis but, instead, along the entire front, from the Black Sea to the Baltic, as well as in Finland. Soviet advances increased the sense of threat and foreboding on the part of the Germans.

In the face of Soviet successes, the treatment of Hungarian Jews reflected the continuing synergy between Hitler's war strategy and the war against Jews—and his attempt to ensure just such a synergy. Hitherto, despite serious antisemitic acts, the Hungarians had refused to carry out a variant of the Final Solution. However, once occupied, Hungarian officials cooperated eagerly, motivated (as, in part, the Germans were) by the benefits sought from the seizure of Jewish assets. The postwar communist regime typically refused to return the seized assets.[30]

Elsewhere also, the seizure of assets played a role in encouraging active cooperation with the Holocaust. This was the case, for example, with the bounty hunters responsible for the capture of many Dutch Jews, most of whom, having been transported to Poland, were killed in Auschwitz or Sobibor. As an instance of national variations, the Dutch proved more active as bounty hunters than did the Belgians.[31]

The seizure of assets paid the costs of the Holocaust, as German officials were keen to calculate and demonstrate to each other as part of their rationalization of policy. This seizure was also designed to aid the German economy, an economy under tremendous pressure from the growing strains of a war that was becoming more difficult as the Soviet Union and United States successfully deployed their economic strength. As such, the Holocaust was an aspect of the attempt to transform, through large-scale violence, the socioeconomic structure of Europe, notably Eastern Europe. This attempt does not necessarily make the vicious policy an aspect of some sort of perverted modernization but, rather, underlines the extent to which part of the context for the mass slaughter was the drive for plunder on the part of a regime that, despite its preposterous claims to culture, was very primitive in its methods and goals. This element underlines the extent of participation in the Holocaust, a point driven home in 2015 by the conviction in a German court of Oskar Gröning, who had taken part in the seizure of money from Jews arriving at Auschwitz II.

The distribution among the non-Jewish German population of goods seized from German and foreign Jews was designed to help further bind the public to the regime as well as to provide the public with compensation for the burdens of the war, not least Anglo-American bombing. On the night of July 27–28, 1943, Hamburg was heavily damaged in a firestorm created by British bombing with massive casualties resulting. This attack created a crisis of public confidence in the Nazi regime. Goebbels, who had been given responsibility for sorting out the aftermath of the bombing of cities, was particularly concerned about the morale of bombed civilians. The evacuation of civilians to the countryside spread alarm about German weakness. That November, the British air offensive on Berlin, which was to last until the end of March 1944, was launched. Initially, city authorities across Germany had seized the possessions of Jews as a form of opportunistic plunder that took forward the already arbitrary use of tax and other criteria in the prewar years to acquire goods on forced terms. In turn, this process of seizure became systematized. The distribution of seized goods indicated the range of the spoils system, led to pressure from below for more plunder, and underlined the extent to which Jews were being mistreated: 674 trainloads of household goods from the apartments of deported French Jews were sent to Germany.[32] Clothes, furniture, and bedding taken from Jews were provided to Germans who had lost possessions in Allied bombings. It would be all too easy when referring to compensation in this form to write of "Germans who had lost everything in Allied bombing," the rebirth of the post-Versailles idea of Germans as victims. However, that English phrase and scholarly analysis scarcely capture the reality that those who thus received the benefits of expropriation, theft, and murder were alive, whereas the Jews who had had these goods taken from them had been killed or were close to death. There is no equivalence. Indeed, the use of the bodies of the slaughtered, notably their gold teeth, had echoes of cannibalism.

The redistribution of plunder reflected the attempt to maintain civilian morale (for non-Jews) and was in accordance with the War Damages Law, decided on November 30, 1940, which decreed that there would be full compensation for any war damage suffered by civilians in future. This law was intended to counter Allied bombing, demonstrate community, and provide the Nazi Party with legitimacy as the helper in times of distress. Thus, the social order was to be ensured by the spoils system.

This "racist form of crisis management"[33] was part of a broader pattern of looting. Other parts of German life "benefited," to again misuse language as is all too easy when writing on this subject.[34] For example, watches taken from Crimean Jews were used for the military. The files of ghetto and camp administrations included many requests from soldiers, policemen, and civil servants for watches and jewelry.[35] Much else was simply seized.

The seizure of Jewish goods as a means to bind the people to the regime and its cause and to support the war effort was also seen among Germany's allies, notably in the case of Romania. There, motivated by his murderous antisemitism, ethnic-nationalist corporatism, and desire to avoid the social travails of World War I, Marshal Antonescu, the Romanian dictator, saw Jews' possessions as both problem and opportunity. In practice, rampant greed affected this policy from top to bottom, with most of the property stolen not only by the state from its Jewish citizens but also from the state by its agents and others. Corruption in this process was frequent, and there were many corruption trials. Greed and the opportunity for gain helped in Romania to ensure that there was a high level of local initiative and variation in the seizure of Jewish goods.[36]

The pronounced theft dimension of the Holocaust, like that of murder, brought together old antisemitic themes, in this case the belief in secret and fabulous Jewish riches, as well as more recent ideas of hostility to the free market and, paradoxically, violent opposition to Jews as alleged communist fifth-column agents. Moreover, central power and local initiative in government both played a role in this process, as did the state and those who did not work for state agencies. The attempt by both the government and some of the Christian population to gain from the expropriation and plunder of the goods of Hungary's Jews was important to how the Jews were treated in 1944.[37]

The process of seizure of property varied greatly, as did the identity of those involved, whether perpetrators, bystanders, or victims. As such, the seizure mirrored the Holocaust. The perpetrators were not only the officials and agents of state, party, military, and police but also neighbors, former friends, and other locals. In the case of the heirs of those who lost their property (and often their lives), the theft was to be compounded by the postwar situation, as bureaucrats, courts, and owners notably but not only in Germany and Austria, made the restitution of goods and property very difficult. Frequently, the context was one of a continuing antisemitism that contributed to a new iteration of the legalized theft of the Nazi years, for example arguing that those who had fled had left voluntarily. The postwar plunder of Jews was also seen in Eastern Europe.

The wartime plunder, as already noted, was a matter not only of the seizure of the goods, jobs, and property of Jews but also the use of their bodies. The actual details deserve frequent reiteration in order to make absolutely clear what happened. Personal pieces of jewelry, such as wedding rings, were seized, as were gold fillings from teeth, which were extracted with hooks and pliers. Moreover, the hair and skin of the dead were used. The bodies were burnt to ashes, which were at times used as fertilizer. Synthetic petrol was also a product. The detailed lists kept of the goods that were plundered, both in the camps and in other stages of the treatment of the Jews, indicate a concern for profit, as well as a conviction that keeping such records was acceptable as well as necessary. Yet, although such listings may seem to show administrative sophistication, that was far from the case.

The use of slave labor was also an important aspect of a plunder of resources, not least because it was obtained as part of a system that included the destruction of skilled Jewish manpower and, more generally, the deliberate elimination of the Jewish role in the economies of Europe. This slave plunder became more important to the Germans as the war continued, and that, in turn, became a more prominent factor in the treatment of Jews.[38] With German forces no longer advancing after late 1942 (other than in local counterattacks), there was no more prospect of obtaining forced labor, Jewish or non-Jewish, by conquest. That meant that existing sources of slave labor had to be used more carefully, including the (to the Germans) undesirable categories of Jews and Russian prisoners of war.

Nevertheless, *care* is a very relative term. Jews who were moved to labor camps were treated in a particularly brutal fashion, and to ensure that they could be readily thus treated (and with less chance for resistance), they were segregated in distinct teams. The food was limited and of poor quality, the barracks were not heated, sanitary facilities were primitive, the clothing was inadequate, and the work was brutally arduous. Shifts were long, there was no concern with safety, many of the workers lacked relevant experience, and there were frequent beatings and shootings. Those who were ill or who collapsed through exhaustion were shot.

These conditions were true not only of Jews working under the control of the SS but also of those working under other German agencies, not least the Organization Todt (OT), which was the key construction agency for the German war machine. Headed from 1942 by Albert Speer, the OT was responsible for a range of war construction projects including the extensive underground facilities built to safeguard weapons production from Allied air attack. At Nuremberg, the case against Speer noted, without specifically referring to Jews: "He proposed the use of internees from the concentration camps in the armament factories. Now, in view of the wretched physical condition of the prisoners, no profit but only the extermination of the prisoners could be expected from this measure."[39] Jewish workers were sent in 1944 from Auschwitz and directly from Budapest in Hungary to build facilities at Kaufering and Mühldorf, which were satellite camps of Dachau, near Munich. The workers were brutalized; many were killed, and in September–October, the remaining Jews were transported to Auschwitz for gassing. Also in 1944, the camp at Gusen in upper Austria, a subcamp of the Mauthausen main camp that had begun to manufacture aircraft parts the previous year for Messerschmitt and Steyr-Daimler-Puch, was expanded with underground factories for the production of jet fighters. Death rates for the prisoners were high as a result of terrible living and working conditions. In 1945, moreover, Jews from Auschwitz were dispatched to the Mittelbau concentration camp in order to work in the underground Nordhausen factory manufacturing V-weapons (rockets), which were largely fired at Allied-held Antwerp and at London.

A large number of Jewish slave laborers were employed in private industry, where death rates were also high. This was an aspect of the Holocaust that was scarcely hidden from the public eye, and another reason why the thesis of popular ignorance is implausible, although after the war this work was largely overlooked. Thus, the Quandt family concealed its close links with the Nazis. The family business used forced labor to make armaments and batteries for U-boats, with some of the labor taken from satellite concentration camps. Many workers died, in part as a result of exposure to toxic metals. Unsuccessful efforts were made to stop a German television documentary on these matters, *The Silence of the Quandts*, being broadcast in 2007.

Both as individuals and as a group, Jews suffered what Germans intended, albeit to very differing degrees, as a deliberate retribution for their Judaism. Sadism, thus, became not only public policy but also supposedly sanctified in the cause of racial justice and necessity. The imposition of suffering thereby appeared a duty to cleanse the world as much as it clearly was a pleasure to the large number of sadists called forth by total domination and indulged by German military success and Nazi ideology. This sadism emerges clearly in eyewitness accounts of the camps and, indeed, of all aspects of the treatment of the Jews. To refer, for example, to the mistreatment of workers in the camps is to use not only misleadingly sanitized language but also to fail to explain the situation.

The German and German-allied assault on Jewry included a deliberate destruction of Jewish knowledge, culture, and sites, for example prayer books, ritual objects, synagogues, synagogue decorations, and menorahs, all of which were destroyed. Synagogues were blown up. In German cities, air-raid shelters were built on the sites of synagogues. Cemeteries were not so much desecrated, as still happens frequently at the hands of neo-Nazis today, but destroyed, with the gravestones used for construction purposes. In Salonika, they were used for road building and the creation of a military swimming pool. There were also assaults on the memory and culture of other communities, for example, the German and Soviet treatment of Ukraine, part of a larger mistreatment of the Ukrainians,[40] but not on this scale. The Yiddish culture of Eastern European Jewry was particularly hard hit, and it is appropriate that the Holocaust is known in Yiddish as the *Churban* (Destruction). This attack was as part of the German determination to destroy the Jewish past, and thus what was held to be the Jewish grip on the present and threat to the future.

Ironically, at the same time there was an attempt to collect examples of Jewish culture, as if of an anthropology of the dead. This was not so much an annexation of Jewish culture as part of a process of anatomization. In another aspect of plunder, Jewish "spiritual power" was to be collected, and the Nazis created museums of Jewish material culture, notably the Jewish Central Museum in Prague. The collections were designed to celebrate the destruction of the Jews, to mark the triumph of the Germans, the new "chosen people," who would control the future, and to hold onto the relics of Jewish civilization. This goal reflected the centrality to Nazi thought of what was considered to be the Jewish issue. The Jewish role in European culture was also destroyed, with efforts ranging from the attempt to extirpate the major Jewish contribution to European science and the arts, prominently through the burning of books, to the renaming of institutions, buildings, and streets that carried Jewish names. There was an attempt to obliterate the legacy of philosemitism. Thus, in 1942, the Germans destroyed the statue at Lunéville, in Lorraine, of Abbé Henri Gregoire (1756–1837), a key figure in late Enlightenment thought who had made efforts on behalf of Jewish emancipation. Gregoire was to be an unpopular figure under Vichy.

Having demonized Jews, the Germans (like other antisemites before them) were in the dangerous position of feeling both strength and vulnerability toward them. A belief that communism was led by Jews helped make the latter appear more diabolical. Indeed, the killing of Jews was excused by some perpetrators, particularly among Hitler's allies, such as Ukrainian, Lithuanian, and Latvian collaborators, by reference to the alleged Jewish role during Soviet occupation as well as with reference to communist atrocities—real, alleged, or apparently projected. This theme continued (and continues) to be expressed after World War II but has multiple flaws, not least issues of proportionality, the inaccurate characterization of the vast majority of Jews, and the extent to which cover is thereby provided for longer-term antisemitism, well before Stalin.

With their target clearly identified, the Germans were able to plan and execute a barbarous rolling massacre that reflected the one-sided nature of a power relationship in which the perpetrators of slaughter were in no physical danger.[41] As Hitler's reliance on will was revealed inadequate in German war making—not least with this reliance leading to a failure to set rational military and political goals—the slaughter of Jews, which remained sensible to Nazis, was left as a vicious way to convince him that he still had willpower and could achieve something with it, as he felt he had to do. Fearing, from the late summer of 1942, that final victory might be out of reach, if it was not already, Hitler was determined to fight on in order to destroy Europe's Jews, which he appeared able to do, as well as to achieve a moral victory for his concept of the German people, and thus control the future.[42]

Furthermore, increased difficulties led to the radicalization of the military, as Nazi commitment came to play a greater role in appointments and promotions. After the unsuccessful bomb plot of July 20, 1944, in which a group of German officers, a few outraged by the Holocaust, narrowly failed to kill Hitler and overthrow his regime, the bulk of the military command rallied to Hitler, and the Nazification of the army was pushed by Heinz Guderian, the new chief of the general staff. Moreover, the repression of disaffection and of any sign of defeatism by the Nazi surveillance system, presided over by Himmler (who had also become minister of the interior in August 1943), helped ensure that there was no repetition of the German collapse of 1918, while the judicial system willingly responded to Hitler in dramatically increasing the harshness of its sentences.[43]

Reflecting the mobilization for total war ordered in July 1944, the *Volkssturm*, a compulsory local defense militia for men between sixteen and sixty, was placed under the control of Himmler and Martin Bormann, the party secretary, and not under that of the army. This militia was designed to inflict casualties on the advancing Allies such that their morale—it was believed—could not tolerate and also to indoctrinate the civilian population for a total struggle.

Indeed, it has been argued that, imbued by Nazi ideological assumptions, the German leadership, or at least part of it, continued to believe that it could win even after the summer of 1944. Victory was held to depend on stronger will, as well as on new technology, such as rockets and jet aircraft, to be built, safe from air attack, in underground factories in murderous conditions by forced labor, as well as on improved tanks and, even more, submarines. This will was seen as within the racial potential of the Germans in what was presented by Hitler as "a struggle for existence" and by Himmler as a "people's war in which one race and one nation wants to and must annihilate the other."[44] The idea of war against Jews remained central. The belief that the Allies were dominated by Jewish cliques opened the possibility that the Aryan majorities in Britain and the United States might appreciate that they should not die for Jews and communists or that their supposedly Jewish-run leadership would panic. The counteroffensive launched by the Germans in the Ardennes on December 16, 1944, *Unternehmen Wacht am Rhein* (Operation Watch on the Rhine), which led to the Battle of the Bulge, was made possible by the transfer of troops from the Eastern Front. This operation, for which the Germans massed about 200,000 troops, was designed to lead to the defeat of the Anglo-American armies and possibly to the collapse of their will to fight, which, however, was a serious misjudgment of German prospects. This offensive provides another context within which the continued slaughter of Jews appeared pertinent: to create a Jew-free Europe not only if Germany won but also if it lost. Yitzhak Katznelson, a Polish Jewish teacher murdered in Auschwitz, remarked, "German children who have not yet killed a Jew are raised to do so, educated to it, dedicated to it by murderous parents and murderous teachers."[45]

The number of Jews who could be killed, however, diminished as the war continued. In part, this was because so many had already been slaughtered, as was the key element in Poland. Deportations from there to the extermination camps, however, continued into 1944, as the Germans slaughtered those they had already confined. Over 67,000 Jews were deported from Łódź to Auschwitz II in the summer of 1944, the ghetto being liquidated at the end of August in accordance with orders from Himmler on June 10. In response to this order and the resulting need for more killing facilities, nearby Chełmno, the first extermination camp, was reopened.[46]

More generally, the frenetic yet methodical pace of the killings in 1944 reflected the collapse of the Nazi empire and the still-potent determination to kill Jews. As a result, the key aspect in the chronologies and geographies of the Holocaust remained that of German military fortunes.[47] In their breakthrough attacks in Ukraine in March and April 1944, the Soviets drove the Germans back across the Bug, Dniester, and Prut rivers. Operation Bagration, the destructive attack launched on Army Group Center on June 23, led to the conquest of Belarus and the pushing back of the Germans into central Poland. Lublin was captured by the Soviets on July 23 and Lwów on July 27. Further north, they took Tallinn on September 22 and Riga on October 15. Romania surrendered to the Soviet Union on August 23 (and had already downplayed its anti-semitic policies), Finland signed an armistice on September 2, and, threatened by the advancing Red Army, Bulgaria declared war on Germany on September 5. On October 11, Hungary concluded a preliminary armistice with the Soviet Union.

Meanwhile, the Germans continued their killing; indeed, on May 26, 1944, Hitler pressed the necessity of doing so in a speech to *National-sozialistischer Führungsoffizier* (National Socialist leadership officers), who were army officers responsible for teaching ideology, a group established in December 1943. Their courses indoctrinated large numbers of troops with the need to wipe out Jews. Aside from the slaughter of the Łódź Jews, 10,000 Slovak Jews, for example, were deported to Auschwitz in August–October 1944. Giving evidence in 2015 in the case of Oskar Gröning, a former SS man on trial for complicity to murder 300,000 at Auschwitz, Max Eisen, a Slovak Jew taken there in 1944, testified to being sent first for a shower in Auschwitz I: "There was a man from my town in his 20s, he had very thick glasses and he dropped them when the water came out. He went on his hands and knees to try and find them and one of the SS guards came and kicked him and kept stamping on him and I can remember his ribs were cracking. He killed him right there on the spot."[48]

Deportations to Auschwitz from the "model" concentration camp at Theresienstadt, whose filmed inmates, in order to deceive observers, were initially supposed to receive better treatment, continued until the end of October. Out of the 141,162 Jews sent to Theresienstadt, 33,456 died there, while 88,162 were deported to concentration camps. The role of the influential elders among the Jews in Theresienstadt, for example Benjamin Murmelstein, was subsequently to cause controversy, but in reality they had very little influence.

On the distant Aegean Island of Rhodes, an Italian possession until taken by the Germans in September 1943, Jewish women and children were seized in July 1944, shipped to Piraeus, the port for Athens, and then taken by train to Auschwitz. Thus, as the farthest tendrils of the Reich collapsed, Jews had to be killed first before the Germans pulled out. Considerable effort was devoted to seizing the Jews on Rhodes, and at a time when vessels were limited. It was only on November 28 that there were the last gassings at Auschwitz, and then only in response to the advancing Soviet threat to Upper Silesia. In practice, however, in the face of growing casualties and logistical difficulties after the major advance of the summer, and in response to stiffening German resistance as Germany was neared, the Soviet offensive stalled in late 1944, not least because major German forces remained on the flanks of the advance westward through Poland.

The driving back of the Germans was therefore important in reducing the number of potential victims for slaughter. In some areas, this driving back meant that Jews with partisan groups or in hiding could come out. That, however, could also expose them to the hostile attentions of the Soviet NKVD, which was intensely suspicious of partisans and those who might be associated with them, not least in Poland. Nevertheless, this was far less of a threat than that posed by the Germans.

Other areas where large numbers of Jews had survived were conquered or reconquered by the Allies, most significantly much of Italy in 1943–44 and France and Belgium in 1944. The German commander in Paris surrendered on August 25, three days after the last transport of Jews left France for Auschwitz, and on September 3, Brussels was captured. Rome fell to US forces on June 5, 1944, and Florence on August 4. These areas and cities, therefore, were no longer open to German pressure for deportation or to the possibility that deportation might become more effective. Changes in allegiance by Germany's allies, or the prospect of such changes, similarly lessened the possibility of expansion or intensification of the Holocaust. This was the case in Bulgaria and Finland, although in Hungary the Germans seized the initiative for long enough to ensure the slaughter of large numbers of Jews. However, because Hungary was not conquered by the Germans until 1944, the large-scale killing of Jews there only began that year, so the percentage of Hungarian Jews who survived the war was higher than that in Poland. It was not only killing that continued until the end of the war, particularly mass shootings, but also a neglect of those held in the camps that led to high rates of death through malnutrition and epidemics. The last proved particularly serious.

Meanwhile, the Soviet advance resulted in the overrunning of extermination camps or their sites: Maly Trostinets, Sobibor, Majdanek, and Treblinka were captured in Operation Bagration, the major offensive in the summer of 1944, and Auschwitz on January 27, 1945. The Germans, however, razed camps to the ground when they finished using them or were forced to evacuate them. Although they did not have time at Majdanek to destroy the evidence of their activities, this happened, for example, to Sobibor and Treblinka after they were closed in November 1943. This destruction was an aspect of German deception and one pushed forward by the extent to which the war was no longer moving in the Germans' favor. At the end of November 1944, Himmler, who was already maneuvering for position after the likely fall of Hitler, not least hoping for possible alignment with the West, ordered the destruction of the gas chambers at Auschwitz. As another sign of awareness of guilt, the SS also destroyed deportation schedules, which made it difficult to reach agreement on the number of victims. In 1943–44, in order to destroy evidence, there was an unearthing of victims who, once killed, had been buried rather than burned, and now, these bodies were burned—for example, at Ponary near Vilnius, from September 1943 to April 1944. On February 16, 1945, a decree ordered the destruction of files dealing with the Holocaust in order to prevent them from falling into Allied hands.

Already at Krasnodar in July 1943, the first trial by the Soviets on the charge of participation in German war crimes made public a case of mass murder of Jews. Those convicted were publicly executed.[49] Such action did not lead the Germans to cease killing, but it encouraged them to destroy evidence, although that was not always done. Thus, the "execution book" at Mauthausen concentration camp seized by the Allies revealed 36,318 victims. Trials in the Soviet Union, combined with a conviction of Jewish influence in the leadership of each of the Allies, helped ensure that Nazi leaders felt that they were committed to (and in) the Holocaust and that there was no turning back from their destiny. At the same time, the destruction of evidence most lastingly stole the individuality of the murdered as it made it harder to trace the fate of many.

The Allied insistence on unconditional surrender, enunciated at the conference at Casablanca on January 14–24, 1943, made any compromise peace unlikely and underlined this sense of Nazi committal. It would, however, be foolish to blame the continued German commitment to the Holocaust in some way on the Allied insistence on unconditional surrender, whether or not that blame is an example of the persistent German narrative of victimhood. In practice, the German commitment was centered on ideological fervor and an unwillingness to accept failure, and both were seen in the German willingness to continue fighting and to take very heavy casualties. The Allied insistence was a military absolute different in character from the moral absolute of German depravity and also lacked full knowledge of the latter. Hitler was determined to fight on to achieve what he regarded as a moral victory for his concept of the German people, a heroic apotheosis through violence involving the destruction of the Jews and the inflicting of such casualties on the Allies that their morale could not tolerate it. Hitler also wished to divide the Allies in order to make a separate peace, and the goal of unconditional surrender was the best means to thwart this wish.

As an instructive indication of more long-term German attitudes, the movement of Jews by forced marches from areas about to be conquered by Soviet forces was carried out so that their forced labor and the genocide could both continue. That movement from Auschwitz began on January 18, 1945. Although a few Jews risked death by escaping in the chaos, large numbers were shot, bludgeoned, or died during these marches. The repeated sadism of the guards, especially toward those deemed stragglers, is appalling. Testimony read out at the Nuremberg trials in 1946 about events in Belarus in March 1944 commented on the killing of women and children as prisoners were forced to march from one camp to another: "One woman was walking with three children. One of the children fell down. The Germans shot at him. Horrified, the mother and the two other children looked back; the monster soldiers shot them down one by one. The mother cried out in agony, but her shriek was interrupted by a direct shot."[50]

The prisoners were forced to endure punishing marches on low rations and with little night-time shelter, while their scanty clothes did not keep out the effects of a very harsh winter. The provision systems that had supported the concentration camps, however harshly, collapsed. Murder, freezing, exhaustion, and hunger combined to kill large numbers. How many died on these marches is unclear, in part because the record-keeping apparatus of German brutality was ending, indeed collapsing, but the figure for Jews, who were the majority on the marches, may be between 250,000 and 400,000. This was scarcely the "industrial" slaughter seen at work in the extermination camps. Instead, there was an inherent chaos, but one that was deadly as well as horrific for the victims involved.[51] Jews who were too ill to take part in the marches were slaughtered.[52] Aside from marches, many Jews were put into open rail cars, where they froze to death, not least as the trains were frequently stranded in open sidings and their passengers left without food. Some trains, however, carried Jews to concentration camps in Germany such as Buchenwald and Dachau. Anglo-American prisoners were treated far better on the marches designed to move them away from advancing Allied units. Those too weak to walk were moved by carts and trucks, there was food, and the guards were not brutal. More generally, Allied prisoners were aware of the brutal treatment of Jews to a degree that throws light on German awareness.[53]

Alongside the killing of Jews during the marches, there was widespread disease, both on the marches and in the camps. Like many others there, Anne Frank died of typhus in Bergen-Belsen in 1945. Moreover, the killing at this point, when victory was impossible for Germany, indicated not pointlessness but, instead, the centrality of race warfare to Nazi policy, particularly as additional options were closed down by defeat. In January and February 1945, plans were still being drawn up to deport Jews in mixed marriages and the children of such marriages to the surviving camps.

The killing went on. For example, Hungarian Jews deported to Mauthausen were murdered "out on the street" at the start of 1945 by police, *Volkssturm*, and Hitler Youth members. As in the concentration camps, Jews were treated more harshly than others involved in the death marches, such as prisoners of war. This treatment in large part reflected the views and determination of officials acting on their own initiative, in part to cover their guilt and complicity in the Holocaust, as the central impetus behind slaughter slackened with the growing collapse of the regime. Killing and murderous maltreatment against Jews on these marches continued into April 1945, as in that from the Helmbrechts work camp to Prachatice in Czechoslovakia, and even into the early days of May.

This killing reflected the extent to which Nazi activity continued in the face of the Allied advances, notably the Soviet offensive launched on April 16. This continuation was despite Hitler first being surrounded by Soviet forces in Berlin (April 25) and then, on April 30, committing suicide as they fought their way through to his bunker.[54] In his "Political Testament," dictated the previous day, a raving Hitler held Jews responsible for the war and thus for the destructive bombing of Germany and also for the very killing meted out to Jews. This rhetoric was very similar to the antisemitic response of Wilhelm II to defeat in World War I and indeed of many other Germans to defeat in both world wars. Similarly, even at this late stage, and underlining the continued role of Nazi ideological fervor, German field forces killed deserters; carried out massacres in the field, for example, of captured Polish troops and of surrendered Georgians and Dutch civilians on the island of Texel off the Dutch coast; and tried to break through Soviet forces to relieve Hitler in Berlin. On May 7, however, the Germans surrendered unconditionally, the surrender becoming effective the next day.

THE GERMAN PUBLIC AND THE HOLOCAUST

From the outset of the killing, not all German commanders, troops, and officials responded to Jews in a brutal fashion, and those who did not comply were not generally punished, although, aside from peer group pressure, there were cases of penalties for some who did not take part. Nevertheless, there is no record of anyone being punished for refusing to join the *Einsatzgruppen*, the special police battalions, or the SS units active in the camps. Similarly, although in most cases, private companies sought concentration-camp prisoners as slave labor, those that did not were not punished. This ability to choose how to respond underlines the extent of complicity in the Holocaust. Moreover, beside the executioners, there were planners, organizers, implementers (for example, in the train system), and apologists.[55]

Furthermore, in Germany and Austria, local people who did not join in the persecution of camp inmates and, instead, helped them were generally not harshly punished, unlike in Eastern Europe, where the punishments were savage and often immediate. Poles who helped Jews were murdered in the extermination camps. This variety of responses highlights the issue of individual responsibility and removes from the

guilty the convenient argument that they were in some way passive victims of an all-powerful system and ideology. Knowledge and complicity
are issues because Hitler did not announce the Final Solution publicly—
so also is indoctrination, such as that of the young in the Hitler Youth or
the League of German Girls.[56]

A valuable case study makes it clear that the people of the German
city of Osnabrück (from which the major deportation of Jews occurred
on December 13, 1941) knew of the persecution of Jews that was happening, even if only a minority took part in antisemitic acts; the same is true
of the Austrian town of Mauthausen, near where there was a concentration camp.[57] More generally, widespread public acceptance of a policy
of social exclusion also affected those with at least one Jewish grandpar-
ent.[58] At the same time, intermarriage complicated the response of many
individuals. It ensured that some Jews were helped by fellow Germans,
but it did not lead to an openness to the plight of others. At the individual
level, however, the wartime career of Oskar Schindler, the subject of
Thomas Kennedy's 1980 book, *Schindler's Ark*, and a very successful 1993
film, Steven Spielberg's *Schindler's List*, exemplifies the possibilities for
individual action. Initially as a means for profit, the corrupt Schindler
looked after a Jewish labor force, 1,300 strong, whom he then took expensive and risky steps to save from slaughter. Schindler's strategy worked
during the period in which some SS agencies placed more emphasis on
slave work than on murder. It is indicative of the influence of visual images and, more particularly, significance of films, that tourists in Cracow
are now taken to see where the film was shot.

A lack of knowledge was pleaded by many Germans after the end
of the war. In some cases, this can be shown to be inaccurate. Leni
Riefenstahl, a friend of Hitler's who had made key Nazi propaganda
films in 1933–36, continued to be a propaganda filmmaker during World
War II. She was subsequently to deny knowledge of Nazi killings, but the
evidence reveals that she was a liar. This has been proved in two cases. In
1939, in Poland, she saw the killing of thirty Jewish civilians in the town
of Konskie after they had dug a mass grave in the town square, a very
public act of slaughter. Riefenstahl denied being there, but photographs
by a German soldier prove the contrary. In 1940, Riefenstahl used Roma
(Gypsy) children from a transit camp as extras, after which they were

returned to the camp. She subsequently declared that they all survived the war—when, in fact, most were killed at Auschwitz—and expressed racialist views later in life.[59]

Clearly, the extent of knowledge varied, as did the contrast pointed out by Richard Pipes between a German fetish over cleanliness and adulation of pet dogs and a corresponding lack of concern for other humans. Nevertheless, Germans were not segregated during the war: soldiers, in particular, came home on leave; businessmen and others traveling in conquered territory witnessed killing; and knowledge or rumors of killings in "the East" and of the ghettos were widespread. The extermination camps were far less in the forefront of attention, but rumors, nevertheless, circulated widely. The railway workers who transported Jews did not live in a vacuum. Moreover, Jews who worked in public places, as Victor Klemperer (who was married to a non-Jew) did in a factory in Dresden, were clearly discriminated against and thus mistreated, and many disappeared as they were deported. Arrests and deportations were often carried out in public, and government propaganda unequivocally presented Jews as enemies to be destroyed. Germans internalized this by ignoring neighbors and others who were Jewish and by insisting that they be kept out of air-raid shelters and otherwise segregated.[60] The death marches of concentration camp inmates in the closing months of the war took place in plain sight.

In German propaganda in the closing years of the war, the Jewish threat became more prominent as a theme, not less. Jews were presented as the source of not only communism but also of the British and American plutocracies allegedly responsible for bombing Germany. SD reports revealed that air raids were regarded among the public as a reaction to German persecution of Jews, a belief that indicated the highly misleading extent to which Jews were believed to influence, if not dictate, US and British policy, a view taken by Hitler. That so many Germans thought the air offensive was retribution for antisemitic measures indicates that they knew what was being done to Jews, if not in detail, then at least in its outlines.

In the spring of 1943, over 70 percent of radio broadcasts focused on aspects of the supposed Jewish threat, including the likely fate for Germans (non-Jewish Germans) if Jews took their revenge through the

Allies. Anglo-American bombing and the example of the Polish officers shot by the NKVD at Katyn were blamed by the regime on Jewish influence. Thus, Germany was to be united under the threat of imminent and timeless Jewish atrocities, a bizarre inversion of the actual fate of Jews. This approach not only looked toward self-serving postwar German ideas of victimhood, ideas that are still very much current, or indeed stronger, but also testified to the extent to which it was difficult to be able to listen to the radio and not understand that the regime saw itself as involved in an existential struggle with Jews—and one that was waged as war.[61]

From a different direction, the widespread willingness to serve Nazi goals and, in doing so, fulfill a personal role by denouncing others, including spouses and friends,[62] denunciations that helped the Gestapo in their campaign to arrest Jews, suggests that more people would have taken an active part against Jews had they been asked to do so. In mid-1944, Goebbels received a number of unsolicited letters suggesting that Jews be used as human shields within German cities to deter bombing and that Jews be hanged (i.e., publicly) in reprisal for Germans killed in the bombing.

Such responses have been presented as aspects of a more general moral brutalization of German society, although the extent to which antisemitic legislation and violence had been accepted both before the war and in its early years indicates that this brutalization was already present before the war went wrong for the Germans (as most would have seen it at the time) and stimulated further hatreds.[63] The Anglo-American bombing that the *Luftwaffe* very conspicuously, despite the deployment of major resources, failed to stop also encouraged Hitler in his flights of antisemitic paranoia, as he blamed it on Jews.

That those who were asked to become killers mostly did so reflects the widespread nature of a willingness to participate in or, at the least, condone the killing.[64] Alongside this, racial-eugenicist ideas were widely held. They were not only common among intellectuals but also widely diffused in society, not least because, in some form, they proved readily understandable and could be assimilated by existing prejudices, such as antisemitism.

Racial-eugenicist ideas, but not genocidal ones, were long term, indeed almost a staple of Western thought in the period, with characteristics believed to pertain to particular races, as in the British idea about Indian "martial races" that should be recruited: Gurkhas, Sikhs, or Rajputs, but not generally shorter and darker southern Indians, such as Tamils. Eugenicist ideas reflected anxiety about the consequences of competition between the races and also about the "racial health" of certain nations. In particular, industrialization, urbanization, and their alleged consequences were believed to challenge or compromise racial health, and cosmopolitanism to threaten racial identity and character. This belief led to widespread support for eugenics on the Left, for example in Sweden, as well as on the Right. Resulting policies included the incarceration of those deemed physically and/or medically unfit, measures to prevent them having children, and, in some contexts, sterilization.

This was violation and violence. If it was violence totally different in nature, lethality, and scale to that of the Nazis, it also helped explain how in Germany and, to a degree, among its allies, barriers against cooperating in Nazi killing were overcome as officials and others adapted willingly, and even enthusiastically, to the murderous treatment of Jews. Moreover, many came to see this brutal treatment as a moral duty that was essential to the destiny of the German race and thus to European civilization. The fate of the latter was very much to the fore in German and allied propaganda, for example that of Vichy, which is instructive given that the Holocaust was a clear sign of a fundamental civilizational breakdown.

Those in the field who opted not to kill did not necessarily take this course because of opposition to the idea of the slaughter. Frequently, instead, it was the means of killing that were disliked, or there was a sense of personal unsuitability for the task. Crucially, there was widespread Nazism among Germans and Austrians.

On July 7, 1944, referring to the German treatment of the Hungarian Jews, *The Times* of London claimed that "the responsibility . . . rested on the German people." Only a few thousand Jews survived the war inside Germany with the help of non-Jews. This small number, nevertheless, invites the question about whether individual Germans could have done more, although the terrible and insistent pressure of a totalitarian police state has to be borne in mind. The stress here is on an argument not only that the Holocaust was central to the Nazi regime but also that its implementation was dependent on features of the German society of that period. That does not mean that all Germans played a role—that was very much not the case—but instead that social values, norms, and organization, including the institutions of civil societies, contributed directly to Nazi success in this sphere. Hitler and Himmler orchestrated the Holocaust and benefited to that end from structural forces in, and facets of, German society, although the brutalization of the latter, already pronounced, became even more apparent as the war went badly. The functionalist interpretation, which, in explaining the Holocaust, stresses initiatives by German officials responding to particular problems, appears pertinent as far as the mechanics and, to a degree, the timing of the slaughter are concerned, but otherwise is less valid.

The issue of individual and collective German responsibility is highlighted by the postwar risings against communist rule in East Germany, both unsuccessful and speedily suppressed in 1953 and, in contrast, rapidly successful in 1989. These risings indicated the possibilities of resistance to totalitarian rule, even if, as with the use of Soviet forces in Hungary in 1956 and Czechoslovakia in 1967, this resistance could be swiftly crushed. The use of tanks against demonstrators by the government in Romania in 1989 did not prevent the overthrow of the latter, albeit at the cost of the lives of over 1,000 demonstrators. Although far less violent, the 1989 events in East Germany showed that totalitarianism had its weaknesses, a point that invited reconsideration of not only communist East Germany but also of Nazi Germany. SD reports indicate that the Nazi surveillance system also had weaknesses. This is an instance of the way in which subsequent events help reformulate the questions asked.

Reading back from 1989 to the opposition to Hitler underlines the extent to which this opposition lacked active public support on any scale. Prudence in the face of a brutal totalitarian Nazi regime played an important part, with the regime both far more brutal and powerful than its communist counterpart in East Germany in 1989 and in the midst of a war. However, ideological and practical support for the regime also played a role.

The churches certainly acted in postwar Eastern Europe, particularly but not only in Poland, to sustain public distance from communism in a way that they largely failed to in Germany, Austria, and Germany's allies in the case of the Nazis.[65] In part, this failure was because aspects of Nazi ideology and policy reflected the aspirations, or at least inclinations, of powerful constituencies within the churches or could be interpreted as doing so. In this respect, antisemitism was an aspect of the antiliberal and anticommunist nature of much church thought and notably of many Catholics. There was also a core religious element to antisemitism, with alleged Jewish guilt for the death of Christ playing a prominent part in the Catholic liturgical season of Lent and in popular reenactments of the Crucifixion. As in Vichy France, very much a Catholic state, opposition to what were seen as metropolitan and cosmopolitan tendencies lent added bite and direction to often-vicious antisemitic inclinations.

Moreover, in Germany and elsewhere, much of the clergy was more concerned about ministering to its flock than about other developments in society. State terror also played a role. In 1935, Göring declared that clerical interference with state policies would not be tolerated, which led to arrests by the Gestapo. The treatment of clerical opponents became much harsher in Germany once World War II began. This harshness, which could include being sent to concentration camps and executed, was the response, for example, to German Catholic clerics ministering to Polish laborers. In the majority of cases, however, there was no need for Gestapo action against priests helping Jews, as such action was unusual and generally restricted to Christians of Jewish descent. Bernhard Lichtenberg was a conspicuous exception in the Berlin diocese. He was arrested in 1941, imprisoned, and in 1943 died of pneumonia while en route to Dachau.[66]

Clerics tended to be hostile to communism, an atheistic movement, and to those on the Left who could be seen as crypto-communist. The association between communists and Jews, made by the critics of both, further helped to marginalize Jews. Nationalism and an emphasis on obedience to secular authority contributed to these attitudes in Germany and among its allies. Thus, Clemens von Galen, the Catholic bishop of Münster, who publicly criticized Nazi policies of euthanasia in 1941, did not protest against the Nuremberg Laws, *Kristallnacht,* or the deportation of the Jews in his diocese. In his preaching, the Jews were presented as denying God's truth by turning against Christ. In my experience of visits in the 1970s and 1980s, that was not pointed out in Münster when Galen's opposition to Hitler was emphasized.

Catholic intellectuals found many aspects of Nazi policy attractive,[67] while in Austria, aside from the very much dominant Catholics, the small-scale Protestant Church also tended to welcome the *Anschluss*. Earlier in 1933, when German Protestants considered the issue of Jewish converts, the report from the theological faculty in Erlangen recommended that the Church demand the resignation of Jewish converts from office. From its inception with Martin Luther, German Protestantism had an antisemitic heritage and was historically strongly associated with German nationalism. Many leading Protestant theologians praised Hitler strongly, although Dietrich Bonhoeffer, a Lutheran cleric and theologian who criticized the Nazis, was hanged at Flossenbürg concentration camp in 1945.[68]

In addition, the Church of Jesus Christ of Latter-day Saints, the Mormons, collaborated with the state, removing Jewish references from liturgical practices and hymnals and pursuing means of cooperation. After the war, these efforts were ignored in the creation of a largely misleading account of wartime resistance and difficulties.[69]

The churches can be seen to have played a role not only in terms of their policies (or lack thereof) at the time but also with reference to their longer-term part in encouraging the notion of insider and outsider. Scholarship on the medieval Church has argued that this distinction legitimated persecution and made it necessary and legal. This situation was important to later manifestations of persecution. There is also an instructive parallel with popular support for the Inquisition in the early modern period (sixteenth to eighteenth centuries). Although reviled in Protestant Europe and criticized by "progressive" Catholic intellectuals, the Inquisition, much of which was directed against the persistence of Jewish religious and social practices, appears to have enjoyed a considerable amount of popular support. Reflecting the situation across much of Catholic Europe, the frequent *autos-da-fe* (burnings), organized at the behest of the Inquisition in the lands of the Crown of Aragon in Spain in the late sixteenth and early seventeenth centuries, were popular because those punished were mostly outsiders. In the kingdom of Valencia, part of Aragon, the Inquisition's attempts to repress the worst excesses of erroneous doctrine were seen as laudable, and it continued in the eighteenth century to display an impressive capacity to attract fresh recruits.[70]

If antisemitic messages, explicit or implicit, still came from the pulpit in the 1940s, they were far more systematically pushed in Germany and German-occupied Europe through government propaganda. This propaganda included not only frequent diatribes, for example, on the radio and in the press, but also the use of film, especially *Jew Süss* (1940), which by 1943 had been seen by over twenty million Germans as well as in allied states such as France, and *The Eternal Jew* (1940), a supposed documentary that compared Jews to rats. *Jew Süss* misrepresented an episode from the eighteenth century that ended with the public hanging of the Jewish central character. The film couched its propaganda in the form of a historical narrative in which a fiendish Jewish moneylender covets and terrorizes a virtuous Aryan maiden, an aspect of a supposed threat to pure German women. He is publicly executed. In film and elsewhere, the lesson of an apparently endless struggle between Germans and Jews was repeatedly driven home. It provided a key background to hostility that was both organized and spontaneous.

Support for the Holocaust is an aspect of the more general issue of backing for Nazism. This is complex because, aside from the many and serious pressures of totalitarianism and a police state,[71] Nazism meant different things to particular individuals and groups, and at distinct moments. The same was true, for non-Jews, of the state antisemitism that culminated in the Holocaust. This variety ensures that questions about the degree of support are dealing with a moving target. This is even more the case because, however vicious, the disorganized and incoherent nature of Nazism contrasted with the greater consistency and interior logic of Soviet communism, which itself was also extremely vicious. The latter, moreover, had far longer to implement its policies, and it benefited from the extent to which it gained total power after victory in a civil war that had permitted the terrorization of real or alleged domestic opponents. Thus, communist authority and strength in the Soviet Union started from a different basis than that of the Nazis in Germany. Soviet communism was a more effective totalitarianism as a system of state control: it was supported by the Russian tradition of autocracy that looked back

to the fifteenth century. The Soviet state was more powerful and centralized than its German counterpart, in part because, despite the Depression in 1933, Germany was economically a well-off place, whereas the
Soviet Union in 1921, when War Communism and the civil war ended,
was not.

As with Italian and Spanish fascism, the incoherent nature of Nazism
was also an aspect of its strength, as it ensured that the movement could
reach out to a large number of constituencies of support by representing itself directly or through its intermediaries in these constituencies
in very different lights. Furthermore, in reaching out differently, there
was an opportunity to respond to what were seen as popular drives and
discontents. Although there were core groups and regions of support,
not least young men (which does not mean all young men), backing for
Nazism, while varying regionally, was wide ranging across German and
Austrian society, attracting women and older men as well. Consent as
well as coercion, collusion as well as coping, were all seen in the response
to a set of ideas and practices that could be emotionally gripping and
cohesive as well as frightening.[72] Moreover, far from limiting support
for the Nazis, antisemitism provided themes for expanding it, not only
with Christian antisemites but also as a way to try to appeal to left-wing
views by (falsely) presenting the unattractive side of business and finance
as Jewish.

Resistance to Hitler in Germany was patchy. Instead, reflecting the
extent to which the war, as much as Nazism, brought major changes in
Germany, the cumulative pressures of defeat and of a failure brought
home by Allied bombing led, alongside social dissolution, to a degree
of greater brutalization rather than to resistance. Yet in Germany from
the outset, as well as the sense of destiny that helped give force to Nazi
plans, governmental confidence in popular responses was variable. In
addition to fanatical support for the regime, which continued until the
very end of the war, failure and disillusionment led to a fall in morale and
to dissidence. However, the weakness of popular resistance on behalf of
the Nazis during and after the Allied conquest in 1944–45 was a demonstration of their *eventual* unpopularity and did not mean that there had
been a lack of consent earlier. Indeed, rather than social fragmentation
playing a crucial part in support for genocide or acceptance of it, as has

been argued in the case of the wartime German empire,[73] social cohesion may well have been responsible, at least in part, alongside other factors such as ideology and terror, for this support in Germany.

BRITAIN AND THE UNITED STATES

The question of what could have been achieved by Allied pressure to ameliorate, slow down, or limit the implementation of the German extermination policy is long standing. This issue is one that was widely raised after the war, not least over the past two decades, with claims that Allied pressure could and should have limited the Holocaust. In large part, this debate focuses on whether Allied bombing could have disrupted the rail routes to the concentration camps and, indeed, the camps themselves. In 1961, British secret reports were revealed showing plans to bomb Auschwitz, which were, in the end, turned down. In 2008, at Yad Vashem in Jerusalem, President George W. Bush stated that the Allies had failed in their response to Auschwitz: "We should have bombed it." Discussion frequently underplays the range of demand on Allied air power and the distance of the extermination camps from Western air bases, although the I. G. Farben works at Auschwitz were bombed, while in 1944, British and US aircraft reached Warsaw in order to drop supplies to help the uprising there. However, the Soviets, who were reluctant for the Western Allies to assist the pro-Western Polish Home Army leading the uprising, would not let the aircraft land on Soviet airfields.

Allied air capability increased in December 1943 with the introduction of the P-51D Mustang, a first-rate fighter that, fitted with external underwing drop tanks to carry extra fuel, had an operating range of 600 miles. This extended the range within which bombers could be escorted, but for British-based aircraft, this still excluded Hungary and Poland. The superiority of American interceptors, already demonstrated with the P-47 Thunderbolts introduced in April 1943, was taken further with the Mustangs. In late February and March 1944, these aircraft used their superiority over German interceptors in escorting Anglo-American raids in clear weather on German sites producing aircraft and oil, not least during "Big Week" in late February. Despite the increased range of Allied planes, bombing Hungary and Poland still posed serious extra challenges. The normal maximum range for the American B-17 and B-24 bombers operating from East Anglia in Britain was 750 miles, although greater range could be gained by adding auxiliary fuel tanks or reducing the bombload. Greater range, however, meant increased exposure to interception and the loss of aircraft, as well as less time over the target and less bomb tonnage. There was also no shortage of strategic targets in Germany, as "Big Week" showed. Had the killing of Western Europe's Jews taken place in Western Europe, then the situation as far as range, though not targets, would have been very different, but the emphasis in target acquisition would still have been on military and military-industrial targets, notably, in 1944, preparing for the invasion of France, as with the destruction of bridges across the Loire and the Rhone in order to lessen the chance of a rapid deployment of German reinforcements to Normandy.

By 1944, similarly, Hungary was easily within the range of Allied air bases in Italy: in November 1943, the Fifteenth US Army Air Force had moved its base to Foggia in southern Italy. This potent air unit focused, however, not on disrupting the deportation of Jews in 1944 but on attacking German oil supplies (especially the Romanian oilfields at Ploesti), the aircraft industry (particularly at Wiener Neustadt in Austria), and transport links. All were crucial to the German war effort. Target, not range, was the key issue, and the range of Allied aircraft was not the reason why the Germans deported Jews to Poland for killing.[74] The German ability to repair damaged railways rapidly is worthy of mention, as are the difficulties of precision bombing, a point made abundantly clear elsewhere.

Prior to the outbreak of the war, the British government was already aware of the mistreatment of German Jews. In late 1939, in response to German propaganda about Allied atrocities and concerning the role of the British in establishing concentration camps during the 1899–1902 Boer War, the British government presented to Parliament *Papers Concerning the Treatment of German Nationals in Germany 1938–39*, which were then published by the Stationery Office. They left no doubt of the murderous nature of the treatment of Jews, not least as a consequence of incarceration in the concentration camp at Buchenwald. The tortures there were detailed at length. Of the 2,000 Jewish prisoners who arrived at Buchenwald on June 15, 1939, the death of 110 in the first five weeks was reported.[75]

It took a while, however, for the outside world to understand the full extent and implementation of German policy in the shape of the Final Solution. In large part, the Allied focus was on other issues, primarily and understandably the conduct of the war, but it was also difficult to understand that genocide was being carried out, that the killing was in pursuit of a systematic plan, and the nature of this plan.[76] For Jewish leaders outside occupied Europe, in Palestine, Britain, and the United States, including the Jewish Agency, the organization headed by David Ben-Gurion for establishing a national home for Jews in Palestine, this indeed also took a while to grasp fully. Their experience was of pogroms, not genocide, an experience and assumption that affected the attitude of some Jews when confronted by German rule and trying to understand rumors about German intentions.

The Allies became aware of the large-scale killing of Jews in part through the interception and deciphering of German radio traffic, which revealed, from July 18, 1941, that Jews were being killed by German units operating in the Soviet Union. The ciphers used by the German regular police, who played a significant role in the mass slaughter, could be read, although not the Gestapo messages. Whether more public use should have been made of these reports is controversial but fails to take note of the urgent British need to maintain secrecy in order to retain interception and code-breaking capabilities.[77]

Subsequently, aside from disbelief about the extermination camps and the policy of total extermination, the Allies did not appreciate the scale of the killing, as shown by the US government's response in August 1942 to the report by the World Jewish Congress. The Allies were also wary of proposals for deals or rescue ideas, seeing them as possible German ploys.[78] There may have been a reluctance, not least on the part of the US State Department, to acknowledge German action in case it provided the basis of demands for action on behalf of Jews, such as relaxed immigration quotas. German deception,[79] as well as conflicting accounts, made it difficult to confirm reports or to piece together the entire picture, and the information that arrived in the West was frequently of events and developments that had already occurred.[80] Allied

intelligence agencies focused anyway on German strategy and war production. Meanwhile, the German deception indicates that, alongside
an ideological commitment to the Holocaust, there was an awareness
of its criminality, in addition to instrumental reasons for concealment.

Information supplied by Emmanuel Ringelblum, who was to be
killed by the Gestapo in Warsaw in 1944, about the killing at Chełmno
led to the BBC reporting it on June 2, 1942. On June 20, *The Times* of
London printed news of the murder of one million Jews "either by being shot or by being made to live in such conditions that they died." The
following month, Eduard Schulte, a prominent German businessman
opposed to the Nazis, was able to pass on information that the Germans
were planning the genocide of Jews, the basis of the Riegner telegram
sent that August by Gerhart Riegner of the World Jewish Congress. To
escape the Gestapo, Schulte fled to Switzerland in 1943. In August 1942,
the Greek Catholic Metropolitan of Lwów sent a report to the Vatican
about the mass murder of Jews in Ukraine. In November 1942, Jan Kar-
ski (real name Jan Kozielewski), a Polish agent who had entered and
left the concentration camp at Bełzec disguised as a guard, arrived in
London. He was able to provide an account of the killing to the Polish
government-in-exile, Anthony Eden (the British foreign secretary), and
President Franklin D. Roosevelt. In response, on December 17, 1942,
the Allied governments produced a declaration attacking "this bestial
policy of cold-blooded extermination." By then, the Jewish Agency had
also made the facts at its disposal public and had called for action. On
November 24, *The Times* of London reported the "systematic extermination" of Jews in Poland, followed, on December 4, by referring to a
"deliberate plan for extermination." In his Christmas Eve broadcast in
1942, Pope Pius XII declared "Mankind owes that vow to the hundreds
of thousands of persons who, without any fault on their part, sometimes
only because of their nationality or race, have been consigned to death
or to a slow decline."

Once the fact of large-scale mistreatment, even genocide, was understood, the Allies were, however, unwilling to focus on this issue, in
part because it did not seem to have any effect on the defeat of Germany.
The US government proved particularly reluctant to emphasize the
Holocaust. Antisemitism in the State Department and other sectors of

government, including part of the military leadership, may have played a role, but there were also policy issues. Aside from concern about popular antisemitism in the United States, as well as anxiety that the conflict would be presented as a Jewish war and thus serve isolationist goals—and also the argument that reports about German atrocities in Belgium in World War I had been misleading or counterproductive—the Holocaust did not correspond to the government's distinction between Nazis and Germans. This was a distinction important to publicly expressed US war goals, with the Anglo-American Atlantic Charter of August 1941 referring to "Nazi tyranny," and to postwar planning, with the desired unconditional surrender of the Nazis designed to lead to the rehabilitation of the Germans.[81]

There was also a sense (as in the Soviet Union) that Jews were among many victims of the Germans and that attention should not be diverted from the war in which Americans were fighting. Partly as a result of the latter and, more generally, of the range of the war news and the pressures this created for news reporting and layout, including a bitter war with Japan, newspapers such as the *New York Times* not only did not wish to but also could not focus on the Holocaust.[82] Nevertheless, on March 9, 1943, Congress passed a resolution condemning the "mass murder of Jewish men, women, and children" and demanding due punishment. At the same time, the State Department issued a report recording the "cold-blooded extermination" of Europe's Jews.

Among the British public, absorbed with war news and its own efforts to get by, there appears to have been a widespread lack of interest.[83] It was also difficult to understand and credit the full extent of German actions and plans,[84] although, on March 11, 1943, the *Times* of London reported that two million Jews had been killed and, on June 1, 1943, that the killing was spreading to the Balkans. That year, the Mass Observation Survey in Britain noted public sympathy for Europe's Jews and concern about an absence of government action on their behalf.[85] However, the government itself was worried that stressing the issue might lead to a rise in antisemitism and support for the banned British Union of Fascists, not least if the Germans were able to present the conflict as a Jewish war. There was certainly latent antisemitism, as indicated by the false rumors that circulated in London during the Blitz (German bombing offensive) of 1940–41 that Jews had gotten into the air-raid shelters first and that others had been successful in leaving London to take refuge in the countryside.

There was also British concern about the implications for Palestine. At the Anglo-American Bermuda Conference in April 1943, a conference held at the same time that the Germans were attacking the Warsaw ghetto, the proposal by the Jewish Agency for an approach to Hitler to ease the position of Jews was turned down, as was the plea for Britain to ease Jewish immigration into Palestine. Indeed, the conference simply decided to open a Jewish refugee center in North Africa, which certainly did not match the gravity of the crisis. The British feared that encouraging Jewish immigration to Palestine would stir up Arab antipathy and thus help the German war effort.[86] Indeed, such immigration was seen as a German plan to that end.

As a result, the British government had no time for the Biltmore program, announced after a meeting of American Zionists in the Biltmore Hotel in New York in May 1942, which called for Jewish sovereignty over an independent Palestine as a way of providing a postwar refuge. On November 6, 1944, Field Marshal Alan Brooke, chief of the Imperial General Staff, recorded in his diary: "A difficult Chiefs of Staff at which we discuss the problems of the partition of Palestine for the Jews. We are unanimously against any announcement before the end of the war, but our hand may well be forced."[87] The British experience of the Arab Rising in Palestine in 1936–39 set a worrying precedent.

British governmental concerns led to the refusal to accept Jewish illegal immigrants into Palestine. Instead, many were forced to remain in neutral countries, such as Turkey, or were interned in the British Indian Ocean colony of Mauritius. Their circumstances there were considerably better than those the Germans had intended for Europe's Jews on nearby Madagascar.

More information on the Holocaust was received as the war continued, including, by the summer and autumn of 1944, reliable reports of events at Auschwitz and Majdanek.[88] In July 1944, Allied pressure on the Hungarian government, which was considering abandoning Germany, helped persuade it to stop the deportations. By then, Allied successes, notably the range of Allied bombers operating since late 1943 from Italy, as well as the changes arising from Soviet advances, made this pressure more effective.

Earlier in 1944, authorized by Himmler after the idea had been agreed to by Hitler, Eichmann had initiated an approach over Hungarian Jews. In May, he proposed, via Joel Brand, a key member of the Jewish Relief and Rescue Committee, and the Jewish Agency to exchange Hungarian Jews, on a pro rata basis, for trucks, coffee, cocoa, tea, and soap—the trucks, he promised, were only to be used for the war against the Soviet Union, which, itself, was given trucks by the United States. The British opposed negotiations, correctly seeing them as a way to sow disunion among the Allies, but the Americans persuaded the British to maintain the link in the hope that it might help Hungarian Jews. Without even being aware of the provisions about the trucks, Soviet opposition led to the abandonment of the approach.[89]

In practice, the German proposal was probably intended to divide or discredit the Allies. The willingness of German leaders to trade Jews was only episodic and pales into insignificance beside the general determination to slaughter them. Indeed, Eichmann was to criticize the idea of slowing down for diplomatic ends the slaughter of Hungarian Jews. More generally, Hitler was willing to ally with Stalin in 1939–41 but not to make any deal with or over Jews. This made unviable Himmler's tentative approaches in late 1944 and early 1945 to Jewish organizations and others, in Switzerland and Sweden, for some sort of deal involving favorable treatment for at least some Jews. These approaches were linked to his unsuccessful and deluded attempts from 1944 to maneuver for advantage and safety as he saw Germany approach defeat. His efforts to contact the Americans and British in 1945 through Count Folke Bernadotte, the vice president of the Swedish Red Cross, involved opportunistic offers to end the Final Solution. Himmler also gave orders at this stage intended to minimize the killings during the death marches.

After the war, Jewish anger and Anglo-American guilt combined with a concern to establish the facts of wartime policy in discussions of whether the Allies could have done more. In part, there is a misleading tendency to focus on the real or supposed wrongs of Britain and the United States, rather than the evil of Nazi Germany or—not that it is so directly pertinent in this issue—paranoid mass murder by the Soviet

government. Whether or not Britain and the United States should have
done more, it has been argued that obtaining victory was regarded as
of greater importance at the time.[90] Indeed, more specifically, it was
generally claimed that winning the war was the way to rescue Jews. For
the many Jews saved as Allied forces advanced in 1943–45 (late 1942, if
Morocco and Algeria are included), this was true, although many others
were slaughtered by the Germans then. The harsher fate of Jews in Tunisia, a French colony that was occupied by German forces in late 1942,
compared to Morocco and Algeria, French colonies that were occupied
by US and British forces, is more generally instructive. By late 1944, it is
unclear what would have been achieved by bombing the camps. Most of
the killing had already taken place, and the Germans were preparing to
dismantle Auschwitz, which was liberated by Soviet forces on January
27, 1945.

Looking back to before the war, it is possible to note the refusal by
both Britain and the United States to take more Jewish immigrants from
Germany and occupied territory and to link this to the wartime failure
to do more to help. In the particular case of British policy over migration to Palestine, there is a link, but it is far from clear that this is more
generally pertinent. Concerned about domestic opinion, neither the US
nor British governments wished, during the war, to create the impression
that the conflict was being waged on behalf of Jews, not least because it
was feared that this would play into the hands of German propaganda.
Allied antisemitism doubtless played a role in what were presented as
pragmatic considerations, but the central fact was that the vast majority
of Jews were under German control and received no mercy.

FOUR

Germany's Allies, the Occupied, and Neutrals

THE ANTISEMITIC COMMITMENT OF THE NAZI REGIME HELPED ensure that the extensive German alliance system registered this hatred. Indeed, toward the end of the war, Hitler was increasingly using cooperation with the Holocaust as a test of loyalty for Germany's allies, a further instance of the link between the war and the Holocaust. That context should not underplay the strong and autonomous antisemitic impulses of many of Germany's allies, for example, Romania under General Ion Antonescu, its dictator from 1940 to 1944, but, nevertheless, there can be little doubt that these impulses were encouraged by the Nazis. Furthermore, had the German government taken a different position, then its strength within the alliance would have led to corresponding pressure that could have affected outcomes. This would also have been the case had Italy under Mussolini been the dominant party in the Axis alliance system, as antisemitism, though present, was not a key drive or policy for him, and certainly not to the extent shown by Hitler. However, among Germany's allies and within Germany itself, antisemitism was not simply or solely a matter of government policy. Instead, it rested on potent elements in society and public culture, not least the determination to see Christianity as a key ingredient for national identity. Antisemitism also drew on hostility to communism, and the two can be seen in the "crusade" of anticommunist fascist troops that invaded the Soviet Union in 1941.

ROMANIA

Of Germany's allies, there was particular support for extermination from
the Antonescu government. There was a long tradition of Romanian antisemitism, and it had been an issue in diplomacy in the late nineteenth
century. One of the most difficult subjects to settle at the Congress of
Berlin in 1878, an international congress addressing Balkan issues, had
been Romania's harsh treatment of its Jewish minority. As Romania, in
May and June 1940, realigned its foreign policy away from Britain and
France and toward alliance with Germany, the cabinet decided on a raft
of antisemitic legislation, notably, on July 9, the removal of all Jews from
the civil service and, on August 8, the redefinition of the legal position of
Jews so as to deprive them of political and civil rights.

Antisemitic violence also became frequent from the summer of 1940,
with about 200 Jews killed in the Dorohoi massacre in June. Like the
massacre at Galați that summer, it was carried out by troops withdraw-
ing from Bessarabia, which Romania had been forced to cede to the
Soviet Union as a consequence of the Nazi-Soviet Pact of the previous
year. These massacres were followed by the killing of Jews by the Fascist Legion of the Archangel Michael that autumn and winter—notably
in January 1941 in the capital, Bucharest. Meanwhile, under a series of
decrees issued from October 1940 to March 1941, Jewish property was
expropriated while all Jewish employees were to be dismissed by the
end of the year. In July 1941, Jews were excluded from military service, a
badge of citizenship, and, instead, males from eighteen to fifty were made
liable for labor service.[1]

Unlike its Bulgarian and Hungarian neighbors, the Antonescu government was a keen supporter of the slaughter of Jews, which was not
solely a policy for conquered regions. Instead, the policy was applied
in Romania itself with, for example, a brutal pogrom in Iași, the capital
of the province of Moldavia, in June 1941, in which at least 4,000 Jews
were slaughtered, a slaughter that was later blamed on the Germans.
This policy was also followed from June 1941 for the nearby sections
of the Soviet Union occupied by the Romanians, particularly Bessarabia (now Moldava), northern Bukovina, and Transnistria (now part
of Ukraine between the Bug and Dnestr rivers). In order to further a

policy of Romanization, the Jews of Bessarabia and northern Bukovina were deported to concentration camps in Transnistria where they were used for labor; many were slaughtered, notably by being shot, buried, or starved to death. The lack of food, housing, or medical assistance provided them in Transnistria contributed to the high death rate. An estimated 154,000–170,000 Jews were sent there in 1941–43, but due to prior residents, more than that number died there. Little was done about the typhoid that also killed many.

When the city of Odessa fell to the Germans and Romanians in 1941 after a long siege (August 10 to October 16), the victors killed at least 20,000 Jews in a murderous pogrom in what was an important cosmopolitan city. This was a major episode in the Holocaust and one that receives insufficient attention. The Romanian army played a leading role: aside from the mass shootings of Odessa's Jews, there were also other forms of slaughter including burning Jews alive. Within Romania, there was little secret about these and other killings. The international commission established by the Romanian government in 2003 concluded that between 280,000 and 380,000 Romanian and Ukrainian Jews were killed in territories under Romanian control. There was a brutal interplay with the Germans, as Jews were force marched to the Bug in order to move them into the German sphere of control, only to be killed by the Germans if they crossed.

In large part, the Romanian government was motivated by anti-semitism. There was also a political dimension, as in much of the violence in this (and other) regions. Antonescu, who stated that "there is no law" as far as Jews were concerned, claimed, as did colleagues, that Jews were pro-Soviet and, therefore, a threat to Romania—in fact, traitors. This was a parallel to the Turks' treatment of Armenians in 1915 as pro-Russian. The slaughter in Iași in June 1941 was planned by Romanian military intelligence as Romania moved to war with the Soviet Union. Aside from those killed in the town, many died from a lack of food and water while on trains moving them to concentration camps. On August 18, 1941, Hitler told Goebbels that Antonescu had taken more radical steps than the Germans had yet pursued. Antonescu took a close interest in the Romanian Holocaust, gave direct orders for the slaughter, and criticized commanders whom he thought too soft. In practice, there was scant difficulty; the soldiers carried out their murderous orders.[2] The anti-Soviet dimension appears to have been particularly significant for some Romanians, as well as for ethnic Germans in Transnistria, whose militias killed as many as 50,000 Jews in late 1941.[3] Killing Jews seems to have been a way of relieving fears about communists, but at the same time, as elsewhere, it is necessary not to underplay the role of anti-Jewish hatred. This position had a variety of aspects. Thus, in 1942, the Heroes' Cult secured the expropriation of a Jewish cemetery on the edge of Bucharest and prepared a detailed plan for exhuming all the graves in order to establish a large heroes' cemetery of wartime dead, although this was not pursued.[4]

The Antonescu government deported some Jews to German extermination camps in late 1942 but stopped this policy as the war increasingly went badly for the Axis. This decision ensured that most of the Jews of Wallachia and Moldavia, those areas that had been Romanian prior to 1918, were not deported to the German extermination camps.

CROATIA, SERBIA, AND SLOVAKIA

Other allies were also very happy to cooperate with German intentions. The collaborationist regime of Ante Pavelić and his *Ustasha* movement, installed in Croatia in 1941, slaughtered Jews there and in Bosnia, with about 80 percent of the community being killed—although in terms of numbers killed, the far more numerous Serbs, who were Orthodox unlike the Catholic Croats, were their major victims. As in Germany, there was an emphasis on racial and cultural purity as central to national identity and redemption.[5] The Croat regime proved very willing to deport Jews for slaughter by the Germans, but the majority had already been killed, and in conditions of great brutality. Jews, like Serbs, were hacked to death and burned alive in barns. The type of killing was similar to that seen in Rwanda in 1994. The religious dimension of the slaughter was readily apparent in the option given Jews and Serbs of conversion and in the support of some of the Catholic clergy for the *Ustasha* campaign. Conversion was not an option offered by the Germans. In total, nearly 45,000 Jews were killed or handed over to the Germans, and with no public criticism from Pope Pius XII about this genocidal policy of a

Catholic state, although no diplomatic recognition was given to the new state. Instead, it was the Italian military that helped to end the genocide by advancing farther into Croatia in late 1941 and offering protection to Jews and Serbs. Few Jews were left to send subsequently to Auschwitz after Italian control ceased in 1943 to be replaced by that of Germany.

Within Serbia, the collaborationist regime also cooperated in the Holocaust, although the Germans were in control there, with the army assisted by the ethnic German minority. Serbia was declared "free of Jews" in August 1942.

The Slovak regime of the People's Party under Jozef Tiso, a Catholic priest and firm ally of Hitler, introduced antisemitic legislation and forced labor. From 1942, the regime also deported its Jews, including baptized Christians of Jewish origin, to the extermination camps rather than slaughtering them in Slovakia: 10,000 Jews were sent to Auschwitz from August 28 to October 27, 1944. The Germans did not need to put much pressure on Tiso to support the deportations, and there were few exemptions. As with Pavelić in Croatia, Tiso was convinced he had a duty to free Slovakia from Jews in order to ensure a regenerated Christian nation, one in which the Catholic Church would be a leading force. For Tiso, the Holocaust also matched a corporatist social politics of creating a Christian Slovak middle class, one able to provide self-respect and not be subordinate to Hungary or to supposedly foreign interests, the last a policy that was interpreted in an antisemitic fashion.[6]

HUNGARY

In 1941, Jews living in Hungary's extended territories—which, after recent gains, included much of former Romania, Czechoslovakia, and Yugoslavia—but who lacked Hungarian citizenship were deported to southern Poland. There, they were slaughtered by the Germans at Kamenets-Podolsk. Nevertheless, the Hungarian government of Miklós Kállay, in power from March 1942 to March 1944, although antisemitic, did not deport Jews who were Hungarian citizens. Indeed, the Hungarian attitude was considered a problem by the Germans at the Wannsee conference in 1942. Well aware that the Germans were trying to kill all Jews, the government tried to follow Italy's more cautious policy.

However, the overthrow of Mussolini in July 1943 and the German takeover of northern and central Italy that September limited the options for Hungary. After German troops occupied Hungary on March 19, 1944, Kállay was replaced by the pro-German general Döme Sztójay (who was to be convicted of war crimes and shot in Budapest in 1946), and the situation changed. A Reich plenipotentiary was installed to ensure that the new pro-German government complied fully with German demands. A ghetto was established in Budapest on April 16, and the Hungarian police actively assisted the SS in deporting Hungarian Jews, 437,000 in total, to Auschwitz from May. The majority of Jews were killed, while all Jewish property was confiscated in a fruitless effort to balance the Hungarian budget. In reality, much of the property thus to be stolen was, instead, stolen by state functionaries or by private individuals.

However, Hungarian policy then switched again. In part, the change in policy was due to the tide of war in Eastern Europe, which had already led Romania, once exposed to the Soviet advance, to change sides. Concern about the fate of Hungarian Jews, accentuated by pressure on Admiral Miklós Horthy, the regent of Hungary from 1920 until 1944, from the pope, Britain, the United States, and Sweden, led to the end of the deportations in July; a new government, under General Geza Lakatos, was appointed on August 29. Nevertheless, many Jews were still killed by the Arrow Cross and other Hungarian fascist movements. There was a particularly serious and murderous pogrom in October 1944, the month in which a German-supported coup by Hungarian fascists led to the installation of an Arrow Cross regime under Fevenc Szalasi.[7] In Budapest, Jews were lined up along the bank of the Danube and shot, their bodies falling or being pushed into the river, a fate marked by a monument installed in 2005 of sixty pairs of shoes made of iron set into the embankment: the Arrow Cross frequently forced the victims to take their shoes off so that they could use or sell them. The Danube was referred to as "the Jewish Cemetery." The city did not completely fall to Soviet forces until February 13, 1943.

BULGARIA

Not all of Germany's allies persecuted Jews to death. In Bulgaria, as the government moved closer to Germany in 1940, antisemitic legislation was passed. This was designed to make it easier to segregate Jews, who were no longer permitted to have Bulgarian names nor Jewish ones with Bulgarian suffixes. Jews were also made to wear the yellow star. Moreover, restrictions were placed on their freedom of movement. The Purity of the Nation Act banned mixed marriages. As relations with Germany became even closer, with Bulgaria joining the Axis on March 1, 1941, taking a role in the attack on Yugoslavia and Greece on April 6, and annexing territory from Yugoslavia and Greece (in Macedonia and Thrace, respectively), pressure on Jews increased. In part, this was in response to demands on the government from Adolf-Heinz Beckerle, a committed Nazi, who became German envoy in October 1941. Jewish organizations were banned, Jews lost their civil rights, and their businesses were compulsorily purchased. In accordance with German pressure, Jews were removed from the important tobacco industry. In August 1942, Jews in the occupied territories in Thrace and Macedonia were deprived of their Bulgarian citizenship, and the following March, after arrest by Bulgarian policemen, they were deported to Treblinka. Over 11,000 were slaughtered, a point that needs to be born in mind when considering the account of Bulgaria's supposed exceptional humanitarian status.

There was also a plan drawn up by Aleksandur Belev, the head of the Commissariat for Jewish Affairs, with the connivance of the cabinet for the secret deportation of 6,000 Jews (out of 55,000) from prewar Bulgaria, that is, Bulgaria excluding the wartime conquests. The secret was not kept, however, in part because Belev's outraged mistress informed the press, and there was a chorus of anger, which contrasts markedly with the situation in Germany, France, Romania, and most of allied or occupied Europe. The Orthodox Church attacked the proposed step, as did a range of workers' organizations, including railway workers, and such middle-class professional groups as doctors and lawyers. Government supporters in parliament signed a petition against the deportation. Once the petition was submitted to King Boris III, he vetoed the deportations of Jews from prewar Bulgaria.

Another secret attempt to deport Jews from prewar Bulgaria was unsuccessful in May 1943, with Metropolitan Stefan of Sofia prominent in the opposition. For Boris III and others, a key issue was national sovereignty and the need for Bulgaria to retain control of its citizens.[8]

Bulgaria's Jews, instead, were sent to work camps within Bulgaria, camps that did not compare in brutality with the concentration camps of the Germans and Croats. It is possible that concern about postwar punishment by the Allies was also an issue, as the war was now moving against the Germans. Indeed, in March 1943, Boris admitted that he no longer thought German victory likely. While the slaughter of Jews in Germany continued as the war went badly for the Axis, in Bulgaria and Romania there was a different response.

Beckerle finally backed down, arguing that the Bulgarians were used to multiethnic life and lacked the antisemitism found across much of Europe and that Germany would be unwise to compromise its political influence in Sofia by trying to force the Bulgarians to yield.[9] All Bulgarian antisemitic legislation was repealed on August 17, 1944, as Soviet forces advanced into the Balkans. Bulgaria declared war on Germany on September 5.

ITALY

Elsewhere, as with other aspects of complying with a new order increasingly based on German notions of their own superiority, there could also be a notable lack of zeal in implementing persecution. In fascist Italy, this was the case with Mussolini, who had a Jewish mistress and lacked commitment to the killing, although recent scholarship has emphasized his racism.[10] As with Germany, a personality cult focused on the Italian leader meant that his views and, less consistently, what were believed to be his views were of great significance.

At the same time, the incoherent diversity of Italian fascism ensured an extremely varied response to Jews, both Italian and foreign. It was acceptable in Italy in 1938 to ban Jewish teachers from teaching and to forbid marriage between Jews and non-Jews.[11] These measures were readily enforced. However, compared to Germany and Austria, there was less antisemitic feeling among the population and less support for deportation and mass murder.[12] At the same time, alongside sympathy for the Jews they knew, there was an unwillingness to extend sympathy to others, let alone to protest on their behalf. Moreover, there were many involved in the Italian dimension of the Holocaust, not least in seeking to profit from the despoliation of Jews. In Italy's colony Libya, where state control was stronger and antisemitic policies were more pronounced than in mainland Italy, Jews were sent to concentration camps, notably Giado, where poor conditions led to the death of many.

Italian fascism sought a stronger state: there was not the commitment to race seen with Germany. Indeed, Italy and Italian-occupied territory, such as Dalmatia, Nice, and parts of Greece, were safer for Jews than other German-allied states—for example, Vichy France and Croatia—and as a result, many Jews took refuge there, while others sought to do so. However, the Italian treatment of Jews varied, and the truth needs to be disentangled from retrospective sanitization, of which there has been plenty.[13] Italian forces on the Eastern Front, where 60,000 troops served in 1941 and 220,000 in 1942, did not match the Germans in the habitual deliberate brutality of their treatment of Jews but did nothing to stop it. In contrast, issues of control and status vis-à-vis Germany played a role in the unwillingness to deport Jews from the Balkans while, notably in response to Croat atrocities, "the Italians eventually devoted special attention to the rescue of the Jews."[14] Quite a number of French Jews found refuge in the Italian-occupied zone of Southeast France. The Italian authorities were aware of the arrival and location of Jews, but not terribly interested. The Italians also refused to deport foreign Jews from Italy, while the forced labor of Italian Jews was not lethal, and there were Jewish army and naval officers who remained hidden "behind desks" for years after 1938. The Italian government and military, not the Vatican, were the key elements in this situation, although they were also the bodies with power. At the Ferramonti camp—which began operating in June 1940 with 160 Jews from Rome and contained, when it was liberated by the British in 1943, 1,604 Jews and 412 non-Jews—there were no killings or deportations to German-controlled Europe. Conditions were humane, and death rates by natural causes were low. The camp included two synagogues.

The situation did not change until Germany seized Italy and Italian-occupied territory following the overthrow of Mussolini on July 25, 1943, and the Italian armistice with the Allies on September 3, 1943. The official German military occupation on September 10 meant an assumption of power. The position of Italy's Jews then deteriorated in those areas the

Allies were unable to liberate. Even if orders to round up Jews could be sabotaged by high-ranking officials, diplomats, and church networks, the fate of Italy's Jews was dependent on German determination to apply the policy. The key individual was Herbert Kappler, head of the SS and Gestapo in Rome; he was imprisoned in Italy after the war but escaped in 1977. On September 15–16, 1943 the first deportation and killing of Jews occurred by Lake Maggiore, followed by many deportations in the areas of Bolzano, Merano, and other parts of the territory under German control. On September 23, the German police issued an order declaring all Italian Jews subject to deportation. On October 16, the Jews of Rome who could be seized were rounded up by the SS, although over 4,000 were able to take shelter in church properties.

The fascist Republic of Salò, the Italian Social Republic created in northern Italy in 1943, was a German puppet state headed by Mussolini, whom the Germans had rescued in September. This republic passed more antisemitic legislation than Mussolini had earlier, proclaiming the Jews officially to be "foreigners and enemies," and collaborated in deporting Jews to slaughter in the extermination camps: it did not need to be coerced and most of the arrests were carried out by the Italian authorities, who also handed over to the Germans their census information on Jews. On September 23, the Republic of Salò was given responsibility for organizing and managing the arrest of the Jews in the provinces. Buffarini Guidi, the minister for the interior, acted accordingly, and in December, the first Jews were moved from the many provincial concentration camps to the newly established national concentration camp in Fossoli, which became the linchpin for deportation to Germany. Bounties were paid for Jews arrested. The last convoy of Jews transported them from Trieste to Bergen-Belsen on February 24, 1945.

In practice, there was tension between the Germans and the Salò government over control and goals. Some officials were accused of being pro-Jewish, including Guidi and Mussolini himself. Others, notably Giovanni Preziosi, were clearly antisemitic. Preziosi had translated *The Protocols of the Elders of Zion* into Italian in 1921. In March 1944, Preziosi, although greatly disliked, was allowed, under German protection, to organize a Department for Demography and Race and, the following April, an Inspectorate for Race, which gave him access to the 1938 census of the Jews. Mussolini's attitude was ambivalent. Although not antisemitic, he did not prevent article I from being included in the Verona Manifesto of November 14, 1943. This article stipulated that those "belonging to the Jewish race were foreigners and enemy."

Figures vary, but about 8,500 Jews living in Italy were deported, mainly to Auschwitz, of whom only about 1,000 survived. About 7,750 were killed in Italy by the Germans, sometimes with the help of Italian officials. At the German-run San Sabba camp outside Trieste, about 5,000 Jews were killed, some gassed, and others made to dig graves and then shot. In the former ghetto in Venice, the list of names of those killed is a poignant memorial. However, about 35,000 Jews avoided being arrested and/or deported. Of these, some 29,000 hid in cities and the country, often under false names, and frequently helped by the local population. Others escaped to the Allied-occupied South and to Switzerland or found shelter in church buildings. About 2,000 Jews joined the partisan resistance. Not all ordinary people followed the policy of the authorities, and many Jews survived because of the generosity and bravery of such people.[15] After the war, Guidi was arrested by partisans, found guilty of war crimes by an Extraordinary Court of Justice in Milan, and shot. Preziosi had already committed suicide. His ally in antisemitic "philosophical" ranting Julius Evora was acquitted in 1951, but another, Roberto Farinacci, was executed by partisans after capture.

FINLAND

A more distant ally, Finland was unenthusiastic about the Holocaust. Himmler visited Helsinki in July 1942 to press for the handing over of foreign Jews (who numbered 150–200). The Finnish secret police drew up lists, but there was opposition in both the government and among the public. Eight foreign Jews were handed over in November 1942, of whom only one survived the war. The Finnish government did not cooperate thereafter, and no further Jews were deported. Finnish Jews fought alongside their compatriots against the Soviet Union in 1939–40 and 1941–44 and against the Germans in 1944–45.[16]

JAPAN

Japan also proved unwilling to implement German pressure for participation in the Final Solution. There was very little antisemitism in Japan, and indeed, the Japanese had had very little contact with Jews until the late nineteenth century. The Jewish population under Japanese rule increased from 1931 as a result both of Japanese conquests and of Jewish emigration from Europe. The conquests brought under Japanese control areas where some Jews already lived, such as Manchuria, where they were part of the large Russian population that had left Russia as a result of communist victory in the Civil War, and also Shanghai (conquered in 1937). Jewish emigration from Europe in the 1930s ensured that more Jews came to areas that were to be conquered by Japan, such as the Philippines (conquered in 1941–42), which had taken about 700 refugees, as well as to Japan itself. There was even a plan to provide Jews with a form of shelter in Manchuria or Shanghai (the Fugu Plan), although this idea was dropped as the Japanese government strengthened its ties with Nazi Germany. One Japanese diplomat, Chiune Sugihara, who is sometimes described as "Japan's Schindler," was vice-consul in Lithuania and saved the lives of about 6,000 Jewish refugees by issuing them transit visas in contravention of the order from the Foreign Ministry of Japan. His achievement was not duly recognized by the Japanese government until recently.

About 19,000 Jews were confined in Shanghai, but the Japanese rejected German pressure for their slaughter. This contrasted with the extremely murderous Japanese policy toward the Chinese and, to a lesser extent, Koreans.[17] The Jews were isolated in a ghetto and the conditions were poor, as they were for Europeans as a whole. About 2,000 died of privation and disease, the latter owing something to inadequate sanitation.

OCCUPIED EUROPE

The range of response scarcely glimpsed in Germany, but seen far more among its allies, was also witnessed in occupied Europe, although it is necessary to note the pressures the German occupiers imposed on the collaborating governments and authorities in occupied countries. As with Russia, Germany, Austria, Hungary, and Turkey after World War I, defeat led to disorientation and to the opportunity for new political outcomes. Some who, prewar, had been on the margins politically now came to the fore as collaborators, although, as in Vichy France, members of the existing establishment were also involved. Most of the occupied peoples focused on their own concerns, a feature of the extent to which defeat, occupation, and totalitarian rule lead a demoralized populace to atomize and to concentrate on their own private concerns. If these excluded Jews, whether neighbors or not, the process also excluded many non-Jews, but there was a contrast. In part, it was a matter of antisemitism and, in part, a response to the new political environment. This was a compound of powerlessness and determination to secure the most acceptable position under occupation. Both led to an attempt to continue government as usual, an attempt that greatly played into the hands of the Germans.

This was a general situation, but, in the specific case of the Holocaust, it led to large-scale cooperation in aspects that were necessary to German purposes, not least in identifying and segregating Jews and then deporting them. Antisemitism was an aspect of the collaboration with an active role in the Holocaust across German-allied and German-occupied Europe. Other factors also played a role. These included the desire to benefit personally by seizing the property of Jews. Thus, the war hit hard at civil society. In particular, the war helped precipitate the dissolution of what had been multiethnic communities, as the fault lines of earlier tensions were exposed in a totally one-sided fashion. At the same time, the situation did differ across Europe, in part as a result of the nature of civil society and in part due to the particular impact of German policy and the policies of its allies. For example, the majority of the close to 60,000 of the prewar Greek Jewish population of 72,000 moved to the extermination camps came from German-occupied Greece, but many of them came from Bulgarian-occupied Thrace and Macedonia, for Bulgaria cooperated in the Holocaust in its occupied territories.

BALTIC REPUBLICS AND UKRAINE

There was active and large-scale cooperation in the Holocaust across much of occupied Europe, perhaps more in Lithuania, Latvia, and

Ukraine than anywhere else in Eastern Europe. There are the complications alongside antisemitic activity of understanding Christian–Jewish relations under enormous duress. The relevant historical-sociological context is that people largely got along until the situation dramatically changed. Jews were a key part of commercial life for many centuries in western.

Ukraine (west of the Dneiper River) and in Lithuania (both of which were part of the Polish-Lithuanian Commonwealth, formed in 1569) and, more recently, in Latvia. Denied the opportunity to become members of the nobility and to own land or even to work on it as peasants, Jews in this region, initially invited to settle in these areas during the time of Casimir the Great (r. 1333–70), took up trades as craftsmen, artisans, and estate managers. In villages and towns, Jews congregated in the area in which the Catholic and Orthodox peasants came to sell their grain and handicrafts to Jewish buyers and merchants, to purchase items from the Jewish artisans, and to drink in taverns owned by Jews. Everybody knew everybody else in terms of personal disposition and behavior; there was a broad spectrum of acceptance, friendliness, resentments, rejection, and nasty conduct, which could be extremely violent, involving the murder of many Jews. Prior to the Holocaust, the major murderous episodes in Eastern European history directed against the Jews were the Khmel'nyts'kyi Ukrainian revolt of 1648–54 and the Russian pogroms of the early 1880s and the early 1900s. In addition, the Golden Charter of the 1768 uprising in western Ukraine ordered the killing of all Jews and Poles, while many Jews were slaughtered in 1918–21 during the Russian Civil War. If, for the most part, the majority of people in Poland and Ukraine got along on a day-to-day basis, that did not mean that there were not serious undercurrents of suspicion and dislike, as well as local open altercations. The two principal causes were Catholic and Orthodox antisemitism and ethnic-occupational stratifications.

During the interwar period (1919–40), the three Baltic Republics (Estonia, Latvia, and Lithuania) each had a broad range of political parties, an increasing move to political authoritarianism, and no pogroms against Jews. People did not necessarily like one another, but they could cooperate on a day-to-day basis. Despite the hazards of the Baltic Republics' tumultuous birth and of the interwar period, civil society operated reasonably. This is all the more remarkable in view of the fact that these small, recently independent countries had political parties and supporting constituencies that were pressing for monoethnic countries and viewed with suspicion the Poles, Germans, and Russians who lived in them, as well as Jews.

But once they lost their independence in 1940, the Baltic Republics became geographical expressions as well as decivil societies as external totalitarian regimes, first Soviet and then German, thrust their anti-humanitarian ways of life on them. Under extraordinary stress, including economic dislocation, loss of political and social freedoms, large-scale arrests, the terror of the brief 1940–41 Soviet occupation, and acute disorientation, the worst aspects of human behavior burst through. In Lithuania, as Soviet rule collapsed in 1941 and subsequently under the Germans from 1941–44, the Lithuanian police, other collaborators, and local village denouncers collected and murdered Jews, at times with gusto. Most people, one hopes, probably found the massacres repugnant, but with society collapsing in the face of hatred and fear, they kept their mouths shut. This is a reminder of the multiple layers of culpability, participation, disengagement, denial, and positive helpfulness. Cooperation, for example from much of the local police, was useful to the Germans, and many of the tasks of deportation and murder were allocated to local collaborators. The major killers were the Germans; they instigated the killing, and their responsibility was central. Nevertheless, in some cases, collaboration in the Holocaust began before the German invaders arrived in 1941, or in their absence. This was true of Latvia, Lithuania, and Ukraine, with some of the hatred for Jews attributed to the allegation that they had allied with the communists—as a very small number, indeed, had done. As such, slaughtering Jews was an aspect of the collapse of communist control. Thus, in Latvian towns such as Daugavpils and Riga, before the arrival of German troops, Jews were seized by armed Latvian gangs and killed without anyone stopping them. These were particularly vicious pogroms. The same occurred in several Lithuanian towns, such as Kaunas (Kovno), where 2,500 Jews were killed, and in Ukrainian towns such as Lwów and Tarnopol. In killing at close quarters, this, like that by the German *Einsatzgruppen*, was a killing different from the standard conception of the Holocaust as

carried out by Germans in extermination camps. Moreover, the Lithuanians and Ukrainians involved were just as willing as the Germans to
kill women and children. At Kaunas, the killing was applauded by some
of the local people. Elsewhere, there was less cooperation, for example, in
Brest-Litovsk in eastern Poland, where neither the Poles nor the Belarus-
sians supported the 1941 killings.

Subsequently, many Lithuanians and Ukrainians were prominent
in supporting the German war effort. This involved many Lithuanians
as concentration-camp guards and as killers of Jews in the field, for example, in Belarus in 1941. Lithuanian units took part in antipartisan
operations in which Jews were killed and also in suppressing the Warsaw
ghetto in 1943. Ukrainians were prominent among the guards at several
of the extermination camps, particularly Bełzec, Sobibor, and Treblinka.
Latvian police units shot Jews, as in 1943, when they closed down labor
camps near Vilnius. Local ethnic Germans, for example, those among
the "Black Sea Germans," also slaughtered many of their Jewish neighbors.[18] Most of the Estonian Jews fled in 1941, the remainder being killed
by *Einsatzgruppe* A. There was local collaboration in the slaughter by the
Estonian Home Guard.

Although Salaspils camp near Riga was considered a concentration
camp for Jews from Germany, and Jews were used to help build it, the
camp instead served primarily to detain political prisoners. In November and December 1941, many German Jews were taken to the Jungfern-
hof concentration camp near Riga. The camp was dissolved in March
1942 and the Jews taken to Biķernieki forest, where they were shot.

FRANCE

The situation in France exemplified the room for contrasts. Once
conquered in May–June 1940, France was largely divided between a
German-occupied zone under military governance and a zone, about
40 percent of the country, left under the control of a pro-German
French government, voted into office in July 1940 and based at the
town of Vichy. In the German-occupied region, the trajectory seen
elsewhere in occupied Europe was followed, with a move eventually
toward large-scale deportation to the extermination camps in Eastern

Europe. These roundups were entrusted to the French police, and they focused on foreign Jews. In addition, Alsace-Lorraine was annexed anew by Germany, and Jews were deported from there in October 1940, while Italy gained control of part of France.

From the outset in Vichy France there was a willingness to discriminate against Jews; it did not require much German prompting, let alone pressure. Within the Vichy elite, there was only limited support for fascism, as opposed to a more broadly based conservative nationalism that was particularly open to Catholic activism. The religious, cultural, political, and social fault lines of the Dreyfus Affair, which had begun in 1894 with the unwarranted conviction for treason of a Jewish army officer, reemerged. The agrarian, ruralist, Catholic values advocated by the government of Marshal Philippe Pétain were directed against metropolitan and liberal values with which Jews were associated, as Vichy strove to create an ostentatiously Christian France. In doing so, it took forward the late 1930s antisemitic revival in France, which had been linked to opposition to Jewish refugees.[19] In 1940, the new situation saw the citizenship of many naturalized Jews revoked, and foreign Jews were interned. There was also legislation to define who were Jews and to exclude them from government posts, including teaching. The issue of definition, not least the competing criteria of race and religion, led to fresh legislation in 1941 and further limitations on employment and commerce. In both zones, Jewish property was subject to confiscation, with the relevant measures introduced in Vichy in July 1941, although, as was the norm with Vichy prior to July 1942, the application of antisemitic measures was highly inconsistent. Vichy, indeed, was an aspiration and ideology but also a range of ideas and practices, a point that can differently be made about the Holocaust but only if accepting its fundamental genocidal thrust.

The complexity of Vichy could influence scholarship, but, unsurprisingly, memorialization is directed by the general direction of policy. Thus, the separate Police for Jewish Affairs was established by the Vichy Minister of the Interior. Such measures were intended to demonstrate a desire to cooperate with the Germans.

Vichy attitudes were also displayed in France's colonies, where German oversight was very limited. Thus, there were major purges of Jews in Guadeloupe, which was under Vichy from 1940 to 1943, and in Madagascar, under Vichy in 1940–42. In French North Africa, Jews lost civil rights in Algeria, while many were moved to forced labor camps such as Bedeau and Djelfa, although the situation did not become still more menacing until an SS unit arrived as part of the deployment of German troops to Tunisia from November 1942. The rapid Allied defeat of the Germans in Tunisia was important to the survival of most Tunisian Jews.[20]

In 1942, Vichy handed over foreign Jews for deportation to the camps. Having rounded up on July 16 over 27,000 non-French Jews in Paris and its suburbs, about 10,000 were sent to Auschwitz between July 17 and August 31, including, in the first transport, children, who had not been requested. Over 2,000 foreign Jews were sent from the detention camp of Les Milles near Marseille to Auschwitz. These deportations were very different from the restrictions on immigration displayed pre-war, not least because now the policy was explicitly antisemitic as well as being murderous in effect. The extent to which these deportations were handled by the French authorities and by French railwaymen, both focused on serving the system,[21] was concealed postwar, but most of those deported in 1942 were not under German control until handed over for movement out of the country. Vichy, however, resisted handing over French Jews, in part because of a critical public reaction. German authority was greater because, on November 11, 1942, German troops were sent into the Vichy zone. The roundups in 1943 were mostly by the SS, not the French police. The Vichy government knew that Jews were being sent to slaughter and, indeed, fewer than 3 percent of the 75,000 deported survived, in comparison to 59 percent of the 63,000 French non-Jews deported mostly to the concentration camps at Ravensbrück and Buchenwald. This contrast underlines the problematic nature of postwar commemoration that failed to distinguish Jewish from non-Jewish victims, for example, the Day of Remembrance of the Deportations that was instituted in 1954.

The killings did not trouble Vichy, but the government was concerned that being seen to back German policy over French Jews would compromise Vichy's position in its contest with anti-Vichy forces within France. In the event, French Jews were rounded up in 1943–44, including in Marseille, Nîmes, Avignon, and Grenoble. In 1944, a more extreme government, which, as in Hungary, was imposed by the Germans, encouraged the *Milice française* (far-Right militia) to round up Jews, including French Jews. That January, the *Milice* leader Joseph Darnand became Vichy police minister, and the *Milice* increased to over 35,000 members.[22] The result was that nearly one-third of the Jews deported from France were French. Darnand was executed in France after the war.

The French public itself was split. There was protection for the Jews, particularly in the Protestant-dominated Cévennes Mountains, and, at the individual level, there was much help from French people for Jews, both compatriots and, albeit to a lesser extent, foreign Jews. The Catholic Church included those willing to criticize the deportations, such as Pierre-Marie Gerlier, cardinal archbishop of Lyon, Jules-Géraud Saliège, archbishop of Toulouse, and Pierre-Marie Théas, bishop of Montauban, who was imprisoned by the Gestapo in 1944, and to take risks to help Jews—alongside many others who preferred to accept, indeed support, Vichy, which also benefited from widespread antisemitism. In 1941, Cardinal Alfred Baudrillart, a fervent anticommunist and distinguished scholar of eighteenth-century diplomacy who backed Vichy,[23] called for men to join the League of French Volunteers against Bolshevism, but most French bishops responded icily. The majority of French Jews, especially children (some of whom were given over to adoption and brought up as Christians), survived the war within France, but foreign Jews found the situation far bleaker.[24] This contrast was more generally the case across Europe, with officials being more willing to give over foreign Jews in order to assuage German pressure. Furthermore, these Jews had far fewer links with, and in, local society and, in practical terms, were also less able to evade seizure.

NETHERLANDS

The raft of antisemitic measures seen in prewar Germany was rapidly introduced in the Netherlands after it was conquered in May 1940. From August, Jews were no longer permitted to become civil servants, and those already in civil service positions could not be promoted. In October, all civil servants had to sign a declaration that they were "Aryan"

or "wholly or partially Jewish," and the latter were sacked the following
month. From January 1941, the systematic registration of all Jews in the
Netherlands began, and physical attacks became common. In February, there were the first deportations, and a broadly based protest in a
number of towns on February 25 was harshly suppressed. Antisemitic
measures were stepped up that summer. From the summer of 1942,
102,000 Jews—three-quarters of the 140,000 Jews in the Netherlands
in 1940—were seized, taken to the Westerbork transit camp in the eastern Netherlands, and then deported and killed. If some of this activity
rested on the individual initiative of bounty hunters, much was due to
the cooperation and efficiency of the Dutch civil service and police and
the willingness of most of them to please the Germans.[25] The ratio of
Jews deported and killed was far higher than in Belgium (40 percent) or
France (25 percent), and the total number was also higher. About 24,000
Jews went into hiding. The most famous deportee, Anne Frank, a child
from a German Jewish family that fled to the Netherlands in 1933, hid
from 1940 only to be betrayed and deported to Bergen-Belsen in 1944.
Her diary, published in 1947, is very poignant about life in fearful hiding.
The Dutch also provided more volunteers for the SS than the French or
Belgians. Some Dutch historians have argued that the non-Jewish Dutch
population was latently hostile to Jews or, at least, indifferent. Queen
Wilhelmina only mentioned the Jewish deportations once in her radio
broadcasts from London.

BELGIUM

Almost 25,000 Jews, 40 percent of Belgium's total, were deported, with
twenty-seven trains sent from Mechelen to Auschwitz between 1942 and
1944; another 5,000 Belgian Jews were sent to Auschwitz from Drancy.
The role of the SS in Belgium was limited by the determined opposition
of the German Military Administration, which was largely focused on
military and economic goals. The Belgian civil authorities proved accommodating to German measures, for example, the regulations of October
28, 1940, which decreed the registration of Jews and their exclusion from
public functions. As a reminder of the importance of local variations, the
civil authorities of Brussels refused in the summer of 1942 to distribute

yellow stars or to use the police to arrest Jews, while, the same summer, those of Antwerp did both. On April 14 and 17, 1941, Flemish fascists had moved into the Jewish quarter in Antwerp and burned two synagogues, the sort of riot not seen in France or the Netherlands. Flemish collaboration in Antwerp was in part due to well-devised German propaganda hailing the different, Aryan character of Flanders as distinct from the French-speaking Walloons in the rest of the country. In the latter, the authorities of Liège were more compliant with the Holocaust than those of Brussels, not least in drawing up a list of Jewish-owned enterprises before the Germans asked for it. Such contrasts contributed to the character of the Holocaust as the interplay of an ever more brutal, insistent, and oppressive German drive to control and kill, with a response ranging from eager cooperation to successful defiance.[26]

POLAND

In Poland, however, admittedly in very adverse circumstances, there was active or complicit hostility to Jews, including a massacre on July 10, 1941, of between 200 and 400 at the town of Jedwabne near Białystok, part of Poland under Soviet occupation from 1939 to 1941. What happened there is controversial. Claims that 1,600 Jews were killed, and by the Poles, have been qualified by research indicating, instead, that a smaller number of Poles, encouraged by antisemitic priests and Gestapo agents, cooperated with the German killers. In 2001, President Aleksander Kwasmiewrski laid a wreath at the site of the massacre before apologizing for it.[27]

   In Poland, there was antisemitic hostility that preceded the war and continued after it. There was also, nevertheless, much help on the personal level, particularly in sheltering Jews.[28] Aside from killings elsewhere, 1,500 Poles who tried to assist Jews died in the extermination camp at Bełzec. Due to their own hatred of the Poles, the Germans did not give them the opportunity to collaborate in killing Jews that they offered to Ukrainians, for example, of the Organization of Ukrainian Nationalists (OUN), and Balts.[29] However, a postwar pogrom at Kielce in July 1946 against Jews trying to return home from Auschwitz, in which forty-two Jews, including women and children, were killed, led many of the few thousand Jews in Poland who had survived the Holocaust to emigrate. The pogrom drew on false reports of Jews abducting children.

SCANDINAVIA

Cooperation was minimal in Denmark, which was conquered in 1940, and most of its Jews survived. Denmark indicates that a willingness to rescue Jews could exist and be overwhelmingly successful in a country that was not removed from the antisemitism and racism seen elsewhere in Europe. The Germans began to round up Jews for deportation on October 1, 1943, but, forewarned, the resistance, drawing on wide public support, was responsible for spiriting about 7,000 Jews to Sweden overnight, and only 472 were caught and deported.

The refusal of the Danes to cooperate set a standard some Norwegians failed to meet. In Norway, collaboration, notably by the police, was more common: 728 Jews were sent to their deaths in German camps. The Danes, however, were at the top of the Nazi "Nordic hierarchy." This had an ameliorating effect on the German occupation of Denmark and provided the Danes a certain window of opportunity to let their better side shine through.

NEUTRALS

French action serves as a reminder of the extent to which imperial systems—in this case, that of the Third Reich—depend on consent and cooperation. Much of this is provided within a context in which coercion, overt or implicit, plays a role,[30] but consent and cooperation are nonetheless important. Moreover, the nature and extent of consent and cooperation reflect not only the hard power on which coercion is based but also aspects of soft power, including cultural and ideological influences. These could be seen, for example, in the international alliance structure that supported Germany. In the case of Sweden and Switzerland (both neutral), important economic and financial benefits accrued to the Nazi system as well as to both countries.[31]

These benefits included profit at the expense of Jews: for example, the expropriation by banks and insurance companies of money belonging or owed to Jews and dealing in gold seized from Jews. Revelations about Swiss practices led to widespread international criticism and became the focus for demands for restitution in the 1990s, notably in the United States, with the D'Amato inquiry on the Swiss banks and the Volcker committee's report on dormant accounts. Revelations about the Swiss also affected public culture, as with the depiction of the crooked Swiss banker in the James Bond film *The World Is Not Enough* (1999). During the war, the Swiss National Bank purchased large amounts of gold from the German Reichsbank in order to maintain its gold reserves.

Few Jews were given refugee status by these neutrals: Switzerland took in only 7,000 before the war and another 21,000 during it. Many Jews seeking refuge were denied entry, which could be the equivalent of a death sentence. The neutrals' support for Germany reflected not simply "realist" considerations of relative power, as was stressed after the war, but also ideological factors. In the latter, racism was prominent, and, alongside pan-Aryanism, in Switzerland and Sweden there was a degree of antisemitism that led to a reluctance to help Jews. The Swiss government largely abandoned to their fate Swiss Jews living in German-occupied territory, and its bleak attitude greatly affected postwar restitution.[32] However, Swedish diplomat Raoul Wallenberg made major efforts to save Hungarian Jews and did so for about 4,000 by handing out Swedish visas. Italian Jews deported to slaughter were not moved by train via Switzerland; on the other hand, far from this being a serious impediment, the best route to Auschwitz lay further east via Austria. In the statistics prepared for the Wannsee conference in January 1942, Eichmann included as Jews to be slaughtered those from the neutral countries, such as Ireland, Portugal, Spain, and Switzerland, as well as the 330,000 British Jews once Britain had been overcome. There was space at Auschwitz for such slaughter.

Spain remained neutral but provided assistance to Hitler, including about 47,000 volunteer troops sent to fight the Soviets. Francisco Franco, the dictator, an antisemitic racist, shared in Hitler's belief that Judaism, communism, and cosmopolitanism were linked threats and that Jews were responsible for the alliance against Hitler. Franco did not want Spain to shelter Jews. A decree of May 11, 1939, prevented entry of "those of a markedly Jewish character," and another of October 23, 1941, banned the passage for Jews on Spanish ships to the New World. Few Jews were given shelter, although as the Allies did well, Franco became more accommodating.[33]

In Ireland, there was a reluctance to heed the plight of Jews that in part reflected the strength of antisemitism in a strongly Catholic country, as well as markedly pro-German and anti-British attitudes of the Taoiseach, Eamon de Valera. He was aware of the slaughter of Jews by 1943 but showed little interest in their plight. Looking back to the example of cooperation in the previous world war, the nationalist Irish Republican Army (IRA), which wished to force Britain out of Northern Ireland, sought money and arms from Germany. After the war, the Irish government was not helpful to Jewish refugees, while films of the concentration camps were treated critically as propagandist.[34]

Turkey remained neutral, indeed signing a friendship pact with Germany in 1941, until it joined the Allies in February 1945. There was a propaganda battle in the meantime, with pro-German writers, notably Yunus Nadi, offering antisemitic copy, but about 100 German Jewish exiles were allowed to teach in the universities and the official news agency was philosemitic. However, in response to German pressure on neutrals in 1942 to repatriate their Jewish citizens, the Turks denaturalized 3,000 to 5,000 Jews living abroad, mostly in France, and many ended up in extermination camps. Moreover, antisemitic legislation was passed during the war. Transit visas for Jews en route to Palestine were most common in late 1944 after the tide of war had changed toward the Allies. Now, Turkey claims an undeserved degree of help to Jews during the Holocaust.

Alongside neutral states came neutral international organizations such as the papacy and the Red Cross. Each found it difficult to understand the nature and scale of the problem, and both were subsequently criticized, and understandably so, for lacking moral courage and for their inability to produce a credible response. In the case of the Red Cross, concern about the consequences for Switzerland may also have played a role. The World Jewish Congress found the role of the Red Cross unsatisfactory. The heads of the German Red Cross were aligned with the German government, and as a result, Jews received no support from it.[35]

CONCLUSIONS

There were clearly potent constraints due to German occupation and pressure; there was resistance, and there are major issues in conceptualization and methodology. Nevertheless, the extent of cooperation, complicity, and collaboration across Europe was concealed after World War II, helping ensure that the Holocaust was far more than an episode that can be discussed simply in terms of German causes, goals, and actions.[36] Nazis were the key, but their wider impact was in part dependent on a degree of cooperation that constituted a more general crisis of European culture and, indeed, Western civilization. This reflects the extent to which the Nazi challenge was a civilizational collapse. Something went terribly wrong with Western civilization, whereby a basic constituent group (ancient Hebrews/Jews) was being exterminated, indeed cannibalized in metaphorical and physical senses, by others who regarded themselves as purported representatives and defenders of Western civilization. These events understandably raise the question of whether the Holocaust was a specific calamity and crisis, a stand-alone event, or part of something much larger: a crisis in Western civilization wherein fundamental directions were lost. This is both an epistemological and a philosophical question, as well as one of historical links and turning points. Alongside a general tendency to look at notions and practices of nationalism and imperialism, there was the malign influence of Marxist-Leninist teachings and practices on totalitarian and quasi-totalitarian European thinkers from the late 1910s. Thus, by the early 1920s, the antisocietal, would-be transformative policies of the Bolsheviks and the associated mass murder was widely understood, for example by Hitler. The burgeoning Nazi movement was able to scope out, conceive of, and plan future moves that earlier antisemitic parties had not.

FIVE

Memorialization

THE TRUE SCALE OF THE GERMAN KILLINGS, AS OPPOSED TO the fact that there were many, did not become widespread public knowledge until the liberation of the concentration camps propelled it to the attention of the outside world. This awareness was from July 1944, when the first major camp, Majdanek, was discovered by the Soviet army. The Soviet press provided full details of the gas chambers, and radio and film treatment followed, although no coverage was given to the targeting of Jews,[1] while the Western powers found it difficult fully to grasp the enormity of what the Soviets reported. The liberation of Auschwitz and about 7,000 prisoners who had been left behind, mostly due to ill health, followed on January 27, 1945, which is why that date was later chosen as Holocaust Memorial Day. The extermination camps at Bełzec, Sobibor, and Treblinka had been demolished by the Germans. Photographic evidence of the killing was now available in the West.

Bergen-Belsen was liberated by the British on April 15, 1945, and Buchenwald, Dachau, and Mauthausen by the Americans on April 11, April 29, and May 5, respectively. For the British, Bergen-Belsen, where over 10,000 unburied dead were found, was a shocking revelation, one spread round the world by BBC filming and by cinema newsreels, although the 2014 documentary *Night Will Fall* indicated that a documentary made shortly after, *German Concentration Camps Factual Survey*, was never shown possibly due to changing political priorities. American and Soviet cameramen also played a role in documenting the camps.[2] At Bergen-Belsen, where 30,000 of the 70,000 dead were Jews, malnutrition and typhus were key killers. Plans to use Bergen-Belsen as a camp for displaced persons were hastily discarded. The camps, indeed, lent urgency to the cause of displaced persons but not specifically to that of Jews. In part, this reflected the widespread nature of disruption during, and as a result of, the war. This disruption extended to the experience of liberation; it entailed a difficult process, beginning with immediate sheer survival and extending to subsequent movement for safety and the handling of settlement anxieties and wishes, which fed through into the developing Cold War. Liberation meant handling the psychological aftermath.[3]

The liberation of the camps also led to pressure for action against those responsible in and through international law. *Genocide* was a term first used in print in *Axis Rule in Occupied Europe: Laws of Occupation— Analysis of Government-Proposals for Redress* (1944) by the Polish jurist Raphael Lemkin. Joining the Polish army in 1939, he was wounded, managing to evade capture by the Germans, but lost forty-nine relatives in the Holocaust.[4] Genocide was not a charge used in the Nuremberg trials of German leaders, *Holocaust* was not a term employed in the trials, and Jewish survivors of the Holocaust were not called as witnesses there. Nevertheless, the "mass murder" of Jews was an aspect of Count Four of the indictments at Nuremberg and discussed in the trials. Moreover, in 1948, genocide was made into a crime by a United Nations convention. At Nuremberg, estimates of between 4.5 and 6 million Jewish victims were given by the prosecution. The use of a documentary film, *Nazi Concentration Camps*, shown to the court in November 1945 as proof of criminal wrongdoing, was a major juridical innovation.[5] The role of film in the understanding of the Holocaust countered both the destruction of evidence by the Germans and the degree to which the victims could not speak.

The war was followed by a series of trials of those directly responsible for the Holocaust, especially the commandants of concentration camps. For example, Max Koegel and Martin Weiss were tried, convicted, and executed in 1946, while Rudolf Höss was executed outside Auschwitz in 1947. The Nuremberg Military Tribunal tried twenty-four *Einsatzgruppen* leaders in 1947–48, sentencing fourteen to hanging, although some sentences were later reduced. After the large number of postwar trials,[6] however, the Holocaust receded somewhat from attention as efforts were made in the West (but not the Soviet Union) to forget the war and as Germany and German guilt were reconceptualized with the new divisions and alignments of the Cold War. Further trials were downplayed or abandoned. Moreover, certain prominent Nazis were treated very gingerly, in some cases because of assumptions about their value.

One such officer was SS *Obergruppenführer* Karl Wolff, who had been chief of staff to Himmler from 1936 before becoming head of the SS in northern Italy. In 1945, he arranged the capitulation of all German forces in Italy and was given a degree of immunity, which ensured he escaped justice until tried by West Germany in 1962 and convicted of being an accessory to murder in the shape of the deportation of Italian Jews. Sentenced in 1964 to fifteen years imprisonment, he was released in 1971 on the grounds of ill health. Wolff, who lived till 1984, had also been involved in the Holocaust as chief of Himmler's personal staff from 1936 to 1943, for example making sure there were sufficient deportation trains in 1942.[7]

There is no best way to discuss the legacy and memorialization of the Holocaust. The period covered by this chapter increases all the time. So also does the complexity. This is reflected in the length of the chapter, the organizing principle of which is geography by state, group of states, or international connections. That organization, however, implies a failure to employ a typology in terms of perpetrators, victims, and bystanders. This failure has an unfortunate legacy, as perpetrators and victims are not considered separately. Such an approach poses problems, not only on moral but also on methodological grounds. Memorializing the Holocaust and dealing with its legacies mean different things to and among the descendants of perpetrators, victims, bystanders, and survivors. On the other hand, memorialization is focused in terms of the experience of specific states and the challenge of expounding their wartime conduct and legacy. That the particular priorities of the public reflect national issues is not simply because the frame of perception is generally national—although that was not the case for most victims, notably those taken from one country to be slaughtered in another, as with many killed in the concentration camps. Although the killings were recorded, both officially and sometimes by photograph, all victims were to be made invisible as part of an intention to absent Jews from Europe, indeed the world. The terms of the memorialization of the war and indeed history could challenge this purpose, but, conversely, could fulfill it.

GERMANY

Having fought to ensure unconditional surrender and the destruction of German militarism, the United States and Britain now sought a new Germany. The Cold War with the Soviet Union, which became readily apparent from the Berlin Crisis of 1948–49, and the desire first to get their occupation zones to work and then to normalize West Germany and revive it as a pro-Western democracy ensured that other issues took precedence over memorialization. As a result, relatively little attention was paid to the Holocaust in the 1950s. This choice also reflected the nature of the earlier prosecutions, which had focused on proving a Nazi conspiracy to aggression, and thus war guilt, rather than on detailing the actual Nazi crimes. With the emphasis on Nazi perpetrators and not on victims, the notion of collective Jewish suffering was downplayed. Furthermore, in the trials, the Anglo-American focus on documentation led to a stress on the concentration camps they had liberated and on Auschwitz, rather than on the extermination camps for which less documentation was readily available, particularly Bełzec, Sobibor, and Treblinka. This emphasis on documents was at the expense of eyewitness accounts, although using German documentation ensured that the Nazi state was exposed by its own records. There was also a failure to bring out the major role of the German army and police and of collaborators in the Holocaust.[8]

The new West German government preferred to ignore the Holocaust and to downplay the Nazi era. One of the first laws passed by the newly constituted *Bundestag* (parliament) in 1949 was a widespread amnesty, with similar further measures in 1951 and 1954. Israel, with the strong support of the United States, did manage to force a reluctant West German government to agree in 1953 to pay compensation for crimes against Jews. Underlining the political character of the treatment of the past, the Social Democrats were readier to engage with the issue of Jewish reparations, whereas the more reluctant Christian Democrats who, under Konrad Adenauer, were the governing party tended to claim a separation of Nazis and Germans and to emphasize aspects of what they saw as German victimhood. Many voted against the reparations that, in the end, came to over 100 million Deutschmarks. In contrast, in Berlin, the Allied occupation authorities in 1949 imposed the restitution of identifiable property to victims of Nazi oppression.

Both West Germany and East Germany, newly created by the Soviet Union from its occupation zone to rival West Germany, publicly rejected the Nazi system and its works, including the Holocaust. Nevertheless, many West Germans were inclined to criticize what they saw as the Allies' verdict on the war, not least complaining about what they claimed was the "victors' justice" of the Nuremberg and other trials. This criticism was a key aspect of the self-serving presentation by Germans of themselves as victims of the war. Issues of widespread German responsibility were shunned and, instead, Hitler and the Nazi regime were held accountable for World War II, as they also were for the failure of the attack on the Soviet Union. Defendants at Nuremberg frequently claimed that they had been misled, that senior figures had denied that mass murder was being committed, and that the German people were sympathetic to German Jews.[9]

Postwar polls, however, indicated that many Germans thought the Jews partly responsible for what had happened to them and also that antisemitism remained strong and was, indeed, encouraged by the Allied treatment of Jews. A British army officer (the father of an acquaintance of the author), learning German from a schoolmaster, reflected to him on the terrible destruction the war had wrought on Germany only to be told, "At least there are no more Jews." Visiting Germany in 1950, Hannah Arendt discerned a widespread refusal to face what had happened.[10] Many Germans appeared to have learned nothing about themselves. The idea of a responsibility derived with the West German claim to be the sole legal successor to the Reich was not matched by a comparable sense of responsibility for the Holocaust.

In many senses, this shunning of the recent war and denial of Germany's atrocities repeated the experience of the years after World War I, when there had also been a German rejection of war guilt. Many Germans developed a long-standing and self-serving account of victimhood that looked back to 1918–19, and even Prussia's defeat by Napoleon in 1806, and then to the experience of being bombed by the Allies in World War II[11] and, subsequently, to the brutal, forcible postwar driving of Germans from Eastern Europe. Most Germans claimed to know nothing about atrocities. *Wehrmacht* accounts of the war with the Soviet Union were drained of atrocities and focused, instead, on the effort made to protect Europe from the Soviet threat and on Soviet atrocities. This reluctance and evasion deserves as much attention as the Western repositioning of West Germany as an ally in the Cold War. The collapse of de-Nazification as a policy as the Cold War took hold made denial and evasion more possible. Many Germans, moreover, equated Hitler with Stalin.[12]

During the chancellorship of Konrad Adenauer from 1949 to 1963, many former Nazis were employed in responsible positions in West Germany, for example Theodor Oberländer, the minister of refugees in 1953–60. Hans Globke, the chief of staff of the Chancellery from 1953 to 1960 and a key ally of Adenauer, had been an active bureaucrat under the Third Reich, not least in drafting antisemite measures.

Few were tried for war crimes and the even fewer who were convicted received very light sentences. Insofar as there were trials, attention was directed on Nazism and not on the wartime crimes of ordinary Germans, whether military or not. Instead, in a running together of wartime disruption and the problems of occupation, these supposedly ordinary Germans were presented as separate from, and victims of, the Nazis. For example, among the first cases investigated by West German courts in the late 1940s and 1950s were the killings of ordinary German civilians in the last weeks of the war by hardcore Nazis, notably SS squads.[13]

Reintegration and amnesty were key themes in government policies that enjoyed much public support. The governing Christian Democrats were particularly sympathetic toward ex-Nazis, in part because their electoral constituency, and that of their Bavarian Christian Social Union (CSU) ally in government, included many former Nazi sympathizers. Other parties were also lenient toward ex-Nazis, although some prominent Social Democrats, such as Kurt Schumacher, the head of the opposition Social Democrats until his death in 1952, had been held in concentration camps. Schumacher publicly accepted German responsibility for the Holocaust. Most West Germans, however, proved very willing to ignore or downplay the evidence of the extermination camps, which were now in communist-run Eastern Europe. Insofar as there was blame, it was focused on the SS and the Nazi Party, not on the army and the administration. Moreover, albeit at a modest scale, antisemitic opinions continued to be expressed.

Postwar West German historical scholarship also contributed to the sanitized view of Germany's past, leading to the propagation of a misleading and self-interested account of the Nazi years. The reality was far bleaker. Numerous academics had profited personally and knowingly from the removal of Jewish colleagues, while many had been involved in work that contributed directly to the regime's propaganda and planning, as well as to other activities.[14] These academics went on to profit in the postwar order, which prevented anything approaching scholarly impartiality. Thus, Hermann Albin (1885–1969), who was a key figure in work on the "German East" that looked toward large-scale racial slaughter, became chairman of the Association of German Historians and president of the Historical Commission of the Bavarian Academy of Sciences. Politics played a major and continuing role because senior academic appointments were very much under the control of the government. Albin was given the title of adviser by Franz-Josef Strauss, the conservative head of the CSU from 1961. Membership of the Hitler Youth generation and/or the Nazi Party also could be related to a reluctance to accept widespread complicity in the Holocaust.[15]

The reception elsewhere of academics who had successfully pursued their careers in the Hitler years frequently failed to confront the challenge of their wartime roles. Thus, in editing and translating Theodor Schieder's biography of Frederick the Great, the British historian Hamish Scott described it as "firmly within an established German— and German nationalist—tradition," and Schieder's career under the Third Reich was presented as involvement "with the Ostforschung School of German historians who emphasized their nation's decisive contribution to the development of 'Slavic areas in Eastern Europe.'"[16] This evaluation did not face up to the politics of Schieder (1908–84), who pursued a racially oriented social history and warned about the supposed dangers of Germans mixing with other nations. The primary purpose of Schieder's research was to justify German supremacy. As a member of the Nazi

Party, he was the author of the "Memorandum of October 7, 1939," calling for expulsion of millions of Jews, Poles, and Russians from Eastern Europe in order to create room for German settlers. Schieder's suggestions were later incorporated in the *Generalplan Ost*. Having held posts during the war, Schieder held a position at the University of Cologne after the war and worked as a highly respected historian for the West German government. In 1952, he headed the government commission for researching the expulsion of Germans from Eastern Europe; from 1962 to 1964, he was the rector of the University of Cologne. From 1965, he headed the research section of the History Department. Schieder was also president of the Historical Commission of the Bavarian Academy of Sciences and president of the Academy of Sciences of Rhine-Westphalia, and from 1967 to 1972 chaired the German Historians' Association.[17]

The German attitude after World War II was, nevertheless, different from that after World War I. While it is true that there was not much discussion about German war crimes after World War II, this was also due to the fact that most Germans were busy surviving, finding their relatives, or getting jobs. When plans for the creation of a new German army became public, the strong reaction against it in Germany showed that lessons had been learned. After World War I, most Germans had quite a different perspective on the issue of rearmament. Most were keen to rearm in order to lessen the possibility of defeat in any future war.

Seeking to integrate West Germany into the West as the front line against communism led, from the 1950s, to German nationalism's re-formation, with the creation of a "new" free West Germany and, in particular, a new West German army. This required an acceptable presentation of recent history, one in which Nazism was seen as an aberration, while resistance to Nazi policies was emphasized. There was particular stress on the military plotters who unsuccessfully sought to kill Hitler and overthrow the Nazis in July 1944. They were emphasized as part of a positive evaluation of the German army, which was presented in terms of a Prussian, not Nazi, tradition and regarded as a background to the German contribution to the Cold War. In practice, these plotters were scarcely democratic, while the nonmilitary resistance enjoyed only limited support. Nevertheless, this resistance was very important for the construction of an acceptable postwar German identity and, indeed, justifiably remains so. *Wehrmacht* veterans mirrored postwar accounts of German victimization by seeing their Eastern Front service as a period of grievous hardship.[18] This framing did not encourage scrutiny of the actual conduct of the army during World War II.

Within the West, not only the exigencies and ideological suppositions of the Cold War, both of which were influential[19] (and seen with former Fascists in Italy), but also the pressures for Western European integration encouraged an overlooking or acceptance of a German self-image as victims of Nazism. Conversely, the experience of the war and the desire to neutralize German economic power and nationalism by integrating it into a supranational structure were the driving forces behind European integration. European integration was popular in West Germany because many Germans realized that it was the only way back into the international community after what their country had done during World War II.

Pressures for integration included ideas of a Western bloc—Western Europe, or United States of Europe—that looked toward the plan for the European Defence Community and, more successfully, to the establishment of the European Coal and Steel Community in 1951 and the European Economic Community (EEC) in 1958. This was the result of the Treaty of Rome of 1957, which, in pledging to work for "an ever closer union of the peoples of Europe," understandably did not leave room for the recollection of German popular support for Hitler. Nations with a shameful past can only really focus on the future, and the EEC became a vehicle to move quickly from the past. Focusing on the future made shedding the past easier. The established narrative was that European unification was a reaction against the horrors of the war.[20] Ironically, aspects of the EEC looked back to wartime talk of a new economic order that was advanced by collaborators with Nazi Germany, especially in France. In 1940, Robert Schuman—later, as the French foreign minister (1948–52) and president of the EEC Assembly (1958–60), a key figure in the creation of the EEC—had, as a member of the National Assembly, voted for the fall of the Third Republic, the prelude to the establishment of Vichy. Yet at the same time, the EEC owed much of its genesis to anti-Nazi Catholic politicians such as Adenauer. However, the reluctance in West Germany to insert the Holocaust in the historical narrative and analysis and in memorialization was also more widely seen. Holocaust memory, indeed, was confronted mainly by adapting the old frameworks of antifascism and antitotalitarianism.[21]

A comparable integration occurred in Eastern Europe with the formation of the economic bloc of Comecon (1949) and the security bloc of the Warsaw Pact (1955). The continuity between Nazi Germany and both the Soviet occupation and East Germany as totalitarian regimes was indicated when the concentration camps at Buchenwald and Sachsenhausen were used for detaining political prisoners. East German scholarship tended to neglect the Holocaust or to mention it either as a product of capitalism, specifically needs for labor and capital, or of an attempt to divert attention from the failings of capitalism and the Nazi system. Compensation was not paid to Jews. This was because East Germany perceived itself as an anti-Fascist state and not in the tradition of previous German states, whereas West Germany saw itself explicitly as the legal successor of the German Reich. In East Germany, the victims of Nazi killing were presented as opponents of fascism and not as Jews. Indeed, the latter were treated as passive victims rather than active fighters against fascism, who were honored if communist. As in West Germany, antisemitism itself continued, while, for example, in Potsdam, synagogue ruins were swept aside.[22]

The situation subsequently changed, both in Germany and in other states that had played a role in the Holocaust, either as sites for murder, sources of collaboration, or, allegedly, as overly disengaged observers. The attempt to contain the effects on Germany's image by blaming the atrocities specifically on the Nazis, thus presenting the bulk of the population as victims, was eventually challenged in West Germany, especially in a debate about the complicity of the military, which was indeed pronounced and cumulative.[23] In occupied Serbia, for example, the mass killing of Jews was carried out by the army from 1941.[24] By the late 1950s, there was a willingness to engage with misconduct by generals, although not yet with responsibility for the Holocaust.[25] Similarly, in 1960, Theodor Oberländer, a cabinet member in Adenauer's government who had played a major role in 1937 in developing an idea of turning Polish peasantry against Polish Jews, was dismissed in response to accurate reports of the mass murder of Jews in Lvov by Ukrainian forces under his command in 1941, although it was alleged that the evidence used against him was fake and, indeed, part of the East German attempt to discredit West Germany as a new Nazi state. Oberländer had been minister for refugees and expellees, those Germans forced in large numbers from Eastern Europe.

In West Germany, growing pressures on the somewhat complacent collective myth of general social and cultural changes were increasingly important: specifically, the rise, from the 1960s, of a generation that did not feel responsibility for Nazism, the decline of deference toward the former generations, and the need to explain what had happened to those who had not lived through the war as adults. There was also the influence of the US and British occupation, the awareness of US and British political practices, US consumer culture, and the pull of American and British youth cultures in fortifying younger Germans' resolve to question their elders' past. The political and cultural agendas were no longer shaped by the pressures of postwar reconstruction, nor by the evasion of responsibility through presenting wartime conduct as that of uninformed bystanders. Indeed, an aspect of the 1968 generation's critique of its predecessors was the charge that the latter did not mark a break from the wartime cooperation with Nazism and had not accepted individual responsibility. The radical Left accused its predecessors of being the Nazi generation.

It was now argued that coming to critical terms with the past was an aspect of anchoring democracy in Germany. Moreover, human rights became increasingly important in the political agenda. This argument also reflected the rise of the Social Democrats who, from 1969 to 1982, occupied the Federal Chancellery. Visiting Warsaw in 1970, the new chancellor, Willy Brandt, knelt before the Ghetto Monument, a powerfully symbolic gesture of official atonement, one made by an individual not in any way linked to the wartime state: Brandt had fled, first to Norway and then Sweden. Brandt went on to visit Israel in 1975, the first visit by a West German chancellor.

In part, the shift in German attitudes was due to a growing awareness of the atrocities committed by the Nazi regime, notably due to the establishment in 1958 of the Central Office for the Investigation of National Socialist Crimes, and to a desire to rebut East German propaganda.

Aside from the Eichmann trial in Israel, the 1958 Ulm *Einsatzkommando* trial (the basis for more wide-ranging prosecutions) was followed by the illustrations in Gerhard Schoenberner's *Der gelbe Stern* (1960) and then by the trial that opened at Frankfurt in 1963 of twenty-three men involved in Auschwitz. Those accused in the so-called Auschwitz trial included the two deputy camp commandants. It was the most public and largest trial of Holocaust perpetrators in West Germany before a West German court and under West German law. This trial brought the Holocaust to the forefront of public knowledge. Witness statements left no doubt of what had occurred and also provided an opportunity for public testimony by survivors. A wall of silence was broken. In 1964, members of the court made an official visit to Auschwitz. The trial had a Cold War dimension, with Friedrich Kaul, the lawyer for the East German civil plaintiffs, being instructed by the East German government to use it as a propaganda opportunity, while the visit to Auschwitz was encouraged by the Polish authorities. Both despite and because of this dimension, the West German authorities and the court, which were under the spotlight, did not allow the trial to be used to discredit the idea of trying war criminals, as the key defense lawyer, Hans Laternser, wanted. However, in what, in some respects, was an unsatisfactory outcome, it proved difficult to bring together collective responsibility and individual guilt. The prosecution sought to put Auschwitz as a whole and the Holocaust into the frame, whereas the defense sought to have the accused individually charged. In the event, the accused were judged in accordance with penal law and not the Nuremberg criteria. Furthermore, it has been argued that by focusing on the crimes of individual Auschwitz figures, the trial could not engage with the wider parameters of German responsibility.[26]

The 1963–65 Frankfurt Auschwitz trial was not alone. Karl Wolff was finally tried and convicted as an accessory to the mass murder of 300,000 Jews for having supervised their deportations to Treblinka. The most senior official to be tried in a German court, he was sentenced in 1964 to fifteen years' imprisonment but was released, ostensibly for health reasons, in 1969.[27] Meanwhile, some German scholars focused more on the SS and the Holocaust. Holocaust survivors such as Simon Wiesenthal directed attention to surviving Nazis who had been involved in atrocities. Among those Wiesenthal tracked down was the Austrian-born commandant of first Sobibor and then Treblinka, Franz Stangl, who had escaped to Italy and Syria in 1948 and then to Brazil in 1951, was arrested in Brazil in 1967, extradited to West Germany, and in 1970 given a life sentence. This shift was matched by an increased focus on the Holocaust from outside Germany.[28]

Within West Germany, there developed an influential determination to treat the Holocaust as the defining moment in public responsibility. Thus, in place of the notion of the Germans as in some ways victims of the Nazis[29] (an idea that continued to be pushed especially hard in Austria for the Austrians) came the view that the Germans had collaborated. A recognition of this collaboration was seen as important to the health of German democracy and as crucial to public education. From 1962, the Länder (provinces), the level of government responsible for education, extended the teaching of history to cover the Hitler years, including the Holocaust. Becoming effective from 1967, this was a major step in a process of public education over the Holocaust and one that ensured that the Germans became better informed on the Holocaust than other Europeans, notably those in Eastern Europe. Alltagsgeschichte (the history of everyday life), often by local historians using oral history, was an important development in the 1980s, and the history of local Jews began to become an increasing focus. There was also the phenomenon of Stolpersteine, an attempt from 1992 to recover the names of all those murdered by the Nazis, which was not confined to Jews, but in which they were prominent. This involved a concrete cube bearing a brass plate giving the names of those murdered that was installed where they lived. This memorial is more insistent because widespread.

Nevertheless, there were still important lacunae in public education and a lack of agreement about how best to interpret the information. Moreover, there was a reluctance to commemorate key sites. The Bavarian government, for example, was opposed to spending money to maintain Dachau as a memorial, and the same was true of the local council.

On the extreme Right, Holocaust deniers were active, such as Wilhelm Staglich, who had been part of the Auschwitz military defense system, author of Der Auschwitz-Mythos (1979), a book confiscated nationwide in 1980. The Hitler Diaries, by Konrad Kujau, a German serial forger, that was exposed as a fraud in 1983 may have been a neo-Nazi attempt to rehabilitate Hitler as it implied that he sought to resettle Jews on occupied territory rather than to slaughter them.

The presence of such deniers and, more generally, of neo-Nazis, who were responsible for acts such as the desecration of Cologne synagogue in 1959, as well as the electoral success of the far-Right NPD during the 1960s led to support for an emphasis on the need for public education about the Holocaust. This also encouraged a more positive response to foreign representations of the Holocaust as, crucially, in January 1979, when the US television series of that name was broadcast to an audience of about twenty million, over 40 percent of television viewers in West Germany.

The emergence of the Holocaust as a central issue in Germany, France, and the United States from the 1970s and more particularly in the 1990s rested on complex social, cultural, and political reasons.[30] These included, and not only in Germany, a reaction against Holocaust denial by the resurgent extreme Right, a denial that became central to its mythology and discourse.[31] In addition, the opening of archives in Eastern Europe and the Soviet Union made the status quo no longer viable. Growing interest in and reference to the Holocaust marked an important change in how people saw World War II, while the Holocaust also became a legitimate academic subject. Moreover, a wider frame of reference developed. This was seen, for example, in the United States with the opening, in 1993, of the large US Holocaust Memorial Museum on a prominent site in Washington, DC and with the passage of the Nazi War Crimes Disclosure Act in 1998. To implement the latter, the Nazi War Criminal and Imperial Japanese Records Interagency Working Group was established.[32] Developments within individual countries encouraged pressure for action elsewhere, while a general atmosphere of scrutiny encouraged institutions to open archives in response to criticism. Thus, in the early 1980s, the International Committee of the Red Cross opened its wartime archives. Many businesses found it necessary to demonstrate and make amends for their relations with the Third Reich, although some did not.

In German historiography, there was a bitter controversy about the relationship between the Nazi period, both the Nazis and the Germans as a whole, and the longer-term trends in German history, a controversy that had a direct relevance to heated debates over the legitimacy of the West German political system and was linked with challenges to the dominant conservative (and, to an extent, gerontocratic) character of postwar West German historical scholarship. The *Historikerstreit* (controversy among historians) of 1986–87, which linked discussion of the Holocaust to the question of how best to present national history, was played out in a very public fashion, with many articles appearing in prominent newspapers. In part, this was a product of the attempt to normalize German history made by historians close to Chancellor Helmut Kohl, the leader of the conservative Christian Democratic Party, which gained power in 1982. This normalization was taken to mean making German history more acceptable in order to ground national identity and seek inspiration.

Kohl, who remained chancellor until 1998, saw such a step as a necessary basis for patriotism, national pride, and spiritual renewal, a theme taken up more generally on the German Right, but one that scarcely focused on issues of ethical concern. Kohl himself had earlier voted against abolishing the statute of limitations for murder, an abolition that left ex-Nazis vulnerable to prosecution. Officials in the Kohl government perceived the establishment of the Holocaust Memorial Museum in Washington as anti-German and unsuccessfully attempted to change its contents by including references to the anti-Nazi resistance and to postwar German history.[33]

In the controversy, the degree to which Nazism could be seen as a historical episode rather than as a characteristic inherent in longer-term trends, and the degree to which the Holocaust arose from specific German characteristics rather than being an aspect of more widespread violence, were debated. So also was the extent to which the German state had a historical mission specifically to resist advances from the East, that is, the Soviet Union. This approach was pushed by conservative historians such as Andreas Hillgruber, a veteran of the Eastern Front, who presented in *Zweierlei Untergang: Die Zerschlagung des Deutschen Reiches und das Ende des europäischen Judentums* (Two kinds of ruin: The fall of the German Reich and the end of European Jewry, 1986) a moral equivalence between the Holocaust and the end of German power in Eastern Europe while also praising the *Wehrmacht* and the generals who opposed the July 20 bomb plot. This attitude led to the claim that German iniquities had to be considered against this background, with Ernst Nolte arguing that the Nazis were a reaction to communism and presenting Hitler as trying to thwart what he saw as a Jewish communist threat. Furthermore, Nazi activities were depicted as in part emulating the communists, but in a way that seemed to minimize the Holocaust.

The argument that the Germans had to fight on to resist the Soviet advance was also that of German generals in the final stage of the war. This self-serving argument did not stop them mounting fierce resistance to Anglo-American forces, including directing the reserves involved in the Battle of the Bulge counteroffensive against them rather than against the Soviets. Fighting on, of course, also provided more time for the Holocaust, not that this was the main purpose of the generals, although it was indeed a factor for Nazi leaders.

Kohl's attempt at a reevaluation was unsuccessful in that it led to much criticism both within Germany and internationally. Nolte and others were attacked by a number of prominent scholars, including Jürgen Habermas. They argued that Nolte was trying to relativize or historicize Nazi activities and thus limit them and reduce the collective and individual responsibilities of Germans. Instead, the Nazi enterprise was presented by Habermas and others as unique in its criminality.[34]

An essential issue in the *Historikerstreit* was the fact that the Holocaust was seen as implying the problem, indeed issue, of the legitimacy of West Germany. This legitimacy was challenged by East Germany, and that was one reason why the controversy petered out once German unification became a prospect, which ended this challenge.

In the same period as the *Historikerstreit*, Kurt Waldheim, the former secretary-general of the United Nations (1972–81), became president of Austria (1986–92). He served in these positions despite wartime involvement in anti-Jewish atrocities in Yugoslavia and Greece: Army Group E's intelligence staff, of which he was a member, played a role in the deportation of Greek and Yugoslav Jews to slaughter, as well as in brutal antipartisan operations. In response to criticism, Waldheim publicly claimed that Jews were trying to ruin the reputation of his generation. Taking up earlier Nazi themes, Waldheim linked this accusation to a purported international conspiracy, with Jewish pressure against him being presented as centered in the United States, where Waldheim was now treated as an undesirable alien.

Waldheim's persistent evasions and downright lies came to explain and symbolize the extent to which this episode was regarded as a key aspect of the Austrian reluctance to accept the legacy of the Holocaust, and one that contrasted markedly with the greater engagement in West Germany. Indeed, on May 8, 1985, in the ceremony held in the *Bundestag* marking the fortieth anniversary of the end of World War II, Richard von Weizsacker, the West German president, recognized the Holocaust as an aspect of the war and emphasized individual and collective responsibilities while also presenting defeat and surrender in 1945 as a liberation for Germany.[35]

Austrians, in fact, played a disproportionately prominent role in the SS and the Holocaust. From January 1943, the Reich Main Security Office was headed by Ernst Kaltenbrunner, formerly head of the SS and police in Austria.[36] Eichmann was brought up in Austria; Globocnik was born in Trieste when it was Austrian and became active in Austrian Nazism, eventually becoming *Gauleiter* of Vienna. Franz Stangl was commandant first of Sobibor and then of Treblinka. Austrians were regarded as being particularly cruel concentration-camp guards (and became guards out of all proportion to their numbers) and, in addition, were very active in the deportation of Jews from the Netherlands. Judging by public-opinion polls, antisemitism, which was potent during the Nazi years,[37] remained strong, as did a disinclination to note the presence, let alone significance, of Jews in Austria's history. The investigations of Holocaust perpetrators were not driven home in Austria. However, Holocaust memorialization has become more prominent and, from 1991, a commemorative service financed by the government has existed to provide guides at Holocaust sites.

Meanwhile, scholarly work on key aspects of Germany during the war, particularly the army, the police, and the judiciary,[38] presented them critically as actively supporting Nazi aims. The greatest controversy was caused by the *Wehrmacht* exhibition, arranged by the Hamburg Social Research Institute and that toured Germany and Austria from 1995, drawing 800,000 visitors in thirty-four cities by 1999. The approximately 1,500 photographs of *Wehrmacht* soldiers involved in atrocities had a major impact on the public and led to much discussion and contention, including hostile demonstrations in Dresden and Munich and a terrorist attack by right-wing extremists at Saarbrücken in 1999. The thesis that the army, instead of solely the SS, had been active in the Holocaust cut across the argument that the troops were patriots fighting for their country.[39] The visitors' books to the exhibition of photographs revealed generational differences in the responses, with the young being most critical of the *Wehrmacht*. The traditional German military narrative, purposefully crafted by German generals in their memoirs and interviews after the war, placed the blame for the Holocaust on the SS and political leaders. This whitewashing enabled the parallel but separate study of the war in terms of military campaigns and the Holocaust. This narrative, however, was destroyed by scholarly studies, notably the multivolume history of the war produced by the *Bundeswehr's Militärgeschichte Forschungsamt*. As a result, the military and Holocaust elements were integrated, although far less so at the popular level.

A reluctance to accept the implications of wartime action was seen in Nuremberg in 1997. Criticism of the granting by the city council that year of honorary citizenship to Karl Diehl, a local industrialist who had used concentration-camp workers, led to a bitter controversy in which the majority of the council supported Diehl. This was an instance of the extent to which a critical remembrance could be resisted, notably at the local level.[40] Conversely, and more generally, there has been major debate about compensation for forced laborers, which, in many respects, has been a cornerstone for a new way the German government and companies have tried to come to terms with their past. Class actions brought against German companies in the United States in the late 1990s encouraged restitution, most centrally through a public-private foundation.[41] In 2009, the trial for the blackmail of Suzanne Klatten, Germany's wealthiest woman, by a gigolo, Helg Sgarbi, provided an opportunity to discuss the extent to which leading German companies had been implicated in the Nazi regime. Klatten, the owner of much of BMW and Altana, is granddaughter of Günther Quandt, a key figure in the armaments industry, a member of the Nazi inner circle, and the first husband of Magda Goebbels. The Quandt factories used concentration-camp labor, which was treated atrociously. After the war, the Quandts refused interviews and denied historians access to their wartime archives.

The capacity of totally different historical works to ignite public interest in this field was shown by the response to Daniel Goldhagen's depiction of a large number of Germans as *Hitler's Willing Executioners* (1996) and also with the 2000 libel trial in Britain arising from David Irving's work. The former episode juxtaposed an often-critical scholarly response with a more engaged populist reception accepting Goldhagen's somewhat simplistic and ably marketed case, especially in the United States, although also with young German audience members in his 1996 tour.[42] Antisemitism has been seen at work in the highly critical reaction among important sections of German opinion and in German-controlled publications,[43] although the prejudices this reaction drew on were more complex and, in part, reflected institutional, historiographical, and political drives within Germany.

Criticism of Goldhagen, a sociologist and political scientist by training, also focused on what was presented as an oversimplistic thesis, poor methodology, questionable conclusions, a combative manner (an antisemitic trope), and the desire to build a career on presenting himself as a taboo breaker. This ensured that there was scholarly criticism of Goldhagen from the Left as well as, more prominently, from the Right. German Jewish commentators were divided in their response to Goldhagen. There was a lack of consistency in his running together evidence of Germany wishing to exclude Jewishness and the determination to kill Jews, not least because exclusion could be achieved by assimilation or forced emigration. Goldhagen also provided the Holocaust with an inherent past in German political culture and society that exaggerated the earlier unique centrality there of antisemitism. At the same time, he reminded readers of the centrality of Jew hatred in Germany.

The Irving libel trial arose from a case brought in 1996 by Irving against Deborah Lipstadt, author of *Denying the Holocaust* (1993), and her publisher, Penguin, over her claims that Irving had falsified history in the shape of Holocaust denial. Irving was presented by supporters as being denied the ability to present his views, but the exact opposite was in fact the case. Irving is frequently described as a historian, but this is only true insofar as he writes about the past: he has not been trained as a scholar and has not held an academic or other related post as a historian. Irving had appeared for the defense in 1988 in the second trial in Toronto of Ernst Zundel for Holocaust denial. The prosecution called Christopher Browning, a distinguished scholar and specialist on the Holocaust, noted for *Ordinary Men: Reserve Police Battalion 101 and the Final Solution in Poland* (1992), who, in the face of attacks from Zundel's defense team on the methodology of history, underlined the role of facts as opposed to simply opinions. Zundel was convicted.

The Irving libel trial judgment of 2000 indicated anew that historical evidence could be deployed effectively within the constraints of legal cases, as the trial served as an opportunity to assert and demonstrate historical truths, in this case the horrors of the Holocaust, which was done, in particular, by the historian Richard Evans. This demonstration, both of the truths and of Irving's misuse and denial of them, ensured that Irving lost his case. The judge, Charles Gray, remarked that Irving's ideological slant was "anti-Semitic and racist," and the case led to the publication of a number of reviews of the evidence, as well as accounts of the trial including the film *Denial* (2016). Irving lost his application for appeal and was forced into bankruptcy.

Irving was subsequently arrested, tried, and imprisoned in Austria in 2006 for Holocaust denial on an earlier visit, again an episode that led to extensive coverage. In this trial, Irving accepted that the Holocaust involved the murder of millions of Jews and that Hitler knew about it, a point he had earlier denied in his *Hitler's War*. Holocaust denial is a criminal offence in Austria (since 1992), as also in Germany, where, in 1994, it was made a form of racial incitement.[44]

The very different Goldhagen and Irving controversies indicate that the Holocaust remained an issue capable of engaging much interest and generating much comment, the first in the United States and Germany in particular, and the second in Britain. Indeed, the saliency of the Holocaust, both in its own right and not least as a touchstone for wider tensions, emerged powerfully in both cases.

Separately from but related to persistent debates among historians, the controversial nature of the recent German past has a direct impact in German domestic politics and, possibly, on German foreign policy. The former was seen in 2003, when a controversy arose over a speech by

Martin Hohmann, a backbencher from the then-opposition Christian Democratic Party, declaring that Germans should not, as a result of their support for Hitler, be treated as a "guilty people." Hohmann's statement was indeed designed to deflect criticism onto those whose brutal treatment under Hitler formed the prime charge, Jews, because he claimed they were themselves guilty of a prominent role in communist atrocities, a claim also made on behalf of antisemitic nationalists in Eastern Europe. After a fortnight's controversy, Hohmann was expelled from the party. Concerns that his attitude was related to and might encourage antisemitism were linked to claims that antisemitism was related to growing opposition to Israel's policies toward the Palestinians.

Hohmann lacked the significance of Philipp Jenninger, who in 1988 had to resign as president of the German parliament, but his argument was resonant in a country in which part of the population—an increasing percentage of which had had no experience of the war—was fed up, even resentful, with being urged to remember the Holocaust. This remembrance was central in German education, with the Nazi period a compulsory subject. However, as indicated by the response to Goldhagen's 1996 *Hitlers willige Vollstrecker* (*Hitler's Willing Executioners*), some German historians and senior journalists were unwilling to move from a form of abstract condemnation and a depersonalization of the Holocaust to confront the argument of widespread German willingness to engage in a slaughter characterized by sadistic antisemitism. The popular response to Goldhagen's book tour in 1996 was far more positive.

In policy terms, the German government had taken a more significant step when, for thirteen years after the fall of the Iron Curtain, it offered all Jews from the former Soviet Union automatic residency. As a result, by 2006, there were 115,000 Jews in Germany, most from a Soviet background. In comparison, over one million moved from the Soviet Union to Israel in the same period, although possibly as many as 100,000 returned to the former Soviet Union, in large part to take advantage of the greater economic opportunities there. Moreover, German compensation for Holocaust suffering was extended, with payments from 1997 for unpaid work carried out in the ghettos, which was followed, under the ZRBG (so-called ghetto pension) indemnity law of 2002, by allowing former residents of any ghetto incorporated into the German Reich to qualify—a law that, however, excluded most ghettos and most of those used for forced labor. As also with belated Swiss interest in the wartime role of Swiss banks, fear of legal action inside and outside Germany, and notably in the United States, played a role in this compensation.

The official federal government memorialization in Germany is reflected powerfully in the Memorial to the Murdered Jews of Europe, which was finally opened in 2005 after a long period of controversy, four years after the Jewish Museum in Berlin opened. A large and much-visited work the size of two football fields, built close to the Brandenburg Gate and the site of Hitler's bunker in Berlin, its design was, however, a source of dispute, as was the extent to which it represented a real break with the past. The need to coat the stones (designed to represent a Jewish cemetery) with antigraffiti spray reflected anxiety that they could be defaced by neo-Nazis. Similarly, the Ohel Jakob synagogue, a complex comprising synagogue, Jewish museum, and community center, which opened in Munich in March 2007, faced neo-Nazi opposition, including, in 2003, a plot to bomb the construction site. The synagogue's dedication in 2007 was protected by 1,500 police and by metal-detecting gates.

As another cause of controversy over the Berlin Memorial, the antigraffiti spray was manufactured by Degussa, a subsidiary of which had produced the Zyklon-B gas used in the extermination camps. The memorial was presented not simply as a response to the past, but also as a warning. In 2004, Wolfgang Thierse, the speaker of the German parliament, praised it not just as a memorial to mark the Holocaust but also for being "about the future: a reminder that we should resist antisemitism at its roots."

This, indeed, was an urgent issue for a Germany where racism has been resurgent, especially in the former East Germany, where neo-Nazi support remains strong. In 1992, as an attempt to challenge memorialization, there was an antisemitic firebomb on the parts of Sachsenhausen where Jewish prisoners were held. Racism there can be seen not only as an aspect of the failure of the communist system in public education but also as a consequence of the fall of that system. Concern helped lead the German government, in 2007, to propose to make Holocaust denial a crime across the European Union. Brigitte Zypries, the justice minister, claimed: "We should not wait until it comes to deeds. We must act against the intellectual pathbreakers of the crime." In part, resurgent racism was a product of the economic difficulties that followed German reunification, particularly high male unemployment in the former East Germany, but there were also powerful cultural and ideological currents of hostility and fear that led, for example, to attacks on Jews, Africans, and Turkish guest workers, synagogues, and asylum hostels. These currents reflected the persistence of neo-Nazi beliefs, agitation, and symbols, although the extreme Right was scarcely specific to Germany. At the same time, the Jewish community in Germany greatly increased, in large part due to the large-scale immigration from Russia. As a consequence of this and of the earlier devastation in the Holocaust (followed by the emigration of Jews who ended up in Germany as a result of the enforced population movements of displaced persons in 1945–46), Germany came to have the fastest-growing Jewish community in the world. The community in Munich, for example, is now over 9,000 strong, an instance of the total failure of the Nazis even in their heartland. In 2001, a new synagogue opened in Dresden, the first to be built in the former East Germany since the Nazi years. In 2006, the first rabbis to emerge from German rabbinical training since the Nazi years graduated.

Furthermore, Jews became more central in German life as an aspect of public apology and absolution. This was both symbolic and also played a role in particular crises. Thus, in 2007, when Gunther Oettinger, the Christian Democratic premier of Baden-Württemberg, landed in controversy for his funeral eulogy for a predecessor, Hans Filbinger—who had had to resign for his wartime role as a military judge (and SS officer) in occupied Norway—he met Charlotte Knobloch, the head of Germany's Central Council of Jews, as part of the process of apology for the controversial eulogy. Chancellor Merkel, who demanded an apology, was a centrist whose views were very different from those of Filbinger and Oettinger. Filbinger was all too characteristic in his murderous pseudo-legalism.

The relationship remained complex. By 2011, Germany was spending over 2 million euros annually on youth exchanges with Israel, and in 2012, Germany agreed to contribute 1 million euros annually to Israel's Yad Vashem Holocaust Memorial until 2021. However, in 2011, the German Ministry of the Interior suggested that a fifth of the population had latent antisemitic tendencies.[45]

Reflecting different national issues, memorials and cemeteries are important sites for contestation as well as commemoration.[46] This is not only true of specific Holocaust sites, such as Auschwitz, which became a World Heritage Site in 1979. Thus, President Ronald Reagan of the United States caused a stir on a state visit to West Germany in 1985 when, joining the German chancellor, Helmut Kohl, he visited the military cemetery at Bitburg. The controversy arose because the cemetery contained the graves of forty-nine members of the Waffen-SS. They were not SS concentration-camp guards and, by the time they died, the Waffen-SS was no longer a volunteer army. Only fifteen of the forty-nine were registered in SS personnel files. Nevertheless, the Waffen-SS was a vicious organization (indeed, a criminal one in clear breach of international law), and Reagan had been advised not to visit Bitburg. However, he heeded Kohl's pressure to do so. Reagan described these soldiers as being as much victims of the Nazis as those who had suffered in concentration camps, a truly bizarre equivalence but one that reflected the sense that he had to say something about the camps.[47] Reagan also visited Bergen-Belsen.

The continuing emphasis on German victimhood raised uneasy reflections. This emphasis focused particularly on the impact of Allied bombing, an issue stressed by Nazi propaganda. In the 2000s, in a highly inappropriate and self-serving relativism, the bombing was frequently presented anew as a war crime, one that leveled the playing field in terms of German war guilt and atrocities and even offered some sort of comparison with the Holocaust, a highly offensive approach and one unconsciously endorsed by liberal-inspired reconciliation processes. This literature proved very popular in Germany. Appearing in 2002, Jörg Friedrich's *Der Brand: Deutschland in Bombenkrieg, 1940–1945* rapidly sold 500,000 copies in Germany. He implied an equivalence between the Holocaust and the bombing, employing terms to describe the first with reference to the second. In 2006, the parliamentary deputies of the National Democratic Party, a neo-Nazi organization, referred to "a Holocaust in bombs." In response, a civic declaration outlining a "framework for commemoration" acknowledged Dresden's role in the Nazi system and its crimes, including against the city's Jews.

That issue was not alone. The hugely popular 2013 television series *Unsere Mütter, unsere Väter (Our Mothers, Our Fathers)* was on the whole critical, but the inappropriate sympathetic concern for the protagonists extended clearly to excusing the willingness of German soldiers to commit atrocities by blaming it on indoctrination and compulsion, a mistaken approach; 7.6 million Germans saw the final episode.[48] The series caused complaints in Poland, as the depiction of the Poles suggested a degree of antisemitism there. A branch of relativism focused on the dictatorial character of East Germany, which, despite its cruelties, scarcely approximated to Nazi Germany.

A bizarre form of German victimhood occurred in 2015 when the Goebbels estate won a lawsuit before the Munich appeals court over the copyright of his diaries, a verdict upheld in a subsequent decision. The case was brought in 2014 against Random House Germany by the estate because royalties were not paid out for the use of his diaries in a biography published by Peter Longerich. The case was brought on behalf of Goebbels's heirs by Cordula Schacht, the daughter of Hitler's minister of economics, Hjalmar Schacht, president of the Reichsbank.[49] Rainer Dresen, the lawyer representing Random House Germany, argued for the suspension of copyright laws, in this case on legal and moral grounds. Dresen also made a private and public offer to Schacht for Random House to pay the royalties so long as the funds were donated to a Holocaust charity rather than going toward the estate, but she refused, insisting the money go to Goebbels's relatives. Dresen argued that the Bavarian government had been actively obstructive in the case by refusing to accept that it had copyright as a result of a sale of the rights by Goebbels in 1936. Cordula Schacht had been a legal adviser to François Genoud, a Swiss banker (1915–96) who supported Hitler and also financed the legal defenses of Eichmann and Klaus Barbie, as well as supporting the Ayatollah Khomeni during his exile in Paris and being a friend and financial adviser of Amin al-Husayni, the bitterly antisemitic grand mufti of Jerusalem who was most impressed by the gassing of Jews. The executor of Goebbels's will, Genoud had purchased the rights to the diaries in 1955, transferring his interest in them to Schacht in 1996. The case was particularly scandalous for a number of reasons, not least that Goebbels saw the diaries as a future money spinner.

Alongside the tendency of many Germans to focus on the travails of veterans and of those expelled from further East at and after the close of the war and to ignore the enthusiasm with which many—both individuals from these groups and among their compatriots—participated in the numerous crimes of the Third Reich, there has come a major effort to remember these crimes.[50] Indeed, in 2014, Chancellor Angela Merkel, in leading a rally against antisemitism, declared, "It is our national and civic duty to fight antisemitism." Since the 2011 trial of John Demjanjuk, who worked as a guard at Sobibor, evidence that defendants must have known about the murders taking place around them has sufficed. In 2022, Irmgard Furchner, a personal assistant to the head of the Stutthof concentration camp, was convicted accordingly.

Anxiety among Jews about the German Far Right rose from the mid-2010s as it became more prominent. Established in 2013, the Alternative for Germany (AfD) movement became the third most important party in the federal elections of 2017, winning 12.6 percent of the vote and being particularly strong in Thuringia, where it played a key role in the 2020 controversy over the election of a minister president. In 2021, the AfD fell to fourth place, with 10.3 percent. Much of the ire of the movement was directed against Muslim immigrants, who, in part, inherited some of the hostility toward Jews, although in a very different context.[51]

The Germans continue to confront the difficult task of making a coherent national history that has integrity.[52] However, to a greater degree than elsewhere, by far the foremost difficulty for this task arises from the past intentions, attitudes, and conduct of the nationals of the country itself.

FRANCE

Germany's wartime allies and collaborators also came to grips with the Holocaust, although often with considerable reluctance and only to a partial degree. This process was most contentious in France, where the Vichy legacy proved difficult to overcome, in part because of a determination not to accept the nation's role in the Holocaust and also because of the strength of the Gaullist myth about a powerful and unifying French Resistance. Moreover, aside from continuing active antisemitism in France, there was only limited governmental support for the restitution of goods and buildings seized from Jews or for indemnification.

The French role in the Holocaust was neglected both in the French account of the recent past and in the French treatment of Germany. Thus, at Nuremberg, François de Menthon, the French prosecutor, did not refer to the Holocaust, while, in France, prominent figures from Vichy were criticized and tried for treason but not for cooperation in mass murder. In Alain Resnais's 1955 documentary about the deportation, *Nuit et brouillard* (Night and fog), a film commissioned by the Comité d'Histoire de la 2e Guerre Mondiale with the support of the Ministry of Veterans' Affairs, the French licensing authorities censored a shot briefly showing the kepi of a French policeman among those guarding deportees who, furthermore, were not identified as Jews.[53] The film was also withdrawn from the Cannes Festival as a result of a formal protest to the French government by the German foreign ministry.

This process of denial was given added force by the search for assurance and prestige that finally culminated in the formation of the Fifth Republic in 1958 and the presidency of Charles de Gaulle from 1958 to 1969. His refusal to collaborate during the war was presented as the quintessential cause of the new France, and the fact that he was now president apparently vindicated the French of 1940–44 and, more generally, French history, as did the widespread exaggeration of the popularity and effectiveness of the wartime Resistance. This idea of a national resistance also held no particular place for Jews. In the Memorial to the Martyrs of the Deportation, inaugurated in 1962 in Paris by de Gaulle, there was no mention of the major role taken by Vichy. This remained the case for the information displayed at the entrance there in 2014. De Gaulle's attempt to create a collective memory involved sidestepping, indeed ignoring, many of the complexities of the war.

This situation was to change, in part because of developments specific to France itself, but in part due to both the greater weight that the Holocaust came to have in the collective Western consciousness and the less reverential approach to the past that was an aspect of the cultural changes of the 1960s. Scholarship played a role, particularly the book *Vichy France: Old Guard and New Order, 1940–1944* (1972), by the American Robert Paxton. In place of the presentation of Vichy and collaboration as something forced on France by the Germans, Paxton, by extensively employing German archival material (the French archives were closed to him), argued that the Vichy regime had been popular and also keen to collaborate in order to win German support for a reconfiguration of French society that was to mark the triumph of Vichy's antiliberal ideology. Similarly, in 2009, it was a foreign work that demonstrated how readily French artists and intellectuals had collaborated: Frederick Spotts's *The Shameful Peace: How French Artists and Intellectuals Survived the Nazi Occupation*. This book caused a furor in France.

Paxton's approach was unacceptable to many of those in academic authority in France, and there were difficulties in publishing a French translation of his book. Moreover, Marcel Ophuls's documentary about the occupation in Clermont-Ferrand, an industrial center near Vichy, *Le Chagrin et la pitié* (*The Sorrow and the Pity*), eventually released at the cinema in 1971, was not shown on French television until 1981. The government in 1969 had already banned the television transmission of this tale of collaboration, which, however, was shown that year on television in Germany, Switzerland, the Netherlands, and the United States. The lengthy documentary was largely based on interviews.

De Gaulle himself publicly indicated his critical view of Jews in a press conference on November 27, 1967, when he called them "a people sure of themselves and domineering." While this remark was a response to Israel's sweeping success over Egypt, Jordan, and Syria in the Six-Day War earlier that year, it was also all too indicative of the role of antisemitism in the unwillingness to face the French past. Similar remarks were to be made by prominent Belgian politicians in the 2000s.

Sympathetic postwar views about Vichy's wartime conduct continued to be expressed, as in François-Georges Dreyfus's *Histoire de Vichy* (1990), which presented itself as an assault on an anti-Vichy "vendetta" waged by Paxton and others. Dreyfus was later to criticize Chirac for recognizing Vichy's role in deportation. Nevertheless, growing interest in Vichy's complicity in the Holocaust and the less-deferential character of French society, especially after the unrest of May 1968, combined to provide a more conducive atmosphere for the pursuit of the truth by journalists, scholars, and others. Documentaries, films, memoirs, and novels were published, and Louis Malle's film *Lacombe, Lucien* (1975) created considerable controversy because it made fascism seem attractive and presented its French protagonist as working voluntarily for the

Gestapo.[54] Marcel Ophuls's documentary *Hotel Terminus: Klaus Barbie* (1988), about the brutal head of the Gestapo in Lyon from 1942 to 1944, won an Oscar.

Research by journalists also played a role. In October 1978, the news magazine *L'Express* published verbatim an interview with Louis Darquier de Pellepoix, who in 1942 had been appointed Vichy commissioner for Jewish affairs (thanks in large part to German support for this virulent antisemite). Darquier claimed in this interview that the Holocaust was a hoax and that only lice were gassed at Auschwitz, which provided the title for the interview, "In Auschwitz, They Only Gassed Lice." Darquier also claimed that the research by Serge Klarsfeld, a Holocaust survivor and president of the Association of Sons and Daughters of Jewish Deportees from France, and his wife Beate on the names of Jews deported from France was a "Jewish invention." Klarsfeld's research, which showed the large numbers deported, had been published that year as *Le Mémorial de la déportation des Juifs de France*. He recorded the names of each of the 75,000 Jews (51,000 foreign, 24,000 French) sent by train to the camps; only 2,500 returned.

This interview caused a sensation, with the National Assembly (parliament) debating it the following month. In part, there was anger that Darquier was living in Spain where, like many Nazis, he had been given refuge by Franco. Sentenced to death in France in absentia in 1947, Darquier had not been hunted down. Moreover, in 1978, he could not be extradited because his sentence, for collusion with the enemy (rather than for mass murder), had lapsed in 1968 as a result of the statute of limitations. In part, the anger rebounded more widely because Darquier himself drew attention to the more favorable fate of his wartime rival, René Bousquet, secretary-general to the Vichy French police in 1942–43. Bousquet had been able to stay in France and even to pursue a successful career despite having agreed to use French police to arrest Jews and having pressed for the deportation of foreign Jews to Eastern Europe.[55]

This interview and the resulting consideration of Bousquet's position helped encourage a sense that France had failed to address the issue of Vichy's complicity in the Holocaust, specifically rounding up Jews for deportation to Auschwitz. Further journalistic research provided fresh light on the same process. In 1981, the press first revealed the major role of Maurice Papon, wartime secretary-general at the Prefecture of the Gironde, in the deportation of Bordeaux's Jews. Postwar, Papon had become a government minister and a key member of the French establishment. As police chief of Paris under de Gaulle, he had also been responsible for the violent suppression of postwar demonstrations. In 1983, Klarsfeld emphasized the role of the Vichy authorities in his book *Vichy–Auschwitz*. In 1987, Klarsfeld acted as prosecuting counsel in the trial of Barbie, whom he described as the "butcher of Lyon." Five years later, Barbie's headquarters became the site of the Center for the History of the Resistance and Deportation.

Politics also played a major role, as scores were settled with those who could be tainted for their roles under Vichy. Most prominently, although only indirectly, these included François Mitterrand, president from 1981 until 1995. A civil servant under Vichy, Mitterrand was a friend of Bousquet, who was assassinated in Paris by Christian Didier, a pursuer of Vichy figures, in 1993, just before he could be tried for his role in rounding up Jewish children for deportation to slaughter in Germany.

Judicial proceedings further helped encourage interest and controversy, especially the capture and trial in 1994 of Paul Touvier, head of the collaborationist *Milice* in Lyon, and the trial, in 1997–98, of an unrepentant and aloof Papon. Evidence of the role of Vichy in the Holocaust was thus publicized. Robert Paxton gave evidence, a responsibility several French historians refused to accept.[56]

Aside from Mitterrand and his connections, there was also criticism of the wartime role of the French communists. Their general secretary, Georges Marcais, was accused of volunteering to work in Germany, while Serge Mosco's film *Des Terroristes à la retraite* (1985) claimed that in 1943 the communist leadership had deliberately committed the Jewish Resistance units to particularly hazardous operations and then betrayed them while claiming credit for their exploits. The Communist Party tried and failed to stop the film being shown on television.

In 2003, Kurt Schaechter took legal action against the SNCF, the state-owned rail company, for deporting his parents to Sobibor and Auschwitz, a symbolic case designed to highlight the range of responsibility. In 2009, the Conseil d'État recognized the responsibility of the Vichy government in the deportation of Jews. This ruling established, for the first time, a legal recognition of France's role, as the Conseil d'État accepted (correctly) that France had acted independently and not simply under pressure from the German authorities. At the same time, the Conseil d'État argued that postwar compensation was sufficient and that no more needed to be provided. However, in 2010, the SNCF expressed remorse for transporting Jews to German extermination and concentration camps. In part, this step was taken to ensure a better chance at obtaining well-paying contracts for high-speed rail lines in the United States. In 2011, this step was followed by a formal public apology directly to Holocaust victims, while the company handed the station of Bobigny over to local authorities in order to create a memorial to the Jews transported from there to the camps. In 2015, France approved an agreement with the United States to pay $60 million in compensation to foreign nationals who had been deported to extermination and concentration camps on French trains. Previously, French citizens who were victims had been paid $60 million under a 1946 scheme.

The Holocaust and its part in the debate about France's role in the war helped focus a more complex refashioning of the recent French past, creating a demand for the recognition of events and memories that had been ignored in the public account[57] and that were challenged by Holocaust deniers.[58] In 1994, Klarsfeld published *Le Mémorial des enfants juifs déportés de France.* On July 16, 1995, the anniversary of the major roundup of Jews in Paris in 1942, Jacques Chirac, Mitterrand's long-time opponent and eventual successor as president from 1995 until 2007, accepted national responsibility for the wartime treatment of Jews. This created pressure for a new public memory. It was a major condemnation of the Vichy regime and a step that Mitterrand had refused to take in 1992. Indeed, Papon had only been arrested after Mitterrand's death. The argument that Mitterrand had sought to make, maintaining the line of his predecessors, that the true France did not commit crimes, was shattered; it was also clear that there had been a considerable cover-up effort.

The responsibility was more seriously Mitterrand's than his predecessors because of the extent to which by the 1980s, and even more the 1990s, other governments were coming to grips with wartime collaboration and postwar moral cowardice, not to say, in many cases, complicity; in his refusal to accept collective responsibility, Mitterrand shared the attitudes of Kohl, his friend and political ally. Chirac, in contrast, referred to Holocaust denial as a crime against truth and a perversion of the soul, and he made July 16 a national day of mourning. In 2004, the French education ministry distributed to schools DVDs with excerpts of *Shoah* (1985), Claude Lanzmann's influential (and nine-and-a-half-hour-long) film about the Holocaust (in Eastern Europe, not France), as part of its attempt to combat antisemitism.[59] It was certainly a blow against French Holocaust deniers. The use of *La Shoah* in France to describe the Holocaust is a potent testimony to the impact of Lanzmann's work and, more generally, of film.

The weight of the past continued to play a major role in French politics. With the Right divided between the Gaullists and the far-Right National Front (FN), under Jean-Marie Le Pen, both struggled for appropriate historical references. The Gaullists argued that the National Front looked back to Vichy, and, indeed, it did make such references, not least in the 2002 presidential election, when the Vichy slogan "Work, Family, Country" was deployed. Le Pen, who came second to Chirac in that election, had been fined 1.2 million francs (£171,000) in 1987 for declaring in a radio interview that the Holocaust was a detail of history, an instance of his more general pattern of antisemitic and racist rhetoric. In 2009, Le Pen repeated the phrase in the European Parliament in Strasbourg: "I just said that the gas chambers were a detail of Second World War history, which is clear."

Marine Le Pen, who succeeded her father as head of the FN in 2011, offered a different historical focus, concentrating on immigration rather than World War II. She faced charges in 2014 for comparing the spillover of Islamic prayers into the streets to the Nazi occupation, an approach, implicitly criticizing Vichy, which to a degree dissociated her from her father's favor for Vichy and his association with antisemitism. A rift between the two over the latter became public later in 2014.

The relationship between past and present was at stake in France in 2004, when Chirac sought an appropriate context for a call to act against a rising wave of antisemitism and racism. He traveled to Le Chambon-sur-Lignon, a village in the Massif Central that had sheltered Jews from the Holocaust,[60] in order to declare: "Faced with the rise of intolerance, racism and anti-Semitism[,] . . . I ask the French to remember a still recent past. I tell them to remain faithful to the lessons of history, a so-recent history." Praising Chambon (a majority Protestant village where the Catholic Church is weak) as a model for modern France because its people had rejected "the infamy of the Vichy regime," Chirac linked a call for modern vigilance to a demand that the horrors of the past be understood. The Holocaust Memorial opened in Paris in 2005. Alongside Vichy, although as a lesser topic, German actions in France were also very much at issue. In 2006, Chirac praised the vindication a century earlier of Alfred Dreyfus, a Jewish army officer wrongly sentenced for treason amid much controversy and publicity in 1894. In 2007, in a major ceremony at the Panthéon in Paris, Chirac honored the Righteous of France, those who had helped Jews during the German occupation. Nikolas Sarkozy, president from 2007 to 2012, maintained Chirac's position as part of the stand of showing that the established Right was the appropriate custodian of the republican legacy, a point long contested by the Left. His successor, François Hollande (r. 2012–17), a Socialist, followed Chirac, not Mitterrand. In 2022, Emmanuel Macron (r. 2017–), delivering a speech at the Holocaust Memorial at Pithiviers train station, condemned the Vichy leaders for their role in the Holocaust as part of a broader attack on antisemitism and historical revisionism.

Aside from the politics, the Natzweiler-Struthof concentration camp in Alsace and the Gurs internment camp near the Pyrenees, from which Jews held in dire circumstances under Vichy were deported to the concentration camps, are particularly pointed reminders.

BELGIUM AND THE NETHERLANDS

Holocaust denial is currently a criminal offence in France (since 1990, the Gayssot Law), as it also is in Western Europe, in Austria, Belgium, Germany, the Netherlands, and Spain. In 2007, Belgian prime minister Guy Verhofstadt apologized in parliament for the role Belgian officials played in denouncing Jews to the Germans and/or deporting them. This was the first apology by a senior Belgian governmental figure in parliament, and it was an occasion that was different from the inauguration, in 1970, by then prime minister Gaston Eyskens, of the *Memorial National aux Martyrs Juifs*. Verhofstadt had, as prime minister, first apologized in

2002 at Malines/Mechelen—the deportation center and now the location of the Jewish Museum of Deportation and Resistance—and then, in 2005, at Yad Vashem in Jerusalem. His speech included the need for information on the Holocaust to be part of school education, although in Belgium, responsibility for this rests with regional rather than federal authorities.

In 2007, Verhofstadt also attended the unveiling in the *Mont des Arts*, in the center of Brussels, of memorial plaques to the "Just," non-Jews who helped Jews escape capture. The unveiling took place on May 8, the day that commemorates the end of World War II for Belgium. Verhofstadt paid tribute to the Just and argued that their contribution was a reminder of the need for tolerance at all times. As an instance of the manner in which the Holocaust could now conflate different forms of public memorialization, the town authorities agreed to name the path containing the plaques the "Alley of the Just"; the minister of defense, whose responsibilities include war victims, unveiled the plaques, one in French, the other in Flemish. The national anthem followed by the "Last Post" was played by a military band, and after a minute's silence, the European "anthem" from Beethoven's Ninth Symphony was played. Whether this was an appropriate choice, not so much because of Beethoven's national background as because of the European theme, is left to the reader to consider. All the Belgian radio stations put the ceremony as the first item on their lunchtime news programs.

In his speech, Verhofstadt noted that the Ceges (*Centre d'Etudes et de Documentation Guerre et Sociétés Contemporaines*) report, commissioned by the *Senat* in 2003, describing the role of the Belgian authorities during the Nazi occupation, had been received, and that it had described them as docile at best and with some directly collaborationist activities. The closing remarks of the report were that "the Belgian state had adopted a docile attitude in providing a collaboration unworthy of a democracy toward a policy that was disastrous for the Jewish population, both Belgian and foreign." In response, Verhofstadt announced an expansion of Holocaust compensation.

In 2002, the Buysse Commission was set up to work with Jewish representatives in Belgium in directly allocating public and private funds. In 2007, an additional fund was established to help those not covered by the original grant. In total, the Belgian government had already contributed to the establishment of a fund of 110 million euros for compensation for Holocaust sufferers.

The postwar conduct of the Dutch was shameful, with a callous indifference to returning Jews and a reluctance, until the mid-1960s, to acknowledge what had been done. It is instructive, however, that the Dutch have not shared a popular opprobrium for wartime conduct comparable to that of the French. The dockers' strike in Amsterdam in February 1941 on behalf of their fellow Jews gave the Netherlands a reputation for resistance to German demands, which until fairly recent times survived the true facts of widespread collaboration. Feelings of guilt may have played a role in Dutch support for Israel in the Arab-Israeli wars of 1967 and 1973 and were cited in 1973 as a reason by Bram Stemerdink, the minister of defense, who on his own authority decided to send missiles to Israel. Dutch public understanding of cooperation in the deportations essentially dated from the mid-1960s, particularly the publication of historian Jacob Presser's study *Ondergang* (1965). That year, but not earlier, the government offered to pay toward the Auschwitz Memorial. Only in 1995, however, did the monarch, Queen Beatrice, acknowledge the fate of Dutch Jews. This acknowledgment has been further advanced by the erection of statues, including that of a dock worker to commemorate the strike when the first arrests of Jewish men took place, and "Lotty's Bench," in 2017, to mark the poor treatment of Jews returning from the concentration camps. That was also the title of an important 2019 book by Gerben Post that looked at this memorialization. The Jewish theater from which many Jews were deported is now a monument. Also in 2019, the state-owned rail company Nederlandse Spoorwegen paid compensation for moving Jewish deportees by train, worth over E40 million (£35 million), to Holocaust survivors after resisting reparation demands for decades.

Consideration of Anne Frank is perhaps the most widespread way in which children in the United States, Britain, and elsewhere come into contact with the Holocaust. However, a survey of 2,000 Dutch people in December 2022 by the US-based Claims Conference found the Dutch worse for Holocaust denial than similar surveys in Austria, Britain, Canada, France, and the United States. In this survey, 32 percent of the Dutch born after 1980 did not know that Frank died in a concentration camp, while 23 percent said that the crimes of Nazi Germany were untrue or exaggerated, a percentage that fell to 12 for the Dutch people as a whole surveyed. Of the Dutch people surveyed, 29 percent believed that two million or fewer Jews were killed, a number that rose to 37 percent among those born after 1980.

ITALY

In Italy, the treatment of Jews, particularly after the antisemitic legis-lation of 1938,[61] was and is an issue in the contest over the reputation of Benito Mussolini and the debate over the popularity of the Fascist Republic of Salò in northern Italy in 1943–45. This issue also relates to that of the Italian position in the Balkans, part of which was occupied by Italian forces in 1941–43. As with other countries, postwar politics rapidly came to the fore and led to a determination to overcome the past. In this case, that meant excusing it. Thus, in 1946, there was a gen-eral amnesty for those charged with Fascist crimes, with very few war crimes trials and Fascist officials given posts in the new administration. In contrast, the communists emphasized the resistance to Germany and the Salò Republic, as they had been prominent in it. The rival Christian Democrats preferred to focus on the nineteenth-century *Risorgimento*, the struggle for national unification.[62]

A long-standing contest over the Italian past is directly linked to the legitimacy of current political groupings that look to the past for evidence of their probity and of the iniquity of their opponents. The Italian Social Movement (MSI), the Fascist Party, tried to break with its past in order to move from the political margins. As late as 1992, the MSI marked the seventieth anniversary of Mussolini's seizure of power by donning black shirts and giving the Fascist salute, but in 1994–95, the leader Gianfranco Fini changed the MSI into the more moderate Alleanza Nazionale (AN). This party sought acceptance, especially by rejecting antisemitism. A positive appraisal of Mussolini was offered by Silvio Berlusconi, the prime minister in 1994–95, 2001–6, and 2008–11, but was rejected by the Left. In 2023, on Holocaust Remembrance Day, Giorgia Meloni, the new prime minister who came from the AN, described the Holocaust as "the abyss of Humanity," criticized the 1938 racial laws passed by Mussolini, and pressed for efforts to combat all forms of antisemitism.

Serious questions have also been raised about the role of Eugenio Pacelli, Pope Pius XII (r. 1939–58), the wartime pope who has been accused of antisemitism and of failing to act against the Holocaust, not least in Rolf Hochhuth's 1963 play *Der Stellvertreter: Ein Christliches Trauerspiel* (The deputy, a Christian tragedy; published in English as *The Representative*). The pope has been criticized, more specifically, for failing to block the deportation of Jews from Rome, and also for his stance over the treatment of Jews in Croatia, France, and the Netherlands.[63]

Conversely, it has been claimed that communist misinformation played a role in such charges and that Pius XII was more sympathetic to Jews than is generally believed and also was active on their behalf.[64] In responding to the German treatment of Jews, the Catholic Church was certainly aware of the hostility to religious interests of communism, an atheistic movement. The Church, moreover, feared that criticism of the Germans would lead to problems for Catholics. Indeed, in May 1943, Dutch Jews baptized as Catholics were arrested and deported to their deaths by the Germans in response to a pastoral letter from the Dutch Catholic bishops opposing the deportation of Jews. In contrast, Protestant Jews were not deported.

The previous Christmas, 1942, the pope used his radio message to criticize the Final Solution, as he did again in June 1943, but, fearing an invasion of the Vatican City, he did not respond when the Germans rounded up Rome's Jews that October. Indeed, later that year, in response to German raids on Church properties in Rome, the Vatican instructed that only Jews who had been baptized as Catholics should be given shelter. Already in 1939, Pius had shown a failure to provide leadership when he said nothing about the German killing of Polish Catholic clergy. In his apologia of June 1945, the pope argued that his radio messages had been the sole effective means he had to influence German Catholics in the face of the power of evil. In practice, while concerned about the fate of Nazi victims, Pius emphasized diplomatic restraint in order to avoid even greater German violence, although, from the perspective of Jews and many others, this greater evil was already very present. Political considerations played a role in Vatican deliberations, including a wish to keep communism at bay.

The papacy, like other church authorities across Europe, did little to oppose the Holocaust by influencing either Germans or others—both those active in the Holocaust and those who did nothing—and this remains a serious moral failing. The extent to which the Holocaust was dependent on the cooperation of non-Germans, many of whom were Catholic, underlines the importance of this issue. Pius XII, for example, did not match the brave denunciations of Alojzije Stepinac, the archbishop of Zagreb in Croatia. The papacy failed to pass on in public denunciations the knowledge it had of the Holocaust and did not provide the leadership of the Church that the hierarchy, clergy, and laity needed and that some sought.[65] Foreign Protestant churches, while primarily concerned about the plight of coreligionists in Germany, were increasingly aware of the nature and immorality of Nazi antisemitism, but also did or said relatively little.[66]

Blaming Pius XII for not having done enough to criticize the Holocaust may be appropriate and fair (and not only in retrospect), and Pius would have been regarded as more heroic had he suffered detention as Pius VII did under Napoleon. Arguments may be made for Pius XII as pope, but he was a terrible Christian. His wartime role was at best prudent (but only in a narrow sense) or at worst truly appalling, and this was also true of many Catholic prelates, in Hungary, for example, and also many Catholic clerics in the United States, notably Father Charles Coughlin, a radio demagogue who blamed communism on Jews. Yet, alongside underlining the complexity in the relationship between Pius XII and Hitler, the Vatican, and the Nazis, it is necessary to underline the extent to which Church authorities outside Germany receive blame for something that individuals and secular institutions within that country were better placed to act against.

After the war, Pius XII devoted scant attention to the aftermath of the Holocaust as far as Jewish victims were concerned, while he was also not interested in improving relations between Christians and Jews.

Instead, he sought to ensure that no blame was attached to the German Church. An opponent of de-Nazification policies, Pius XII was keenly anticommunist. Moreover, even though he probably did not approve, elements of the Catholic Church helped German and Croatian war criminals to escape to Spain and South America, including Eichmann, Mengele, and Pavelić. It is not surprising that subsequent support for the beatification of Pius XII, the preliminary step to canonization as a saint, aroused much criticism.

In contrast, Pius's successor, John XXIII (r. 1958–63), favored a better relationship with Jews. This led to the Second Vatican Council's decision in 1965 to absolve Jews from responsibility for the death of Christ, a key thesis in Christian antisemitism. *Nostra Aetate*, the Declaration on the Relation of the Church with Non-Christian Religions, bluntly stated, "Whoever despises or persecutes this [Jewish] People does injury to the Catholic Church." Paul VI (r. 1963–78), who had served in the Vatican diplomatic service in wartime, was considerably less positive but did not reverse this step. Moreover, John Paul II (r. 1978–2005) was to call Jews the "elder brothers" of the Christians.

The rejection of the Second Vatican Council by Catholic traditionalists was motivated primarily by the opposition to its modernized liturgy. However, the movement drew on a strand of antisemitism, notably in France but also elsewhere, as with the American Holocaust denier Hutton Gibson, the father of the actor Mel Gibson. Monsignor Marcel Lefebvre, the superior general of the Spiritan missionary congregation, founded the "Priestly Confraternity of Pius X," which rejected many of the council's reforms. In 1976, he was suspended from the public exercise of his priestly and episcopal functions for forming this confraternity. Defying the suspension, Lefebvre consecrated bishops to carry on his work without the mandate of the pope, for which schismatic act he was excommunicated by John Paul II in 1988. The four bishops he had ordained were also excommunicated. In 2009, there was considerable controversy over the remission of these excommunications by Pope Benedict XVI (r. 2005–13), as one of the bishops, the British-born Richard Williamson, claimed that fewer than 300,000 Jews were killed in the Holocaust. Chancellor Merkel was unusually forthright in demanding an unambiguous clarification from the pope that there could be no Holocaust denial.

The controversy led to a renewed airing of long-standing contention over the wartime conduct of both the papacy and of traditionalist Catholics. Moreover, the particular issue of the German-born Pope Benedict's membership in the Hitler Youth caused controversy.

Less attention was devoted to Benedict's account of the Third Reich, which, in presenting the Germans as victims, neglected the role of complicity. At Auschwitz in 2006, Pope Benedict announced: "I come here as a son of that people over whom a ring of criminals rose to power by false promises of future greatness and the recovery of the nation's honor, prominence and property, but also through terror and intimidation, with the result that our people was used and abused as an instrument of their thirst for destruction and power."

His attitude, which matched a strand of German victimhood, contrasted with that of his Polish predecessor, John Paul II, who was more willing to address the questions of antisemitism and Catholic complicity.[67] However, before Pope Benedict visited the Yad Vashem Holocaust Memorial in Israel in 2009, he was pressed by its head, Avner Shalev, to include in his speech a reference to the memory of the Holocaust, and the pope indeed made a powerful denunciation stating that the act by the "godless" Nazi regime would never be forgotten or denied. He also laid a wreath on a stone covering the ashes of people killed in the Holocaust and met Holocaust survivors.

The Vatican was sufficiently affected by the greater centrality of the Holocaust in public discussion to take a role in the debate over Pius XII. In 1998, its Commission for Religious Relations with the Jews issued a defense of the pope in its report *We Remember: A Reflection on the Shoah*, but this was a one-sided approach to the evidence and less than convincing in its judgment. Five years later, the Vatican declassified archival material relating to Pius XII in an attempt to indicate his "great works of charity and assistance" toward those persecuted by the Nazis. In 2009, on his visit to Yad Vashem, Pope Benedict indicated that he did not wish to visit the museum exhibit accusing Pius XII of failing to act to save Jews from genocide. The caption there declared: "When the Jews were deported from Rome to Auschwitz, the Pope did not intervene." The Vatican lobbied to have the caption changed, claiming that Pius followed behind-the-scenes diplomacy to save Jews. Pope Benedict's support for the beatification of Pius was controversial. His successor, Francis (r. 2013–), opened the Vatican Secret Archives to scholars, visited Auschwitz II in 2016, and in 2022 emphasized the need never to repeat the "unspeakable cruelty" of the Holocaust and stressed the need to teach the young about the Holocaust.

EASTERN EUROPE

In Eastern Europe, communist totalitarianism was presented by the communists as very different from its Nazi rival, although in fact, there were many echoes, including the use of some of the same apparatuses of oppression.[68] For example, in East Germany, Sachsenhausen concentration camp was employed anew as a detention center, as was Mühlberg.

Communist criticism of the Nazi regime and its collaborators was often, in practice, matched by antisemitic policies. In its wartime propaganda, the Soviet Union downplayed the Holocaust, with Stalin redrafting war reports in order to direct attention from the extent to which Soviet victims of Nazi killing were Jews.[69] Stalin was acutely aware of how to play off ethnic rivalries as a divide-and-rule strategy to channel resentments away from coalescing into a potentially threatening anti-communist resistance bloc. Inserting Communist Party member Jews into high party and government positions was one method for accomplishing that. In part, antisemitic policies reflected attempts to ground communist governments in a populist nationalism and, in part, rifts within communist regimes—as a result of which Jewish communists, who had been influential, were widely purged.

In the Soviet Union, antisemitism in part was accepted as a way to cope with popular attitudes. This was particularly so with the impact on limited local housing of Jewish returnees, notably from central Asia, in formerly occupied areas, particularly Ukraine, where Kiev was freed from German occupation in late 1943.[70] A large number of Polish Jews had been deported to Soviet labor camps in 1939–41, and others who could had fled the Germans as they advanced in 1939 and 1941.[71]

Jews were presented as unpatriotic cosmopolitans, the wartime Jewish Anti-Fascist Committee was suppressed under Stalin in 1948, and its leaders were executed in 1952. In 1948, the Propaganda Department of the Central Committee of the Communist Party stopped the publication of *The Black Book of the Destruction of Soviet Jewry* and ordered all copies destroyed. There was a determination not to raise Jewish consciousness or consciousness about Jews.[72]

The satellite states followed suit. Zionism was a major charge against Jewish communists who were purged, but with a macabre twisting of truth, all too characteristic of both communists and Nazis, some Jews were accused of wartime collaboration with the enemy. Factions within the Communist Party used antisemitism and the charge of Zionism against rivals—for example, in East Germany and Romania and, very prominently, in the Slánský trial in Czechoslovakia in 1952, where there was a marked upsurge in antisemitic propaganda. Slánský, the Jewish general secretary of the party, was executed.

The following year, Soviet Jewish doctors were denounced in *Pravda* as a "Zionist terrorist gang," antisemitic attacks occurred in the Soviet Union, and it is possible that this crisis would have led to the deportation of Soviet Jews to the East, a distant Jewish homeland in the Jewish Autonomous Republic, Birobidzhan, which had been founded in the early 1930s in eastern Siberia. This deportation was but one of Stalin's fantasy schemes. Another was packing Soviet Jews into boxcars and running them off the rails and over the cliffs on the western shore of Lake Baikal into the lake itself.

Stalin's death cut short such ideas. However, the support shown to Israel by the United States from 1967 and, conversely, Soviet backing for Egypt, Syria, and pan-Arabism strengthened communist antisemitism. Indeed, in the bizarre world of Soviet propaganda, Zionists were accused of cooperating with the Holocaust in order to give birth to Israel.

In 1968, there was an antisemitic campaign in Poland as the Polish Communist Party (formally the Polish United Workers' Party) sought to dislodge Polish Jews from Poland. Many Polish Jews were compelled to emigrate. This campaign originated from tensions within the party; in the aftermath of Poland's de-Stalinizing moment in October 1956, when Wladyslaw Gomulka, who had a Jewish wife, came to power, there were several factions within the party that were dormant or semi-active at various points. Seeking to topple Gomulka, the faction headed by Mieczyslaw Moczar, the authoritarian and antisemitic minister of the interior from 1964 to 1968, attacked what he termed "the Zionist Infiltration."

Linked to the communism, antisemitism, and hostility to Israel that characterized governmental attitudes was a practice of downplaying the extent to which Nazi atrocities were aimed at Jews, a situation linked not only to antisemitism and politics but also to communist ideology in the shape of the treatment of religion as reactionary and because of the communist emphasis on a united Soviet struggle with fascism and victimization by it.[73] This downplaying was seen in the memorialization at the camps. For example, Auschwitz, which became the metonym for the Holocaust, was presented as a symbol of Polish resistance, with the communist nationalist account organizing and/or subsuming local, regional, nationalist, and Catholic narratives. Communist purposes extended to anti-imperialist displays in which the Germans were used to criticize US foreign policy. Jewish victims were not mentioned, and the museum there, on which work began in 1947 as a memorial to the "martyrdom of the Polish nation and other nations," was used to disseminate a communist view of events, which was also the case with the International Auschwitz Committee established in 1954. Polish and Soviet works made mention of the large numbers killed without identifying the fact that many were Jews. In part, this choice reflected the argument that communism, a movement that supposedly was axiomatically opposed to religious or racial prejudice, took precedence over other identities, so that in this light, Jews should not be treated as separate—but whereas churches were rebuilt in Poland, the effort did not extend to the synagogues and the ghettos.[74] At Sachsenhausen in East Germany, the Sachsenhausen National Memorial, inaugurated in 1961, was intended to symbolize the "victory of anti-Fascism over Fascism."

The Soviets rarely referred to the "Holocaust," preferring to mention the extermination or destruction of the civilian or peaceful population. Babi Yar was presented as the slaughter of "peaceful Soviet citizens," and the inscription there did not mention Jews.[75] Auschwitz I, not Auschwitz II, the site of the killing of most of the Jews, was for a while the only part of Auschwitz that could be visited. *The Historical Atlas of Poland* (1981) claimed that over six million Polish citizens were killed during the war, without giving a figure for the Jews. It also stated that in Auschwitz, four million people "of various nationalities" perished.[76] The Romanians and Czechoslovaks adopted a similar position, a stance encouraged by the extent to which these post-1945 states sought to be monoethnic and, to that end, adopted assimilating approaches toward Jews that in practice entailed denying their particular experience.

It would, however, be misleading to suggest that the communist period was one of unchanging indifference or even hostility. There were signs prior to the fall of the communist system—for example, in the early 1980s in Poland—of greater interest in Jewish perspectives, and there were efforts to bring academics together in order to find a basis for discussion.[77]

The fall of the Iron Curtain led to the publication of new sources from former communist states relating to the Holocaust. For example, the former ghetto in Kaunas had been bulldozed in 1964, leading to the discovery of the buried secret account of the history of the ghetto police written in 1942–43. News of it was suppressed by the Soviet authorities, and access only followed Lithuanian independence. In 1996, access to the relevant collections in the Romanian National Archives was granted to American and Israeli historians. Somewhat differently, the microfilm onto which his diaries had been copied at Goebbels's request in 1945 was discovered by a German historian in a Moscow archive in 1992 and published between 1993 and 2008. Photography also came to the fore, with opportunities to record the remains of a devastated culture.[78]

However, now the key emphasis in Eastern Europe was not on Nazi killings but on communist and Soviet oppression, replicating a tendency seen earlier among exiles. From the late 1940s, displaced non-Jews, many refugees from communism, were frequently antisemitic and angered by recognition of Jewish suffering.[79] The focus was encouraged by new revelations. For example, in Belarus, the mass graves at Kuropatny, where the Soviet NKVD (secret police) had slaughtered at least 100,000 people between 1937 and 1941, were exhumed from 1988,[80] reviving and popularizing Belarussian nationalism in the crucible of anger. As Eastern Europeans came to see themselves as victims of communist rule who had played no role in the regime (a largely misleading view), while communism was presented as a foreign ideology, the sufferings of others such as Jews were neglected. Moreover, the tendency seen earlier in the century to link communism with Jews, a tendency very much pushed by Nazi Germany and its allies, was revived in the 1990s, with antisemitism playing an explicit or implicit role in some populist nationalism. Furthermore, the long-held tendency to emphasize Christian victims of Nazi persecution as much as or more than their Jewish counterparts continued. This was seen, for example, in the contest between Catholic and Jewish interpretations of Auschwitz,[81] which had been visited by over twenty million people by 1997. The fall of the Iron Curtain was followed in Auschwitz's museum by an emphasis on the German killing of Poles. The tendency in Eastern Europe in the 1990s to think of societies as nations that were not pluralistic helped lead to Jews being largely ignored.[82]

Throughout Eastern Europe, there was also a reluctance or failure to acknowledge the degree of local complicity in the Holocaust.[83] Furthermore, in Bulgaria, Croatia, Hungary, Romania, and Slovakia, wartime regimes that had collaborated with Hitler received far more sympathetic attention than had been the case under the communists. Ion Antonescu, dictator of Romania from 1940 until 1944, had actively persecuted Jews and collaborated with Hitler, being executed for war crimes in 1946. However, in the 1990s, he was proclaimed as an anti-Soviet nationalist, and cities rushed to name streets after him. Antonescu was celebrated in 1994 by a large commemorative exhibit opened in the National Military Museum.

Although not seen as antisemitic, this process was an aspect of the expression of traditional themes that included antisemitism. Indeed, in 2003, an official government press release managed to state that no Holocaust occurred in Romania. International press criticism led to its retraction, and efforts to improve relations with the United States and Israel encouraged a change in policy. In 2004, the Romanian president, Ion Iliescu, made the first official acknowledgment of the country's role in the Holocaust. The previous year, he had established an international commission to report on the subject, which it did in 2004, making it clear that senior decisionmakers had been responsible for large-scale killing. Iliescu was an ex-communist, and it is unclear whether a right-wing leader would have made the same decision. Indeed, it is improbable, while Iliescu had scarcely been eager to take the step. It owed much to

Romania's determination to ground itself in the West, notably through membership in NATO and the European Union, a determination that had already led Romania to support the United States in its "war on terror." There was a similar process in neighboring Moldova in 2003. From 1998, the Romanian Ministry of Education sought to improve education about the Holocaust, a process also seen in Moldova where, in 2006, secondary school teachers were instructed to organize activities dedicated to Holocaust remembrance. In 2005, the Romanian government established the National Institute for the Study of the Holocaust in Romania and chose an official annual remembrance day: October 9. In 1941, this was the date on which the deportations of Jews from Bukovinia to Transnistria began. Nevertheless, monuments to the Jews slaughtered in Romania are largely invisible. Almost all are found in Jewish cemeteries and inside, or in the courtyard of, synagogues. They are thereby hidden from the non-Jewish population. Public spaces where Jews were killed are not marked by memorials.[84]

It was not only in Romania that the willingness to acknowledge the Holocaust was linked to politics. In 1996, when the Polish foreign minister apologized to the World Jewish Congress for antisemitism and the Kielce pogrom, the apology was by an ex-communist, Dariusz Rosati. Only in 2004 did the Polish president officially acknowledge that maltreatment by Poles was an aspect of the wartime devastation of Poland's Jews. This was followed in 2006, when President Lech Kaczynski joined Jewish leaders in breaking ground for the Museum of the History of Polish Jews in the heart of what was once the Warsaw ghetto. Opened in 2014, the museum has exhibits on the Holocaust, but its primary purpose is intended to be covering the large Jewish community that once flourished there. In addition, there are plans to build two memorials to Polish Christians who rescued Jews during the Holocaust. Nevertheless, there is evidence of a deliberate perpetuation of myths advanced by some Polish nationalists about Polish-Jewish relations, including an exaggeration of Jewish support for communism and a misleading marginalization of Polish antisemitism.[85]

In 2001, Hungary established a Holocaust Memorial Day, followed in 2002 with the Holocaust Memorial Center. As a reminder of the variety of national memories, the Hungarian Holocaust Memorial Day is

April 16, the date the Budapest ghetto was established in 1944. Subsequently, the government established a commission to commemorate the seventieth anniversary of the 1944 deportations and, in 2013, Tibor Navracsics, the deputy prime minister, declared that the Hungarian state had, in 1944, turned on its own Jewish citizens. Thus, he did not seek to shift the blame to the Germans, as many had done. On the other hand, there have been accusations of whitewashing wartime collaboration, while the government's treatment of Hungary's Roma (Gypsies) has been a matter of great controversy and has led critics to make references to the war. In the 2000s and 2010s, nationalist opposition politicians actively pushed antisemitic themes. The opposition Jobbik party, the "Movement for a Better Hungary," includes members who commemorate old blood libel accusations, claim Jews orchestrated World War II, and call the Holocaust the "Holoscam."[86]

In Lithuania, the process of exonerating anticommunists extended to include celebrations of "heroes" and "freedom fighters" who fought in and alongside the SS, such as Jonas Noreika: in 1991, Lithuania gave a general pardon to wartime collaborators, and the issue caused fresh controversy in 2023. The Third Reich had won considerable support among those who had been ruled by the Soviet Union since the Russian Civil War, particularly non-Russians,[87] and this made the issue of postcommunist commemoration and history more problematic and troubling. At the same time, there was and is a range of nationalist opposition to wartime cooperation with Germany and its subsequent extenuation, both politically and with reference to the Holocaust. Denial of the Holocaust is currently a criminal offence in Eastern Europe, in the Czech Republic, Lithuania, Poland, and Romania, but that is only a limited guide to the diverse complexity of public memory about World War II and its place in national historical narratives. Thus, in Lwów in the 1990s, far-Right Ukrainian nationalists freely expressed antisemitic sentiments: others had killed Jews in 1941. In 2015, state recognition was granted to pro-German Ukrainian nationalist militias that had killed Jews and Polish civilians before resisting the Soviet regime. From 2015, researchers and journalists are supposed to present "fighters for Ukrainian independence" as heroes.

The Holocaust is rarely mentioned in Ukraine. The wartime killings are largely attributed to Soviet hatred of the (Christian) Ukrainians, a matter in which the Poles (and Jews) became involved. The real victims are presented as the (Christian) Ukrainians, and the "real Holocaust" as the "Holodomor," the prewar famine in 1932–33 engineered by Stalin and the ruthless collectivization schemes in which several million peasants died. Coined in the 1970s, the term *Holodomor* clearly alluded to the Holocaust and implied that it was a genocide against the Ukrainian people.[88] Ukraine today is a fusion of prewar Soviet-held territory and territory annexed from Poland and Czechoslovakia in 1945. The Holodomor took place in the first, but the torch of grievance was taken up by the former Polish citizens who did not suffer it but who lived in a region where Jews were largely wiped out and their collective memory expunged.[89] The Holodomor has become a huge element of their history and culture. Expatriates in Canada and the United States are especially active in this process of remembering and commemorating. In Lithuania, some commentators have blamed "Judeo-Bolsheviks" for what they present as a Soviet genocide from 1944.[90] These views are also seen among émigrés.

Aside from tensions within countries, the Holocaust also became an issue between them, although less so than the more widespread pattern of occupations, killings, and forced movements that Eastern Europe experienced in the 1940s. Responsibility for actions was the main topic for debate—or, more usually, diatribe—but there was also dissension as to the national identity of the victims. In particular, wartime territorial divisions became an issue, as commentators strove simultaneously to inflate the number of their own victims and also to assert territorial interests. This dissension continues to this day, with Russia describing victims from areas seized by Stalin in 1939 (eastern Poland) and 1940 (Estonia, Latvia, Lithuania, and part of Romania) as "Soviet citizens." These areas, which were conquered by the Germans in 1941 and reconquered by the Soviets in 1944, indeed largely became part of the Soviet Union in 1945. Others reject this interpretation, and it became critical at Auschwitz, where the Polish government refused to permit Russia to reopen its exhibition unless it acknowledged the Polish viewpoint. This led to a war of words. Romania and Hungary offer clashing interpretations of the situation in Transylvania, which was transferred to Hungary in 1940 as a result of German pressure.

The determination of ex-communist states to win international acceptance, not least in order to provide a degree of protection against a resurgent Russia, led them to face, to some degree, the international significance of the Holocaust, particularly the significance in the United States, the key to NATO membership, and Western Europe, the key to European Union membership. This encouraged a symbolic process of apology. Thus, in 1995, Algirdas Brazauskas, the president of Lithuania, addressing the Knesset (Israeli parliament), publicly apologized for the Lithuanian role in the Holocaust. In Lithuania, where Soviet discrimination had been replaced, after independence, by a more overt antisemitism, there was a move to a less grudging official stance in the 2010s. In 2012, the government agreed to pay $50 million to the Jewish Heritage Foundation as compensation for unlawfully taken Jewish property and to pay $1 million to help destitute Holocaust survivors; 2013 was a memorial year to mark the seventieth anniversary of the destruction of the Vilnius ghetto.[91]

Attending memorials was a crucial mark of political finesse. In 2007, seeking to make all the correct gestures at a time of great sensitivity about memorialization, Estonian prime minister Andrus Ansip, to mark the anniversary of the end of World War II, attended ceremonies at a Holocaust memorial outside Tallinn, as well as at a cemetery commemorating soldiers who had died in Estonia fighting for the Soviets and the Germans, and at the recently and controversially moved monument to Red Army casualties in the war.

Discussion of the Holocaust was not only a question of memorialization in Eastern Europe, where, for example, cinema engaged with the Holocaust from the approach of history and memory.[92] Aside from the relevance of the Holocaust to continuing antisemitism against surviving Jewish communities, an issue made more pertinent by the large-scale active cooperation in the Holocaust displayed in Eastern Europe, there was the issue of ethnic violence and alleged genocide in Eastern Europe in the 1990s. The end of communism led to a major upsurge in national consciousness. This highlighted the role of ethnicity in national narratives and thus could lead to the underplaying of minority groups, including Jews, and/or the use of the Holocaust to validate these national narratives, with the particular sufferings of the Jews ignored or minimized.[93]

The use of ethnic considerations to advance nationalist territorial assertion and aggressiveness in the former Yugoslavia led to often-murderous ethnic cleansing, principally of Serbs by Croats, of Muslim Bosnians and Kosovars by Serbs, and to massacres in Bosnia.

These brought on Western intervention and, in support of this intervention, there were frequent direct references to the Holocaust on the "never again" theme. Indeed, an understanding of the grasp of visual images on the imagination led President Bill Clinton to press people to see the film *Schindler's List* (1993). There were also arguments that Bosnia was different from the Holocaust, not only because of the organized nature of the latter but also because Bosnia was more in the pattern of brutal ethnic cleansing.[94] This interpretation was contested by the argument that a systematic murder of Muslims that amounted to genocide was being carried out by the Bosnian Serbs.[95]

The need to legitimate German participation in the military intervention in Kosovo led Chancellor Schroeder to put the ethnic cleansing in the former Yugoslavia in the same category as the atrocities of the Third Reich. Although this may not have been his intention, Schroeder's approach implicitly relativized Nazi wartime misdeeds, providing opportunities for German expellee organizations to demand a greater public profile in the official narrative.[96] In 2015, Russia vetoed a British-drafted United Nations resolution condemning the 1995 Srebrenica massacre by Bosnian Serb forces of 8,000 Bosnian Muslims as a "crime of genocide." This would have been the first formal recognition by the UN Security Council that the worst atrocity in Europe since 1945 was an act of genocide. In turn, Vitaly Churkin, the Russian permanent representative to the United Nations, described the wording as "politically motivated," as if his response was not. In practice, the contrasts are far more apparent than the similarities, although these killings were in part in the pattern of violence in Yugoslavia in the 1940s.

Wartime collaboration with Germany was not only an issue in France and Eastern Europe, although in much of Europe, it has been downplayed as an issue. This has been true, for example, of collaboration by German allies, such as Finland, and by neutrals, such as Portugal, Spain, and Sweden. In Sweden, there is relatively little readiness to discuss why Sweden was not only not at war with Nazi Germany but, instead, willingly supplied militarily crucial goods. In that sense, there was active support for the system that made the Holocaust possible. Interestingly, detective fiction has served to direct attention to obscure corners of Swedish life, including wartime support for Germany. This support has been repeatedly linked in fiction to political extremism, corruption, and individual psychoses.

THE UNITED STATES

By the 1990s, the Holocaust was a key episode in US historical consciousness, although the relationship between this situation and the level of Holocaust denial is unclear. In 1993, a poll carried out by the Roper Center for Public Opinion Research suggested that nearly a quarter of Americans were unconvinced that six million Jews had been slaughtered. The opening of the Holocaust Memorial Museum in 1993, together with a series of news items, contributed to general Holocaust awareness. There was also the question of whether Nazis had taken refuge in the United States or elsewhere with US connivance. Ivan Demjanjuk, a Ukrainian who had become a US citizen, was accused of being "Ivan the Terrible," a feared guard at Treblinka. With considerable public interest in the case, his US citizenship was revoked and, in 1986, he was extradited to Israel, where he was convicted. In the event, the conviction was overturned by the Israeli Supreme Court in 1997, and Demjanjuk was released because, although he had probably been a guard at Sobibor, he was not the same Ivan he was accused of being. Also in the 1990s, pressure from the United States, notably class-action lawsuits, was crucial in forcing the Swiss to pay compensation for their wartime conduct.

Widespread interest in the Holocaust also served public purposes, including the continued moralization of US foreign policy. This focused on iterations of World War II, notably the theme of the "Greatest Generation," and whereas the Japanese attack on Pearl Harbor provided the moral grounding for the war in the Pacific, the Holocaust gave moral force and purpose in the war against Germany. This rationalization was an aspect of retrospective validation and the rewriting of the past because the Holocaust had not played a role in US policy during the conflict or in earlier public debate about the move toward confrontation with Germany in 1941. This retrospective justification was also seen with other powers. In part, it reflected the horror of the Holocaust, but the move away from state interest and geopolitics toward, instead, interventionist humanitarianism as an explanation judged sufficient for war also played a role.

The Holocaust as theme and justification was subdued in America immediately after the war itself and for over three decades thereafter. The Holocaust played a role within US public discussion in the late 1940s, especially in encouraging support for the foundation of Israel, which, in 1948, the United States was among the first to recognize de facto (de jure following in 1949). Nevertheless, the Holocaust was not a central subject or theme in recent history, neither for public education nor for reference in discussion. Nazi horrors were a subject for films, with Orson Welles's *The Stranger* (1946) including footage of the concentration camps. In it, Welles played Franz Kindler, an escaped Nazi crucial to the Holocaust using the cover of a New England teacher. At the same time, however, a toxic effect of the early stages of the Cold War was that US intelligence was recruiting Germans who had been involved in the Holocaust in order to acquire their experience against the Soviet Union.[97] Moreover, prior to the war, Hollywood had been reluctant to criticize the Nazi regime.

After the war, the Nazi issue came to the fore in George Stevens's film *The Diary of Anne Frank* (1959) and Stanley Kramer's *Judgment at Nuremberg* (1961), while Sidney Lumet's *The Pawnbroker* (1964) depicted a Holocaust survivor, but the Holocaust was not a major theme. Indeed, it was ignored in most US and British war films. As far as wartime horrors were concerned, the focus was on Japanese cruelty to American and British prisoners of war: for example, the Bataan Death March of American and Filipino prisoners in the Philippines in 1942 and the use of British (and other) prisoners to construct the Burma Railway in murderous conditions in 1942–43. The German atrocities that attracted attention were similarly focused on the United States and Britain, such as the massacre by SS troops of American prisoners near Malmédy in December 1944 during the Battle of the Bulge.

Moreover, the integration of Germany into Western defense structures encouraged American leaders to look more favorably on Germany.

Dwight Eisenhower, the supreme commander of the Allied Expeditionary Force who, in 1945, was much affected by his visit to Buchenwald, was in 1950 appointed NATO's first supreme commander with operational responsibility for its forces in Europe. In this role, he became more favorable to the wartime conduct of the *Wehrmacht*, declaring in 1951 that "the German soldier fought bravely and honorably for his homeland." The myth of a clean *Wehrmacht* was important to US public and popular culture during the Cold War,[98] and in the early stages of this political hostility, the Holocaust was a minor theme in US public consciousness. The popularity of the film *The Student Prince* (1954) reflected that accounts sympathetic to German culture worked well for US audiences with their troops then in West Germany. The extent to which Heidelberg was earlier a center of Nazi sympathy was, of course, ignored.

The situation changed from the 1970s, not least with six important television miniseries: *Holocaust* (1978), *Playing for Time* (1980), *The Wall* (1982), *Wallenberg: A Hero's Story* (1985), *Escape from Sobibor* (1987), and *War and Remembrance* (1988–89), a series that depicted Auschwitz and the Babi Yar massacres in Ukraine. It has been argued that "the Holocaust had become an effective moral catharsis for American viewers after the Vietnam war," not least because the Americans emerge by extension in a heroic and unproblematic light as opponents of the Nazis,[99] but that is overly reductionist and negative. It is also relevant, as with other countries, to consider national developments as, in part, an aspect of wider developments and to note the reevaluation across the West noted earlier in this chapter.

Marvin Chomsky's series *Holocaust*, which won a US audience of 120 million viewers, was particularly important, both for Jewish viewers, for whom it asserted, demonstrated, or underlined the centrality of the Holocaust, and for non-Jews. The use of a soap-opera format, focusing on a particular family in the four episodes—the fictional Weiss family of Berlin, most of whom are finally killed—helped make it more accessible. The series followed Chomsky's series *Roots* (1977), which had had a similar impact for African Americans. The *Holocaust* series also helped establish the term as the normal one in the United States.

Moreover, aside from the Holocaust, the Nazis came to play a greater role in Hollywood as an existential threat to humanity, one, moreover, in touch with occult forces and therefore anti-Christian, not least with Steven Spielberg's highly successful films *Raiders of the Lost Ark* (1981) and *Indiana Jones and the Last Crusade* (1989).[100] Neither film was Holocaust focused. A humorous tone was adopted with *The Producers* (1968), but the sinister nature of the Nazis was frequently reiterated, as in *Marathon Man* (1976). The film *Boys from Brazil* (1978) used Mengele to support its theme of the danger of a revived Third Reich. Albeit without Holocaust references, Nazi selective-breeding policies were important to the James Bond film *A View to a Kill* (1985). *Schindler's List* (1993) was a revolutionary event in Holocaust education. US high schools and universities paid to take students to the film or showed it, and when the film was re-released in 2018, there were free educational screenings. Many American students have studied the Holocaust and are aware of its general events, unlike in the 1980s. Yet a survey released in 2018 by the Conference on Jewish Material Claims against Germany found that many Americans believed the number of Jews killed in the Holocaust was "substantially less" than six million, and that about 45 percent of Americans, including 49 percent of millennials, could not name a single concentration camp.

A different strand of concern for Jewish issues came from American evangelical Christians. Much of this powerful constituency had been fairly antisemitic in the early twentieth century, but, in the last quarter of the century, it became actively pro-Israeli. In good part, this shift reflected the belief that the ingathering of the Jewish exiles to Israel would forward the "millennium," although this theological notion could be antisemitic, as some Christians believe that if Jews do not accept Christ as their Messiah on the Day of Judgment, they are condemned for eternity to damnation. A concern with Jewish causes was an aspect of evangelical Christian support for Israel. That Israel was a close ally of the United States from the late 1960s, replacing the marked tension between them in 1956–57 during and after the Suez Crisis, contributed to the same end, not least as many Americans felt isolated, particularly during and after the Vietnam War. That the Holocaust became more prominent in US public memory was an extraordinary departure, as it related to events in foreign countries that did not involve Americans as perpetrators or victims. As such, the only real comparison for Americans was with the New Testament account of suffering and fortitude: Jews and Jesus.[101]

This prominence, however, helped ensure that the Holocaust was drawn into America's culture wars. This was notably seen with claims by counterculture critics that the Holocaust was detracting attention from varied ills attributed to the United States, such as slavery, the Vietnam War, and the fate of the Native Americans. Claims that charges of genocide should be extended to these cases in US history were linked to the argument that a focus on the Holocaust thwarted such an extension.[102] A lack of comparability made this a poor case, and it was weakened further by the intemperance of the polemic and its lack of historical awareness. Alleged comparability between the Holocaust and the treatment of the Aborigines has proved a comparable issue in Australia. It was also argued in America and more widely that the Holocaust was deliberately used to divert criticism from Israel's occupation of Arab lands, especially from 1967—an unconvincing claim.

The United States has the largest number of Jews in the world, in large part due to emigration from the Russian Empire in the late nineteenth and early twentieth centuries. Indeed, a major geographical reordering of Jewry was a key consequence of the Holocaust and thus of its location as the working through of murderous, racially based nationalism.[103] The slaughter of about a third of the world's Jews meant a crucial shift in the distribution of Jews in proportional terms: from Europe to North America and Israel. Within Europe, the shift was to the margins: from Eastern and central Europe, notably Germany, Austria, Poland, and Hungary, to Britain and Russia. Postwar movements accentuated this tendency. The harsh or, at best, callous treatment of Jews after World War II, not only in Eastern Europe, especially Poland, but also in France, Belgium, and the Netherlands, encouraged further emigration to the United States, particularly after immigration restrictions eased with the passage of the Displaced Persons Act in 1948.

The Jewish community in the United States was reticent in drawing attention to the Holocaust or pressing for support for Israel in the late 1940s and 1950s, as it focused on integration and combating domestic antisemitism and also did not associate closely with the victim status of European Jewry. However, its attitude changed in the 1960s, not least as the Holocaust was increasingly incorporated into US consciousness. A growing activism on the part of American Jewry, which reflected the degree of their integration into US society as well as their confidence following Israeli victory in the Six-Day War of 1967, led not only to increased pressure on behalf of Israel but also to a focus on the Holocaust. This pressure and focus reflected major and insistent fears about the security of Israel, not least because the Six-Day War of 1967 was followed by renewed Arab pressure on Israel that culminated in the Arab attack in the Yom Kippur War of 1973.

The US Jewish community funded, and continues to fund, the establishment of Holocaust museums, memorials, lectures, and academic posts. This reflects not simply the relative wealth of American Jewry and its practice of generosity for public causes but also the extent to which, in the United States, it is possible for bodies other than the government to take such initiatives. Privately funded museums and academic posts are less prominent in Europe. As the Holocaust survivors in the United States died out, so there was a determination to erect museums, including one in Houston in 1996, as a different form of memorialization and one to serve both the Jewish community and the remainder of the population. The first US Holocaust museum, that in Los Angeles, was founded by Holocaust survivors in 1961 but gained its permanent home in 2010. At the same time, there is a variety of narratives. The National Museum of American Jewish History in Philadelphia, established in 1976, focuses on the experience of immigration and offers a memorialization very different from the Holocaust Museum in Washington, DC.

In 1995, at the time of the fiftieth anniversary of the end of the war, the emphasis was on filmed oral interviews. Concern about the loss of memory, alongside an awareness of the weight given to oral evidence, led to Steven Spielberg's support for what became the Survivors of the Shoah Foundation. Claude Lanzmann's lengthy film *Shoah* (1985) focused on interviews with those involved in the Holocaust, divided between Jewish survivors, Polish bystanders, and German perpetrators (who excused themselves as unaware of what happened). Filmed interviews were an instructive testimonial to late-twentieth-century public culture, as they brought together new technology with the authority of the participant and the determination to bear individual witness. As such, they were aspects of what has been termed the "memory boom."[104] Already from 1979, the Fortunoff Video Archive for Holocaust Testimonies, established at

Yale University, had been compiling lengthy interviews.[105] This contrasted with the reluctance among many surviving victims to discuss their traumas, a situation that did not change for some until the 1980s and 1990s.

Among the US Jewish community, memorialization of the Holocaust reflects collective mourning but is also a response to concerns about the challenges to Jewish identity in the liberal culture and society, both of the United States and of American Jewry. Thus, the Holocaust is seen as a cohesive experience of Jewishness and one that should serve as a living memory, even though most American Jews are not Holocaust survivors or their descendants.[106] Commemoration of the Holocaust also underlines an international quality to, and consciousness of, Jewishness that is under challenge from the powerful assimilationist tendencies in US society.

The theme is frequently one linking suffering to resistance, as with the New York memorial that reads, "This is the site for the American Memorial to the Heroes of the Warsaw Ghetto Battle April–May 1944 and to the six million Jews of Europe Murdered in the Cause of Human Liberty." The latter is an instructive phrase, as the killing reflected racial and (to a degree) religious hatred. The key issue was not human liberty as a political issue of democratic power but rather as the right to be of any race or religion. In Philadelphia, the monument to the Holocaust erected in 1964 declares "Now and Forever enshrined in memory are the six million Jewish Martyrs who perished in concentration camps, ghettos and gas chambers. In their deepest agony they clung to the image of Humanity, and their acts of resistance in the forests and ghettos redeemed the honor of man. Their suffering and heroism are forever branded upon our conscience and shall be remembered from generation to generation."

This account exaggerates the extent of resistance but is an assessment that was attractive in the 1960s. By the 2020s, with survivors and veterans dying, the Holocaust is a distant memory for most Americans, including Jews. The Holocaust itself has been so internationalized and universalized that the specific conditions associated with the slaughter of Jews has frequently been transmogrified into any atrocity on the world stage so that, despite the Holocaust museums and other aspects of public education, Holocaust awareness sometimes displays only limited awareness of the actual circumstances of the slaughter. Moreover, the position of Israel has for many observers been converted from David to Goliath, while concern about the victimization of African Americans in US history and the American present trumps that of Jews in wartime Europe.

The complexities of the American response to Jewish history, the Holocaust, and Israel were highlighted during the administrations of Barack Obama (2009–17). In 2009, in Cairo, in what was presented as his address to the Islamic world, he rejected the legitimacy of continued Israeli settlement construction in the occupied territories, a rejection in line with the criticism of the settlements by Obama's predecessors. Instead of stopping in Israel on his way home from Cairo, Obama visited the Buchenwald concentration camp in Germany before commemorating the sixty-fifth anniversary of D-Day. The focus on the Holocaust led many Israelis to fear that Obama did not appreciate their nation's biblical roots. By visiting Dresden as well as Buchenwald, Obama risked suggesting some sort of parallel. In turn, in 2013, on his first presidential visit to Israel, Obama endorsed the Israeli account and visited not only the Holocaust Memorial at Yad Vashem but also at the Israeli national cemetery at Mount Herzl the grave of Theodor Herzl, whose Zionist activities preceded the Holocaust. The continuing salience of the Holocaust was very differently shown in 2022 as George Santos, a Republican who won the New York Third Congressional district from Democrats, claimed to be Jewish and that his grandparents had survived the Holocaust as Ukrainian-born Jews who fled to Brazil. In fact, there is no proof, and it is clear that he misrepresented his heritage.

Holocaust diminishment in America takes the forms seen elsewhere, including attempts to erase the specificity of the Jewish experience, to universalize the Holocaust, and to find a Christian meaning in it. There are also deniers, while antisemites in America, as elsewhere, may view the Holocaust as a failure rather than deny it ever happened. "The Jews Will Not Replace Us" was the mantra of some of the neo-Nazi torch-carrying White supremacist demonstrators in Charlottesville in 2017; some blamed Jews for COVID-19. The *Daily Stormer* website is virulently antisemitic, and there is a popular narrative that is anti-Israel.

AUSTRALASIA

In Australia, institutions and museums were established by Holocaust survivors or their children in response to the rise of Holocaust denial in the 1980s. Among the Australian Jewish population, the percentage who were Holocaust survivors was higher than anywhere, bar Israel. The Jewish Holocaust Museum and Research Centre in Melbourne, established in 1984, was followed by the Holocaust Institute of Western Australia in Perth in 1990 and the Sydney Jewish Museum in 1992. A survivor guide at the Melbourne museum explains the role of David Irving: "Getting older, we became aware that our Voices can't be heard forever. The Irving interview was a turning point for me. I thought to myself, I am still alive and he tells me there was no Auschwitz. A lot of people reacted to that. A lot of survivors rang up the Holocaust Centre, wanting to deposit their memories, where before they couldn't talk about it. Since then I made it my policy to talk at forums when I am asked to."

These museums operate not solely for the Jewish community but also more generally, being used, for example, as part of student assignments.[107] The understanding of the Holocaust has parallels with that in the United States, with emphasis on the success of the Jews who escaped it by settling in Australia alongside some criticism of the Australian government of the 1930s for not allowing in more Jewish refugees. As elsewhere, trials of those involved in Nazi atrocities increased public consciousness. In Australia, this was the case with the War Crimes Act trial of Nikolay Beresvsky in 1992, a trial that had a symbolic political role in underlining Australia's multicultural identity. Sensitivity increased. Thus, Tony Abbott, the Australian prime minister, was obliged to apologize in February 2015 when he claimed that the previous Labor government was to blame for a "holocaust" of job losses in the defense sector. The following month, he withdrew a reference in Parliament to the Labor Party leader, Bill Shorten, as "the Dr. Goebbels of economic policy." His remark led to a parliamentary row in which Michael Danby, a Labor MP who is Jewish, walked out, remarking that it was "silly to use an example of the ultimate evil in politics."[108]

In New Zealand, the pattern of commemoration was similar to that in other major centers of Jewish activity in the Anglo-Saxon world and in Israel: in other words, there was a time lag. There have been no distinctive initiatives in New Zealand. In 2007, the Wellington Holocaust Research and Education Centre, which aimed to collect and record the accounts of Holocaust survivors who fled Europe and came to New Zealand, was opened by the representative of the head of state, Governor General Anand Satyanad. The legacy of Holocaust survivors also emerged in a volume produced in 2003, *Mixed Blessings: New Zealand Children of Holocaust Survivors Remember.*[109]

In Britain, the pattern of public attention also followed similar contours to those elsewhere in the Anglo-Saxon world. However, there was the addition of the powerful irritant of the British Mandate in Palestine until 1948, which exposed the British authorities there to violent pressure for decolonization from both Jews and Arabs. Moreover, although very much a minority opinion, there was a strain of fascism in British society that, under the malign inspiration of Oswald Mosley, peddled Holocaust denial.[110] The National Front had an average vote of 3.3 percent for the fifty-four constituencies it contested in February 1974, but by 1983, this had dropped to just over 1 percent for fifty-eight constituencies, and the party did not take part in the 1987 general election. Antisemitism, however, had a broader basis in Britain, albeit one smaller than across most of continental Europe.

The Holocaust became more prominent as a theme in Britain from the 1970s and, particularly, from the 1990s. The Jewish community in Britain played an important role, but Holocaust consciousness was much wider in its context and impact. Concern about World War II criminals led Canada, Australia, and Britain to pass legislation in 1987, 1989, and 1991, respectively, that would enable their prosecution for crimes committed abroad and long ago. Margaret Thatcher supported the legislation, which arose from an inquiry commissioned by the government in 1988 that produced the Hetherington Report. An active All Party Parliamentary War Crimes Group investigated a number of issues. For example, in 2002–3, it forced the reexamination of files and urged the prosecution of British citizens, formerly Ukrainian by inclination or nationality but

Polish by birth, for war crimes committed while members of the Four-
teenth Galician Waffen SS Division and other units. Attention was also
devoted to the Channel Isles, the sole part of the United Kingdom to be
occupied by German forces. Some of the local administrators prepared
a list of the Jewish or part-Jewish population and cooperated in their
subsequent roundup and deportation to concentration camps, which led
to discussion of what would have happened had mainland Britain been
successfully invaded.[111]

Holocaust consciousness was an important aspect of the rise of individual memory and the individual story seen, for example, in television
stories and newspaper articles such as "The New Anne Frank," a long article about the journal of Rutka Laskier, a Holocaust victim from Poland,
published in the *Sunday Times* of June 17, 2007. The piece owed much
to the voice offered by Rutka's half-sister, the daughter of her father (he
survived Auschwitz and later remarried). Number seven on Amazon's
top ten was then Ruth Kluger's *Landscapes of Memory: A Holocaust Girl-
hood Remembered.*

Aside from the key influence of Hollywood, the centralized character of the British educational curriculum was important, with Nazi Germany and the Holocaust being a major subject in the teaching of history,
although this led to complaints from Muslim bodies in the 2010s. Nevertheless, the Holocaust retained this status in the national curriculum
for history when it was revised in 2013. The central role of the Holocaust
was indicated by the cynical discussion of how best to teach it in Alan
Bennett's iconic play *The History Boys* (2004), which in 2014 was voted
the "Nation's Favourite Play" in a poll undertaken for English Touring
Theatre. The prominence of the Holocaust in Britain has been indicated
in many ways. For example, Studylink, which provides group travels for
students, put a photograph of Auschwitz on the front cover of a leaflet
distributed in 2007 without feeling it necessary to explain what it was.
As the leaflet included trips to World War I battlefield sites and D-Day
landing sites, the choice of illustration was indicative. Visits under the
Berlin headline included to the "House of Wannsee Conference" and to
Sachsenhausen concentration camp and, under Cracow, to Auschwitz-
Birkenau, the wartime ghetto, and Schindler's factory. More generally,
in Britain and elsewhere, the Holocaust became the key foreign and

global locator of a world war that was otherwise presented essentially as a national narrative, focusing, in the case of Britain, on Dunkirk, the Battle of Britain, the Blitz, and D-Day.

Holocaust awareness in Britain was underlined by active engagement by the BBC, with major television series, especially *The Nazis: A Warning from History* (1997), which was subsequently sold to over thirty countries, and *Auschwitz: The Nazis and the "Final Solution"* (2005), which was produced for the BBC and the US Public Broadcasting System and transmitted in over a dozen countries. The sensitivity of apparently antisemitic references to the Holocaust was indicated in 2005 when the left-wing mayor of London, Ken Livingstone, compared a critical Jewish journalist to a concentration-camp guard, a remark similar to that made in 2003 to MEP Martin Schulz by Silvio Berlusconi, then Italian prime minister, leading, in each case, to much controversy—as did allegations of antisemitism focused on Labour under the leadership in 2015–20 of Jeremy Corbyn. In 2023, there was a controversy when Gary Lineker, the lead BBC football commentator, compared the language used to launch a new government asylum policy with that of Nazi Germany, a case of Holocaust diminishment that he tried to dodge by referring to free speech criteria.

Government support was important for the designation in Britain of Holocaust Memorial Day, held on January 27, the anniversary of the liberation of Auschwitz-Birkenau.[112] In 2015, on a state visit to Germany, Queen Elizabeth II visited the concentration camp at Bergen-Belsen, a visit that received much sympathetic attention in Britain. A large and impressive exhibit was opened in 2021 in the Imperial War Museum, while a "temporary" Holocaust Education Centre opened in Victoria Tower Gardens by Parliament in 2015. The following year, Prime Minister David Cameron announced that a national memorial and permanent underground learning center would be built there "to show the importance Britain places on preserving the memory of the Holocaust." The High Court, however, ruled in April 2022 that the planning decision was unlawful in that its siting was in the wrong place and the planning process had overlooked this. There had indeed been much controversy over the location, with the Jewish community divided over the site, many preferring it to the Imperial War Museum site. In turn, in 2022, however, the new prime minister, Rishi Sunak, wrote to the Conservative Friends of Israel: "It is important that the Memorial is built in Victoria Tower Gardens as soon as possible—a fitting memorial that will send a powerful signal of the importance that we attach to remembering the Holocaust and learning the lessons of the past."

In Britain, the Holocaust Educational Trust, founded in 1988, spreads knowledge not only in order to increase knowledge of the Holocaust but also because the Holocaust is seen as more generally directly applicable for today and the future. The highly effective Trust seeks to inform teachers and also takes large numbers of schoolchildren (and others) to Auschwitz on the "Lessons from Auschwitz" project, which has won the support of the British government.[113] The Trust's program has also helped increase sensitivity to genocide in the modern world, such as in Darfur, where the genocide of Black Muslims by Arab Muslims from the 2000s has also been of concern to American Jews, including director Steven Spielberg. Israel is visited by some of the Trust's tours.

Scholarship was part of the trend emphasizing the Holocaust, with it increasingly present as a theme in the history not just of Germany but also of the world. For example, two of the thirty-one chapters in the *Companion to Europe 1900–1945*, part of what is intended to be the definitive series Blackwell Companions to European History, are devoted to the Holocaust, one of which, by Harold Marcuse, "Memories of World War II and the Holocaust," argues that an internationalization of recollection both decontextualized and universalized the experience of World War II.[114]

The memorialization of the Holocaust has been strongest in Israel, where it is known in Hebrew as the *Shoah* (catastrophe), although there is a stronger current of emphasis on the history of Israel, in part thanks to the collective identity represented by conscription. While diaspora Jews have claimed and do claim the Holocaust as a moral and historical justification for the creation of the state of Israel, that claim was originally rejected in Israel. Zionists know that the dreams, efforts, and moral and historic justifications for a Jewish state long preceded the Holocaust.

Indeed, the Holocaust was not as central in Israeli histories of Israel in the founding generation as it has become since the 1980s. Even today, there is a stronger recognition in Israel (compared to the diaspora) that Israel is not a product of the Holocaust (historically) and does not need to refer to the Holocaust to justify its existence (morally). Instead, the primary justification for most Israeli Jews is still Jewish nationhood. In this respect, Israelis' historical and moral justification for their state is essentially that of other nationalities. The Holocaust is incorporated into this narrative by being seen as a warning about the consequences of defeat and the need for Israeli Jews to embrace self-defense and self-reliance and also as a call for Jewish nationalism, given that diaspora Jews who rejected Zionism could not practice self-defense.[115] Aside also from addressing the powerful need to remember, memorializing the Holocaust helped to underline a commonality of experience. This was important because the creation of Israeli identity faced serious challenges, as the different sources of Jewish immigrants had had extremely varied experiences and challenges. In response, although the Zionist ideology and practice were already strong prior to the war, the Holocaust played a central role in Israeli self-identification, not least with the establishment in 1953 of Yad Vashem in Jerusalem as "The Memorial Authority for the Holocaust and Heroism," a Holocaust memorial, museum, and archive. It became a spiritual home of Holocaust remembrance, although, of course, it was not a Holocaust site nor in the lands where the Holocaust took place. Yad Vashem, in part, thus represented an assertion of the role of the Holocaust as a living Jewish memory separate from the sites of killing in Eastern Europe. A new museum for Holocaust history was opened in Yad Vashem in 2005.

In 1953, all Jews killed in the Holocaust were granted "memorial citizenship" in Israel. Israel itself was presented as the safeguard against there being another Holocaust, as it was to be the safe haven of all Jews and a land in which, under the "law of return," all Jews could become citizens. This right owes something to the Holocaust but more to a common feature of nationalism, as most countries have a similar law about those seen as nationals.

The sense of a safe haven was appealed to by Ariel Sharon, Israel's prime minister, when, in 2004, in response to antisemitic outrages in

France, he called for French Jews to emigrate to Israel. This call was repeated in 2015, to the anger of the French government, by Binyamin Netanyahu, the prime minister, in response to antisemitic terrorist murders
in Paris. The outrages were committed by French Arabs who, as a group,
had little interest in the right-wing French extremism that had concerned
earlier Jewish commentators, still less in the legacy of Vichy. Sharon
was reflecting a more widespread theme of the diaspora—specifically,
Europe as the site of *Shoah* and Israel as the land of rebirth but one that
requires continued vigilance to ensure its protection. As a subtext, Israel
was also seen as a protection against the destruction of Jewish ethnicity
and religion through assimilation.

Presented as a moral and historical justification for the state's founding and survival, the Holocaust helped Israel win international sympathy
and support. This was particularly the case with the United States, both
from Jews and, even more significantly, from non-Jews, and with West
Germany, which, aside from diplomatic support and financial compensation, sold Israel munitions, including tanks, although also funding pro-
Palestinian organizations in Israel.[116] Netanyahu claimed in 1998 that "if
the state of Israel had not been founded after the Holocaust, the Jewish
future would have been imperiled" because it would have been more difficult to win US support. Indeed, fifty years earlier, Chaim Weizmann,
head of the World Zionist Organization and soon-to-be first president of
Israel, was able to write to US president Harry S. Truman: "The choice
for our people, Mr. President, is between statehood and extermination."
In 1948, this was certainly not true of world Jewry, but in the face of Arab
pressure, it seemed true for Israel's Jews.

More to the point, it was an appeal that was difficult to reject in
the aftermath of the Holocaust, although the aftermath led Britain,
determined to maintain strict limits on Jewish migration to Palestine,
into confrontation and conflict with the Zionist movement, which accused the British government of failing to provide succor to Holocaust
refugees. The British government was concerned that such immigration
would lead to a violent Arab response that would destabilize Palestine.
Jews trying to reach Palestine were intercepted by the Royal Navy, detained, and interned in Cyprus, then a British colony. The British presence in Palestine was brought to an end in 1948, with the government,

financially exhausted and abandoning some major imperial positions, keen to get the problem of containing tensions between Arabs and Jews off its hands. The United Nations (UN), the successor to the League of Nations under which Britain had held Palestine, took over the decision about its future and decided in 1947 to divide the land between Arabs and Jews, which was what the British had recommended doing before the Holocaust and what Britain was doing in India: partitioning the land into India and Pakistan. Thus, partition, which led the UN to decide on a Palestinian state that was in practice partitioned, largely by Jordan, as well as a Jewish one, was not dependent on the Holocaust. Preventing and then settling conflict in Palestine was the UN goal, not creating an Israel that, among other facets, could help absorb a lot of European Jews who were refugees in Europe.[117]

In the Israeli context, the Holocaust was given a distinctive historical background. The theme of Jews fighting back linked the brave (but doomed) defense of Masada against the Romans in CE 73 to the Warsaw ghetto rising in 1943. This theme sought to counter the feeling, not least in Israel, where there was criticism among Zionists from the diaspora,[118] that, due to passive acquiescence, not enough had been done to resist the Holocaust and that the Jews, and therefore Israelis, appeared in some fashion weak. In 1948–49, the establishment of Israel as an independent state was contested by attacks from much of the Arab world, so the threat of genocide appeared an urgent one in underlining the need to fight back. Holocaust Day, designated in 1959, marks the anniversary of the 1943 Warsaw ghetto rising. It is actually Remembrance Day for the Holocaust and Heroism, and this name reflects the stress on the need to fight back that is seen as crucial to Israeli society. This emphasis is also presented in the Yad Vashem museum, where armed resistance to Nazism is presented as an exemplary episode. On Remembrance Day for the Holocaust and Heroism, two minutes of silence are observed at ten a.m., and traffic stops. The date, April 19 (10 Telvet), links a national memorial occasion joining the Holocaust to modern Israel to a traditional religious day of mourning for the beginning of the destructive siege of Jerusalem by Nebuchadnezzar of Babylon in 588 BCE. This connection was part of the process of relating Jewish cultural continuity to the national identity and calendar. The Chief Rabbinate of Israel has chosen to observe the day as a general mourning day for Holocaust victims whose dates of death are unknown. In doing so, the day is provided with a range of meanings related to particular groups in Israeli society, notably the more secular and the religious: those whose emphasis is on the national community and those more concerned with Jewish identity.[119]

The seizure of Adolf Eichmann in Argentina by Israeli agents in 1960, and his subsequent trial and execution in Israel in 1961–62,[120] was a key moment in maintaining Holocaust consciousness as an active principle. The trial was extensively reported across much of the world, including on US television, and this broadcast the testimony offered by Holocaust survivors. The Holocaust also underlined the hostility in Israeli society and culture to what could be seen as, or associated with, German antisemitism, particularly the music of Richard Wagner and Richard Strauss, both of whom were antisemitic and whose music was favored by the Nazis, with Hitler particularly keen on that of Wagner.

The extendable meaning of the Holocaust was indicated when what had been a specific historical episode was also used as a symbol of the travails of the Jews through history. As far as Israel was concerned, this ensured that an account of the Holocaust that had most meaning for the large numbers of Jews who had emigrated there as refugees from Europe in the late 1940s, and who had played a key role in Israel's early history, could also be a crucial identifier for the large number of Jewish refugees from Muslim countries who became proportionately more important in the 1970s and 1980s.[121] Similarly, in France, the large number of Jewish immigrants from the former colonies of Morocco, Algeria, and Tunisia who arrived in the 1960s absorbed the travails of the Jews of metropolitan France during the Vichy years as an aspect of their history. Israeli pressure on behalf of persecuted foreign communities of Jews, such as those of Ethiopia, reflected not only the traditional obligation and practice of helping fellow Jews notably in distress but also the impact of Holocaust consciousness. There is not a contrast between diaspora and Israeli consciousness and identity comparable to that between the Armenian diaspora and the Republic of Armenia: the commemoration of the Armenian massacres of 1915 has proved more significant for the diaspora than for the republic.[122]

THE ISLAMIC WORLD

Partly as a result of the role of the Holocaust in Israeli consciousness and international support, but more generally reflecting the persistence of antisemitism, there is also a tradition of Holocaust denial or minimization, one intended to lessen what is seen as the consequences of the Holocaust in terms of support for Israel. To Arabs, the Holocaust has been employed to give historical and moral justification for the state of Israel. Indeed, although there is enormous variety, many Europeans present this historical narrative—namely that, whatever the longer-term background, the Jews have been granted statehood by the nations because of the Holocaust. In contrast, a majority of Israelis and Americans justify the state of Israel on the grounds of Jewish nationhood.

A variant on the former view is the claim that the Palestinians similarly suffered a holocaust. In the Arab-Israeli war of 1948–49, there were certainly, on both sides, murderous actions designed, more generally, to drive away members of the other community. These included the massacre of 254 Arabs at Dir Yassin on April 9–10, 1948, by the Lohamey Herut Yisrael (Fighters for the Liberation of Israel; Stern Gang to the British). However, aside from the degree to which both sides carried out massacres—and there is controversy about some of the latter, including Dir Yassin—neither the overall circumstances nor the scale in any way correspond to the Holocaust. Arab commentators who argue some sort of equivalence are following post-1945 German Nazis, who also drew attention to Dir Yassin by way of trying to argue that the Jews would be murderous given the chance, and that this somehow justified wartime Nazi policy. The difference in scale and intentionality makes such a comparison pointless. Some Arab commentators accept that there was a Holocaust devastating European Jewry but question why the consequences had to include the establishment of the state of Israel. In short, they present the Palestinians as victims, not only of Israel and the United States but also, more tenuously and at one remove, of Hitler.

As an aspect of widespread paranoia, a key Muslim theme of victimhood focused in the 2000s on the allegedly malign goals of a Jewish conspiracy directing US foreign policy, and much else, in pursuit of Israeli goals. In specific terms, the terrorist attacks of September 11, 2001, are frequently blamed on Israeli intelligence or held to be fabrications. Much of this violent paranoia is reminiscent of Nazi rhetoric, and, as with the Nazis, it is appropriate to take what is said as a serious indication of dangerous beliefs and absurd assumptions instead of treating it as a meaningless rant or one that is not central to intentionality. In both cases, there is also a hysterical tendency to blame problems on others and to see no agency in oneself for working to understand and improve the situation, other than the supposedly redemptive use of violence in a Manichean context in which right and wrong are clearly differentiated and necessarily opposed in a struggle for existence.

A Holocaust denier, a position he presented as centrally related to opposition to Israel and the West, Mahmoud Ahmadinejad was president of Iran from 2005 to 2013. He came in a tradition of Muslim leaders downplaying the Holocaust, although there are exceptions. Arab nationalists tended to view Hitler and Mussolini favorably because they shared an opposition to the Anglo-French dominance of the Middle East, which had gathered pace from the 1880s. The most prominent Arab supporter of Hitler was Hadj Amin ei-Husseini, the mufti of Jerusalem, a religious official who had played a key role in the Arab revolt in Palestine in 1936–39, a movement against Jewish immigration. He became a German propagandist, raised Arab troops for German service, and was assured in person by Hitler on November 28, 1941, that Arabs and Germans were joined in friendship by antisemitism and that the Germans would seek the annihilation of the Jews in the Middle East. As a result of genocide within Europe and conquest outside it, the Germans would block any Jewish homeland in Palestine. The pro-German prime minister of Iraq Rashid Ali ei-Ghalani, who was overthrown by the British in May 1941, supported antisemitic policies and was responsible for fomenting several days of anti-Jewish rioting in Baghdad that led to many Iraqi Jews being massacred. Rashid fled, eventually to Germany, where he was a major propagandist for the Nazis. He returned to Iraq after the pro-British monarchy was overthrown in 1958 in a left-wing nationalist coup.[123]

One of the reasons why Arab public figures tend to downplay the Holocaust and even deny it is that admitting the Holocaust happened as it did is tantamount, in their eyes, to granting legitimacy to European Jews (thought of as European colonizers), before the war and after, emigrating to Mandate Palestine, later Israel. More generally, the Arab presentation of European history is quite different from that of most Europeans. Given the prevalence of rabid antisemitism in the television and literature of Muslim countries—for example, in Egypt and Syria—as well as in the comments of some Muslim clerics, it is scarcely surprising that many have been unreceptive to films about the Holocaust. Malaysia, for example, was not alone in banning *Schindler's List*. There is no comparison in Muslim public treatment of the Holocaust to the complexity offered by the film *Don't Touch My Holocaust* (1994), by the Israeli filmmaker Asher Tlalim, with its consideration of Israeli and other responses.[124] In contrast, Egyptian television programs frequently deploy crude antisemitic themes. Moreover, in Western Europe—for example, in Britain—Muslim communities have also showed themselves reluctant to participate in public and interdenominational commemorations of the Holocaust. This remains a problem, and in 2015, David Cameron, the British prime minister, referred in a speech to the toxic character of antisemitic Islamism.

Mahmoud Abbas from 1968 was part of the ruling circle of the Palestine Liberation Organization, becoming its chairman in 2004. In 2005, he became president of the Palestinian National Authority. In 1982, Abbas received his PhD from Moscow State University for a dissertation published in 1983, titled "The Other Side: The Secret Relationship between Nazism and Zionism." It challenged the estimate of the number of victims and argued that Zionists had cooperated with the Nazis in order to ensure Jewish emigration to Palestine. However, in 2014, Abbas denounced the Holocaust as a "heinous crime."[125]

In 2005, Ahmadinejad, a millenarian who seeks an anti-Western pan-Islamism, referred to the Holocaust as a "fairy tale" serving Israeli ends. In 2006, he presided over a conference in Tehran held to examine "the myth of the Holocaust." This conference, the luminaries of which included David Duke, a discredited leader of the racist American Ku Klux Klan movement, received a lot of critical attention in the West, and deservedly so. It echoed the ludicrous argument among some Muslims that Jews, Israel, the United States, or a combination thereof were responsible for the September 11, 2001, attacks on New York and Washington, DC. In 2009, Ahmadinejad argued in an address to a UN conference at Geneva that World War II was a cause of what to him was unwelcome international support for the foundation of Israel.

Iran's drive to develop a nuclear capability, linked to its success in already acquiring a medium-range missile delivery system, threatens Israel with modern-day destruction that would kill millions of Jews (and large numbers of non-Jews), the event of which would inevitably be compared to a second Holocaust. Iran has deployed the Shahab missile that, with a range of 812 miles, is able to reach Israel.

CONCLUSIONS

Closing the chapter at this point not only underlines the long-standing applicability of the Holocaust, most obviously in Jewish contexts,[126] but also highlights the issue of diminishment by comparison that is addressed in the next chapter. This issue captures a tension in the memorialization of the Holocaust between a focus on what happened in the 1940s and, in contrast, an understanding of memorialization that encompasses later comparisons, with all the problems entailed by such comparisons. As far as a focus on the 1940s is concerned, such a focus entails an element of greater historicization than the alternative, not least as the 1940s recede and, in particular, appear less approachable to those growing to maturity in the twenty-first century. In contrast, the approach to memorialization that encompasses comparisons with later or current events raises the issue of whether comparisons are appropriate and, if so, which ones and to what purposes. In particular, there is a contrast between analogies and suggestions of equivalence.

At present, claims for restitution continue to provide items of news and for reflection. In particular, there was the question of the treatment of items disposed of by Jews during the Nazi period. The extent to which, as was almost invariably the case, oppression linked to the Holocaust was responsible for the fact and terms of sales was a key issue, particularly with forced sales.[127] This led in a number of states to changes in the law or its practice, notably with the Holocaust (Return of Cultural Objects) Act of 2009, which enabled British national institutions to return such objects. More recently, art galleries have been active in returning to the descendants of Holocaust victims works they acquired from the 1930s on.

The acknowledgment of the existence of the Holocaust and rejection of the example and legacy of the Holocaust, in place of an earlier elision,[128] became a central theme in the European Union,[129] notably from the 1990s and, even more, the 2000s. In part, this was because the Holocaust could be employed against the Far Right, while it also served to express a commitment to human rights and antiracism and testified to a repentance by the EU's leading power, Germany. The European reconsideration of how best to present the Holocaust was an important aspect of a wider international engagement with restitution and memorialization. In this, the Stockholm International Forum of 2000 played a major role. The forum was followed by subsequent Stockholm conferences and by the establishment of an international task force. The institutionalization of Holocaust memory was a key theme. In the Stockholm Declaration of 2000, member states declared their intention to include the Holocaust in the education system, while in 2005, January 27 was chosen as the official remembrance day.[130] For example, in Denmark, aside from Holocaust Memorial Day, a Department of Holocaust and Genocide Studies was established at the Danish Institute of International Studies. In addition to undertaking scholarly research, this department provides public lectures as well as books and other kinds of educational material to Danish schools.[131] This initiative owed much to the publication of a survey demonstrating a serious ignorance of World War II and the Holocaust on the part of Danish youngsters.

However, aside from the political ambiguities, elisions, and opportunism involved, attempts to argue for an equivalence between communism and Nazism, a long-standing theme revived after the fall of the Iron Curtain in 1989, posed major difficulties. These attempts took on governmental energy from the 1990s, as in the 2008 Prague Declaration on European Conscience and communism, and were especially advanced by the new members of the EU from Eastern Europe. These attempts proved highly disruptive in the 2000s and 2010s, capturing the extent to which the expansion of the EU has made it difficult to project any historical account other than one that is at once vacuous in generalities but illuminated by particular episodes held to be of specific importance. At the same time, as this chapter has indicated, the Holocaust's very ability to focus and intertwine memories helps give it a form of "multidirectional memory."[132]

SIX

The Holocaust and Today

THE WIDE-RANGING NATURE OF HOLOCAUST REFERENCES, BUT also their detachment from the events in question, was exemplified in June 2015 when Dimitris Kammenos, an MP for Independent Greeks, a coalition partner in the left-wing government, tweeted a photoshopped image of the infamous gates of Auschwitz with the slogan changed from *Arbeit macht frei* to "We live in Europe" in Greek. This message was aimed at Germany, the principal player in the European Union, because the Greeks, and notably the Greek Left, largely blamed Germany for austerity programs. Moreover, there had been frequent comparisons in Greece between Hitler and Chancellor Merkel. The MP's Auschwitz image was criticized by the Greek Central Board of Jewish Communities as shameful because it "trivializes in the most hideous way the sign." In turn, Kammenos claimed on June 24 that there had been a "misunderstanding," writing on Facebook: "Maybe the comparison was unfortunate but my country is experiencing an economic holocaust."

Leaving aside the totally inappropriate, not to say narcissistic, nature of the comparison—and narcissistic self-importance, indeed, frequently plays a key role in the use of Holocaust comparisons—there is also an antisemitic dimension. The party, Independent Greeks, had previously been condemned by Greek Jewish organizations for a "serious antisemitic act" after its leaders and Panos Kammenos, the defense minister (who is not a relation of Dimitris Kammenos), accused Jews of not paying taxes.[1] This antisemitism is served by the misappropriation of the Holocaust, for it is linked to a totally inaccurate presentation of Jews as villains, both as not paying taxes and through being prominent in international financial organizations, notably in the United States. The latter approach taps into traditional antisemitism as well as recurrent paranoia.

It is all too easy, in light of the unwillingness of so many to confront the past, if not the continuation of active antisemitism, to focus on prejudice and hatred. As a result, it is pleasant to emphasize signs of reconciliation. In Poland, the Jewish Claims Conference, which administers money from restored Jewish property, funds reunions between Jews who survived the Holocaust and Poles who gave them shelter at great personal risk. The meetings are encouraged by the Polish government in order to challenge Poland's unenviable reputation as an antisemitic society, but that does not lessen the positive and life-enhancing tales of heroism, humanity, and fortitude that emerge. The meetings also provide an instance of the personal dimension of victimhood, which is all too often lost or overshadowed by the understandable stress on the scale of the slaughter.

Another aspect of the emphasis on the individuality of victimhood, which has become much stronger with the development of oral history, was shown in 2007, when the Jewish Museum of Deportation and Resistance in Mechelen, Belgium, opened an exhibition that included the photographs of 1,200 of the 1,636 prisoners on board Transport XX, which left Mechelen for Auschwitz on April 19, 1943. This exhibition was made more prominent because the photographs were not displayed only for the museum's visitors but, instead, outside along a stretch of the road next to the Dossin Barracks, which was the holding prison for the deportees.

As far as Polish antisemitism is concerned, the country's Jews had been reasonably well integrated into Polish society during the early modern period, the sixteenth to eighteenth centuries.[2] There were major strands of antisemitism by the interwar years (1918–39), however, and during the acute strains of World War II, the situation was far less positive. Alongside the honorable behavior of many individual Poles and the horror of the murderous German occupation, there was a widespread indifference to the fate of the Jews, not least on the part of the Polish government-in-exile in London, which was unwilling to see Polish Jews as full citizens. This was a long-standing attitude that was accentuated for many Poles by their identification of Jews with communism, not least with its existential challenge to Christianity. This perspective was encouraged by the willingness of some Jews, confronted by Polish antisemitism, to welcome Soviet occupation of eastern Poland in 1939. The same was true of the Soviet occupation of Lithuania in 1940. The Polish government-in-exile based in London was affected by antisemitism, but that was not the view of all exiled Poles or the organizational policy. Moreover, some members were responsible, through the government-in-exile's own intelligence operatives in occupied Poland, for providing Western governments with information on the unfolding dimension of the Holocaust in Poland.[3] Other governments-in-exile tended to neglect the issue of antisemitic legislation and, indeed, the onset of deportations. For example, it was only in September 1943 that the Belgian government-in-exile condemned collaboration in Belgium with the persecution of the Jews.

DENIAL

Holocaust denial is abhorrent as well as ridiculous, a veritable Death of History,[4] but "denial never went away."[5] It is reasonable and necessary to question the motives and integrity of all Holocaust deniers and to impugn the worst of intentions to them. They are mad, bad, or both, although a description of deniers in terms of madness is a calumny on the insane. No one of judgment and morality can deny that Jews were the foremost category of people, from start to finish, that the Nazis wished to exterminate. More generally, antisemitism and Holocaust denial are symptoms of a poorly developed civil society,[6] or one with perverse values. Holocaust denial in some form or other is unfortunately far from a fringe opinion in the Muslim community. Moreover, it is part of a more general Muslim pattern of the portrayal of Jewish history: for example, the denial of a positive, or any, Jewish role or place in the Moorish-ruled medieval al-Andalus, now Andalusia in Spain.

DIMINISHMENT

The Holocaust serves for many as a paradigm within which other atrocities are understood and presented—indeed as a form of "year zero" in this case. This process helps make it more central but can also lead to a degree of misunderstanding, if not much worse. An issue very different from Holocaust denial—one, in certain respects, made more insidious by the fact that most of its numerous supporters are not in any respect Holocaust deniers—is the downplaying of the Holocaust by comparison. Here, an issue is not so much comparison with other genocides, notably that of Tutus in Rwanda in 1994, for they also are deplorable and disgusting,[7] but rather comparison with episodes that, however distasteful and cruel, were not genocidal.

Two examples are the attempt by Germans, no longer on the Far Right but now also in the mainstream, to argue that the German experience in 1943–45, first of heavy Anglo-American bombing and then of being brutalized and driven from Eastern Europe, is in some way comparable to the Holocaust. This is absurd, not least because no genocide was attempted, even by Joseph Stalin. Moreover, whether or not the bombings, which also inflicted considerable damage on the German economy and demoralized German society, constituted war crimes, they were not genocidal.[8] Most German commentators do not appear to show the same concern about German bombing during the war, including the use of rockets against civilian targets, notably London and Antwerp, in 1944–45. Linked to this point is that attempts to relativize the combatants (in part in pursuit of transnational history) by stressing the common horror of war, the experience of combat, the miseries of occupation, and the strains of the "home front" all miss the element of German intentions.

Separate to the specific German critique of Allied bombing comes the argument that the bombing campaigns of World War II, indeed bombing itself, as well as the Holocaust, were rooted in Western imperialism, with "genocidal weapons" making possible "dreams of genocide." In this approach, the British and Americans are treated like the Nazis.[9] The unscholarly and indeed quasi-hysterical nature of such arguments scarcely needs underlining, while the suggestion that genocide required sophisticated weaponry was hardly demonstrated by Croatia in 1941 or Rwanda in 1994. In particular, the rate and nature of killing in Rwanda indicated that "industrial" processes are not a necessary condition for mass killing: many of those slaughtered were killed by the use of machetes and other handheld weapons.

There has been the reiterated comparison of the Atlantic slave trade, which was obviously very malign, to an African holocaust, which is also absurd. It underrates the major role of African agency in the slave trade, in the shape of supplying enslaved Africans, and that the intention of the slave trade was not to kill Africans, still less to reorder the racial geography of conquered territory, but instead to ensure plentiful, pliant, and relatively inexpensive labor.

The downplaying of the Holocaust by historical comparison also draws in part on the worthy goal of using the widespread horror that the treatment of the Jews inspired, and continues to inspire, to elicit a similar reaction on behalf of other persecuted groups: past, present, and apparently imminent. In the Soviet Union, for example, terror and government-tolerated famine killed at least eleven million people in Stalin's "peacetime" years (1924–41, 1945–53), warped the lives of the remainder of the population, and made casualties of faith, hope, and truth. As with the Germans, the Soviets used cattle cars to deport victims by rail. In Ukraine from 1991, independence brought public attention to the Soviet government's complicity in the mass famine that began in 1933 and led to pressure for its recognition as a genocide. In 2010, Stalin and colleagues were convicted posthumously of genocide in a Ukrainian court. That year, *Stalin's Genocides* by the American academic Norman Naimark pressed for discussion of genocide in the case of Stalin. The treatment of Ukrainian peasants as enemies of the people who deserved to die led Naimark to conclude that the Ukrainian famine was genocide—so also with the treatment of allegedly dangerous and traitorous Poles and Germans in the western borderlands of the Soviet Union in 1932–33, most of whom were killed. Naimark's comparison of Hitler and Stalin argued that dekulakization and the Ukrainian famine were attempts to eliminate a class of people, while the nationalities most brutally attacked by Stalin were destined for elimination, at the very least as self-identifying nationalities.

Naimark concluded that both systems were genocidal by their very character, not only their ideological motivations but also their Promethean transformative aspirations. This approach was also taken by Timothy Snyder and by the Russian writer Aleksandr Solzhenitsyn. Communist policies were certainly murderous on a massive scale and directed at the destruction of entire social categories, a goal some see as akin to racial extermination.[10]

The routinely murderous secret police was the military of this war, a crucial prop to a Soviet government that used large-scale violence and insistent surveillance. Moreover, very large numbers were imprisoned in the gulags, which effectively were concentration camps that, as a source of forced labor, played some role in the Soviet economy, although the deprivation to the general civilian economy attributable to the removal of skilled, semiskilled, and unskilled labor to the camps meant that normal civilian technical and other contributions were nullified. Civilian economies are better able than forced-labor ones to determine opportunity costs, but that was not the nature of communist or Nazi assumptions. Ironically, the many Jews sent to the gulags in 1939–41 from newly occupied areas—eastern Poland, the Baltic republics, and Bessarabia—were more likely to survive World War II than if they had remained in their homes. Similarly, the Chinese communist state slaughtered very many in the 1950s and 1960s, notably in the "Great Leap Forward" of 1958–62, although famine and famine-induced disease killed far more of the many millions who died.

The large-scale massacres of Armenians in the Turkish empire in 1915, massacres and "ethnic cleansing" in which about 1.5 million were killed or otherwise died, are instructive, not least in terms of the subsequent and continuing Turkish tendency to minimize or deny them and to extenuate and contextualize the episode in terms of Armenian support for Russia, one of Turkey's wartime opponents, as well as to emphasize the suffering of the Turkish population. Thus, books that detail the massacres can expect to be denied publication in Turkey, while those who speak on the subject in Turkey can anticipate not being invited back to lecture. The episode was part of a wider process, one in which Turkish nationalism helped turn a polyglot empire into a sectarian state only of Muslims. Turkey's denial of the Armenian massacres has been linked to the Holocaust debate (which, in fact, is not a case of comparing like with like) and, thus, to the question of Turkey's membership of the European Union, as Holocaust denial there is now a crime.[11]

Nevertheless, large-scale killing alone, however reprehensible, does not compare with the Holocaust, because the attempt to define and destroy an entire ethnic group and its complete culture represents a different scale and intention of assault, indeed a global assault. The scale and intentions underlying the slaughter of Tutsi in Rwanda in 1994 were genocidal, but whereas the Holocaust aimed to make Jews everywhere victims, this was not the intention of the Armenian massacres nor those of the Rwandan Tutsi.

This point about the attempt to destroy an entire ethnic group helps address the charge that focusing on the Holocaust has led to a failure to consider adequately the extent to which the Germans also slaughtered large numbers of other groups,[12] as well as killing many Germans who were not Jewish—in short, that the Holocaust is an incomplete perspective on Nazi policies and practice. This issue is seen, for example, in the question of who should be commemorated at Auschwitz and who should be in charge of the commemoration. This issue also resonates with the quest by many Germans for acceptance of their status as victims: if attention is moved from the slaughter of the Jews, then the Germans can emerge as one of the peoples who suffered grievously in the 1940s. This is a presumption that strikes many non-Germans as ahistorical, ludicrous, and offensive. The Germans who suffered most were, of course, German Jews. Discussing what happened to the large numbers of non-Jewish European civilians during the war does not diminish the Holocaust, but pressure to look at others killed then and on other occasions can become a key issue in the politics of Holocaust diminishment, not least with calls that relevant legislation should include the denial of communist crimes.

Eastern European psychologies of comparative suffering and victimology were, and are, important. The environment was different from that in Western Europe. The scale of destruction and suffering was much greater. People are complicated, and memories, motives, and facility of expression can be twisted (for obvious reason in terms of what the survivors endured), making it all the harder for historians to figure out what people's trains of thought really are and what is behind these thoughts when they enumerate their own ethnic group's sufferings. Since individuals tend to be egoists, they habitually dwell on their own suffering more than on others' and thus neglect the array of quantitative and qualitative data that can help judgment. Egoism, however, does not necessarily make people antisemitic or anti-whatever. If, for example, a Polish Catholic or

Hungarian politician or group is (or is not) a forthright nationalist and has recidivist desires to dwell on his or her own group's sufferings, that does not necessarily mean that he or she is a crypto antisemite. Indeed, he or she might not even be thinking about Jews at all. Here and there, he or she might drop some hints, innuendos, or contorted and obfuscating explanations that are revealing, or perhaps utter none at all. It can be difficult for the interested bystander and the historian alike to probe for what might be the genuine views underneath utterances and the written record. In many cases, there is an implicit sympathy or recognition of the disaster that befell whatever group, but in some cases, there is a gloating over a calamity befalling some other ethnic or religious group. Identity politics point in many different directions, as do relativistic worldviews. If Nazi ideology has some features in common with modern or earlier identity politics, that does not necessarily mean that the latter equates with the former.

The calls to criminalize the denial of communist crimes were strongest from countries that had been occupied by Soviet forces and forcibly converted to communism but were also heard elsewhere. For example, in Denmark, there have been critics who have asked why "only" the Nazi genocides should be officially commemorated and why not also the crimes committed by communist dictators such as Lenin, Stalin, Mao, and Pol Pot. Nevertheless, pressure has been strongest from ex-communist states, and this pressure has affected calls for Holocaust remembrance. Opposition from Estonia and Lithuania affected plans to make Holocaust denial an offense across the European Union. Alongside Latvia, Slovenia, and Poland, Estonia and Lithuania tried but failed, in 2007, to have included in the European Union's criminalization of genocide denial a crime of denying, condoning, or trivializing atrocities committed in the name of Stalin. The thesis of "double genocide" was then advanced in the Prague Declaration of 2008, which was initiated by the Czech government. It enjoyed considerable traction in the European Parliament but was criticized by some Jewish organizations.

Within Germany, there is competition, often acute competition, for attention, including funding between former concentration camps, such as Buchenwald, Dachau, and Ravensbrück, as well as sites in East Germany that commemorate the victims of communism. Within the

Christian Democratic Party, there is pressure for equivalent treatment as, it is argued, all those commemorated were victims of political dictatorship. This was the argument, for example, of Bernd Neumann, head of cultural affairs in Angela Merkel's Chancellery from 2005 till 2013, who as a child had fled Elbing, which Prussia had seized from Poland in 1772. The Central Board of German Jews rejects this equivalence, as it argues that it diminishes the Holocaust. Furthermore, returning the debate to the crucial sphere of military realities, it was very much necessary to rely on Stalin's forces to end the Holocaust.[13] Moreover, these forces included Jewish soldiers.

From the academic perspective, the comparative dimension, currently advocated as transnational history, can provide theoretical support for incorporating communism, as does the success of linked biographies on Hitler and Stalin. However, as a warning of the problems with this dimension, a prominent academic instance of the downplaying of the uniqueness of the Jewish experience is provided by *Poland's Holocaust: Ethnic Strife, Collaboration with Occupying Forces and Genocide in the Second Republic, 1918–1947*, by Tadeusz Piotrowski (1998). A professor of sociology at the University of New Hampshire and a naturalized American of Polish descent, Piotrowski defines the Holocaust as including the victims of both Germany and the Soviet Union. Doing so enables him to divide his study of the Holocaust in Poland into seven chapters, with "Nazi Terror" preceded by "Soviet Terror," and chapters on Polish, Belorussian, Lithuanian, and Ukrainian collaboration preceded by a chapter on Jewish collaboration with both Soviet and German agencies. The overall impression, to put it mildly, is of a seriously unbalanced account and of a hijacking of the term *holocaust*.[14]

More seriously, rising tensions from the 2020s about Russian expansionism under Vladimir Putin led to controversy over wartime conduct, notably in Ukraine. Putin's Russian nationalism very much focused on World War II. The crisis over Ukraine that developed from 2013 and, even more strongly, 2022 led Russian commentators and supporters repeatedly and inaccurately to claim that Ukrainian nationalists were fascists and antisemitic, which was a totally misleading attempt to apply a categorization of some in World War II to the current situation. On March 3, 2014, Russia's foreign ministry referred to "the West's allies" in Ukraine as "outright neo-Nazis." These claims were designed to influence opinion in Russia and more broadly. Historical references were pushed to the fore. For example, the killing of violent pro-Russian separatists in Odessa in 2014 was illustrated in part by photographs of a very different episode: a massacre by the pro-German Ukrainian Insurgent Army in 1943.[15] Such claims certainly helped maintain support for Putin in Russia.

A more pertinent comparison as far as the slaughter of Jews is concerned would be with the Roma (Gypsies), of whom at least a quarter of a million, and possibly up to 1.5 million, were killed by the Germans. As a percentage of the world population of Roma, this is a high figure. Germany's Roma were sent to Auschwitz II following an order signed by Himmler on December 16, 1942. Hitler's attitude toward Jews, however, was very different, as he depicted them as an active and direct threat to the Germans and their mission, which was not a danger he or Himmler saw in the Roma. After the war, discrimination against the Roma continued in both West and East Germany, and until the 1960s, they were not regarded as victims of German wartime persecution.[16] Discrimination continues in Eastern Europe, notably in Hungary and Romania. As far as World War II is concerned, there was also a genocidal dimension to the internecine struggles in Yugoslavia in 1941–45.[17]

Crimes against humanity are certainly all too common, and the Holocaust is far from unique in that light, but that does not establish an equivalence. The latter, nevertheless, has been a strong theme of political diatribe. To each generation, such comparison appears new, but this is not the case. For example, the treatment of the Algerians by the French authorities in the early 1960s was compared to Nazi policies, while subsequent US conduct in the Vietnam War was compared to the Holocaust. These claims were absurd, although in the former there was the Vichyist strand, not least with the role of Papon in French police administration during both the Holocaust and the Algerian War. Addressing US conduct in the Vietnam War, the French intellectual Jean-Paul Sartre advanced the case for genocidal relationships,[18] a thesis that was applied more widely. During World War II, Sartre himself had accepted a teaching post that was vacant because its Jewish holder had been removed. To claim in 1987, as did Jacques Vergès—the defense lawyer to Klaus Barbie, the murderous SS head of the Gestapo in Lyon from 1942 to 1944—that the focus should not be on German crimes against Jews but rather on those of imperial power against peoples struggling for freedom was also to seek to put France, a major imperial power until the early 1960s, in the dock. Vergès's cocounsel, Nabil Bouaitt, argued that the Israeli invasion of Lebanon in 1982 was a holocaust. Barbie was sentenced to life imprisonment.[19] When, from 1967, the radical Left in Germany became critical of Israel, they similarly drew unfounded comparisons with Nazi Germany, the terrorist Ulrike Meinhof referring to the successful Israeli defense minister, Moshe Dayan, as "Israel's Himmler."[20] In 1961, the failure of the British government to condemn Portuguese brutality in their colony Angola against revolutionaries led the Labour politician Denis Healey to imply that this inaction supported "Eichmann-esque" slaughter. Subsequently, the Labour leader Harold Wilson publicly condemned the Wiriyamu massacre of civilians in 1972, in another Portuguese colony, Mozambique, as "obscene savagery [with] no parallel in the scale of genocide since the days of the Nazi massacres."[21] He was wrong in this. British policy in Kenya in response to the Mau-Mau uprising of 1952–57 has also been compared recently to the Holocaust, an absurd argument that in part rests on a confusion of detention camps with extermination camps, a confusion that is either deliberately misleading or extremely foolish.

In Australia, the fate of the Aborigines has often been explicitly compared to the Holocaust, not least as a way of shocking a response. John Howard, the conservative prime minister from 1996 to 2007, criticized what he termed the "black arm-band historical view," namely, claims that the British colonizers acted in a brutal and genocidal fashion and that this was the unacceptable foundation of modern Australia. In the 2000s, there was a bitter controversy over whether academics had exaggerated the numbers of Aborigines killed by the early British colonists. The debate still simmers, but the term *genocide* is not appropriate in connection with colonial Australia.

In New Zealand, the word *holocaust* was used in 1996 in the *Waitangi Tribunal*, which investigated the grievances of Maori against the Crown, in *Taranaki Report: Kaupapa Tuatahi*, its report on Taranaki, a district in the North Island that saw conflict, land confiscation, protest, and dispossession in the nineteenth century: "As to quantum, the gravamen of our report has been to say that the Taranaki claims are likely to be the largest in the country. The graphic *muru* [plunder] of most of Taranaki and the *raupatu* [confiscation] without ending describe the holocaust of Taranaki history and the denigration of the founding peoples in a continuum from 1840 to the present."

This report led to political fallout in 2000. Taria Turia, a prominent Maori who was the associate minister of Maori affairs, gave a "Maori holocaust" speech that caused controversy and for which she apologized to parliament in a personal statement: "I did not . . . mean to belittle survivors of the World War Two Holocaust." However, when asked by Winston Peters, the leader of the opposition New Zealand First Party, which vigorously criticized the idea of special treatment for Maori, whether she felt the use of the term *holocaust* in a *Waitangi Tribunal* report on the treatment of the people of Taranaki gave her license to use the term, she replied: "I believe, yes, you're quite right. I read the *Waitangi Tribunal* report on the devastation of the Taranaki peoples and I acknowledge they used the word 'holocaust,' which in terms of what happened to Taranaki I believe was appropriate." This did not please government supporters, such as Trevor Mallard, the education minister, and clashed with the decision given just days earlier by Helen Clark, the prime minister, that the term *holocaust* must never again be used in a New Zealand context. Days later, the Indigenous Peoples Conference, held in the capital, Wellington, endorsed both the *Waitangi Tribunal* statement and Taria Turia.

In India, the argument is made that the Holocaust was bad but not the responsibility of ordinary Germans. However, there is a widespread view among the educated middle class that the Holocaust was not unique but that American and European imperialists also killed large numbers in pursuit of expansion. A minority view among Indian ultranationalists, one that dates back to wartime cooperation, is that Hitler was a positive influence because he hit hard at the British, who were the colonial power in India. On the part of some commentators, there is a tendency to bring Israeli conduct in Palestine into the debate, which, again, is certainly not comparing like with like.

Not centered on the Holocaust, there is also a more general down-playing of the Jewish experience of persecution. Thus, in the catalogue for the major exhibition *At War*, held in Barcelona in 2004, Jose Mana Ridao wrote of

> the temporal as well as spatial transmigration of stereotypes upon which death and destruction are wont to thrive: the representation of the pre-Columbian Indian coincides with that of today's Muslim, and that of today's Muslim with that of the Congolese native from the time of King Leopold [of Belgium], and that of the Congolese native with the persecuted Jew, and that of the persecuted Jew with that of Leo Tolstoy's Chechenian, and that of Tolstoy's Chechenian with the Chechenian the more recent press depicts. For each and every one of these figures, and for so many others, simple names on an interminable list which would include poor and gypsies alike, Hutus as well as Tutsis, Serbs as well as Bosnians, the stigma is always identical.[22]

More specifically, Godwin's Law, promulgated in 1990, is an internet adage asserting that "as an online discussion grows longer, the probability of a comparison involving Nazis or Hitler approaches 1"—in other words, becomes very strong. Mike Godwin, a lawyer active in internet law, has written about his adage: he wanted people who glibly compared someone else to Hitler or to Nazis to think harder about the Holocaust.[23] This appears readily apparent when, in Britain, both modern agriculture and the fate of hedgehogs have been described as a holocaust.

At the same time, there have also been efforts to make the Holocaust relevant to non-Jews without losing sight of its Jewish character. This is particularly common in the United States, which has a tendency to present the Holocaust as a crime against all, with the Jews as victims. Thus, Michael Berenbaum, project director of the United States Holocaust Memorial Museum from 1988 to 1993, referred to the Americanization of the Holocaust in terms of American values, especially tolerance, pluralism, and human rights. The Simon Wiesenthal Center and Museum of Tolerance in Los Angeles exemplifies the same tendency.[24] A similar policy underlies Holocaust memorial days in countries like Britain. On January 24, 2005, in an address to a special session of the United Nations held to commemorate the Holocaust, Secretary-General Kofi Annan declared that "the evil which destroyed six million Jews and others in these camps still threatens all of us today; the crimes of the Nazis are nothing that we may ascribe to a distant past in order to forget it. It falls to us, the successor generations, to lift high the torch of remembrance, and to live our lives by its light."

In Belgium, Natan Ramet, chairman of the Jewish Museum of Deportation and Resistance in Mechelen, declared of the Transport XX exhibition: "This is a message against racism. This is not a Jewish theme: it has global relevance. If you discriminate against one group of people, this sort of thing can happen." A similar theme was struck from a different context in a press release from the municipality of Boortmeerbeek about the memorial service held to honor the resistance fighters and the deportees who they rescued in 1943: "Today these ethical messages are still important for our youth, our community and for Belgium after what happened a few months ago when a Belgium teenager in Antwerp made a racial carnage and killed a two-year-old Flemish toddler and her nanny. This incident again created an atmosphere of racial hatred. The same meaningless racial cruelty as the Nazi holocaust happened again."[25]

Similarly, in its literature, the Wellington, New Zealand, Holocaust Research and Education Centre declares its aim to "teach tolerance, courage and racial harmony . . . in ways that will inspire following generations, both Jewish and of other faiths, to combat intolerance wherever it occurs and respect the dignity of the lives of every man, woman and child." Israel found itself in difficulties on this subject in 2007 when detaining Muslim refugees from Darfur in Sudan who were arriving as illegal immigrants.

On the global scale, however, the Western culture for which the Holocaust is a key symbol and warning is of receding consequence. This is particularly true of the rapidly declining demographic, economic, political, cultural, and intellectual significance of Europe; in Europe, a major attempt has been made to establish the Holocaust as the point of departure from which, in a conscious reaction, the new Europe has been created. In 2000, a conference in Stockholm called by Goran Persson, the prime minister of Sweden from 1996 to 2006, sought to define a common commemorative framework. It was agreed that the memory of the Holocaust should inform the values of a common European civil society, dedicated to "mutual understanding and justice." Fine sentiments, but on the world scale, Europe is in decline.

There is also the issue of weakening US power and influence. Instead, the demographic, economic, and political weight of China and India are of growing relative importance, and for neither state is the Holocaust a prominent issue. Both states played a major and generally underrated role in World War II, India as part of the British Empire, but war with Germany was not crucial for either. For China in particular, the issue of wartime crimes focuses on Japan, and in Iris Chang's bestseller, *The Rape of Nanking: The Forgotten Holocaust of World War II* (1997), she compares the mass slaughter there in 1937 to Auschwitz, which, again, is a misplaced comparison. In Japan itself, attention to the Holocaust is limited, which, in part, reflects an education system heavily focused on Japanese history. To a degree, antisemitism may be an issue in Japan, just as, more plausibly, it may be linked to a lack of support for Israel, but the key issue is a lack of awareness.

Looking to the future, it will be instructive to see how far Asian public history focuses on episodes in which Asians harmed other Asians—for example, the Hindu-Muslim conflict arising from the partition of British India in 1947, the murderous Khmer Rouge regime in Cambodia in 1976–69, or the "Great Leap Forward" in China in 1958–62—rather than either the iniquities of Western pressure on Asia or episodes within the West, notably the Holocaust. It is likely that, in place of other factors, foreign dominance will be the key issue, for example, British imperialism for India and British and Japanese imperialism for China. The contemporary response to mass killings represents a form of judgment that then serves to condemn particular regimes and related ideologies.

A separate strand of downplaying the Holocaust is represented by Islam. This strand is not simply a case of the clear policy of most Muslim countries but also that of a growing Muslim role in Western Europe. This role will continue, as Muslim birth rates are considerably higher than those of the non-Muslim population. Political consequences already flow, with Western Europe being, in part, influenced as part of an Islamic sphere of consciousness, although not as yet pulled into the sphere of Islamic influence as sometimes alleged. The attitude of Muslim minorities toward the Holocaust has already been thrown into prominence in Britain, with the reluctance of Muslim organizations to take a role in Holocaust commemorations despite marked public and governmental criticism of that reluctance. In France, Muslims have vociferously re-sisted the emphasis on the Holocaust in the educational process and in public commemorations. At the level of the European Union, this question may become more of an issue when, or if, states with a Muslim majority join. Albania, Kosovo, and Turkey are the main possibilities.

Muslim antisemitism is frequently in evidence. At the trial of the terrorists responsible for the murderous bombing of a Bali nightclub in 2003, one of the accused shouted "Jews, remember Khaibar. The army of Muhammad is coming back to defeat you"—thereby bringing the defeat and enslavement of Jews in 628 into the modern age. In February 2015, at a speech in Lyon to mark the anniversary of the 1943 roundup of Jews who were taken to Drancy and Auschwitz, Robert Badinter, French minister of justice from 1981 to 1986, placed antisemitism "masquerading under the name of anti-Zionism" in a sequence referring to an episode from 2012: "When Mohammed Merah, in a Jewish high school in Tou-louse, chased and caught a little girl aged eight as she tried to run away, grabbed her by the hair, and shot her point-blank in the head, he was reenacting the deeds of the SS *Einsatzgruppen.*"

Those arguing for action against ISIS in 2015 and Hamas in 2023 drew comparisons between Nazi hatred toward Jews and the hatred of Islamic fundamentalists toward Jews. Linked to this comparison, caution was presented as equivalent to the Munich Agreement of 1938, which is held to have "resulted in the Second World and the Holocaust."[26]

Attempts to assert an equivalence with the Holocaust reflect in part the centrality of the Holocaust in the collective imagination and indicate its role as a universalizing basis for public comment, indeed, judgment, in order to find a meaning for Humanity. Thus, alongside and as a warning against the possibility of civilizational collapse, the Holocaust serves as a moral absolute and touchstone for those living in its "moral aftermath,"[27] although that practice is criticized by those who search for comparisons or, even more, focus on cultural relativism. Indeed, the Holocaust is a high bar against which other atrocities fall short.

It was arresting to see as an instance of the impact of the Holocaust on popular culture "Daleks in Manhattan, I," an episode of the highly popular British television series (for adults as well as children) *Doctor Who*, broadcast on April 21, 2007. This episode had the evil Daleks, the quintessential and long-standing villains who hate everything, embark on "The Final Experiment." Their victims were divided between those turned into slaves and others intended as food for the experiment. However flawed, these comparisons indicate the extent to which Nazi policy has become the axis of depravity, and the Holocaust its center, making indeed a hell on Earth.[28]

SEVEN

Conclusions

Earth Conceal Not The Blood Shed on Thee.

—The Jewish Monument at Bergen-Belsen

THE CONTESTED MEMORIES OF THE HOLOCAUST ARE NOT AN inconsequential adjunct of the academic scholarship on the events themselves but, instead, are part of their weighty impact on Western culture. The Holocaust, indeed, is now a central aspect both of twentieth-century European history and of the twenty-first century's collective recollection of the past. It can also be seen as a key element in Nazi Germany's war on Europe and on Europe's cultural inheritance. The total racial recasting of Europe with, at the least, the expulsion of the Jews and, eventually, their genocidal destruction was a Hitlerian objective, not a by-product of the war.[1] Those making the war, including the German army, certainly facilitated both this recasting and the resulting Holocaust. Crucially, German soldiers, policemen, and others who refused to take part in the killing were generally not punished. This both suggests that more, indeed many more, could have refused had they chosen to do so and directs attention to the motivation of the killers. It was a motivation to be sought in antisemitic violence as much as the group cohesion often stressed.

Yet collaborators in the killing, especially the very active and large-scale role of non-Germans in Eastern Europe as the killers of Jews, underline the fact that although the prime responsibility was German, it was not simply Germans who were involved. Instead, a side effect of German policy, and deliberately so, was to open a Pandora's box of antisemitism and nationalist hatred and purposefully focus it on killing Jews.

The vicious murder of pogroms was to become systematic genocide. Moreover, the Holocaust provides a peculiarly horrific instance of how the experience of both totalitarian governmental and total war can distort and deform conscience and behavior in environments of mass fear.

This perspective encourages a reconsideration of the relationship between the Holocaust and World War II: the course of the war was of great significance for the development of the Holocaust, although the latter was not totally dependent on it, as vicious antisemitism as part of a worldview of existential hostility was already a key theme in Nazi rhetoric and policy prior to the war. However, both rhetoric and policy were pushed forward greatly as a result of the war. This rhetoric and policy helped to bring to fruition the plans and violence already strong within Nazism while also further radicalizing its followers and ensuring that those who wanted genocidal solutions could pursue their developing objectives. In addition, success in war and, indeed, in prewar brinkmanship and aggression brought large numbers of Jews under the control of Germany directly—or indirectly, through its allies and through the authorities of defeated states. The pace of conquest outran the ability of most Jews to escape. Thus, the fate of "foreign Jews" became of greater significance as more parts of Europe into which they had fled were conquered by the Germans or brought under a degree of control. In addition, the number of "foreign Jews" and the sense that they were an even larger presence served to underline both the disruption of the war and the alleged or apparent "foreignness" of Jews as a whole. Moreover, those Jews who were defined as "foreign" and/or who lived in occupied territory proved particularly vulnerable in many cases. Thus, Bulgaria deported to Treblinka 11,000 Jews from the sections of Greece and Yugoslavia it annexed. In the case of Germany, however, there was a determination to turn on all Jews.

The treatment of Jews also demonstrated the extent to which, for the Germans, there was scant compromise in the outcome intended from the war. Indeed, their treatment exemplified this point while also serving as a key aspect of the outcome that Hitler and the Nazis themselves sought. Insofar as any war deserves the title "total war," that which was directed against the Jews does. Had they been in a position to put up more resistance, this would have served not to deter the Nazis but simply to encourage them to devote more military resources to their genocidal end. As it was, the army played a key role in the Holocaust. Aside from direct killings, it was also crucial in securing the context within which killing occurred. Moreover, the other agencies involved should be considered part of the German war machine, capturing the degree to which, in many states, the military is not simply a matter of the army.

The extent to which the Holocaust was at once Nazi in origin and cause and yet also rested on wider German connivance and participation and, moreover, at once German in origin and cause and yet also rested on a wider European connivance and participation was underlined by subsequent treatment both in Germany and elsewhere toward the killings. This attitude helped ensure that Holocaust denial was not simply an issue about Germany and for Germans. Partly as a result, in 2007 Germany utilized its presidency of the European Union (EU) to ensure the passage of race-hate laws for the entire Union. This was not so much based on the assumption by the German government that non-Germans were also guilty, but rather as a historic obligation and an opportunity to exercise moral leadership. German legislation provided a background, as Holocaust denial was already a crime there. In the event, German hopes of replicating this legislation on the EU scale, and thus of enacting a specific ban on Holocaust denial, failed. Instead, the EU agreed to criminalize "publicly condoning, denying or grossly trivialising crimes of genocide, crimes against humanity and war crimes," although only where "the conduct is carried out in a manner likely to incite violence or hatred." The definition of these crimes was a matter of contention. Use of the rubrics of the International Criminal Court ensured that the Holocaust was included but also that it was far from unique. The massacres in Rwanda and Yugoslavia in the 1990s were included, although not the Turkish massacres of Armenians in 1915. Current political concerns play a major role in determining the legal status of such cases, notably relations with Turkey.

One area of potential comparability is presented by the extent to which the Holocaust was an instance of the vulnerability of groups when multiethnic supranational empires were divided into monoethnic states. In the former, scattered peoples could integrate and be protected by the law, as the Jews were, to an extent, in the Habsburg Empire or the

Bosnian Muslims in Yugoslavia. In contrast, monoethnic states, or rather those that sought to be so, did not have to be persecuting, but such persecution accorded with the aspiration to be monoethnic. In part, this was also an aspect of the challenge of democratic politics, as the transition from multiethnic empires occurred at the same time as the onset of democracy provided the opportunity for populist authoritarianism. Yet whatever the strains of this transition, an outcome in the shape of the attempt to slaughter all of a racial group was not usual.

CHALLENGING OPTIMISM

The Holocaust serves as a global lesson through the internationalization of its remembrance.[2] It has this wider significance, not least (although not only) if the emphasis is placed on "indifference, disinterest, and a striking lack of moral values" on the part of both perpetrators and bystanders, the attitude and role of the latter being particularly instructive. Such an emphasis suggests in part not only that the Holocaust emerged from a historically unique situation but also that genocide was/is more generally latent.[3] This point represents a major qualification of both secular and religious optimism.

As far as secular optimism is concerned, belief in the progress of, even the possibility of perfecting, mankind was challenged by what Primo Levi, an Auschwitz survivor, termed "the feeling of guilt that such a crime should exist." The very fundamentals of human society were all challenged by the Holocaust. This was in part a question of individual values, self-knowledge, and relationships between humans. Each of these was placed under terrible strain, as Jews confronted the appalling circumstances into which they were thrust and also sought to lessen the burden. This confrontation led to a measuring out of time in fragments of survival, to unhinging despair, to acts of selfishness toward fellow victims (as well as many luminous acts of transcendent selflessness), and to such measures as the denial of identity and also suicide, each of which was widespread, as well as to feelings of guilt and a desire for anonymity among many survivors.

Other social fundamentals were also challenged. Language is always a porous and contested medium of communication and form and an occasion and means of sociability. The Nazis took forward the inversion of meaning and morality in communist terminology, brilliantly caricatured in George Orwell's novel *Animal Farm* (1945), and imparted a particular racial dimension as they fervently conceptualized and sought what to any rational observer was a total dystopia. In part, the jockeying for influence and control between Nazi leaders was waged through competing uses of this warped language. As part of their conflation of hyperbole and euphemism, the language of health and cleansing was used to describe slaughter. Nazi euphemism, arguably, is still employed in a misleading fashion when terms such as *Final Solution* are used. Aside from euphemism, there is the problem of the connotations of words and phrases, as with the use of *liquidation* or *extermination*, terms frequently employed to describe vermin, rather than *slaughter*, although the latter is also a difficult term as it is applied to animals. The issue is one of the many that make it very difficult, as well as highly necessary, to write about the subject.

Although not the equivalent of communist and Nazi linguistic inversion, the more recent language of postmodernism is also an obfuscation of the truth and a denial of reality. In its endless and self-obsessed relativism, which is in part a rejection of standard Western civilization moral precepts and methods, as well as its questioning of the existence of facts, postmodernism is not just empty of meaning and value but also an evil perversion of reason. The valuable critical assessment by Richard Evans, in his *In Defence of History* (1997), is worth noting: he argued that Auschwitz was not a discourse and that it trivializes mass murder to see it as a text. The same is true with the obfuscation and denial bound up in the use of illiberal practices and terms in order to limit, indeed suppress, debate.

THEOLOGY AND THE HOLOCAUST

It was not simply secular language and ideas that were to be tested by the Holocaust. Despite the best efforts of religious leaders and thinkers, and arguments about God's inscrutable purpose and the testing of the devout, the notion of an omnipotent and benign, indeed interested and engaged, God also took a savage knock. The travails of the righteous was scarcely a new theme, but the Holocaust drove it forward as an issue, and not only for Jews. The lengthy BBC Radio 4 interview in 2006 with the then chief rabbi of the British Commonwealth, Jonathan Sacks, focused on this point. Although he put up a vigorous case from the religious perspective, it was not one that necessarily convinced those dubious of the acceptance, even confidence, with which such views are advanced. More generally, there was the problem, for philosophers as well as theologians, of "how to continue thinking without yielding to the temptation of false consolation."[4] Confidence in divine purpose was certainly challenged in the case of some Holocaust survivors. In part, it "reflected their understanding of what had happened to them and, in part, it was an aspect of their continued disorientation, sense of emptiness and experience of destruction."[5] Alexander Donat, a survivor of the Warsaw ghetto and of Auschwitz, wrote of the former: "We kept asking ourselves the age-old question: why? why?"[6] Based on an event described by Elie Wiesel (a prisoner in Auschwitz as a teenager) in his book *The Trial of God* (New York, 1979), a 2008 BBC/WGBH Boston television play titled *God on Trial* and written by Frank Cottrell Boyce takes place in Auschwitz. Jewish prisoners put God on trial in absentia, accusing him of breaking his covenant with the Jewish people by allowing the Germans to commit genocide. One response, however, to the question "Where was God?" is "I wondered where was humanity."[7]

Holocaust theology is not a subject discussed by most historians and, instead, is generally handled by theologians. For a historian to discuss the topic may appear both rash and redundant, but it is a key aspect of the legacy of the Holocaust. Moreover, the questions that are central issues in Holocaust theology—"Why did God let it happen?" and "Where was God?"—are of interest from the historical perspective. It is not necessary to be religious to ask whether, first, any discussion of the former question can throw light on the issue of causation and the process of discussing it and, second, whether the latter question throws light on the experience of the Holocaust.

Moreover, these are issues for both Christian and Jewish theologians. In part, this is because the perpetrators were Christian (some nominal, some not) and the victims Jews. The situation reflects the degree to which many other victims of Nazi slaughter were Christian. There is the issue that both common humanity and a shared interest in theological questions make the Holocaust, and its relationship with divine intentions, a matter of importance for Christian and Jewish theologians. In his painting *Crucifixion* (1942), Emmanuel Levy captured a crossover, with a religious Jew nailed on a crucifix and the sign *Jude* nailed above. Similarly, Marc Chagall's crucifixions depict Holocaust imagery.

There are, of course, other dimensions as well. There were key cross-currents that diminished the extent to which the Holocaust was a religious question. However much it drew on antisemitism, the Nazi assault was on a race, not a religion, and avowedly so, and this made it different from the totalitarian assault on religion that church leaders perceived in Nazi policies.[8] The overwhelming majority of Europeans were at the time nominal Christians, but the Nazis were active in a form of secularization and, if they had any religious sensibilities at all, some type of neopaganism. However, in the case of Germany's allies, many of those involved in the Holocaust were Christians and had a clear Christian politico-religious ideology, and this was also true of some Germans. Many Jews who were victims of the Holocaust were not religious, while some had converted to Christianity.

The question as to what extent Nazism itself was a religion or pseudo-religion is linked by some commentators to the issue of whether the Holocaust, and Nazism itself, stands on some sort of charge sheet against atheism, an argument frequently made—for example, by the Catholic polemicist William (Lord) Rees-Mogg in *The Times* in 2007 (he was also critical of communism). Conversely, it is argued that this is a meritless charge and, indeed, can be reversed by arguing that Nazism itself was a religion. That Nazism was not akin to Christianity does not imply that it should not be seen as being a religion or, at least, as a movement with religious elements including, crucially, a messianic leader and millenarian beliefs.[9] From this perspective, the treatment of the Jews can be seen in part as the removal of what was (misleadingly) presented as a rival religion, not only with the slaughter of its members and the destruction of its sites but also with the appropriation of its regalia and sacred books, as if a magic were being seized.

Among the standard theological responses to the central questions about God's role in the Holocaust are arguments that God left humanity with a degree of free will that made the Holocaust possible and also that God was present in the Holocaust and strongly so, not least as Jews courageously and powerfully testified to their faith in the most difficult and extreme circumstances. Literature on the latter includes Yaffa Eliach's *Hasidic Tales of the Holocaust* (1982) and Pesach Schindler's *Hasidic Responses to the Holocaust in the Light of Hasidic Thought* (1990). God suffering in the Holocaust is a major related theme, with the argument, for example, that God was present at Auschwitz.[10] God after Auschwitz has also been presented as "an undamaged standard by which one can measure the full extent of catastrophe,"[11] although others are less optimistic.

The Holocaust, moreover, serves as the key and tangible modern instance of a far longer experience of Jewish persecution, suffering, and loss. While episodes such as the destruction of the temple in Jerusalem in 70 CE by the Romans, the brutal Roman suppressions of Jewish opposition in Israel in 66–74 and 132–35, or the medieval slaughters of Jews, for example, in 1096 in Germany at the time of the First Crusade seem remote if not lost in the mist of time, the Holocaust is a far more present issue. There are also relevant differences, however, in that the German attempt to destroy the Jews throughout Europe was not one with which it was possible to compromise or attempt to escape by conforming to the values of the persecutor, as earlier, with the Roman Empire or the Christian Church. Challenged by Jewish monotheism and difference, the empire and the Church attacked what was an alternative religion, but members of the race could conform to Rome or Christianity, as they could not to Nazi ideology. From this perspective, the Holocaust was very different, although in religious terms, it was the latest in a series of vicious persecutions of Jews that were opportunities for the affirmation of Jewish belief.

Christian theologians have not always handled the implications of the Holocaust sensitively or sensibly. There are issues about the relationship with antisemitism, especially the role of Christians in the killing, a point that can be underlined by considering collaboration and the extent to which some collaborationist regimes and groups—for example, the governments of Vichy, Croatia, Hungary, Romania, and Slovakia—strongly emphasized Christianity as crucial to their identity. There are also the more general implications of the Holocaust for theology, not least in terms of the immanence of evil and barbarism. Some Christian theologians have argued that the Holocaust can be understood alongside the suffering of Christ, a thesis that can have unfortunate, indeed highly unfortunate, implications but that is intended to underline the argument about a central relationship between Jews and Christians and a common bond of pain. This is a frequent reaction from American visitors to the Holocaust Museum in Washington, DC. Other Christian theologians have pressed for the need to address the legacy of Christian antisemitism, not least by revising theology where necessary.

Christian theologians have also been challenged by the evil seen in the Holocaust. In *Christian Theology after Auschwitz* (1976), the Catholic theologian Gregory Baum argued that, in place of an all-powerful God, it was necessary to see God as acting from within, unable to block all movements or human sin but nevertheless able to act as "reviver" because of the divine role as the "forward movement operative in people's lives enabling them to enter more deeply into authentic humanity." Thus, a theological caution about divine power, not to say uncertainty about divine intentions, can match secular pessimism.

At the same time that the slaughter was a terrible episode in Jewish history and a central instance in the theme of a wider, unjust Jewish suffering across the ages, the Holocaust also resonates as a universal question. The latter does not lessen nor qualify the former but is part of it. Indeed, the questions "Why did God let it happen?" and "Where was God?" were seen before the Holocaust, not least in response to the horrors of World War I. The Holocaust added more coal for that fire but did not ignite a secularist withdrawal from religion.

THE ARTS

Religious and theological issues and difficulties have been matched by those of the arts. The limits of representation for all the arts have been debated in the case of the Holocaust. A range of tensions came into play, not least the need to offer a testimony and witness to the enormity that occurred. A profound melancholy provided a key tone. At the same time, taboos, politics, inaccuracy, and fabrication all played a role.[12] There was, notably, a debate about how best to represent the Holocaust on

screen.[13] For example, filmmaker Jean-Luc Godard denounced Spielberg's *Schindler's List* (1993) for presenting too affirmative an account
and for demanding no action from the spectator.[14] Based on a book by
Bernard Schenk, the film *The Reader* (2009) underplayed the degree
of personal responsibility of SS guards, notably of "Schmitz," the role
entrusted to the leading actress, Kate Winslet. This invented character
was linked to Hermine Braunsteiner, a sadistic murderess at the extermination camp at Majdanek who was imprisoned by an Austrian court
for only six months in 1949–50, being sentenced instead to life by a West
German court in 1981. There was first-rate press criticism of the apparent
message of the film and its screenwriter, David Hare, and notably of the
attempt to argue a moral relativism that extenuated some of the guilt of
the participants and, more generally, of wartime Germans, presenting
them alongside their victims as "history's unfortunate little people."

    The Boy in the Striped Pyjamas (2008), often presented as equivalent
to a modern *Anne Frank's Diary* as a way to introduce children to the
Holocaust, has been widely seen as highly problematic because of the
implausibility of even children in the fictional commandant's family
not knowing about the events depicted and due to the somewhat em-
pathetic character of this family. The situation was very different for
Jewish families, which were deliberately broken up, thus contributing
to a fundamental asocial characteristic of the Holocaust even for those
who survived.[15]

    Some films, however, were more successful in depicting the self-
corruption involved in collusion with the Nazis, for example, Istvan
Szabo's *Mephisto* (1981), a powerful account of Gustav Gründgens, a key
figure in the artistic pantheon of Nazi Germany who in 1934 became the
artistic director of the Prussian State Theatre. He was imprisoned by
the NKVD in 1945–46. Gründgens had been criticized in Klaus Mann's
novel *Mephisto* (1949), but a long subsequent legal case found in 1971
in favor of Gründgens's post-mortem personality rights. *The Woman in
Gold* (2015) ably depicts the roles of Austrians in antisemitism in 1938 and
subsequently—notably in seizing paintings from Jews and, later, being
very unwilling to make restitution.

    Aside from scrutinizing the Holocaust, the slaughter was also used
as a way to approach wartime conduct. Thus, in his play *Berlin Hanover*

Express (2009), the Irish writer Ian Kennedy Martin employed knowledge of the truth about the concentration camp at Bergen-Belsen in order to criticize the wartime neutrality of Eire, a neutrality that, despite the honorable conduct of many Irish individuals, was in large part sympathetic, if not supportive, to the German cause.

EUROPE TODAY

Coming to terms with the past involves, in part, considering the present and the future. Much has changed since the writing of the earlier version of this book in 2007. In Europe, there are repeated signs of antisemitism and accompanying physical manifestations in the form of the frequent harassment of Jews, especially those distinguished by dress as Orthodox Jews, and attacks on Jewish institutions and memorials, notably gravestones but also synagogues. Alongside traditional right-wing antisemitism and a rise of left-wing antisemitism, a greatly disproportionate amount of this violence comes from members of Muslim communities. Interfaith collaborative crisis groups have failed to rise to the occasion, in large part due to the attitude of many Muslim community leaders. Moreover, Western European publics have not responded well to the challenge of defending their own civil societies from assault.

The antisemitism across the political spectrum is most apparent on the Left, notably the Far Left, in part as an extension of criticism, often virulent and disproportionate, of Israel. However, in addition, the Far Right is the source of antisemitism, which is a continuation of traditional themes but one that has become more vigorous in recent years. Far from antisemitism only being a matter of economic marginal and social reactionaries, it is more widely diffused across society in Britain, more generally in Europe, and elsewhere, including in the United States. Through the world wide web, there has been an internationalization of Holocaust denial.

The strength of antisemitism in the modern world helps make the Holocaust more directly relevant than some of the academic discussion might suggest. "Death to the Jews!" and "Gas the Jews!" were shouts at pro-Palestinian rallies in Belgium, France, and Germany in 2014, and the French prime minister, Manuel Valls, referred to a "new anti-Semitism."

In response in large part to this antisemitism, there has been an increase in the number of Jews leaving Europe: France, alone, saw 7,000 depart in 2014. Antisemitism was also in evidence in pro-Palestinian and anti-Israel rallies and social media across the world in 2023.

LOOKING TO THE FUTURE

Cultural, political, and generational tensions and changes are all linked to the contested and altering presentation and understanding of the Holocaust. A key element of the political dimension, and notably in Europe, is the struggle between Left and Right over memorialization and within those broad categories. The nature and tone of future politics in particular countries will affect how this argument develops in the public sphere, for example in the relationship discerned between Nazi and communist slaughter.

Generational change encourages a different frame of reference not least because the young can be resentful about the approach of the old or require a new stance.[16] Episodes from the past become more distant. Today, some still have their resonance, for example World War I and the Holocaust, but in an increasingly decontextualized fashion as far as the circumstances of those episodes are concerned. Instead, the emphasis will be on such episodes as universal archetypes, however misleading this can be. Thus, these cases will probably serve respectively as archetypes of futility and racism, which, in practice, misunderstands World War I and underrates the Holocaust. This emphasis on archetypes is a classic way in which history is used. It will be affected by contrary pressures for transnational or amalgamated and national or distinctive history, pressures very much related to the politics of Europe,[17] but not only there. The Holocaust is a key event not only in human history but also in its presentation and understanding.

Notes

Preface

1. See, for example, P. Cooke and B. H. Shepherd, *European Resistance in the Second World War* (Barnsley, 2013); J. S. Corum, O. Mertelsmann, and K. Piirimae, *The Second World War and the Baltic States* (Frankfurt, 2014).

1. Until Barbarossa

1. J. M. Roberts, *The Mythology of the Secret Societies* (London, 1972).

2. J. Osterhammel, *The Transformation of the World: A Global History of the Nineteenth Century* (Princeton, NJ, 2014).

3. V. Caron, "Catholic Political Mobilisation and Antisemitic Violence in *Fin de Siècle* France: The Case of the *Union Nationale,*" *Journal of Modern History*, 8 (2009): 315–18.

4. M. Michaelis, "Fascism, Totalitarianism and the Holocaust: Reflections on Current Interpretations of National Socialist Anti-Semitism," *European History Quarterly*, 19 (1989): 99.

5. W. I. Brustein, *Roots of Hate: Anti-Semitism in Europe before the Holocaust* (Cambridge, 2003); W. Laqueur, *The Changing Face of Anti-Semitism from Ancient Times to the Present Day* (New York, 2008); D. Nirenberg, *Anti-Judaism: The Western Tradition* (New York, 2013).

6. P. Birnbaum, *A Tale of Ritual Murder in the Age of Louis XIV: The Trial of Raphaël Lévy, 1669* (Stanford, CA, 2012).

7. W. Patch, "The Catholic Church, the Third Reich, and the Origins of the Cold War: On the Utility and Limitations of Historical Evidence," *Journal of Modern History*, 82 (2010): 400–1.

8. J. Connelly, *From Enemy to Brother: The Revolution in Catholic Teaching on the Jews, 1933–1965* (Cambridge, MA, 2012).

9. S. Almog, *Nationalism and Antisemitism in Modern Europe, 1815–1945* (Oxford, 1990).

10. J. D. Hansen, *Mapping the Germans: Statistical Science, Cartography, and the Visualisation of the German Nation, 1848–1914* (Oxford, 2015).

11. O. Zimmer, "Beneath the 'Culture War': Corpus Christi Processions and Mutual Accommodation in the Second German Empire," *Journal of Modern History*, 82 (2010): 333–34.

12. P. Appelbaum, *Loyal Sons: Jews in the German Army in the Great War* (London, 2014).

13. C. Ingrao, *Believe and Destroy: Intellectuals in the SS War Machine* (Cambridge, 2013).

14. M. M. Payck and R. Pergher (eds.), *Beyond Versailles: Sovereignty, Legitimacy, and the Formation of New Politics after the Great War* (Bloomington, IN, 2019).

15. C. Ingrao, "The Revolutionary Origins of the Twentieth-Century Holocausts," *Consortium on Revolutionary Europe: Selected Papers, 1997* (Tallahassee, 1997): 32; P. Pulzer, *The Rise of Political Anti-Semitism in Germany and Austria* (Cambridge, MA, 1988); W. Gruner, *The Holocaust in Bohemia and Moravia: Czech Initiatives, German Policies, Jewish Responses* (Oxford, 2019).

16. L. Waddington, *Hitler's Crusade: Bolshevism, the Jews, and the Myth of the International Jewish Conspiracy* (London, 2009).

17. J. C. G. Röhl, *Wilhelm II: Into the Abyss of War and Exile, 1900–1941* (Cambridge, 2014): 1253.

18. M. Roseman, "Ideas, Contexts, and the Pursuit of Genocide," *German Historical Institute London: Bulletin*, 25 (2003): 73.

19. E. D. Weitz, *Weimar Germany: Promise and Tragedy* (Princeton, NJ, 2007): 321.

20. N. Naimark, *Fires of Hatred: Ethnic Cleansing in Twentieth Century Europe* (Cambridge, MA, 2001); V. Solonari, *Purifying the Nation: Population Exchange and Ethnic Cleansing in Nazi-Allied Romania* (Baltimore, 2009).

21. A. E. Steinweis, *Art, Ideology and Economics in Nazi Germany: The Reich Chambers of Music, Theater, and the Visual Arts* (Chapel Hill, NC, 1993); D. B. Dennis, *Inhumanities: Nazi Interpretations of Western Culture* (Cambridge, 2012): 84–105; M. Haas, *Forbidden Music: The Jewish Composers Banned by the Nazis* (New Haven, 2014).

22. V. G. Liulevcius, *The German Myth of the East: 1800 to the Present* (Oxford, 2009).

23. A. Confino, "Why Did the Nazis Burn the Hebrew Bible? Nazi Germany, Representations of the Past and the Holocaust," *Journal of Modern History*, 84 (2012): 376–99.

24. J. Q. Whitman, *Hitler's American Model: The United States and the Making of Nazi Race Law* (Princeton, NJ, 2017).

25. A. Versluis, *The New Inquisitions: Heretic-Hunting and the Intellectual Origins of Modern Totalitarianism* (Oxford, 2006).

26. E. Black, *IBM and the Holocaust: The Strategic Alliance between Nazi Germany and America's Most Powerful Corporation* (London, 2002); D. M. Luebke and S. Milton, "Locating the Victim: An Overview of Census-Taking, Tabulation Technology and Persecution in Nazi Germany," *IEEE Annals of the History of Computing*, 16, 3 (Autumn 1994): 25–39.

27. J. O'Loughlin, M. Flint, and M. Shin, "Regions and Milieux in Weimar Germany: The Nazi Party Vote of 1930 in Geographic Perspective," *Erdkunde*, 49 (1995): 305–14.

28. S. Friedländer, *Nazi Germany and the Jews: The Years of Persecution 1933–1939* (London, 1997); P. Kenez, *The Coming of the Holocaust: From Antisemitism to Genocide* (Cambridge, 2013).

29. B. Zucker, *In Search of Refuge: Jews and the U.S. Consuls in Nazi Germany, 1933–1941* (London, 2001); dealing with Jews from the village of Kippenheim and US officials divided over refugees, M. Dobbs, *The Unwanted: America, Auschwitz, and a Village Caught in Between* (New York, 2019); B. Trachtenburg, *The United States and the Nazi Holocaust: Race, Refuge and Remembrance* (New York, 2018), but see review by R. Medoff on H-Judaic, http://www.h-net.org /reviews/showpdf.php?id=53736.

30. P. Hayes, "Big Business and 'Aryanization' in Germany, 1933–1939," *Jahrbuch für Antisemitismusforschung*, 31 (1994): 254–81; L. M. Stallbaumer, "Big Business and the Persecution of the Jews: The Flick Concern and the 'Aryanization' of Jewish Property before the War," *Holocaust and Genocide Studies*, 13 (1999): 1–27; see, more generally, J. Steimer, *"A Third Reich, as I See It": Politics, Society, and Private Life in the Diaries of Nazi Germany, 1933–1939* (Bloomington, IN, 2023).

31. J. Connelly, "The Uses of *Volksgemeinschaft*: Letters to the NSDAP Kreisleitung Eisenach, 1939–40," *Journal of Modern History*, 68 (1996): 926.

32. H. James, *The Deutsche Bank and the Nazi Economic War against the Jews: The Expropriation of Jewish-Owned Property* (Cambridge, 2001).

33. A. Nolzen, "The Nazi Party and Its Violence against the Jews, 1933–39," *Yad Vashem Studies*, 31 (2003): 245–85; U. Gerhardt and T. Karlauf (eds.), *The Night of Broken Glass: Eyewitness Accounts of Kristallnacht* (Cambridge, 2012).

34. A. Confino, *A World without Jews: The Nazi Imagination from Persecution to Genocide* (New Haven, 2014).

35. C. Dillon, *Dachau and the SS: A Schooling in Violence* (Oxford, 2015).

36. N. Wachsmann, *KL: A History of the Nazi Concentration Camps* (London, 2015).

37. B. Rubin and W. G. Schwanitz, *Nazis, Islamists, and the Making of the Modern Middle East* (New Haven, 2014).

38. J. Steinberg, "The Third Reich Reflected: German Civil Administration in the Occupied Soviet Union, 1941–44," *English Historical Review*, 110 (1995): 632;

J. Matthäus, J. Böhler, and K. M. Mallmann, *War, Pacification, and Mass Murder, 1939: The Einsatzgruppen in Poland* (Lanham, MD, 2014).

39. For a later American academic to flee Warsaw in October 1939 and reach America via Italy, R. Pipes, *Vixi: Memoirs of a Non-Belonger* (New Haven, 2003): 8–11; R. Bessel, "Death and Survival in the Second World War," in M. Geyer and A. Tooze (eds.), *The Cambridge History of the Second World War: III Total War* (Cambridge, 2015): 259–60.

40. M. Fulbrook, *A Small Town Near Auschwitz: Ordinary Nazis and the Holocaust* (Oxford, 2012).

41. C. Browning, "Nazi Ghettoization Policy in Poland, 1939–41," *Central European History*, 19 (1986): 365.

42. For life in this ghetto, M. M. Sutnik (ed.), *Memory Unearthed: The Lodz Ghetto Photographs of Henryk Ross* (New Haven, 2015).

43. J. Moser, "Nisko, the First Experiment in Deportation," *Simon Wiesenthal Center Annual*, 2 (1985): esp. 17–21.

44. C. Browning, "Nazi Resettlement Policy and the Search for a Solution to the Jewish Question 1939–41," *German Studies Review*, 9 (1986): 515.

45. R. D. Müller, *Enemy in the East: Hitler's Secret Plans to Invade the Soviet Union* (London, 2014).

2. Toward Genocide

1. Y. Lozowick, "The Early Activities of Einsatzgruppe C," *Holocaust and Genocide Studies*, 2 (1987): 221–41.

2. D. Wildermuth, "Who Killed Lida's Jewish Intelligentsia? A Case Study of Wehrmacht Involvement in the Holocaust's 'First Hour,'" *Holocaust and Genocide Studies*, 27 (2013): 1–29, at 9, see also fn. 54.

3. G. Wawro, *The Franco-Prussian War: The German Conquest of France in 1870–1871* (Cambridge, 2003): 264–65, 288–89.

4. J. Horne and A. Kramer, *German Atrocities in 1914: Meanings and Memory of War* (New Haven, 2001); J. Lipkes, *Rehearsals: The Germans Army in Belgium, August 1914* (Leuven, 2007).

5. D. Showalter, "'The East Gives Nothing Back': The Great War and the German Army in Russia," *Journal of the Historical Society*, 2 (2002): 15–16.

6. I. Hull, "The Military Campaign in German Southwest Africa, 1904–7," *Bulletin of the German Historical Institute, Washington*, 37 (2005): 41–42; B. Shepherd, *Terror in the Balkans: German Armies and Partisan Warfare* (Cambridge, MA, 2012).

7. M. H. Fisher (ed.), *The Travels of Dean Mahomet: An Eighteenth-Century Journey through India* (Berkeley, 1997): 58.

8. T. Piotrowski, *Poland's Holocaust: Ethnic Strife, Collaboration with Occupying Forces and Genocide in the Second Republic, 1918–1947* (Jefferson, NC, 2007): 221.

9. C. Browning, "The Nazi Decision to Commit Mass Murder: Three Interpretations. The Euphoria of Victory and the Final Solution, Autumn 1941," *German Studies Review*, 17 (1994): 473–81; A. J. Kay, *The Making of an SS Killer: The Life of Colonel Alfred Filbert, 1905–1990* (Cambridge, 2016): 3.

10. C. Hartmann, *Operation Barbarossa: Nazi Germany's War in the East, 1941–1945* (Oxford, 2013).

11. S. Corvaja, *Hitler and Mussolini* (New York, 2001): 236.

12. J. Steinberg, "The Third Reich Reflected: German Civil Administration in the Occupied Soviet Union, 1941–44," *English Historical Review*, 110 (1995): 111.

13. S. D. Kassow, "Inside the Kovno Ghetto," in S. Schalkowsky (ed. and trans.), *The Clandestine History of the Kovno Jewish Ghetto Police: By Anonymous Members of the Kovno Jewish Ghetto Police* (Bloomington, IN, 2014): 1–59.

14. S. Tyas, "Allied Intelligence Agencies and the Holocaust: Information Acquired from German Prisoners of War," *Holocaust and Genocide Studies*, 22 (2008): 10.

15. T. Dupuy, *Encyclopedia of Military Biography* (London, 1992): 644. For another senior figure, Field Marshal Kesselring, lying about the execution of Italian civilians and American troops, R. Raiber, *Anatomy of Perjury: Field Marshal Albert Kesselring, Via Rasella, and the GINNY Mission* (Newark, DE, 2008); K. V. Lingen, *Kesselring's Last Battle: War Crimes Trials and Cold War Politics, 1945–1960* (Lawrence, KS, 2009).

16. T. Anderson, "Germans, Ukrainians and Jews: Ethnic Politics in *Heeresgebiet Süd*, June–December 1941," *War in History*, 7 (2000): 337. For an ethnic German role as well, K. Lada and P. Monteath, "One Day in Israylovka: A Case Study of the Holocaust in Southeastern Ukraine," *Holocaust and Genocide Studies*, 31 (2017): 61–86.

17. D. Wildermuth, "Widening the Circle: General Weikersthal and the War of Annihilation, 1941–42," *Central European History*, 45 (2012): 306–24. For a murderous Ukrainian attack in Tuchyn on July 6, 1941, J. McBride, "The Tuchyn Pogrom: The Names and Faces behind the Violence, Summer 1941," *Holocaust and Genocide Studies*, 36 (2022): 315–33.

18. W. Wolfram, *The Wehrmacht: History, Myth, Reality* (Cambridge, MA, 2006).

19. King's College, London, Liddell Hart Archive, Liddell Hart papers 4/28.

20. M. Wildt, *Hitler's "Volksgemeinschaft" and the Dynamics of Racial Exclusion: Violence against Jews in Provincial Germany, 1919–1939* (New York, 2012).

21. W. W. Beon, *Marching into Darkness: The Wehrmacht and the Holocaust in Belarus* (Cambridge, MA, 2014).

22. E. A. Johnson and K.-H. Reuband, *What We Knew: Terror, Mass Murder, and Everyday Life in Nazi Germany* (Cambridge, MA, 2005): 256.

23. P. Montague, *Chelmno and the Holocaust: The History of Hitler's First Death Camp* (London, 2012).

24. M. Winstone, *The Dark Heart of Hitler's Europe* (London, 2015).

25. L. R. Johnson, *Central Europe: Enemies, Neighbors, Friends* (New York, 1996): 219.

26. P. Witte, "Two Decisions Concerning the 'Final Solution to the Jewish Question': Deportations to Lódz and Mass Murder in Chelmno," *Holocaust and Genocide Studies*, 9 (1995): 325–33.

27. Hansard, House of Commons Debates, 3 September 1939, vol. 351, column 295.

28. A. McElligott and T. Kirk (eds.), *Working toward the Führer: Essays in Honor of Sir Ian Kershaw* (Manchester, 2003).

29. S. Friedländer, "From Anti-Semitism to Extermination," *Yad Vashem Studies*, 16 (1984): 48.

30. R. Gellately (ed.), *The Nuremberg Interviews: Conducted by Leon Goldensohn* (London, 2007): 188–90.

31. S. Friedländer, "From Anti-Semitism": 47.

32. I. Kershaw, *Fateful Choices: Ten Decisions That Changed the World, 1940–41* (London, 2007): 431–70.

33. I. Kershaw, "Improvised Genocide: The Emergence of the 'Final Solution' in the 'Warthegau,'" *Transactions of the Royal Historical Society*, 6th ser. 2 (1992): 73; C. Browning, "German Killers: Orders from Above, Initiative from Below, and the Scope of Local Autonomy—the Case of Brest-Litovsk," in C. Browning, *Nazi Policy, Jewish Workers, German Killers* (Cambridge, 2000): 116–42. For the concurrence of differing levels of causation, A. Wylegala, "Operation Reinhard in District Galicia: Three Levels of Narrative about the Holocaust," *Holocaust and Genocide Studies*, 34 (2020): 478–505.

34. M. Roseman, *The Villa, the Lake, the Meeting: Wannsee and the Final Solution* (London, 2002).

35. J. Noakes, "The Development of Nazi Policy towards the German-Jewish 'Mischling,'" *Leo Baeck Institute Year Book*, 34 (1989): 291–356.

36. J. A. S. Grenville, *The Jews and Germans of Hamburg: The Destruction of a Civilisation, 1790–1945* (London, 2012): 260.

37. Y. Arad, *Belzec, Sobibor, Treblinka: The Operation Reinhard Death Camps* (Indianapolis, 1987).

38. F. Piper, "Estimating the Number of Deportees and Victims of the Auschwitz-Birkenau Camp," *Yad Vashem Studies*, 21 (1991): 49–103.

39. Y. Gutman and M. Berenbaum (eds.), *Anatomy of the Auschwitz Death Camp* (Bloomington, IN, 1994).

40. S. Krakowski and I. Altman, "The Testament of the Last Prisoners at the Chelmno Death Camp," *Yad Vashem Studies*, 21 (1991): 105–23.

41. J. Steinberg, "The Third Reich Reflected: German Civil Administration in the Occupied Soviet Union, 1941–44," *English Historical Review*, 110 (1995): 647.

42. N. Tec, *Resilience and Courage: Women, Men and the Holocaust* (New Haven, 2003).

43. Johnson and Reuband, *What We Knew*: 232.

44. O. Bartov, "The Devil in the Details: The Concentration Camp as Historical Construct," *German Historical Institute London: Bulletin*, 21 (1999): 39.

45. W. Beorn, "Negotiating Murder: A Panzer Signal Company and the Destruction of the Jews of Peregruznoe, 1942," *Holocaust and Genocide Studies*, 23 (2009): 185–213.

46. H. Pringle, *Master Plan: Himmler's Scholars and the Holocaust* (London, 2006).

47. Piotrowski, *Poland's Holocaust*: 31.

48. K. Sakowicz, *Ponary Diary, 1941–1943: A Bystander's Account of a Mass Murder*, edited by Y. Arad (New Haven, 2005).

49. *Trial of the Major War Criminals*, Vol. VI (Nuremberg, 1947): 293.

3. Genocide

1. *Daily Telegraph*, June 27, 2015, 9.

2. C. Browning, "A Final Hitler Decision for the 'Final Solution'? The Riegner Telegram Reconsidered," *Holocaust and Genocide Studies*, 10 (1996): 3–10; T. P. Kaplan and W. Gruner (eds.), *Resisting Persecution: Jews and Their Petitions during the Holocaust* (Oxford, 2020); R. Hilberg, *The Anatomy of the Holocaust: Selected Works from a Life of Scholarship* (Oxford, 2020): 113–46.

3. I. Gutman, *The Jews of Warsaw 1939–43: Ghetto, Underground, Revolt* (Bloomington, IN, 1982). I am most grateful for the advice of David Cesarani. For a comparison, L. Vastenhout, "Remain or Resign? Jewish Leaders' Dilemmas in the Netherlands and Belgium under Nazi Occupation," *Holocaust and Genocide Studies*, 36 (2022): 413–27.

4. S. Schalkowsky (trans. and ed.), *The Clandestine History of the Kovno Jewish Ghetto Police: By Anonymous Members of the Kovno Jewish Ghetto Police* (Bloomington, IN, 2015). K. Person, *Warsaw Ghetto Police: The Jewish Order Service during the Nazi Occupation* (Ithica, NY, 2021).

5. Y. Gutman, *Resistance: The Warsaw Ghetto Uprising* (Boston, 1994).

6. S. Spector, "Jewish Resistance in Small Towns in Eastern Poland," in N. Davies and A. Polonsky (eds.), *Jews in Eastern Poland and the USSR, 1939–46* (London, 1991); B. Shepherd, *War in the Wild East: The German Army and Soviet Partisans* (Cambridge, MA, 2004); H. H. Nolte, "Partisan War in Belorussia, 1941–44," in R. Chickering, S. Förster, and B. Greiner (eds.), *A World at Total War: Global Conflict and the Politics of Destruction, 1937–1945* (Cambridge, 2005): 264, 268; B. Epstein, *The Minsk Ghetto, 1941–1943: Jewish Resistance and Soviet Internationalism* (Berkeley, 2008).

7. Y. Bauer, *They Chose Life: Jewish Resistance in the Holocaust* (Seattle, 1973); J. Glass, *Jewish Resistance during the Holocaust: Moral Uses of Violence and Will* (Basingstoke, 2004); R. Sakowski, "Two Forms of Resistance in the Warsaw Ghetto: Two Functions of the Ringelblom Archives," *Yad Vashem Studies*, 21 (1991): 189–219; S. Erpel, "Struggle and Survival: Jewish Women in the Anti-Fascist Resistance in Germany," *Yearbook: Leo Baeck Institute of Jews in Germany*, 37 (1992): 397–414; R. Rohrlich (ed.), *Resisting the Holocaust* (Oxford, 1998); Z. Barmatz, *Heroism in the Forest: the Jewish Partisans of Belarus* (Jerusalem, 2013).

8. S. Gilbert, *Music in the Holocaust: Confronting Life in the Nazi Ghettos and Camps* (Oxford, 2005): 200. For the powerful account of Shlomo Venezia, a Jew from Salonika who survived being a member of the Auschwitz *Sonderkommando* moving the corpses of those gassed, S. Venezia, *Inside the Gas Chambers: Eight Months in the Sonderkommando of Auschwitz* (Cambridge, 2009).

9. G. Corni, *Hitler's Ghettos: Voices from a Beleaguered Society, 1939–1944* (London, 2002).

10. P. Kenez, "Pogroms and White Ideology in the Russian Civil War," in J. D. Klier and S. Lambroza (eds.), *Pogroms: Anti-Jewish Violence in Modern Russian History* (Cambridge, 1992): 293–313; O. Budnitskii, *Russian Jews between the Reds and the Whites, 1917–1920* (Philadelphia, 2012).

11. D. J. Penslar, *Jews and the Military: A History* (Princeton, NJ, 2013).

12. "Wehrmacht Reprisal Policy and the Mass-Murder of Jews in Serbia," *Militärgeschichtliche Mitteilungen*, 33 (1983): 35; H. Heer and K. Naumann (eds.), *Vernichtungskrieg: Verbrechen der Wehrmacht 1941–1944* (Hamburg, 1995).

13. R. Breitman, *The Architect of Genocide: Himmler and the Final Solution* (London, 1991): 142.

14. S. Friedländer, *The Years of Extermination: Nazi Germany and the Jews, 1939–1945* (New York, 2007): 350.

15. G. Berendt, *Bronna Góra, 1942 roku* (Gdańsk 2021): 202–9.

16. M. T. Allen, *The Business of Genocide: The SS, Slave Labor, and the Concentration Camps* (Chapel Hill, NC, 2002); P. Hayes, *Industry and Ideology: I. G. Farben in the Nazi Era* (Cambridge, 1987).

17. W. Gruner, *Jewish Forced Labor under the Nazis: Economic Needs and Racial Aims, 1938–1944* (Cambridge, 2006). The incoherence of German policy emerges anew in W.W. Mędykowski, *Macht Arbeit Frei? German Economic Policy and Forced Labor of Jews in the General Government, 1939–1943* (Boston, 2018).

18. U. Herbert, *Hitler's Foreign Workers: Enforced Labor in Germany under the Third Reich* (Cambridge, 1977).

19. A. Kochavi, *Confronting Captivity: Britain and the United States and Their POWs in Nazi Germany* (Chapel Hill, NC, 2005); A. Boum and S. A. Stein (eds.), *The Holocaust and North Africa* (Stanford, CA, 2018).

20. F. Piper, *Auschwitz Prison Labour: The Organisation and Exploitation of Auschwitz Concentration Camp Prisoners as Laborers* (Oswiecim, 2002).

21. Gilbert, *Music in the Holocaust*.

22. G. D. Feldman, *Allianz and the German Insurance Business, 1933–1945* (Cambridge, 2001); C. R. Browning, P. Hayes, and R. Hilberg, *German Railroads, Jewish Souls: The Reichsbahn, Bureaucracy, and the Final Solution* (Washington, DC, 2019).

23. G. H. Bennett, *The Nazi, The Painter and the Forgotten Story of the SS Road* (London, 2012).

24. E. A. Johnson and K.-H. Reuband, *What We Knew: Terror, Mass Murder and Everyday Life in Nazi Germany* (New York, 2005).

25. M. Mouton, *From Nurturing the German Nation to Purifying the Volk: Weimar and Nazi Family Policy, 1918–1945* (Cambridge, 2007).

26. M. Mazower, "Military Violence and National Socialist Values: The Wehrmacht in Greece, 1941–44," *Past and Present*, 134 (1992): 129–58.

27. H. Boog, W. Rahn, R. Stumpf, and B. Wegner, *Germany and the Second World War: VI. The Global War* (Oxford, 2001).

28. W. Lower, *Nazi Empire-Building and the Holocaust in Ukraine* (Chapel Hill, NC, 2005).

29. R. Braham, *The Politics of Genocide: The Holocaust in Hungary* (New York, 1981); D. Cesarani (ed.), *Genocide and Rescue: The Holocaust in Hungary, 1944* (Oxford, 1997); R. Braham and S. Miller (eds.), *The Nazis' Last Victims: The Holocaust in Hungary* (Detroit, 1998).

30. R. Zweig, *The Gold Train: The Destruction of the Jews and the Second World War's Most Terrible Robbery* (London, 2002).

31. A. D. van Liempt, *Hitler's Bounty Hunters: The Betrayal of the Jews* (Oxford, 2005).

32. S. Gensburger, *Witnessing the Robbing of the Jews: A Photographic Album, Paris, 1940–44* (Bloomington, IN, 2015).

33. D. Süss's contribution to roundtable on his *Death from the Skies: How the British and Germans Survived Bombing in World War II* (Oxford, 2014), in *Britain and the World*, 8 (2015): 116.

34. For the misuse of language, V. Klemperer, *The Language of the Third Reich: LTI—Lingua Tertii Imperii: A Philologist's Notebook* (London, 2000).

35. H. Loewy, "Diasporic Home of Homelessness: The Museum and the Circle of Lost and Found," *German Historical Institute London: Bulletin*, 34 (2012): 49.

36. J. Ancel, *The Economic Destruction of Romanian Jewry* (Jerusalem, 2007).

37. G. Kádár and Z. Vági, *Self-Financing Genocide: The Gold Train, the Becher Case and the Wealth of Hungarian Jews* (Budapest, 2004).

38. U. Herbert, "Labour and Extermination: Economic Interest and the Primacy of Weltanschauung in National Socialism," *Past and Present*, 138 (1993): 144–95.

39. *Trial of the Major War Criminals* (Nuremberg, 1947), VII, 89.

40. P. K. Grimsted, *Trophies of War and Empire: The Archival Heritage of Ukraine, World War II, and the International Politics of Restitution* (Cambridge, MA, 2001): 196–209; K. C. Berkhoff, *Harvest of Despair: Life and Death in Ukraine under Nazi Rule* (Cambridge, MA, 2004).

41. M. Levene and P. Roberts (eds.), *The Massacre in History* (Oxford, 1999).

42. B. Wegner, "The Ideology of Self-Destruction: Hitler and the Choreography of Defeat," *German Historical Institute London: Bulletin*, 26 (2004): 26–33.

43. N. Wachsmann, *Hitler's Prisons: Legal Terror in Nazi Germany* (New Haven, 2004).

44. D. K. Yelton, "'Ein Volk Steht Auf': The German Volkssturm and Nazi Strategy, 1944–45," *Journal of Military History*, 64 (2000): 1067, 1071; G. L. Weinberg, *Germany, Hitler and World War II* (Cambridge, 1995): 274–86; Howard Grier, *Hitler, Dönitz and the Baltic Sea: The Third Reich's Last Hope, 1944–5* (Annapolis, MD, 2007).

45. Y. Katznelson, *Vittel Diary* (Tel Aviv, 1964) and *Le chant du peuple juif assassiné* (Paris 2005).

46. L. Dobrowski (ed.), *The Chronicle of the Lodz Ghetto* (New Haven, 1987).

47. A. K. Knowles, T. Cole, and A. Giordano (eds.), *Geographies of the Holocaust* (Bloomington, IN, 2014).

48. *The Times*, April 24, 2015, 31.

49. A. J. Kochavi, *Prelude to Nuremberg: Allied War Crimes Policy and the Question of Punishment* (Chapel Hill, NC, 1998): 65; J. Hicks, "'Soul Destroyers': Soviet Reporting of Nazi Genocide and Its Perpetrators at the Krasnodar and Khar'kov Trials," *History*, 98 (2013): 530–46.

50. *Trial of the Major War Criminals* VII (Nuremberg, 1947), 579.

51. D. Stone, *The Holocaust: An Unfinished History* (London, 2023): 223–35.

52. S. Krakowski, "The Death Marches in the Period of the Evacuation of the Camps," in Y. Gutman and A. Saf (eds.), *The Nazi Concentration Camps* (Jerusalem, 1984): 475–91; D. Blatman, "The Death Marches; January–May 1945: Who Was Responsible for What?" *Yad Vashem Studies*, 28 (2000): 155–201.

53. P. Green, *The March East 1945: The Final Days of Oflag IX A/H and IX A/Z* (Stroud, 2012); R. Wallis, *British POWs and the Holocaust: Witnessing the Nazi Atrocities* (London, 2016).

54. J. Russell, *No Triumphant Procession: The Forgotten Battles of April 1945* (London, 1994).

55. I. Haar and M. Fahlbusch (eds.), *German Scholars and Ethnic Cleansing, 1919–1945* (New York, 2005).

56. M. H. Kater, *Hitler Youth* (Cambridge, MA, 2004).

57. P. Panayi, "Victims, Perpetrators and Bystanders in a German Town: The Jews of Osnabrück Before, During and After the Third Reich," *European History Quarterly*, 33 (2003): 451–92.

58. J. F. Tent, *In the Shadow of the Holocaust: Nazi Persecution of Jewish-Christian Germans* (Lawrence, KS, 2003).

59. S. Bach, *Leni: The Life and Work of Leni Riefenstahl* (London, 2007).

60. A. S. Bergerson, *Ordinary Germans in Extraordinary Times: The Nazi Revolution in Hildesheim* (Bloomington, IN, 2004).

61. D. Bankier, "The Germans and the Holocaust: What Did They Know?" *Yad Vashem Studies*, 20 (1990), and *The Germans and the Final Solution: Public Opinion under Nazism* (3rd ed., Oxford, 2002).

62. K. M. Mallmann, "Social Penetration and Police Action: Collaboration in the Repertory of Gestapo Activities," *International Review of Social History*, 42 (1997): 25–43; V. Joshi, "The 'Private' Became the 'Public': Wives as Denouncers in the Third Reich," *Journal of Contemporary History*, 37 (2002): 419–35.

63. N. Stargadt, "Victims of Bombing and Retaliation," *German Historical Institute London: Bulletin*, 26 (2004): 67–69.

64. C. Browning, *Ordinary Men: Reserve Police Battalion 101 and the Final Solution in Poland* (New York, 1992); G. L. Weinberg, *Crossing the Line in Nazi Genocide: On Becoming and Being a Professional Killer* (Burlington, MA, 1997); M. Mann, "Were the Perpetrators of Genocide 'Ordinary Men' or 'Real Nazis'? Results from Fifteen Hundred Biographies," *Holocaust and Genocide Studies*, 14 (2000): 331–66; T. P. Kaplan, J. Matthäus, and M. W. Hornburg (eds.), *Beyond "Ordinary Men": Christopher R. Browning and Holocaust Historiography* (Leiden, 2019).

65. S. Baranowski, *The Confessing Church, Conservative Elites, and the Nazi State* (Lewiston, NY, 1986); R. Ericksen and S. Heschel (eds.), *Betrayal: German Churches and the Holocaust* (Minneapolis, 1999).

66. K. P. Spicer, *Resisting the Third Reich: The Catholic Clergy in Hitler's Berlin* (DeKalb, IL, 2004).

67. O. Heilbronner, "The Place of Catholic Historians and Catholic Historiography in Nazi Germany," *History*, 88 (2003): 291–92.

68. M. Braverman, "Theology in the Shadow of the Holocaust: Revisiting Bonhoeffer and the Jews," *Theology Today*, 79 (2022), https://doi.org/10.1177/00405736221084735.

69. D. Nelson, *Moroni and the Swastika: Mormons in Nazi Germany* (Norman, OK, 2015).

70. R. I. Moore, *The Formation of Persecuting Society* (Oxford, 1988); W. Monter, *Frontiers of Heresy: The Spanish Inquisition from the Basque Lands to Sicily* (Cambridge, 1990); S. Haliczer, *Inquisition and Society in the Kingdom of Valencia 1478–1834* (Berkeley, 1990).

71. R. Gellately, *The Gestapo and German Society: Enforcing Racial Policy 1933–1945* (Oxford, 1990) and *Backing Hitler: Consent and Coercion in Nazi Germany* (Oxford, 2001); G. Eley, "Hitler's Silent Majority? Conformity and Resistance under the Third Reich," *Michigan Quarterly Review*, 42 (2003): 389–425.

72. D. Mühlberger, *Hitler's Followers: Studies in the Sociology of the Nazi Movement* (London, 1991); J. W. Falter, "The Anatomy of a Volkspartei," *Historical Social Research*, 24, 2 (1999): 58–98; H. D. Andrews, "Thirty-Four Gold Medallists: Nazi Women Remember the 'Kampfzeit,'" *German History*, 11 (1993): 293–315; L. Pine, "Creating Conformity: The Training of Girls in the *Bund Deutscher Mädel*," *European History Quarterly*, 33 (2005): 367–85; G. Eley, *Nazism as Fascism: Violence, Ideology, and the Ground of Consent in Germany 1930–1945* (Abingdon, 2013).

73. V. Drapac and G. Pritchard, *Resistance and Collaboration in Hitler's Empire* (London, 2017).

74. M. Gilbert, *Auschwitz and the Allies* (London, 1981); W. Rubinstein, *The Myth of Rescue: Why the Democracies Could Not Have Saved More Jews from the Nazis* (London, 1997); M. J. Neufeld and M. Barenbaum (eds.), *The Bombing of Auschwitz: Should the Allies Have Attempted It?* (New York, 2000); R. H. Levy, "The Bombing of Auschwitz Revisited," *Holocaust and Genocide Studies*, 10 (1996): 267–98; S. B. Erdheim, "Could the Allies Have Bombed Auschwitz?" *Holocaust and Genocide Studies*, 11 (1997): 129–70; E. B. Westermann, "The Royal Air Force and the Bombing of Auschwitz," *Holocaust and Genocide Studies*, 15 (2001): 70–85; J. R. White, "Target Auschwitz," *Holocaust and Genocide Studies*, 16 (2002): 54–76.

75. *Papers Concerning the Treatment of German Nationals in Germany 1938–39* (London, 1939): 33.

76. A. Sharf, *The British Press and Jews under Nazi Rule* (Oxford, 1964): 79.

77. J. Matthäus, *Predicting the Holocaust: Jewish Organisations Report from Geneva on the Emergence of the "Final Solution," 1939–1942* (Lanham, MD, 2019); M. Smith, "Bletchley Park and the Holocaust," *Intelligence and National Security*, 19 (2004): 262–74, reprinted in L. V. Scott and P. D. Jackson (eds.), *Understanding Intelligence in the Twenty-First Century* (London, 2004): 111–21, corrects R. Breitman, *Official Secrets: What the Nazis Planned, What the British and Americans Knew* (London, 1999). For the claim that press reports were censored to avoid public pressure to take refugees, M. Fleming, *Auschwitz, the Allies and Censorship of the Holocaust* (Cambridge, 2014).

78. S. Aronson, *Hitler, the Allies, and the Jews* (Cambridge, 2004).

79. M. Kalb, "Introduction: Journalism and the Holocaust, 1933–45," in R. M. Shapiro (ed.), *Why Didn't the Press Shout: American and International Journalism during the Holocaust* (Hoboken, NJ, 2003): 6.

80. N. Terry, "Conflicting Signals: British Intelligence on the 'Final Solution' through Radio Intercepts and Other Sources, 1941–1942," *Yad Vashem Studies*, 32 (2004): 251–96.

81. S. Friedman, *No Haven for the Oppressed: United States Policy towards Jewish Refugees 1939–1945* (Detroit, 1973); D. S. Wyman, *The Abandonment of the Jews: America and the Holocaust, 1941–1945* (New York, 1984); H. Feingold, *The Politics of Rescue: The Roosevelt Administration and the Holocaust 1938–1945* (New Brunswick, NJ, 1986) and *Bearing Witness: How America and Its Jews Responded to the Holocaust* (Syracuse, NY, 1995).

82. L. Leff, *Buried by "The Times": The Holocaust and America's Most Important Newspaper* (Cambridge, 2005).

83. T. Kushner, *The Holocaust and the Liberal Imagination: A Social and Cultural History* (London, 1994): 186.

84. D. Cesarani, "Great Britain," in D. Wyman (ed.), *The World Reacts to the Holocaust* (Baltimore, 1996): 606–7, and *Britain and the Holocaust* (London, 1998): 12.

85. T. Kushner, *The Persistence of Prejudice: Anti-Semitism in British Society during the Second World War* (Manchester, 1989): 154.

86. B. Wasserstein, *Britain and the Jews of Europe 1939–1945* (London, 1999).

87. A. Danchev and D. Todman (eds.), *War Diaries 1939–1945* by Field Marshal Lord Alanbrooke (London, 2001): 617.

88. M. Salter, *US Intelligence, the Holocaust and the Nuremberg Trials* (Leiden, 2009): 86–91.

89. J. Brand and A. Weissberg, *A Desperate Mission* (New York, 1958).

90. Y. Bauer, *Rethinking the Holocaust* (New Haven, 2001): 202.

4. Germany's Allies, the Occupied, and Neutrals

1. K. Hitchins, *Romania 1866–1947* (Oxford, 1994): 483–85.

2. R. Ionaid, *The Holocaust in Romania: The Destruction of Jews and Gypsies under the Antonescu Regime, 1940–1944* (Chicago, 2000); D. Deletant, *Ion Antonescu: Hitler's Forgotten Ally* (New York, 2006); H. Eaton, *The Origins and Onset of the Romanian Holocaust* (Detroit, 2013); D. Dumitru, *The State, Antisemitism, and Collaboration in the Holocaust: The Borderlands of Romania and the Soviet Union* (New York, 2016); S. Suveica, "Pianos and Paintings from Transnistria: The Plunder of 'Cultural Trophies' during the Romanian Occupation (1941–1944)," *Journal of Holocaust Research*, 36 (2022): 261–80. For the Orthodox clergy as active antisemites, I. Biliuta, "'Christianizing'

Transnistria: Romanian Orthodox Clergy as Beneficiaries, Perpetrators, and Rescuers during the Holocaust," *Journal of Holocaust Research*, 34 (2020): 18–44.

3. E. C. Steinhart, *The Holocaust and the Germanisation of Ukraine* (Cambridge, 2015).

4. M. Bucur, "Edifices of the Past: War Memorials and Heroes in Twentieth-Century Romania," in M. Todorova (ed.), *Balkan Identities: Nation and Memory* (London, 2004): 172.

5. R. Yeomans, *Visions of Annihilation: The Ustasha Regime and the Cultural Politics of Fascism 1941–1945* (Pittsburgh, 2013).

6. J. M. Ward, *Priest, Politician, Collaborator: Jozef Tiso and the Making of Fascist Slovakia* (Ithaca, NY, 2013).

7. K. Ungváry, *Battle for Budapest: One Hundred Days in World War II* (London, 2004).

8. F. Chary, *The Bulgarian Jews and the Final Solution* (Pittsburgh, 1972); M. Bar-Zohar, *Beyond Hitler's Grasp: The Heroic Rescue of Bulgaria's Jews* (Hollbrook, MA, 1998).

9. R. J. Crampton, *Bulgaria* (Oxford, 2007): 266, 271.

10. A. L. Cardova, "Recasting the Duce for the New Century: Recent Scholarship on Mussolini and Italian Fascism," *Journal of Modern History*, 77 (2005): 731–32. For a recent critical view, P. Corner, *Mussolini in Myth and Memory: The First Totalitarian Dictator* (Oxford, 2022).

11. S. Luconi, "Il Gripo della Stirpe and Mussolini's 1938 Racial Legislation," *Shofar*, 22 (2004): 67–79.

12. M. Hametz, "The Ambivalence of Italian Anti-Semitism: Fascism, Nationalism, and Racism in Trieste," *Holocaust and Gender Studies*, 16 (2002): 376–401.

13. G. Schwarz, *After Mussolini: Jewish Life and Jewish Memories in Post-Fascist Italy* (London, 2012).

14. D. Carpi, "The Rescue of Jews in the Italian Zone of Occupied Croatia," in Y. Gutman (ed.), *Rescue Attempts during the Holocaust: Proceedings of the Second Yad Vashem International Historical Conference—April 1974* (Jerusalem, 1977): 465–525, quote 505, and "Notes on the History of the Jews in Greece during the Holocaust Period: The Attitude of the Italians 1941–43," in *Festschrift in Honor of Dr. George S. Wise* (Tel Aviv, 1981): 25–62.

15. J. Steinberg, *All or Nothing: The Axis and the Holocaust 1941–43* (London, 1990); N. Caracciolo et al., *Uncertain Refuge: Italy and the Jews during the Holocaust* (Urbana, IL, 1995); M. Sarfatti, *The Jews in Mussolini's Italy: From Equality to Persecution* (Madison, WI, 2006); S. L. Sullam, *The Italian Executioners: The Genocide of the Jews of Italy* (Princeton, NJ, 2018).

16. H. Rautkallio, *Finland and the Holocaust: The Rescue of Finland's Jews* (New York, 1987).

17. M. Medzini, *Under the Shadow of the Rising Sun: Japan and the Jews During the Holocaust Era* (Boston, 2016).

18. E. C. Steinhart, *The Holocaust and the Germanization of Ukraine* (Cambridge, 2015).

19. V. Caron, "The Anti-Semitic Revival in France in the 1930s: The Socio-economic Dimension Reconsidered," *Journal of Modern History*, 70 (1998): 24–73.

20. E. T. Jennings, *Vichy in the Tropics: Pétain's National Revolution in Madagascar, Guadeloupe, and Indochina, 1940–1944* (Stanford, CA, 2001).

21. L. Broch, *Ordinary Workers, Vichy and the Holocaust: French Railwaymen and the Second World War* (Cambridge, 2016).

22. S. Kitson, *Police and Politics in Marseille, 1936–1945* (Leiden, 2014).

23. Alfred Baudrillart was professor of history at the *Institut Catholique* in Paris from 1894 to 1907, and then its rector until his death in Paris in 1942. Titular archbishop of Melitene from 1928, Baudrillart was declared cardinal priest of S. Bernardo alle Terme in 1935 and was one of the cardinal electors in the 1939 papal conclave that selected Pope Pius XII.

24. S. Zuccotti, *The Holocaust, the French, and the Jews* (New York, 1993); M. Marrus and R. O. Paxton, *Vichy France and the Jews* (Stanford, CA, 1995); D. F. Ryan, *The Holocaust and the Jews of Marseille: The Enforcement of Anti-Semitic Policies in Vichy France* (Urbana, IL, 1996); R. H. Weisburg, *Vichy Law and the Holocaust in France* (New York, 1996).

25. B. Moore, *Victims and Survivors: Nazi Persecution of the Jews in the Netherlands, 1940–1945* (London, 1997).

26. M. Steinberg, *L'Étoile et Le Fusil* (4 vols., Brussels, 1983–86); J. H. Geller, "The Role of Military Administration in German-Occupied Belgium, 1940–44," *Journal of Military History*, 63 (1999): 99–125.

27. M. J. Chodakiewicz, *The Massacre in Jedwabne, July 10, 1941: Before, During, and After* (New York, 2005), corrects J. T. Gross, *Neighbors: The Destruction of the Jewish Community in Jedwabne, Poland* (Princeton, NJ, 2001).

28. G. S. Paulsson, *Secret City: The Hidden Jews of Warsaw, 1940–1945* (New Haven, 2002).

29. A. Ezergailis, *The Holocaust in Latvia, 1941–1944* (Riga, 1996); M. Dean, *Collaboration in the Holocaust: Crimes of the Local Police in Belorussia and Ukraine 1941–1944* (London, 1999); D. Gaunt, P. A. Levine, and L. Palosuo (eds.), *Collaboration and Resistance during the Holocaust: Belarus, Estonia, Latvia, Lithuania* (Berne, 2004).

30. P. Davies, *Dangerous Liaisons: Collaboration and World War Two* (Harlow, 2005).

31. G. Kreis (ed.), *Switzerland and the Second World War* (London, 2000); C. Leitz, *Sympathy for the Devil: Neutral Europe and Nazi Germany in World War II* (New York, 2001).

32. R. Ludi, *Reparations for Nazi Victims in Postwar Europe* (Cambridge, 2012).

33. Stanley Payne, *Franco and Hitler: Spain, Germany, and World War II* (New Haven, 2008).

34. B. Girvin and G. Roberts (eds.), *Ireland and the Second World War: Politics, Society, Remembrance* (Dublin, 2000).

35. J. C. Favez, *The Red Cross and the Holocaust* (Cambridge, 1999).

36. V. Drapac and G. Pritchard, *Resistance and Collaboration in Hitler's Europe* (London, 2017).

5. Memorialization

1. D. Stone, *The Liberation of the Camps: The End of the Holocaust and Its Aftermath* (New Haven, 2015): 36–40.

2. J. Michalczyk, *Filming the End of the Holocaust: Allied Documentaries, Nuremberg and the Liberation of the Concentration Camps* (London, 2014).

3. M. N. Penkower, *After the Holocaust* (New York, 2021).

4. D. L. Frieze (ed.), *Totally Unofficial: The Autobiography of Raphael Lemkin* (New Haven, 2013).

5. L. Douglas, *The Memory of Judgment: Making Law and History in the Trials of the Holocaust* (New Haven, 2001): 23–37.

6. M. J. Bazyler and F. M. Tuerkheimer, *Forgotten Trials of the Holocaust* (New York, 2014).

7. See also T. Boghardt, "Dirty Work? The Use of Nazi Informants by U.S. Army Intelligence in Postwar Europe," *Journal of Military History*, 79 (2015): 387–422, especially 403.

8. D. Bloxham, *Genocide on Trial: War Crimes Trials and the Formation of Holocaust History and Memory* (Oxford, 2001).

9. For example, *Trial of the Major War Criminals* (Nuremberg, 1948), vol. 17, 180–84.

10. N. Frei, *Adenauer's Germany and the Nazi Past: The Politics of Amnesty and Integration* (New York, 2002); H. Arendt, *Essays in Understanding, 1930–1954* (New York, 1994): 249; A. Grossman, *Jews, Germans, and Allies* (Princeton, NJ, 2007).

11. A. Schildt, "The Long Shadows of the Second World War: The Impact of Experiences and Memories of War on West German Society," *German Historical Institute London: Bulletin*, 29 (2007): 35.

12. J. K. Olick, *In the House of the Hangman: The Agonies of German Defeat, 1943–49* (Chicago, 2005); C. Morina, *Legacies of Stalingrad: Remembering the Eastern Front in Germany since 1945* (Cambridge, 2011); J. Lockenour, "Black

and White Memories of War: Victimization and Violence in West German War Films of the 1950s," *Journal of Military History*, 76 (2012): 159–91.

13. P. Wagner, "Imagined Revolutions and Real Executions: Hard-Core Nazis and the Spring of 1945," paper given at the German Historical Institute, London, June 6, 2013.

14. M. Fahlbusch, *German Scholars and Ethnic Cleansing, 1920–1945* (New York, 2005).

15. O. Bartov, "Eastern Europe as the Site of Genocide," *Journal of Modern History*, 80 (2008): 586–87.

16. T. Schieder, *Frederick the Great* (Harlow, 2000).

17. F. Kautz, *The German Historians: Hitler's Willing Executioners and Daniel Goldhagen* (Montreal, 2003): 93; I. Haar and M. Fahlbusch, *German Scholars and Ethnic Cleansing, 1919–1945* (New York, 2006): 11–19; G. G. Iggers and Q. E. Wang, *A Global History of Modern Historiography* (Harlow, 2008): 262.

18. C. Morina, *Legacies of Stalingrad: Remembering the Eastern Front in Germany since 1945* (Cambridge, 2011).

19. R. Moeller, *War Stories: The Search for a Usable Past in the Federal Republic of Germany* (Berkeley, 2001).

20. M. Spiering and M. Wintle (eds.), *European Identity and the Second World War* (Basingstoke, 2011).

21. S. Moyn, "Intellectuals and Nazism," in Daniel Stone (ed.), *The Oxford Handbook of Postwar European History* (Oxford, 2012): 690.

22. J. Herf, *Divided Memory: The Nazi Past in the Two Germanys* (Cambridge, MA, 1997); M. Fulbrook, *The People's State: East German Society from Hitler to Honecker* (New Haven, 2005): 263–64.

23. O. Bartov, *The Eastern Front, 1941–1945: German Troops and the Barbarisation of Warfare* (Basingstoke, 1985), *Hitler's Army Soldiers, Nazis, and War in the Third Reich* (Oxford, 1991), and *Germany's War and the Holocaust: Disputed Histories* (Oxford, 2000).

24. C. Browning, "Wehrmacht Reprisal Policy and the Mass-Murder of Jews in Serbia," *Militärgeschichtliche Mitteilungen*, 33 (1983): 31–37; W. Manoschek, "The Extermination of the Jews in Serbia," in U. Herbert (ed.), *National Socialist Extermination Policies: Contemporary German Perspectives and Controversies* (New York, 2000): 163–85.

25. A. Searle, "Revising the 'Myth' of a 'Clean *Wehrmacht*': Generals' Trials, Public Opinion, and the Dynamics of *Vergangenheits-bewältigung* in West Germany, 1948–60," *German Historical Institute London: Bulletin*, 25, 2 (2003): 49–70; D. Harrisville, *The Virtuous Wehrmacht: Crafting the Myth of the German Soldier on the Eastern Front, 1941–1944* (Ithaca, NY, 2021).

26. R. Wittmann, *Beyond Justice: The Auschwitz Trial* (Cambridge, MA, 2005); D. O. Pendas, *The Frankfurt Auschwitz Trial, 1963–65: Genocide History, and the Limits of the Law* (Cambridge, 2006).

27. K. von Lingen, *Allen Dulles, the OSS, and Nazi War Criminals: The Dynamics of Selective Prosecution* (Cambridge, 2013).

28. L. S. Dawidowicz, *The Holocaust and the Historians* (Cambridge, MA, 1981).

29. M. Sargeant, "Memory, Distortion and the War in German Popular Culture: The Case of Konsalik," in W. Kidd and B. Murdoch (eds.), *Memory and Memorials: The Commemorative Century* (Aldershot, 2004): 199.

30. For accounts from some very different perspectives, Y. Gutman and G. Greif (eds.), *The Historiography of the Holocaust Period* (Jerusalem, 1988); R. Hilberg, *The Politics of Memory* (Chicago, 1996); P. Novick, *The Holocaust and Collective Memory* (London, 1999); T. Judt, "The Past Is Another Country: Myth and Memory in Postwar Europe," in I. Déak, J. T. Gross, and T. Judt (eds.), *The Politics of Retribution in Europe: World War II and Its Aftermath* (Princeton, NJ, 2000): 293–324; N. Finkelstein, *The Holocaust Industry: Reflections on the Exploitation of Jewish Suffering* (New York, 2000); H. Marcuse, *Legacies of Dachau: The Uses and Abuses of a Concentration Camp* (Cambridge, 2001); J. Massad, "Deconstructing Holocaust Consciousness," *Journal of Palestine Studies*, 32 (2002): 78–89.

31. D. Lipstadt, *Denying the Holocaust: The Growing Assault on Truth and Memory* (London, 1993).

32. J. E. Young, *The Texture of Memory: Holocaust Memorials and Meaning* (New Haven, 1993); E. T. Linenthal, *Preserving Memory: The Struggle to Create America's Holocaust Museum* (New York, 1995).

33. J. S. Eder, "From Mass Murder to Exhibition: Museum Representations to Transatlantic Comparison," *Bulletin of the German Historical Institute*, 50 (Spring 2012): 160.

34. O. Bartov, "Historians on the Eastern Front: Andreas Hillgruber and Germany's Tragedy," *Tel Aviver Jahrbuch für deutsche Geschichte*, 16 (1987): 325–45; C. S. Maier, *The Unmasterable Past: History, the Holocaust, and German National Identity* (Cambridge, MA, 1988); R. J. Evans, *In Hitler's Shadow: West German Historians and the Attempt to Escape from the Nazi Past* (London, 1989); P. Baldwin (ed.), *Reworking the Past: Hitler, the Holocaust, and the Historians' Debate* (Boston, 1990); J. Knowlton and T. Cates, *Forever in the Shadow of Hitler? Original Documents of the Historikerstreit, the Controversy Concerning the Singularity of the Holocaust* (Atlantic Highlands, NJ, 1993); S. Berger, *The Search for Normality: National Identity and Historical Consciousness in Germany since 1800* (Oxford, 1997).

35. For an English translation, see G. Hartman, *Bitburg in Moral and Political Perspective* (Bloomington, IN, 1986): 262–73.

36. P. Black, *Ernst Kaltenbrunner: Ideological Soldier of the Third Reich* (Princeton, NJ, 1984).

37. E. B. Bukey, *Hitler's Austria: Popular Sentiment in the Nazi Era, 1938–45* (Chapel Hill, NC, 2000).

38. D. Majer, *"Non-Germans" under the Third Reich: the Nazi Judicial and Administrative System in Germany and Occupied Eastern Europe, with Special Regard to Occupied Poland, 1939–45* (Baltimore, 2003), originally published in German in 1981.

39. H. Heer, "The Difficulty of Ending a War: Reactions to the Exhibition War of Extermination: Crimes of the Wehrmacht, 1941 to 1944," *History Workshop Journal*, 46 (1998): 187–203; C. R. Nugent, "The Voice of the Visitor: Popular Reactions to the Exhibition 'Vernichtungskrieg: Verbrechen der Wehrmacht 1941–1944,'" *Journal of European Studies*, 44 (2014): 249–62.

40. N. Gregor, *Haunted City: Nuremberg and the Nazi Past* (New Haven, 2008); G. D. Rosenfeld and P. Jaskot (eds.), *Beyond Berlin: Twelve German Cities Confront the Nazi Past* (Ann Arbor, MI, 2008). For disagreement about memorialization in Freiburg, T. G. Vanderbeek, "Marginalization and Local Commemoration of Third Reich Victims in Germany," *Journal of Holocaust Research*, 36 (2002): 128–45.

41. S. E. Eizenstat, *Imperfect Justice: Looted Assets, Slave Labor, and the Unfinished Business of World War II* (London, 2003).

42. For a critical view, see R. B. Birn, "Revisiting the Holocaust," *Historical Journal*, 40 (1997): 195–215; R. A. Shandley (ed.), *Unwilling Germans? The Goldhagen Debate* (Minneapolis, 1998); M. Cattaruzza, "A Discussion of D. J. Goldhagen's *Hitler's Willing Executioners*," *Storia della Storigrafia*, 33 (1998): 97–107; G. Eley (ed.), *The 'Goldhagen Effect': History, Memory, Nazism—Facing the German Past* (Ann Arbor, MI, 2000); R. E. Herzstein, "Daniel Jonah Goldhagen's 'Ordinary Germans': A Heretic and His Critics," *Journal of the Historical Society*, 2 (2002): 89–122; J. Vanke, "The Isolation of Daniel Goldhagen: A Response to Robert Herzstein," *Journal of the Historical Society*, 2 (2002): 447–53.

43. R. E. Herzstein, "Daniel Jonah Goldhagen's 'Ordinary Germans,'" *Journal of the Historical Society*, 2 (2002): 102–3.

44. R. J. Evans, *Telling Lies about Hitler: The Holocaust, History and the David Irving Trial* (London, 2002); P. Longerich, *The Unwritten Order: Hitler's Role in the Final Solution* (Stroud, 2001).

45. L. de Villa, "German-Israeli Ties in 2015 and 1965: The Difficult Special Relationship," *International Affairs*, 91 (2015): 838.

46. S. Milton and I. Nowinski, *In Fitting Memory: The Art and Politics of Holocaust Memorials* (Detroit, 1991); J. E. Young, *The Texture of Memory: Holocaust Memorials and Meaning* (New Haven, 1993).

47. G. Hartman (ed.), *Bitburg: In Moral and Political Perspective* (Bloomington, IN, 1986).

48. L. Meissel, "The Innocent Perpetrators: The Portrayal of 'German Victimhood' in *Unsere Mütter, Unsere Väter*," *Journal of Holocaust Research*, 36 (2022): 146–63.

49. On Schacht, P. Barbieri, *Hitler's Shadow Empire: Nazi Economics and the Spanish Civil War* (Cambridge, MA, 2015) complements A. Tooze, *The Wages of Destruction: The Making and Breaking of the Nazi Economy* (London, 2007).

50. H. Heer et al., *The Discursive Construction of History: Remembering the Wehrmacht's War of Annihilation* (Basingstoke, 2008); U. Staiger, H. Steiner, and A. Webber (eds.), *Memory Culture and the Contemporary City: Building Sites* (Basingstoke, 2009), on Berlin; B. Niven and C. Paver (eds.), *Memorialization in Germany since 1945* (Basingstoke, 2010); J. Arnold, *The Allied Air War and Urban Memory: The Legacy of Strategic Bombing in Germany* (Cambridge, 2011).

51. M. L. Kahn, "Antisemitism, Holocaust Denial, and Germany's Far Right: How the AfD Tiptoes around Nazism," *Journal of Holocaust Research*, 36 (2022): 164–85.

52. N. MacGregor, *Germany: Memories of a Nation* (London, 2014): 172.

53. A. Duncan, "The Problematic Commemoration of War in the Early Films of Alain Resnais," in W. Kidd and B. Murdoch (eds.), *Memory and Memorials: The Commemorative Century* (Aldershot, 2004): 210.

54. P. Jankowski, "In Defence of Fiction, Resistance, Collaboration and Lacombe, Lucien," *Journal of Modern History*, 63 (1991): 457–82.

55. C. Callil, *Bad Faith: A Forgotten History of Family and Fatherland* (London, 2006).

56. R. J. Golsan (ed.), *Memory, The Holocaust and French Justice: The Bousquet and Touvier Affairs* (Hanover, NH, 1996); N. Wood, *Victors of Memory: Trauma in Postwar Europe* (Oxford, 1999): 113–42; R. J. Golsan, *Vichy's Afterlife: History and Counter-History in Postwar France* (Lincoln, NE, 2000).

57. H. Rousso, *The Vichy Syndrome: History and Memory in France since 1944* (Cambridge, MA, 1991) and *The Haunting Past: History, Memory and Justice in Contemporary France* (Philadelphia, 2002); A. Colombat, *The Holocaust in French Film* (Metuchen, NJ, 1993); A. Nossiter, *France and the Nazis: Memories, Lies, and the Second World War* (London, 2003).

58. P. Vidal-Naquet, *Assassins of Memory: Essays on the Denial of the Holocaust* (New York, 1992).

59. N. Furman, "Viewing Memory through Night and Fog, the Sorrow and the Pity and Shoah," *Journal of European Studies*, 35 (2005): 180; I. Avisar, *Screening the Holocaust: Cinema's Images of the Unimaginable* (Bloomington, IN, 1988); L. Baum, *Projecting the Holocaust into the Present: The Changing Face of Contemporary Holocaust Cinema* (London, 2005); T. Haggith and J. Neame (eds.), *Holocaust and the Moving Image: Representations in Film and Television since 1933* (London, 2005). For more theoretical, cultural studies approaches, see

J. Hirsch, *Film, Traumas and the Holocaust* (Philadelphia, 2003), and A. Insdorf, *Indelible Shadows: Film and the Holocaust* (Cambridge, 2005).

60. See C. Moorehead, *Village of Secrets: Defying the Nazis in Vichy France* (London, 2014).

61. M. Hametz, "The Ambivalence of Italian Antisemitism: Fascism, Nationalism, and Racism in Trieste," *Holocaust and Gender Studies*, 16 (2002): 376–401; S. Luconi, "*Il Grido della Stirpe* and Mussolini's 1938 Racial Legislation," *Shofar*, 22 (2004): 67–79.

62. M. L. Chirico, R. Cioffi, A. Grimaldi, and G. Pignatelli (eds.), *I Due Risorgimenti: La costruzione dell' identita nazionale* (Naples, 2011).

63. J. Cornwell, *Hitler's Pope: The Secret History of Pius XII* (New York, 1999).

64. M. Burleigh, *Sacred Causes: Religion and Ethics from the European Dictators to Al Qaeda* (London, 2006).

65. M. Phayer, *Pius XII, the Holocaust, and the Cold War* (Bloomington, IN, 2008); R. A. Ventresca, *Soldier of Christ: The Life of Pope Pius XII* (Cambridge, MA, 2013); D. Goldhagen, *A Moral Reckoning: The Role of the Catholic Church in the Holocaust and Its Unfulfilled Duty of Repair* (New York, 2002); D. Kertzer, *The Pope at War: The Secret History of Pius XII, Mussolini, and Hitler* (Oxford, 2022).

66. T. Lawson, *The Church of England and the Holocaust* (London, 2006).

67. *Independent*, May 31, 2006: 22.

68. U. Herbert, "National Socialist and Stalinist Rule: The Possibilities and Limits of Comparison," in M. Hildermeier (ed.), *Historical Concepts between Eastern and Western Europe* (Oxford, 2007): 5–22.

69. K. Berkhoff, *Motherland in Danger: Soviet Propaganda during World War II* (Cambridge, MA, 2012); M. Edele, *Stalinism at War: The Soviet Union in World War II* (London, 2021): 3, 89, 138–42, 152–54.

70. M. J. Blackwell, *Kyiv as Regime City: The Return of Soviet Power after Nazi Occupation* (Rochester, NY, 2016).

71. M. Fulbrook, *Reckonings: Legacies of Nazi Persecution and the Quest for Justice* (Oxford, 2018); M. Edele, S. Fitzpatrick, and A. Grossmann (eds.), *Shelter from the Holocaust: Rethinking Jewish Survival in the Soviet Union* (Detroit, 2017).

72. J. Rubenstein and V. Naumov (eds.), *Stalin's Secret Pogrom: The Postwar Inquisition of the Jewish Anti-Fascist Committee* (New Haven, 2002).

73. Z. Y. Gitelman (ed.), *Bitter Legacy: Confronting the Holocaust in the USSR* (Bloomington, IN, 1997); I. Kukulin, "Russian Literature on the Shoah: New Approaches and Contexts," *Kritika*, 18 (2017): 165–75.

74. M. Meng, *Shattered Spaces: Encountering Jewish Ruins in Postwar Germany and Poland* (Cambridge, MA, 2011).

75. T. C. Fox, "The Holocaust under Communism," in D. Stone (ed.), *The Historiography of the Holocaust* (Basingstoke, 2004): 423.

76. W. Dzaplinski and T. Ładogórski (eds.), *The Historical Atlas of Poland* (Wroclaw, 1981): 34. See also, at a different scale, M. Kucia, M. Duch-Dyngosz,

and M. Magierowski, "The Collective Memory of Auschwitz and World War II among Catholics in Poland: A Qualitative Study of Three Communities," *History and Memory*, 25, 2 (2013): 132–73.

77. W. Bartoszewski, "Some Thoughts on Polish-Jewish Relations," *Polin*, 1 (1986): 287; "Polish-Jewish Relations during the Second World War: A Discussion," *Polin*, 2 (1987): 337–58.

78. Y. Dojc and K. Krausova, *Last Folio: Textures of Jewish Life in Slovakia* (Bloomington, IN, 2011).

79. A. Holian, *Between National Socialism and Soviet Communism: Displaced Persons in Postwar Germany* (Ann Arbor, MI, 2011).

80. T. Snyder, *The Reconstruction of Nations: Poland, Ukraine, Lithuania, Belarus, 1569–1999* (New Haven, 2003): 248.

81. A. Charlesworth, "Contesting Places of Memory: The Case of Auschwitz," *Environment and Planning D: Society and Space*, 12 (1994): 579–93.

82. I. Goldstein, "The Treatment of Jewish History in Schools in Central and Eastern Europe," in C. Koulouri (ed.), *Clio in the Balkans: The Politics of History Education* (Thessaloniki, 2002): 353.

83. E. Zuroff, "Whitewashing the Holocaust: Lithuania and the Rehabilitation of History," *Tikkun*, 7, 1 (1992): 43–46.

84. M. Bucur, "Edifices of the Past: War Memorials and Heroes in Twentieth-Century Romania," in M. Todorova (ed.), *Balkan Identities: Nation and Memory* (London, 2004): 175.

85. J. Grabowski and S. Klein, "Wikipedia's Intentional Distortion of the History of the Holocaust," *Journal of Holocaust Research*, published online February 9, 2023.

86. For criticism of implicit Hungarian equating of the Holocaust and communist domination, R. L. Braham and P. Hanebrink, "The Holocaust in Hungary: A Critical Analysis," *Holocaust and Genocide Studies*, 34 (2020): 1–17.

87. M. Dean, *Collaboration in the Holocaust: Crimes of the Local Police in Belorussia and Ukraine, 1941–1944* (Basingstoke, 2000).

88. Rob Morgan to Jeremy Black, email, August 11, 2015.

89. For an attempt to revive this memory, B. Wasserstein, *A Small Town in Ukraine: The Place We Came from, the Place We Went Back To* (London, 2023).

90. D. Brock, "Double Genocide," *Slate*, July 26, 2015, http://www.slate.com/articles/news.

91. S. Woolfson, *Holocaust Legacy in Post-Soviet Lithuania: People, Places and Objects* (London, 2014).

92. D. Iordanova, *Cinema of the Other Europe: The Industry and Artistry of East Central European Film* (London, 2003).

93. J. Subotić, *Yellow Star, Red Star: Holocaust Remembrance after Communism* (Ithaca, NY, 2019); J.-P. Himka and J. B. Michlic (eds.), *Bringing*

the Dark Past to Light: The Reception of the Holocaust in Postcommunist Europe (Lincoln, NE, 2019).

94. R. H. Hayden, "Schindler's Fate: Genocide, Ethnic Cleansing, and Population Transfers," *Slavic Review*, 55 (1996): 727–48.

95. N. Cigar, *Genocide in Bosnia: The Policy of "Ethnic Cleansing"* (College Station, TX, 1995); E. Becirevic, *Genocide on the Drina River* (New Haven, 2014).

96. T. Berger, *Wars, Guilt, and World Politics after World War II* (Cambridge, 2012).

97. R. Breitman, N. J. W. Goda, T. Naftali, and R. Wolfe, *U.S. Intelligence and the Nazis* (Cambridge, 2005); T. Doherty, *Hollywood and Hitler, 1933–1939* (New York, 2013); B. Urwand, *The Collaboration: Hollywood's Pact with Hitler* (Cambridge, 2013).

98. R. Smelser and E. Davies, *The Myth of the Eastern Front: The Nazi-Soviet War in American Popular Culture* (Cambridge, 2008).

99. F. Manchel, "A Reel Witness: Steven Spielberg's Representation of the Holocaust in *Schindler's List*," *Journal of Modern History*, 67 (1995): 91; M. B. Hansen, "Schindler's List Is Not Shoah: The Second Commandment, Popular Modernism and Public Memory," *Critical Inquiry*, 22 (1996): 311. See also Thomas Elsaesser's chapter in V. Sobchack (ed.), *The Persistence of History: Cinema, Television and the Modern Event* (London, 1996).

100. J. Shandler, *While America Watches: Televising the Holocaust* (New York, 1999); A. L. Mintz, *Popular Culture and the Shaping of Holocaust Memory in America* (Seattle, 2001); N. Finkelstein, *The Holocaust Industry: Reflections on the Exploitation of Jewish Suffering* (New York, 2000); A. Landsberg, *Prosthetic Memory: The Transformation of American Remembrance in the Age of Mass Culture* (New York, 2004).

101. H. Druks, *The Uncertain Alliance: The US and Israel from Kennedy to the Peace Process* (Westport, CT, 2001); E. Stephens, *US Policy toward Israel: The Role of Political Culture in Defining the "Special Relationship"* (Brighton, 2006).

102. L. Friedberg, "Dare to Compare: Americanizing the Holocaust," *American Indian Quarterly*, 24 (2000): 353–80; W. Churchill, *A Little Matter of Genocide* (San Francisco, 1997).

103. B. Liberman, *Terrible Fate: Ethnic Cleansing in the Making of Modern Europe* (Chicago, 2006).

104. K. L. Klein, "On the Emergence of Memory in Historical Discourse," *Representations*, 69 (2000): 127–50; J. Winter, "The Generation of Memory: Reflections on the 'Memory Boom' in Contemporary Historical Studies," *Bulletin of the German Historical Institute Washington*, 27 (2006): 69–92.

105. L. L. Langer, *Holocaust Testimonies: The Ruins of Memory* (New Haven, 1991); M. Rothberg and J. Stark, "After the Witness: A Report from the Twentieth Anniversary Conference of the Fortunoff Video Archive for

Holocaust Testimonies at Yale," *History and Memory*, 15 (2003); G. Hartman, *The Longest Shadow: In the Aftermath of the Holocaust* (Basingstoke, 2003). Hartman is project director of the Fortunoff Video Archive. For the problems of memory, N. Shenker, *Reframing Holocaust Testimony* (Bloomington, IN, 2015) and A. R. Seipp, "Buchenwald Stories: Testimony, Military History, and the American Encounter with the Holocaust," *Journal of Military History*, 79 (2015): 721–44.

106. P. Novick, *The Holocaust and Collective Memory: The American Experience* (London, 1999).

107. Kitia Altman, cited in J. E. Berman, "Australian Representations of the Holocaust: Jewish Holocaust Museums in Melbourne, Perth, and Sydney, 1984–96," *Holocaust and Genocide Studies*, 13 (1999): 202; J. E. Berman, *Holocaust Remembrance in Australian Jewish Communities, 1945–2000* (Crawley, Western Australia, 2001); A. D. Moses, "Genocide and Holocaust Consciousness in Australia," *History Compass*, 1 (2003): 13; A. Alba, "Integrity and Relevancy: Shaping Holocaust Memory at the Sydney Jewish Museum," *Judaism*, 54 (2005): 108–15.

108. B. Lagan, "Abbott Makes Another Nazi Gaffe," *The Times*, March 20, 2015, 38.

109. Edited by Deborah Knowles and published in Auckland.

110. G. Macklin, *Dyed in Black* (London, 2007).

111. C. R. Jorgensen-Earp, *Discourse and Defiance under Nazi Occupation: Guernsey, Channel Islands, 1940–1945* (East Lansing, 2013); G. Carr, P. Sanders, and L. Willmot, *Protest, Defiance and Resistance in the Channel Islands* (London, 2014).

112. D. Stone, "Day of Remembrance or Day of Forgetting? Or, Why Britain Does Not Need a Holocaust Memorial Day," *Patterns of Prejudice*, 34 (4) (2000): 53–59.

113. A. Pearce, *Holocaust Consciousness in Contemporary Britain* (New York, 2014). On visits to Auschwitz, E. Jilvovsky, *Remembering the Holocaust: Generations, Witnessing and Place* (London, 2015).

114. G. Martel (ed.), *Companion to Europe 1900–1945* (Oxford, 2005).

115. T. Segev, *The Seventh Million: The Israelis and the Holocaust* (New York, 1993); R. Linn, "Genocide and the Politics of Remembering: The Nameless, the Celebrated, and the Would-Be Holocaust Heroes," *Journal of Genocide Research*, 5 (2003): 565–86.

116. L. G. Feldman, *The Special Relationship between West Germany and Israel* (Boston, 1984).

117. W. R. Louis and R. W. Stookey (eds.), *The End of the Palestine Mandate* (Austin, TX, 1986); N. Stewart, *The Royal Navy and the Palestine Patrol* (London, 2002).

118. Y. Shain and B. Bristman, "The Jewish Security Dilemma," *Orbis* 46 (2002): 55–56.

119. O. Meyers, E. Zandberg, and M. Neiger, *Communicating Awe: Media Memory and Holocaust Commemoration* (Basingstoke, 2014).

120. Z. Aharoni and W. Dietl, *Operation Eichmann: The Truth about the Pursuit, Capture and Trial* (London, 1996).

121. E. Cohen, *Identity and Pedagogy: Shoah Education in Israeli State Schools* (Boston, 2013).

122. T. de Waal, *Great Catastrophe: Armenians and Turks in the Shadow of Genocide* (Oxford, 2015).

123. D. Motadel, *Islam and Nazi Germany's War* (Cambridge, MA, 2014).

124. O. Bartov, *The "Jew" in Cinema: From the "Golem" to "Don't Touch My Holocaust"* (Bloomington, IN, 2005).

125. *New York Times*, "Mahmoud Abbas Shifts on Holocaust," April 26, 2014, http://www.nytimes.com/2014/04/27/world/middleeast/palestinian-leader -shifts-on-holocaust.html.

126. P. Iganski and B. Kosmin (eds.), *A New Anti-Semitism? Debates about Judeophobia in the Twenty-First Century* (London, 2003).

127. N. Palmer, *Museums and the Holocaust* (Builth Wells, 2000).

128. P. Fritzsche, "The Holocaust and the Knowledge of Murder," *Journal of Modern History*, 80 (2008): 613.

129. T. Judt, *Postwar: A History of Europe since 1945* (London, 2005): 803.

130. R. Clifford, *Commemorating the Holocaust: The Dilemmas of Remembrance in France and Italy* (Oxford, 2013); L. Allwork, *Holocaust Remembrance between the National and the Transnational: The Stockholm International Forum and the First Decade of the International Task Force* (London, 2015).

131. For its homepage, which includes an English version, www.diis.dk.

132. M. Rothberg, *Multidirectional Memory: Remembering the Holocaust in the Age of Decolonization* (Stanford, CA, 2009).

6. The Holocaust and Today

1. *The Times*, June 25, 2015, 35.

2. G. D. Hundert, *The Jews in a Polish Private Town: The Case of Opatów in the Eighteenth Century* (Baltimore, 1992).

3. D. Engel, *In the Shadow of Auschwitz: The Polish Government-in-Exile and the Jews, 1939–1942* (Chapel Hill, NC, 1987), and *Facing a Holocaust: The Polish Government-in-Exile and the Jews, 1943–1945* (Chapel Hill, NC, 1993).

4. M. Shermer and A. Grobman, *Denying History: Who Says the Holocaust Never Happened and Why Do They Say It?* (Berkeley, 2002).

5. A. Pearce, *Holocaust Consciousness in Contemporary Britain* (New York, 2014): 230.

6. Stephen E. Atkins, *Holocaust Denial as an International Movement* (Westport, CT, 2009); Robert S. Wistrich, *Holocaust Denial: The Politics of Perfidy* (Boston, 2012); F. Bobont, "Antisemitism and Holocaust Denial in Post-Communist Eastern Europe," in D. Stone (ed.), *The Historiography of the Holocaust* (Basingstoke, 2004): 464.

7. R. G. Hovannisian, *The Armenian Genocide in Perspective* (New Brunswick, NJ, 1986); R. Melson, "Problems in the Comparison of the Armenian Genocide and the Holocaust: Definitions, Typologies, Theories, and Fallacies," *Jahrbuch für Historische Friedensforschung*, 7 (1999); A. S. Rosenbaum (ed.), *Is the Holocaust Unique? Perspectives on Comparative Genocide* (3rd ed., Boulder, CO, 2009); T. de Waal, *Great Catastrophe: Armenians and Turks in the Shadow of Genocide* (Oxford, 2015).

8. P. Addison and J. A. Crang (eds.), *Firestorm: The Bombing of Dresden, 1945* (London, 2006).

9. S. Lindquist, *A History of Bombing* (London, 2001).

10. S. Courtois (ed.), *The Black Book of Communism: Crimes, Terror, Repression* (Cambridge, MA, 1999); T. Snyder, *Bloodlands: Europe between Hitler and Stalin* (New Haven, 2010).

11. R. Suny, F. M. Göçek, and N. M. Daimark (eds.), *A Question of Genocide: Armenians and Turks at the End of the Ottoman Empire* (Oxford, 2011); W. Gruner, "'Peregrinations into the Void?' German Jews and Their Knowledge about the Armenian Genocide during the Third Reich," *Central European History*, 45 (2012): 1–26.

12. A. Mayer, "Memory and History: On the Poverty of Remembering and Forgetting the Judeocide," *Radical History Review*, 56 (1993): 5–20.

13. P. Novick, "Comments on Aleida Assmann's Lecture," *Bulletin of the German Historical Institute, Washington*, 40 (2007): 31.

14. For criticism of the "double genocide" approach, Michael Pinto-Duschinsky, "Hitler's 'Ecological Panic' Didn't Cause the Holocaust," *Standpoint*, 75 (September 2015): 44–49, a critique of Timothy Snyder's *Black Earth: The Holocaust as History and Warning* (London, 2015).

15. P. Pomerantsev, "Diary," *London Review of Books*, 36/12, June 19, 2014: 42–43.

16. G. Margalit, *Germany and Its Gypsies: A Post-Auschwitz Ordeal* (Madison, WI, 2002).

17. M. A. Hoare, *Genocide and Resistance in Hitler's Bosnia: The Partisans and the Chetniks, 1941–43* (Oxford, 2006).

18. J.-P. Sartre, *On Genocide* (Boston, 1986).

19. A. Finkielkraut, *Remembering in Vain: The Klaus Barbie Trial and Crimes against Humanity* (New York, 1992).

20. U. Siemon-Netto, "The '68er Regime in Germany," *Orbis*, 48 (2004): 87.

21. *Times*, June 20, 1961; N. MacQueen and P. A. Oliveira, "'Grocer Meets Butcher': Marcello Caetano's London Visit of 1973 and the Last Days of Portugal's *Estado Novo*," *Cold War History*, 10 (2009): 29–50.

22. J. M. Ridao, "The Enemy in the Mirror," in *At War* (Barcelona, 2004).

23. M. Godwin, "I Seem to Be a Verb: 18 Years of Godwin's Law," *Jewcy*, April 30, 2008.

24. M. Berenbaum, *After Tragedy and Triumph: Modern Jewish Thought and the American Experience* (Cambridge, 1990); A. H. Rosenfeld, "The Americanisation of the Holocaust," *Commentary*, 99 (1995): 35–40.

25. G. Harding, "Mechelen Remembers," May 3, 2007: 12–13, www .thebulletin.be.

26. Citing friends, allies, and cabinet colleagues of David Cameron, R. Sylvester, "No Appeasement—This Is All-Out War on Isis," *Times*, July 21, 2015: 23.

27. C. Gluck, "Operations of Memory: 'Comfort Women' and the World," in S. M. Jager and R. Mitter (eds.), *Ruptured Histories: War, Memory, and the Post-Cold War in Asia* (Cambridge, MA, 2007): 65; J. Alexander, "On the Social Construction of Moral Universals: The 'Holocaust' from War Crime to Trauma Drama," *European Journal of Social Theory*, 5 (2002): 5–85; D. Levy and N. Sznaider, "Memory Unbound: The Holocaust and the Formation of the Cosmopolitan Memory," *European Journal of Social Theory*, 5 (2002): 87–106.

28. See also B. Crim, *Planet Auschwitz: Holocaust Representation in Science Fiction and Horror Film and Television* (New Brunswick, NJ, 2020).

7. Conclusions

1. A. J. Kay, *Empire of Destruction: A History of Nazi Mass Killing* (New Haven, 2021).

2. J. Surmann, "Restitution Policy and the Transformation of Holocaust Memory: The Impact of the American 'Crusade for Justice' after 1989," *Bulletin of the German Historical Institute*, 49 (Fall 2011): 48.

3. U. Herbert, "Extermination Policy: New Answers and Questions about the History of the 'Holocaust' in German Historiography," in Herbert (ed.), *National Socialist Extermination Policies* (New York, 2000): 43; J. Semprún and E. Wiesel, *It Is Impossible to Remain Silent: Reflections on Fate and Memory in Buckenwald* (Bloomington, IN, 2020) presents an instructive conversation between a Christian and a Jewish survivor; from the human rights perspective, M. Polgar, *Holocaust and Human Rights Education: Good Choices and Sociological Perspectives* (Bingley, 2019). From the perspective of a psychologist, G. Mastroianni, *Of Mind and Murder: Toward a More Comprehensive Psychology of the Holocaust* (Oxford, 2018).

4. J. Cohen, "Post-Holocaust Philosophy," in D. Stone (ed.), *The Historiography of the Holocaust* (Basingstoke, 2004): 484.

5. R. R. Brenner, *The Faith and Doubt of Holocaust Survivors* (New York, 1980).

6. A. Donat, "The Holocaust Kingdom," in A. Friedlander (ed.), *Out of the Whirlwind* (New York, 1976): 176.

7. Reporting Paul Gould, a Viennese Jew whose family was killed, Frederick Schneid to Black, email, August 9, 2015. Samuel Willenberg, a survivor of the escape attempt from Treblinka in August 1943, later wrote of the mass burning of corpses at the camp: "The sizzling half burnt cadavers emitted grinding and crackling sounds. God must have been on holiday. I looked for Him, but there was only beautiful Polish sky" (obituary, *Times*, March 2, 2016).

8. T. Lawson, *The Church of England and the Holocaust: Christianity, Memory and Nazism* (Woodbridge, 2006).

9. R. J. Berger, *The Holocaust, Religion, and the Politics of Collective Memory: Beyond Sociology* (New Brunswick, NJ, 2012).

10. S. T. Katz, *Wrestling with God: Jewish Theological Responses during and after the Holocaust* (New York, 2007). For variety in response, see B. Krawcowicz, *History, Metahistory, and Evil: Jewish Theological Responses to the Holocaust* (Boston, 2020).

11. P. E. Gordon, "Interpretations of Catastrophe: German Intellectuals on Nazism, Genocide and Mass Destruction," in M. Geyer and A. Tooze (eds.), *The Cambridge History of the Second World War: III Total War* (Cambridge, 2015): 653.

12. J. Adams (ed.), *The Bloomsbury Companion to Holocaust Literature* (London, 2014); M. Cosgrove, *Born under Auschwitz: Melancholy Traditions in Postwar German Literature* (Rochester, NY, 2014).

13. F. Weissman, *Fantasies of Witnessing: Postwar Efforts to Experience the Holocaust* (Ithaca, NY, 2004).

14. D. Wheeler, "Godard's List: Why Spielberg and Auschwitz are Number One," *Media History*, 15 (2009): 2000.

15. For example, T. Bower, "My Clash with Death-Camp Hanna," *Sunday Times*, February 15, 2009, and F. Raphael, "Bad Beyond Imagination," *Standpoint*, 10 (March 2009): 54–57; E. R. Adler and K. Čapková (eds), *Jewish and Romani Families in the Holocaust and Its Aftermath* (New Brunswick, NJ, 2021).

16. C. Gorrara, "Not Seeing Auschwitz Memory, Generation and Representations of the Holocaust in Twenty-First Century French Comics," *Modern Jewish Studies*, 17 (2018), https://doi.org/10.1080/14725886.2017.1382107.

17. S. Macdonald, *Memorylands: History and Identity in Europe Today* (Abingdon, 2013).

Index

JEREMY BLACK is the author of numerous books, including *Military Strategy: A Global History, A Brief History of Germany, Strategy and the Second World War,* and *A History of the Second World War in 100 Maps.* He is Emeritus Professor of History at the University of Exeter and a Senior Fellow both of the Foreign Policy Research Institute and the British Foreign Policy Group. Black is a recipient of the Samuel Eliot Morison Prize from the Society for Military History. Follow Black on his website, jeremyblackhistorian.wordpress.com.

For Indiana University Press

Tony Brewer, Artist and Book Designer

Gary Dunham, Acquisitions Editor and Director

Anna Francis, Assistant Acquisitions Editor

Brenna Hosman, Production Coordinator

Katie Huggins, Production Manager

Nancy Lightfoot, Project Editor and Manager

Dan Pyle, Online Publishing Manager

Pamela Rude, Senior Artist and Book Designer

Stephen Williams, Marketing and Publicity Manager